Before the Camera Rolled

Rolled

BY JASON NORMAN

Published in the USA by:
BearManor Media
P O Box 71426
Albany, Georgia 31708
www.bearmanormedia.com

Printed in the United States of America
ISBN   978-1-62933-123-2 (hardcover)

Book & cover design and layout by Darlene Swanson • www.van-garde.com

Contents

Contents

Introduction

*E*ver since I was able to maneuver my own vehicle around (safely or otherwise), the movies have been my place to be. They offer us a chance to step into another world, to forget about reality for a while. They're a place where we can become participants in an outside universe, one filled with laughs, fear, and magic. Worlds where, no matter the odds, the hero almost always finds a way to beat the villain in the end, even if it takes a few sequels to get the job done. The heart of the gorgeous lady, usually of the damsel-in-distress-variety. Where any problem in the world gets solved in two or three hours.

And what of the people we see on the screen? In what other profession can a person spend time as a singing serial killer, blade-handed introvert, mob boss, astronaut, pirate ship captain (four times over!), chocolate factory owner, druggie gonzo writer, and jolly-Olde-England-era police detective? Hell, Johnny Depp did all of that in a matter of years!

Actors get to step back in time, into the future, and sometimes into other worlds. They can be superheroes or evil villains. They can take part in the wars of history, fight battles far from Earth, or become the common everyman (and woman) that so many of us in the audience dream of being. They can be loved, or love being hated. They can go anywhere, do anything... be anyone.

Libraries of books have examined the do's, don't's, why's, and all other sorts of questions and answers about acting. But here's one that hasn't been explored (much!).

How exactly do they get there? What don't we, the audience, get to see? How does one *become* such a character, to the extent that they convince us that they've suddenly morphed into a whole new persona for two or three hours? How do they step out of their normal lives and into those of the characters? Convincing audiences that we're not the person whose name runs through the credits is what wins credibility, fame, fortune, and, to every year's best, even Oscars.

By now, I've answered a few of these questions towards the horror genre in my previous book, *Behind the Screams* (available on the 'net on Amazon, Barnes & Noble, and directly from Bear Manor Media!). Still, that book checked over my personal favorite genre of moviemaking. This one, which was actually begun before *Screams*, broadens the search a bit.

As film fans, we're quite lucky. We only see the final project. The work beforehand, the time and effort spent by everyone at every level of cast and crew, we don't worry too much about that.

Until now. Now we'll wonder and learn a little bit about what came first. About how these people worked themselves into character beforehand. How actors bridge the gap between the people they are and the people they become. About the steps they take to be these people.How they prepare for their roles before filming begins, and stay there so completely for so long.

But want to hear a little secret as to why people act, or at least why I did, and why I think that everyone should step onto a stage at least once in their life? It's not so much the audience's applause, although that definitely adds to it. It's the feeling that comes with acting, a feeling of Utopian invincibility and wonder. As we go through the trip of acting, we'll discuss it more. And by the time we're finished, hopefully you'll be on your way to experiencing it yourself.

Author's note: As I tried to decide who to profile for this work, I knew that I wouldn't be able to do extensive pieces on their entire career. Therefore, especially for those with resumes longer than this book, I focused on my personal favorite performances of theirs. Along the way, you may — heck with it, I'm sure you will! — say something like, "Hey, (actor/actress) was a helluva lot better in (film/TV show) that the one Norman covered in his book! Why didn't he talk about that?"

The answer is, again, that these are my personal favorites. That's a benefit of writing a book; you get to pick and choose who goes in it, and what to talk to them about. Believe me, there's quite a few people in this book that went out of their way to help me out a great deal, some that I didn't think would do so. Different performances mean different things to different people, and that's one of the funnest parts of acting critique; in a picture so large, some parts will seem out of focus to some, but it's the clearest portrait possible for those that worked on it. I hope you like it.

Join me for a journey inside the world of acting. We'll learn about how some of the most well-known faces in the entertainment world became their new personalities. We'll meet people who have scared us, made us laugh, made us cry, and made us cheer, both on the big and small screens. We'll hear from those who specialize in helping others make it to their own respective screens, giving assistance to film stars in the making.

We'll hear a bit from those that have been there and done everything, and from those who've taken the first steps in that direction. We'll hear from people who go out there and give it their all in every role, just because — not for the fame, the money, the prestige, even the large checks: just because it's what they love, which is always right. Together, we'll learn more about getting to the top, and the new set of responsibilities that arrive when we're there.

Let's take a look inside the minds, the talent of those who worked so hard breaking into one of the toughest lines of work... before the camera rolled.

Foreword...

*R*ecently, a young director asked me, "What was *Goodfellas* like?" That's usually what people ask.

Jason Norman captured that.

This book will show various takes of acting, of the experience. *Goodfellas* was unique upon itself, working with Martin Scorsese and Robert De Niro, the experiences that I went through — Jason mirrored how I felt.

His writing style showed a great insight into my experiences on the set. He captured what I tried to explain to him. He pointed out elements of a production that I didn't know or had forgotten. It was more than refreshing: it was a revelation.

The jovial mood that Frenchy (right) spread in 1990's *Goodfellas* wouldn't last, but the acting world's been lucky enough to enjoy Mike Starr's character acting work for decades since.

He shone a light on aspects of what I went through just to get the jobs, and how I was held in such a situation. This book is for someone who's interested in the stories of a specific movie, and for young actors to learn about the character acting process.

This book will be a revelation to a lot of people, because it shows the overall experience of acting. To a person who isn't an actor, someone involved in other aspects of the business, or just a fan, a film buff, this book will shine a new light on the acting experience.

— **Mike Starr, veteran of *Goodfellas* (and a few *hundred* other acting works!)**

Chapter One:

In the Beginning...

When it comes to preparing for roles, the difference between acting and becoming a movie star is the difference between lightning and a lightning bug. Many people would LOVE to be seen on the big screen, to command millions of folding green for a few months' worth of work, but it takes tons of time and effort, and yes, probably a bit of luck, to get that far, no matter how quickly you make it.

Alan Ruck, he of Cameron Frye's infamous "Who do you love?! You love a car!" scene in the comedy cult classic *Ferris Bueller's Day Off* (1986), once said:

"I meet people all the time, and they ask me, 'How do I become an actor? How do I get started?' And I say, 'Well, you gotta get some experience. You have to start acting in the theater, maybe your local community theatre.' And I can see their eyes glaze over, like they're not really thinking about 'acting.' They're just thinking of being in TV shows or being a famous movie star or something. But not about learning how to act."

There's something I need to make clear right off the title page: this book won't make you a movie star. It won't even get you a bit part in a made-for-cable movie or a television pilot or even as an extra in a late-night informercial. That's up to you. That's the decision you'll have to make, and the effort you'll have to put forward. The only person who decides how far you can go in acting, just as with any other field, is the one looking at you in the mirror.

But what this book will do (hopefully) is provide you with a jumping-off point to an acting career. There's no surefire equation to film super-stardom (if there was, we'd all be the next Tom Hanks or Julia Roberts). But inside all of us who dare to dream and work, there's an actor waiting to show their stuff. How often they get to show it and to whom they show it is up to them.

Fame, stardom, and riches should not be the reasons that we get into acting. We should get into it because it's something that we're interested in, something we care about, something that we're willing to work for. And just as with great power comes great responsibility (thanks, Spiderman!), with the realizing of a dream must come the spirit to make it true.

One of the best things about acting is that people can start anywhere and end up at Hollywood stardom. Before Brad Pitt landed in the public eye, he had a gig as a giant chicken doing restaurant shtick. Danny DeVito was a hairdresser. Whoopi Goldberg was a mortician beautician. Steve Martin sewed names on Mickey Mouse ears for Disney for nearly a decade. Sean Connery delivered milk, while Jack Nicholson sorted mail. Michelle Pfeiffer worked at a grocery store, and Jennifer Aniston, Dustin Hoffman, and Gene Hackman waited tables. Jim Carrey was a janitor. Drew Barrymore even went back and forth – *after* working on *E.T.* (1982) and *Firestarter* (1984), she was a coffee shop waitress before the second part of her career got rolling. And on and on.

Point is, no one starts at the top, though people like Barrymore and Abigail Breslin have shown we can make it there before middle school graduation. It's a climb to get there, and some go higher than others. But with acting, as with anything else, it's not where you start; it's where you finish. And it really doesn't matter where you start – where you finish is up to you.

Fortunately, to an extent, we all have experience at acting. It's a profession that starts at work, or on the job – it's just that sometimes we don't get paid much.

We all act every day. Sometimes when we're at a bar, we act all tough, macho, and self-confident to try to charm our way into the heart of that bombshell on the stool next to us, hoping that she'll stick around when she gets to know the real us. When tragedies happen, we act tough for our children to let them know that everything's going to be okay as long as they're with us, and that we have control. How many times have we pretended to be nice to our bosses or co-workers, then groused to friends about what jerks they are?

"Acting is the least mysterious of all crafts," said Marlon Brando, who damn sure knew. "It's hard to imagine anyone surviving in our world without acting. It is a necessary social device; we use it to protect our interests and to gain advantage in every aspect of our lives, and it is instinctive, a skill built into all of us."

The point is, acting is human nature, in every sense of the term. Some of us make a better living doing it than others, but we all do it.

"You have to have at least 75 percent in common with any character you play," said one of the epitomes of acting knowledge, the legendary Nicholson. "You couldn't lose it if you wanted to."

Considering that Anthony Hopkins won an Oscar for playing a cannibal, Forest Whitaker for playing a murderous Ugandan dictator, and Nicholson himself for an obsessive-compulsive bigot (not to mention the different sides of wickedness he showed in *The Shining* [1980] and *The Departed* [2006]), Nicholson's percentage estimate might seem a bit high. But let's step a little deeper into it.

Hopkins didn't get ready for his role by turning a couple of his friends into liver beans and a nice steak, and Nicholson didn't really go insane, just like Whitaker didn't call up a spiritual medium and channel the spirit of Idi Amin. But going beyond that, we can see what made these villains so memorable, if not lovable.

Hannibal Lecter could terrify a statue just by looking at it, but he also had an attractive quality to him. He was the darkest of charmers. Like any good psychiatrist, he was good at making people feel at ease around him, feeling that they could trust him with their secrets. In the most evil of ways, he was charming, soft-spoken, brilliant.

Lecter isn't known as one of Hollywood's most legendary characters because of what he did; he's known because of who he was – a person that you'd find easy to like if not for that little cannibalistic impulse.

Whitaker's portrayal was the same way, and it's the same reason that Uganda fell in love with Idi Amin to begin with – not because of who he was, but because of what he did and how he did it. He showed himself to be a strong uniter, a leader, someone who could say, "Get behind me, and follow a path to greatness!" and got an entire country to listen. Whitaker's character was such that you almost forgot the fact that Amin's regime killed scores of people, because you couldn't help but think that, like Whitaker himself, he was a pretty good guy.

That's one of the biggest keys to playing a real person – if your audience is already familiar with the person before they set foot in the theater, you better have something new about the person to show them. Everyone knew who Ike and Tina Turner were on the stage; it was who they were away from the camera, and bringing them to life as imperfect people instead of performers was what got Lawrence Fishburne and Angela Bassett to the Oscars.

With Nicholson's bigoted Melvin Udall, things went to the extreme, the humorous side of racism. Bigotry isn't funny, but when a character goes to the brick wall side of ignorance (check Carroll O'Connor's Archie Bunker for the watershed example of this), he comes across as almost comedic, like you know the person's an idiot, but you still can't help but laugh at him and even cheer for him as he embarks on a journey he doesn't want to take or even know he's on. Reluctantly as a water torture victim, Udall came around with Nicholson's help, and with Nicholson's natural charisma, he was able to incorporate a shred of common decency inside Melvin that flourished.

So what are some of the first steps to take in acting? Before we pack up and move to Hollywood or New York, before we start calling acting coaches and agents, we've got to get a presentable package together. The following steps are not presented in any particular order, but all should be closely analyzed.

1. Get in character before even trying for a role.

A clean, confident, organized actor makes the best impression on someone looking to cast a role. Of course, there are roles that require a little less makeup and a lot more poundage, but directors and casting crew would rather see an actor or actress at their best before trying to make them into their worst.

Physical fitness is one of the most important first steps to acting success – it's better to start at the top and work your way down when it comes to the physical look. Remember all those resolutions we've made to drop a few pounds here and there? Maybe for New Year's, our birthday, whatever? Go for it! No time like now to shrink a bit!

Despite all those we hear about who intentionally got into sad shape for a role, that isn't something to worry about just yet. Let's get concerned about that sort of thing when there's a few credits behind our name. Right now, physicality is the way to be – and when the decision-makers who might just give us a job in their next production see how devoted we are to ourselves, it's much more likely to impress upon them the effort we'll put into our careers, and theirs.

On the other hand, there are some new things to learn and continue working with to start off our acting careers. It's important to get acquainted with the finest the American film world has ever had to offer. In 1999, the American Film Institute put out the list of top 100 films of all time, filled with such old classics as *The Godfather* (1972), *Psycho* (1960), and top spot winner *Citizen Kane* (1941). Newcomers (well, in the relative sense) like *Fargo* (1996) and *Unforgiven* (1992) made the list as well. It's a great way to journey through the legacy that's turned Hollywood into a worldwide landmark.

"The list is Hollywood keeping the nostalgia alive," says acting coach Clay Banks. "It was 100 films that everybody should watch." After all, who better to learn from than the best?

While getting ready for an audition, particularly one that requires speaking instead of singing, our first critic can be ourselves. During her younger years, remembers Oscar-winning actress Marlee Matlin, "I would take over the bathroom for hours at a time acting out stories in the mirror. Literally hours would go by..., it would be my first training ground for performing."

And one that got her on the acting atlas – she did the same thing to get in character during rehearsals for *Children of a Lesser God* (1986), which she rode all the way to a statuette.

"I created sad faces, happy ones, angry ones," Matlin remembers. "I told stories to the girl in the mirror. I learned how every part of the face and body could communicate emotions, feelings." Beginning before they ever stepped in front of a camera, and continuing throughout their careers, Marilyn Monroe and Oscar-winner Sissy Spacek employed the same technique, as did longtime *Sesame Street* (1969) veteran Bob McGrath.

"I pretended (the mirror) was the camera, verbalizing the scenes," he recalls. "I was looking to see if I convinced myself as to what I was talking about. I would try different positions, if I was walking around or even sitting, trying different positions. If you're standing on a ladder, running, walking, or laying on the floor, it tends to give a different approach to scenes. I wanted to make sure that I knew the lines."

Just as with any kind of acting practice, mirror rehearsal helps us learn our lines through and through, and it helps us develop a sequence of actions that go right along with the spoken requirements.

Acting preparation can start at home, in every sense of the word. Being one's own first audience impression has boosted many wonderful careers!

"That's one of the best pieces of advice for actors: to know the material inside and out," McGrath continues. "That's when you can really create a character. As you go along, you become a little more confident about knowing where you're supposed to be. Everything's a learning experience. If you see something that works, you know you can make it work again. You continue to work, and you continue to grow into what you do."

Keep rehearsing, and think about videotaping yourself while at it to check yourself out later. Many actors are their own biggest critics, but it's OK to be one's biggest fan once in a while.

As an added bonus here, you might want to watch these miracles, especially if you are trying out for a supporting role. Reasons being, you might want to try to react to what these characters are saying. How do you respond to these words, if not vocally? The actions, purely even physical actions, of supporting characters, can make a big difference in the effectiveness of a scene.

Yes, it's important to learn to act. But that doesn't necessarily mean that you have to win a scholarship to Julliard or go to some other prestigious school. A hungry actor – or a poor one – teaches himself to act. The mirror can be a wonderful place to hone the tone of voice, facial expressions, and body language that come from becoming a character. If we haven't convinced ourselves that we're right for the part, it's going to be awfully tough to convince the casting director.

This can help in another way as well: staring into a mirror, recite a monologue – only to yourself. Then think about how you would react and conduct yourself while performing the lines. This helps to put extra emphasis on inner emotion, rather than on voice work. It can help you get an extra appreciation for the characterization.

"I read somewhere that 'art is the search for beauty, and religion is the search for truth,'" remembers Oscar-winner Ellen Burstyn, "and it hit me like a great revelation that it is the search, not the finding. And that search is the process where the art occurs and where the truth occurs. And if, at any time, you think you've found art or you've found truth, it's not alive. It's in that search that you reach and start asking the hard questions… if you're saying 'Oh my God, who is this character? I don't know why she's doing this. Why on earth did she give all that money away? What would make me give that money away?' You start and you follow a trail and as you go along, more questions come up. And it's those questions that ignite you, that get your juices flowing. To me, question is the creative process."

Learning how to act can be rehearsing scenes or reading plays in your own bedroom. It can be taking classes at the local community college – a popular recommendation among acting textbooks and coaches – or it can mean turning our bedroom into a 10-by-10 Broadway, doing the scenes from your favorite plays (it's best to do this with the door locked – having someone walk in and seeing you acting out a scene might make them question your social stability!).

Take a scene from one of your favorite films, perhaps one with a long monologue-type performance, and become a character in the scene. It's best to take a film that you enjoy on a personal level, not only for the quality of the acting. The more personal passion and enjoyment you have for the film, the more likely you'll be to subconsciously put more of that passion and effort into your impersonations. Here are a few effective ones:

a. Faye Dunaway's "no wire hangers!" rant as Joan Crawford in *Mommie Dearest* (1981). One legendary actress showing the dark side of another.

b. Jack Nicholson's courtroom battle with Tom Cruise in *A Few Good Men* (1992). Not only do you get Jack at his most memorable ("I have a greater responsibility than you can possibly imagine!"), but you get to give your own version of the immortal, "You can't handle the truth!"

c. Al Pacino's "I'd take a FLAME-THROWER to this place!" speech near the end of *Scent of a Woman* (1992), or one of his talks in *The Godfather* (1972). He has one of these in almost every film he's ever done, but these two won him Oscars.

d.   Robin Williams' chat to Matt Damon in *Good Will Hunting* (1997), where he uses Shakespeare and a story about his dead wife to get inside Will's head. In a few short minutes, he eviscerates Will's tough-guy persona and brings out the genius inside.

e.   Kevin Spacey's speech to Chaz Palmintieri in *The Usual Suspects* (1995) when he gives the lowdown on the evil, mysterious Keyser Soze. HIS Verbal Kint mixes awe and fear together like peanut butter and jelly, and the fact that you find out that Verbal made it all up just increases the impact.

f.   Peter Finch in *Network* (1976). Take your pick – no way he wasn't winning Best Actor after this showing. "I'm mad as hell, and I'm not going to take it anymore!" is the most well known, but it's hardly the only one.

g.   Samuel L. Jackson's dual speeches in *Pulp Fiction* (1994). He starts and ends the film with the same Bible verse, and manages to put it two opposite and still completely believable ways. Shouting it at the beginning and softly explaining it at the end, this was one for the books (like this one!).

h.   Hilary Swank's plea for Clint Eastwood to help her end things easily from a hospital bed in *Million Dollar Baby* (2004). The best and saddest part of an Oscar-winning work.

i.   James Earl Jones' "People will come, Ray," scene in *Field of Dreams* (1989). One of film's most famous voices does its thing to perfection.

j.   Morgan Freeman's parole committee scene near the end of *Shawshank Redemption* (1994) – the one that actually gets him released. Seconds in, it's easy to believe that this fellow really did spend 30 years in jail.

k.   Marlon Brando's "I coulda been a contender," speech in *On the Waterfront* (1954). So good that Robert De Niro used it to get his own Academy Award in *Raging Bull* (1980).

l.   Mel Gibson's "They may take our lives, but they'll never take... our freedom!" pep talk in *Braveheart* (1995). Another great scene from which, sadly, only one line is commonly recalled.

m.   Humphrey Bogart's final goodbye in *Casablanca* (1942). "Here's looking at you, kid," and everything before it.

n.   *Apocalypse Now* (1979) has at least two options. Robert Duvall's fear that "The war's going to end someday!" and Marlon Brando's spine-freezing "The horror! The horror!" will live forever.

o.   Comedies can be a great way to learn this. Try Bill Murray's speech about the Dalai Lama from *Caddyshack* (1980) or Marisa Tomei's testimonial rants in *My Cousin Vinny* (1992).

These are only some of the cinema's most memorable choices. If you can find another that works, go for it with guns blazing, and keep at it until you've impressed your first and most common audience – yourself. In fact, while these might be good for honing your skills on your own, it might be a good idea to have a lesser-known monologue when you work in front of others: giving the cast and director something they are less familiar with not only gives them an appreciation for your work ethic, but your devotion to learning more about the role beforehand.

Remember – the more passion you show for your role (before, during, and after your tryout), the more your audience – your "other" audience – will appreciate it.

Note: If you're preparing to play an especially strong-willed, intimidating character, it helps to blink as little as possible. According to Oscar-winner Michael Caine, blinking makes a character look weak, a lesson taken to heart by everyone from a cannibal named Lecter to cartoonish supervillian Judge Doom in *Who Framed Roger Rabbit* (1988). Long stretches of staring show intensity and focus – two qualities we want the audience to be receiving when we're in their line of view.

---

2. Got a newspaper, or local web site? Head to the community theater section. Then never, never stop trying.

"Whatever it is, take it," said late acting legend Jack Lemmon. "Even if it's the worst dog of a show and closes after one night. Take any acting role you can get."

There's no such thing as bad experience when it comes to acting.

Long before budding screen stars take the first step into his school, they've got previous opportunities to hone their craft, usually right at home, says acting coach Fran Montano.

"They can do community theater in their area," he explains. "They should volunteer so they can learn about the process when they're working behind the scenes with set design, being a page, running a box office, and trying to get as much theater experience as they can."

Videos, student films, local acting troupes… anything and everything is there for someone who's willing to go out and search for it, even if their first few jobs are far from the stage or camera. If it's practicing a monologue in front of a mirror at home, go for it. If it's reciting the lines from your favorite film, try it. If you're practicing voices while playing various roles reading books to a preschool class, never stop developing your talent, and never stop trying as hard as you can.

Just about every performer profiled in this book has had some on-stage experience of some kind, often between film roles. Patrick Swayze, for example, saw the world playing Prince Charming with the Disney on Parade traveling show.

After all, theater acting offers one chance that we don't get on the screen – an opportunity to see, interact with, and hopefully hold spellbound our audience. We get to stand on stage for the final bow, hearing them cheer, seeing them applaud, and know that we inspired them to do it.

"I want beginning actors to get as much performance experience and knowledge about the business as they can before they get to Hollywood, to see if they even like it," Montano says.

Acting classes can be a two-for-one special. Taking some at the local community college or theater doesn't just make our skills a little better; it can give us a new network outlet. The teachers are there because they themselves have the background and expertise that come from learning how to act – chances are, they have some connections with the local acting scene as well.

"The training stimulates the self and provides an environment where the unconscious can speak," says Oscar-winner Ellen Burstyn. "I've had experiences when I'm playing a character that I think I understand, and suddenly during rehearsal an impulse will come out of nowhere – what was that? So I start paying attention to it, and it takes me on a trail where I can say, 'Oh, I see, she does that because what she's really after is this.' So I start following that trail, and it takes me back to something I have in me, but wasn't paying attention to."

If we can be a class standout, we might score some points with a teacher or director who's looking to put together a production of their own, or knows someone who is. Finding a spot in their mind might just entice them to tell their closest casting buddy, "Hey, there's this person in my class that works really hard and really wants to make an impact. Maybe we should give her a shot in this production!"

It's important to remember that, just as with beggars, budding actors can't be choosers. If directors don't know who you are, they're not going to call you up and say, "Just in case you want to act for a living, I'm looking for people to star in this production. Auditions will be held in this place, at this time..."

Nope, not happening. That's why it's important to never stop auditioning, and never stop looking for places to show your stuff. No matter who's asking for actors, no matter what type of production it is, go for it. If it's a commercial for pet manure carpet removal, go for it. If it's an extra on a school production playing a tree, go for it.

"If you're an actor, you don't stop," said late legendary character actor James Gammon of *Major League* (1989) fame. "If you're an actor, you're an actor. You're going to go to the ballpark, which can be theaters, interviews, anything, and you're going to be swinging away. You're trying to get that rhythm, hit that ball. It's an opportunity for you to meet some wonderful people in the acting world, in the theater world." This leads us to...

---

3. Network the likes of which ABC, NBC, and FX never saw in their lifetimes.

You can never know too many people in this craft, and there can never be enough people that know your name and face. They'll see how serious you are about snaring an acting role, and keep you in mind. Dedication to a craft, devotion to one's work, showing extreme anxiety to take the first and next step in a journey – these are things that make a strong first impression. If you feel that a role is beneath you for whatever reason, acting's probably the wrong profession for you; you're too new to the game to start calling the shots.

"You often will get a role and be shooting as early as the next day," says longtime TV actress Cheryl White. "It's important to focus on the things that you can control. Be prepared for auditions and jobs when you get them. Be a disciplined professional. It is a business and if you waste people's time, it costs them money. But if you do your job, at the highest level of professionalism and artistry that you can, they will want to work with you again. You will build relationships. You will build a career."

At this stage in the game, don't worry about agents; chances are, they're not going to talk to you until your resume fills at least a page. For now, it's up to you to be your own promoter. Talk to people — actors, directors, screenwriters, stage hands, even janitors. You never know when someone might know someone, or when they might have an invaluable piece of advice for you.

"Like most things, (acting) is about relationships," explains Richard D'Alessandro, who's been appearing on screens of all sizes for a quarter-century. "It's about who you know, and who knows you. People hear stories about other people making it overnight, and some people get lucky, but most people make it overnight after 20 years. I like actors who have a steady career; they never hit the top, but they always stay in the middle; you have longevity that way."

It's best to make yourself as reachable as possible. Always have a cell phone at the ready; just make sure to keep it at the vibrating setting in public (loud noises as such have been known to tick passersby off). If you can't get that, or your workplace doesn't allow you to keep one on, grab a pager, a Blackberry, whatever, and be near a phone. Acting jobs can be caught at a second's notice, and lost in the same manner. If someone's doing calls for an audition, they're not going to put it off if you can't come.

While we're here, a word on work while searching for acting success: if you're in an area near the central point of American acting, like Hollywood, and are just holding out for the big break, like many others, it's best to take a job that you (a) don't want to make a career of, and (b) can get a bit flexible with the hours. Try to work somewhere that will not really create a problem with leaving quickly, one that you personally won't mind leaving quickly.

If you're going to be an actor, that needs to be your career and your focal point. Don't get into a position where you might be making a ton of money and in line for a big promotion, only to have to choose whether to lose it all for a shot at acting. You don't want to have to lose much if you miss out on a role. Jobs like waiting tables, working security, stocking at 24-hour places, temp agenices, and substitute teaching are attractive options for people who might just have to drop off a two-week notice quickly.

A few years ago, a young waitress (in training) managed to finagle a week off from work to go star in some five-figure budget flick that no one, not even the studios, ever thought would make it to even 100 theaters.

Quite a while later, she was still hoping for at least fifteen percent on the tabs. The film was being edited and shopped around. But then the jackpot was struck, as a major film company jammed it into theaters.

The film came out, and word started to spread. Less than a week after its release, it had exponentially gained back the budget. It went on to reach the mouths and minds of film fans across America. Before long, people were pouring into the coffee shop for reasons far past the food and drink, asking to pose for pictures and sign autographs. Before she'd even handed in her two-week notice, she was one of the newest faces in the film world's public eye.

It was Katie Featherston – starlette of the *Paranormal Activity* (2007) series.

---

4. Grab What You Can, and Hang On!

It's a good idea to grab contact information of people you meet, and keep a journal of what you learned. Remember that the bit of information that seemed unnecessary at the time might come very much in handy at a later date.

One of the worst things that can happen at any point in an acting career is to get a reputation for being difficult to work with; this can spread like a brushfire, and be almost as destructive. You especially don't want it to happen at the first stages of a career.

"It's all about networking to your pinkie through the door," said Adrienne King, who used the technique to wrangle the lead heroine role in *Friday the 13th* (1980), still being re-made three decades after its premiere. "It's up to you to push it the rest of the way."

Go for every role you can find in every production you can find. Get your name and your face in the local theater community. Not only are you more likely to find a role, but you'll eventually make an impact on the casting directors, the producers, etc. You never know who's going to see you, and who they might know – or even be!

Oh, and one last thing – NEVER let the words, "Open call," "Open audition," or anything that starts with the word "Open," brush you off. Just because anyone can come doesn't mean that everyone will. All too often, potential actors and actresses may see those words and get too intimidated to come.

"After all," they may think, "the place is going to be jammed! Why should I even try? I'm bound to get overshadowed by someone in such a large crowd!"

That's a fallacious assumption, because, again, everything in acting is worth taking a chance in. Many people would like to act, but fewer are willing to put forth the time and effort to make it, and it's too easy to make excuses – and in this book, we'll meet more than one person who overcame all the odds.

"In all the auditions I've ever been to, I've never seen more than 10 or 15 individuals at any casting call," says acting coach Peter Jazwinski. "Sometimes you see hundreds or thousands at an open call, but those are rare!"

Remember the last time you checked out a preview of the next *American Idol* (2002) season and saw a stadium's worth of people who just *knew* that they'd be the next big hit? That's the overwhelming exception – more likely than not, others may decide that the odds against them are so great that they're not worth trying. It's up to you to be the exception to that rule.

And though not all of us were in the Cub Scouts at an early age, we can always follow their motto of "Be Prepared." At an audition, it's always best to go for the gusto and do everything you'd do in the role itself. Do everything you can to get into character long before you walk on the stage. Casting directors want the best, because it's your head — and face, body, etc. — that they're hanging their hat on. They're probably not going to say, "Well, she wasn't the best here, but we'll take a chance on her and trust her to improve by leaps and bounds by the time we get started."

Don't think of auditions as your first chance at the part — consider it your first and last. It's tough to get worked up for something that has little or no guarantee at a payoff, but it's worth it when the part comes your way.

"They want to see it all in the audition, so all the preparation that I do to get the parts is for the audition," says Sarah Joyner, who falls to her death in the opening scene of the 1993 Sylvester Stallone vehicle *Cliffhanger*. "Once you get the part, they kind of expect you to do what you did in the audition. Sometimes there's a logistics change or the script gets re-written, but for smaller roles, you usually do the same thing in the film that you do in the audition."

---

5. Accept rejection, and transform it into competition

The first and last word about rejection is not to get discouraged over not getting certain roles and lines. Know that getting rejected is not something to be feared — it happens to everyone.

Rejection. Get used to hearing that word in acting. Why? Because it's unavoidable. There's many, many other people trying to get involved in the acting world, and many of them will be just as devoted, if not more so, to their dream as you are. Having so many options may be a casting director's dream, but it's an actor's nightmare. That's why it's important to shove each rejection out of your memory and start looking for the next role. The quicker you find a new task, the less time to worry about what you didn't get.

It can be tough to deal with rejection in acting, because chances are the director isn't going to call you up and say, "OK, this was what you did wrong." It's hard to learn from NOT getting a part. But again, everyone gets rejected at some point — maybe many points — in time, but never giving up is the way to think, and once you get that one role, think about how much pent-up aggression you'll be able to finally put into it!

A point of advice might be to see a play you didn't get a role in. Closely watch the person that got "your" role and see what is done with it. Compare the portrayal to your audition, and try to learn from it, to build off of it. That way, next time you audition for the same director or type of role, you'll have a slightly better idea as to what new tactics to utilize.

"I've been 30 years in theater, 20 in film, and it's still hard for me to get jobs I want," says Raoul Trujillo, who stared in *Apocalypto* (2006) and *The New World* (2005), amongst other films and TV shows.

"Go pound the pavement in Los Angeles or New York, and be prepared for intense rejection. If something's really meant to be, it'll come to be. You really have to be prepared to develop a really thick skin and deal with exploitation, to an extent."

Remember, it's worse to quit before you try than to never try at all. That's why rejection is a big part of any actor's life, especially at the start. But the good news about rejection is that it's not always the actor's fault. Remember, the casting director may have a solid picture of what she wants long before the audition process begins. She may be looking for someone of an exact height, an exact weight, an exact age, a mole in exactly the right spot on the end of the person's nose. The important thing is to never, ever stop trying.

But just as with any other type of rejection, it's up to us to put a mute button on those naysayers who try to tell us we shouldn't try. Of course acting's not easy, and paid acting's difficult to find – no one's saying that. But I guarantee you this – **everyone** who has made it big in acting in the past few decades has at some point in time had someone say to or about them, "You shouldn't try, because everyone wants to do that. The competition level's so high, you've got pretty much no chance. You should quit now before you get disappointed."

Those are exactly the type of people that we *shouldn't* listen to. When a person says something like that, what they're emitting is along these lines: "I don't have the guts to try, so you shouldn't either. That way, we'll be even." Remember – it's our life to live, and it's our dream to follow. Never let anyone, even those that might mean well, sour us on realizing our hopes.

Ask yourself: what exactly do you have to lose here? The answer's pretty simple: zilch. Nada. Zero. In another word, nothing. The first time you go to an audition, the first time you go back to an audition after getting rejected, the first time you send out your information to an agency or an acting company, you've taken one more step than thousands of others ever dared. It's going to take time, effort, and dedication, but so does everything else worth doing.

All the people you see on television and the big screen right now were once in the very position you're in; the reason they're there is because they never gave up, and that's what happens when we don't let worthless criticism cloud the vision of our goals. Failing doesn't mean that we tried and didn't get our desired result – it means we didn't have the guts to try.

"If I kept all my bad notices," notes Roger Moore, who brought James Bond to the big screen seven times in the 1970s and 80s, "I'd need two houses."

---

5. Vanquish the Voice!
In my work teaching college English, I spend quite a bit of time on Critical Thinking. People have written books to define the term, so it's best to go one basic feature at a time. Critical Thinking simply refers to the type of education that can't really be obtained from a classroom, and one strong feature is mental

ability with guts involved. It's the willingness to think on one's feet and use them to carry you outside the box. It's the type of education that comes from open-mindedness and experience, things that are all but impossible to learn from a textbook.

Anyway, one of my biggest lessons deals with a thing called the Voice of Criticism. Remember all those people I just talked about, the ones that try to keep you from reaching your dream? They're pretty easy to ignore – just add earplugs. But this Voice is a bit tougher, because it comes from within. It's that pesky little noise you can't help but pick up when you mess up.

You failed a test? "You're a failure!"

You got rejected by that girl at the bar? "You're an ugly anti-socialite!"

You actually got a break? "So what? Everyone gets lucky once in a while, but lightning probably won't strike twice, so you should go ahead and stop trying. It's easier to do what's easy than what's right!"

Sound familiar? Hopefully not, but here's what to do if this verbal virus shows up.

1. **Acknowledge it.**

    The first key to solving a problem is understanding it. We know what the Voice is, and when to expect it. Now that we can put a name to a noise, let's see if we can figure out how to deal with our inner enemy.

2. **Confront it.**

    Remember the last situation when this thing came to visit? Now we know what to do about it. If the Voice shows back up, let it know that you're onto it, and it's in for a battle you'll win!

    Try turning the Voice's statements around to something a little more diplomatic and easy on the ego. If it says, "You're a failure for not getting that part!" just quickly say to yourself (preferably silently, unless you're alone) something like, "OK, you didn't get that part, so what can you take away from it? Was there something that you could have improved on in your preparation? Did you dress right? Did you speak right? Try to find something to do better next time.

    "And hey, who says it was your fault, anyway? Matter of fact, who says it's even your loss? Maybe they had someone in mind before you were even called! Maybe they just don't know talent when they see it! Take all that energy and intensity that you're ready to throw into your acting career and keep it inside – by the time you get a role, you'll be hitting on so many cylinders the casting director won't know what hit him! You'll go the likes of which he's never seen before! Keep working hard, buddy, because it's going to pay off in the long run!"

    The longer version feels a lot better, doesn't it?

"It's important to not take the inevitable rejection personally," says actress Michelle St. John. "That is easier said than done because it is hard to bare yourself emotionally and then have someone say, 'We've gone in a different direction' or 'we've moved on' or 'she's not beautiful enough.' Sometimes producers/directors have no idea what they are looking for and sometimes they know exactly what they are looking for, and as actors our best protection is to do our very best, every time we walk into an audition or a meeting. Maybe we're not right for one role but will be for another."

3. **Keep fighting.**

   Don't be fooled; the voice isn't going to go away overnight, or even over-week! Chances are, it's been in you for quite some time, and it's not ready to leave. That's why you have to keep fighting it. Keep confronting it. Keep using its words against it.

   Eventually, the messages will get smaller and smaller, and you won't notice them as much – but they'll still be there. It's up to you to not let the Voice get the best of you, even for a second. Continue the battle – it's a slippery slope, but the biggest mountain in the world has been climbed.

6. Agents- Who's Good, Who's Not!

Ever seen an advertisement on television for purchasing real estate cheap with the promise that, with the least of efforts, we can sell it high and make about five or six figures in about a month, or some other such venture? How about those ads about people getting rich from stuffing envelopes? Or any other one that included the words "Can't miss!" and "Make money instantly!"? Did you rush to the phone and dial up, already dreaming of the dollar signs rolling in?

Probably not. Because if something seems too good to be true, it probably is. The same concept applies to finding a good agent to get our career going.

If an agent gives you a list of promises about becoming the next Robert De Niro, that's all well and good. But if he or she ends with the words, "All it's going to run you is (dollar amount) up front," take your money and run. A good agent works off commission, not early assurance fees. Once they get you an audition, then you might think about paying for that.

If an agent assures you that they're also qualified to be your photographer or acting coach, it's not just a probable falsehood; it's a conflict of interest. If they require you to work with a specific photographer or coach, see the red flags rising: it's probably not because it's two friends helping one another out; more likely, someone's getting cuts on the downlow.

Treat it just like any other job interview, only you're the employer. Remember, this person's working for you, and you'll eventually end up paying their salary. Ask around, get references, find out who they are and what they're about – what they can do for you. Switch around the JFK inaugural speech: "Ask not what you can do for them; ask what they can do for you!"

7. Headshots

Though most of these steps can be done out of the order written, I put this last because I find it least important. First of all, professional headshots are expensive, and second of all, they shouldn't be done without some experience under your belt. Do some auditions, try to get some roles, and build up your resume and poise before you start worrying about getting a photo. Keep in mind that still cameras and headshot photographers are an audience just like any other kind, so getting experience in front of a theater audience can help your level of self-assurance when you're posing for a single shot.

Headshots are an advertisement, not an audition. If you'd like to be a horror star, don't have pictures taken of yourself looking scared. This isn't the time – yet! – to get in character. Agents, producers, everyone else will see that, and think, "Wow, this person does NOT look comfortable in front of a camera!" They'll think your fear is coming from the setting, not the potential monster chasing you. Headshots are there to show comfort and charisma in the midst of flashing lights, someone with an expression that makes its subject look like there's nowhere else she'd rather be.

It's quite all right to show emotion in a headshot, as long as it's the right kind. Intensity, optimism, friendliness all rolled into a pair of eyes and a wide smile (or pouted, seductive lips, depending on the object) can be the total package for someone looking to get noticed.

Of course, once you have some expertise, once you feel like you can take the next step in acting, by all means, go and get that headshot done! Headshots can be a wonderful manner of self-promotion. Let's be our own public relations firm!

Remember, as with so many other things about acting, what's not usable now might be perfect tomorrow. You never know when someone will take a quick look back through their photos, notice you, and say, "Hey, now *there's* someone who looks the part in abundance!"

Shop around a bit; find out who's got the most experience, the strongest expertise, and, yes, even the finest deals. But get in front of a camera, and get your photos taken and sent around: casting agencies, directors, everyone. At the start of a career, it might be best to get a shot from the chest up; it shows enough of your profile without giving too much away.

If you absolutely want to get a headshot done very early in your career, there's good (read: cheap) ways of going about it. Before you start firing out the funds to a professional, ask around your friends or co-workers. Check at the local schools, like community colleges or technical places, or want ads.

There may be someone with photography as a side business or hobby who can set you up with a great shot for one-twentieth the price of a pro. Remember, just like any other type of art, photography is very open to subjective interpretation. Just because a photo's not taken by a photographer doesn't mean that it won't suddenly grab the attention of a casting director – and just because it was professionally done doesn't mean that it WILL get a second look.

There's plenty of people looking for experience in photography, just like you are for acting, and many will jump at the chance to snap a photo that could kick-start a career – it's their name getting out, as well as yours. They get to use what they've been taught at the same time as you, so everybody can win in a situation like this.

The Audition Process

You've seen a notice for play tryouts, and the production looks perfect for you. Perhaps you've seen the play, or a cinematic variance, before. Maybe you're familiar with the characters in it, and have always thought you could do their job, maybe even a little bit better. For any reason, it's time to take the first step toward the next acting gig.

Prepare beforehand

Try to hunt down a copy of the script beforehand, and familiarize yourself with a character; in many auditions, you'll get to choose the character you are trying out for. Then take all of the steps outlined above, and start developing.

Think of their emotions, their tone of voice, their mannerisms (check the section on Backstories a bit later on for more help in this department). Call ahead to ask the producers what will be expected of you. That makes a good first impression – you cared enough to get acquainted with them and the play beforehand, and now it's up to you to maintain that impression. If you don't get the part you hoped for, the crew might be impressed enough with your work ethic and devotion to give you another role, one that may be just as good, if not better. Know your lines ahead of time – all of them. And know what movements to make, know where you are in character. Know your setting, your past and future, even a few monutes before or ahead. Where have you been, and where are you going from the scene. Make it real. Make it special. Make it yours.

If it's a musical, you'll probably be asked to sing. Pick a song that you're comfortable with, but one that's clean (lyrics with obscentities and other vulgar speech do *not* impress anyone). Pick a song that you're familiar with beforehand. Try singing it along with the music, and then a few times without, since that's probably what you'll be doing at the audition. Forget all those people that go on the *American Idol* auditions and get laughed off the stage – no one worth their salt is going to talk that way to you. The worst thing that can happen is that you don't get the part, and that WILL (not may) happen at some point during your career.

The best thing about auditions is that there's really nothing to lose; if you make it, great. But if you don't, you'll still be meeting people, making contacts, developing your skills. They might not want you the first time, but if you made a strong impact, they'll remember you the next time – and that may be the perfect time. Not only that, but their original choice might not be able to do the role, and if you're their second choice, you're good to go! Finishing second doesn't mean we don't win!

Get there early

To be early is to be on time. To be on time is to be late. To be late is to be left behind.

I didn't invent that quote, but it applies in every professional setting, especially when things like first impressions and reputation establishment are coming into play. You can have the best excuses in the world to be late for an audition or rehearsals, but seasoned directors have heard them all – true or otherwise – before, and your lateness is going to stick in the back of their mind.

"If rehearsal starts at 10 a.m.," said late great character actress Elizabeth Pena, "you get the cup of coffee at nine."

Speaking as someone who can't get out of bed without two alarm clocks and a pair of sodas before 9 a.m. (I was traumatized away from coffee when I was about six when I took a sip of my mother's mug of it and felt like my esophagus had melted), I know that there's all sorts of ways, many of which are much more effective than my own, to get out of bed and get rolling.

This is about planning ahead, another important aspect of professionalism. If you have something big for the next day, especially one whose time expenditure may be difficult to estimate ahead of time, take out a sheet of paper and mark your day off by the hour. Don't just list everything you need to get done – literally write "8 a.m.," then leave a gap before writing "9 a.m.," and so on, all the way until you've gotten around to bedtime. Try to plot out your main priorities for the next day, and the time that you expect to need for them.

Keep it reasonable and realistic; don't try to plan things out to the minute, but get the basics down with your best guesses. Remember that travel, meals, filling the gas tank, and other intangibles need to be taken into consideration with this activity.

Not only will this take a burden off your memory, since you'll be able to glance at a sheet to find out where to be, but it will help keep you on schedule. Will you have half an hour for breakfast, or only 15 minutes? Is the rehearsal location an hour away? If so, do you normally encounter traffic in that area, which might require a bit more time?

Is there anything that you can put off till the next day, or is there anything that should take priority over your rehearsal? There will always be another. Remember that if we try hard enough for long enough, we'll miss a role we felt we had in the bag, and get one that we thought we didn't have a prayer of snaring. One gotten role won't make a career, and one missed one won't kill a career.

Making a schedule for the next day is a good jumping-off point. It shows us a map to success that we just have to follow. It's a place to get the day started long before the sun rises.

Stay in character until the audition ends

By now, you're in character, and you should know the situations at hand. Pretend you're at a job interview for a position you especially want. Walk in with your head held high, exuding confidence. Answer any questions with a strong, serious voice and make eye contact — you're exactly where you should be, and exactly where you intend to stay. This is not the time to appear nervous or off-kilter, especially when you're new to the scene; that may be a part of the character you're portraying, but the judges won't know that you're just acting.

Let them know what you'll be doing; be prepared to discuss the character for whom you are auditioning, why you feel that you should be chosen, and what you can do for the play (remember, this is like a job interview). If you were allowed to choose your audition material, get ready to explain why you chose it in particular.

At the welcome call of "Action," try to lose yourself in the scene. Take yourself away from the stage, the room, or wherever you are, and put yourself where your character is. If you mess up, just keep going; in a theatrical production, that's a situation you may have to face, and showing that you're ready will show them the depths of your preparation.

Let them decide when it's over. If they ask you to stop, do so. Don't stop when you think you're done, and ask, "Is that enough?" That's not the impression you want to make; it shows that you're only there to do just enough, not what they want. Remember, you're there to impress them.

Leave the audition the same way that you would any other job interview. Thank them for their time with a big smile, and stroll confidently (acting or otherwise) out the door.

Before you get the role, you'll probably get at least one callback, when they'll probably ask you to do some scenes from the production at hand. That's why it's important to be familiar with the characters and storyline before you even get into the car to drive to the audition.

Callbacks are a reason to get excited, but not to the extent that anything should be taken for granted. It may mean you've progressed to the next level, but not to the finish line; many performers have to go back several times before they're chosen for any roles, even small ones.

"Getting called back is a triumph in itself," says legendary horror star Robert Englund, Freddy Krueger himself. "Even if I didn't get a certain part, I should still feel good that somebody in the casting office, or several somebodies, liked me enough to give me a second, or third, or even a tenth shot. You have to turn the negative into a positive and take what you can out of the experience, and that could be something as small as a good acting tip, or something as big as getting the producer's contact number."

Remember that *anything* – hair or eye color, age, height, weight, birthmarks, eyelash length, anything, can make the difference between getting the part and not getting it. Sometimes cast members have in mind what they want before they've held the first few auditions, and they might just be looking to thin the herd. That's not fair or right, but it's a dark side of their job, and they probably don't like it any more than the performers they have to turn away – Englund lost roles in *Apocalypse Now* (1979) and *Star Wars* (1977) simply because he was too young at the time. Luck plays as big a role during auditions as it does in any other part of the acting business – we simply don't want it to play too big a part, and we can do this by covering as many bases as possible.

Should you not get picked, you can still get something out of the deal, as Englund pointed out. Whether you're chosen or not, try to get contact information from the crew. After the cast has been picked, give one or more of them a call and ask if they have any tips for you, if they know of any upcoming productions elsewhere, what they liked and didn't like about your audition, anything. Again, it keeps your name in their minds.

Here's something else; auditions need readers, people who aren't trying out, but are the supporting characters in the tryout. They're the ones that read the lines to put the auditioners in action. Contact the casting directors to let them know you'd like to handle the reading duties for the event.

This shows devotion to the craft, and puts your name in their minds as someone with a strong work ethic. Not only that, but if you're new to the auditioning process itself, witnessing it as something of an outsider can give you an up close and more personal view of it than anything else. It's something to remember for when you're the one putting on an impromptu show.

Chapter Two:
Meet The Coaches

"You have absolute control over only one thing, and that is your thoughts. This is the most significant and inspiring of all facts known to humans."

~ Napoleon Hill, *Think and Grow Rich*

Let's talk to some acting coaches around the Golden State, and the city of cinema. Let's get some advice from those who help kick-start acting dreams.

"Before a person comes to my school, I like them to be established," says Emmy-winning acting coach Fran Montano. "They need a place to live, a car, and a job. They're supporting themselves, and they're financially stable. It's important that they plan accordingly. Sometimes a person will show up with a chunk of money and say, 'Okay, I'm ready to live here for six months. Make me a star in six months!' But they need a real commitment to what they're going to do, and they must give it time and work on it.

"A lot of people are impatient," Montano says, "and they want to start working right away. They don't last in Hollywood, and they don't last as actors. Acting is a process; anybody can say a line or write a script, but saying it with a lot of life, emotion, experience, and intention behind it, that's the craft."

"More gold has been mined from the thoughts of men than has ever been taken from the earth." ~ Hill

Some may turn on the television or check out a film and think, "Wow, that looks easy! All I have to do to be an actor is pretend to be someone else! Just change my voice a little and get my facial muscles flowing, and I'll have an Academy Award next year."

According to acting coach Clay Banks, acting carries JUST a bit more challenge than that. Maybe more than a bit.

"If you take a look at anybody that's a master in their profession, from Michael Jordan to Tiger Woods to De Niro and Pacino," Banks says, "the reason everything they do looks so easy is because of all the intense work that they do when we're **not** watching. (Anthony) Hopkins reads his scripts like 250 times before he ever goes in front of the camera. When he gets in front of the camera, he's prepared."

A student's preparation starts long before Banks' first class.

"(Before they come and meet me) they can get focused on what they really want to do," he says, "and decide whether or not they're willing to give a good chunk of their lives to this. Are their lives in a position to handle it? It's the commitment. A lot of people approach acting like it's a business, and it is... *show* business, but there's an artistic side to it. That's something that can't be handled lightly, because it's art.

"Sometimes people take a scene and put it in soil, and say, 'Grow! Grow! Grow!' and it just doesn't work that way. When you're in an artistic profession, the best thing to do is to bring in all the elements. Make sure that the pot is big enough, get the right soil with the right fertilizer, put it in a place where it's going to get light and shade, and water it appropriately. Then it can grow at the rate that nature intended."

Some of his clientele don't even get the seed planted.

"I give actors a one-page script and tell them, 'If you work on this, it's going to improve your acting tremendously,' and most actors don't ever do it," Banks says. "For me, it's an integrity issue. When I work with someone, I want to help them along the way, as opposed to having them just write their check and leave. I'm a real proponent of the instrument as the organic part of acting. For me, if you don't have it in you, you're not bringing it out of you. If you don't have an understanding of life, and behavior, and people, and experience, and emotion, how are you going to recreate that?

"If you had a paint palette with only six colors on it, then everything you draw is only going to have those few colors. But if you experience life, you're opening and awakening yourself to sensory developments – How do things smell? How do they taste? How do they look? If you get into being an artist, your palette grows, with all the colors and everything. You're able to bring that much more shading and depth, and knowledge to things."

"An exercise I have a student do is to ask them to make a significant point of 'experiencing' by going out to the grocery store to buy produce. They set an in-point and an out-point which gives the exercise a beginning, middle, and an end. They go to the produce department and get a grapefruit (or any fruit). Hold the grapefruit. Feel the depth, the dimensions, and the texture. Take your time with it and really look at it. Smell it. Stop time and experience it. When you put it back, how does it line up with the rest of those grapefruit? As you're walking through the produce department, what impressions are you getting? Heighten your awareness of everything."

Though he doesn't have his students read acting books, per se, Eric Stone asks that they peruse one legendary literary tome.

"The first thing that I would suggest would be *Think and Grow Rich*," he says, referring to Napoleon Hill's 1937 (and repeatedly reissued) work, commonly accepted as one of the first and greatest self-help books ever written, compiled over decades of research and hundreds of interviews. "Whether they've done theater all their life as a kid, or just gone to the movies a lot, they want to descend upon Hollywood. There isn't a better approach to Hollywood that I've read than what Napoleon maps out regarding what one should do. It applies to any endeavor one might take. It helps us to lay out a plot. In Hollywood, you cannot separate the artist from the worker. This is an industry town."

He doesn't have them read acting books, he continues, "Because what I want is called, 'the uncarved block.' I want someone who really doesn't know a lot of acting, but really loves it, and someone who is ready to work."

> *"The following are important factors of leadership: unwavering courage, self-control, a keen sense of justice, definitness of decision and plans, the habit of doing more than paid for, a pleasing personality, sympathy and understanding, mastery of detail, willingness to assume full responsibility, and cooperation."* ~ Hill

"What's important for an acting coach, or any good teacher," Banks explains, "is to really have an in-depth understanding of the people that they're working with, and really know where they're coming from. You've got the heart, the soul, the physical appearance of the actor, and all these things factor in and shouldn't be overlooked when a person is chasing a career in acting. I'm not just about building actors for the sake of acting; I'm about building people."

That's because he, like many acting coaches, is about where potential actors have been, where they are, and where they're going.

"When somebody is aspiring to get into the business, and they show up in my acting class," he says, "I watch them, and I want to know where they're coming from. They spend a little time in the studio, and start to get their legs. I'll start seeing, are they taking this seriously, or are they not? Is this a dream, or a job opportunity? Acting is a heightened recreation of the illusion of life, and all of us are in life. You talk with them, and you find out where they're coming from. I've had students come in to the studio that are just oozing with talent, but it's not something that they want to do. That hurts, because you're watching amazing talent that just isn't getting used."

> *"No man achieves great success who is unwilling to make personal sacrifices."* ~ Hill

"People come in and sometimes say, 'I don't even know if I want to be an actor; would you indulge me and let me know what it's about?'" says Banks. "I say, 'As long as you do the work, know your lines, and get along with everyone, no problem. Let's see what you've got.' If they have the right attitude, we're good, and if the superstardom takes off, you've won the lottery."

One doesn't even need a ticket to hit this jackpot.

"When an actor walks through the door, and we hand them a scene, after the cold-reading work, they need to learn their lines to the best of their ability," he says. "It's about the actor's work ethic. If you work with me for six months, and don't put in the time to do enough homework, we have an issue. There's only one rule, and that's to know your lines."

Lessons start with cold-reading a short script.

"It's what we call off-camera rehearsal," he says. "Come knowing your lines, and we go to work on rehearsing the scene."

That's the first week; in the second, Banks' mini-theater becomes a performance place.

"We shoot the scene," he says. "I film the actors with my cameras. We might shoot everything in close-up, because an actor's bread and butter is the close-up. The audience connects with the person in the close-up. The awards are won in the close-up."

His students work on memorization techniques, script analysis, and character work, finishing up with a level near that of actual on-set acting.

"We work on you the actor," Banks says. "All of your emotions, familiar as well as unfamiliar. Let's say you have repressed anger in you, and you just cannot seem to do certain scenes because there's a personal intensity. You need to let go and express your anger… more; it's all OK! The instrument must play all of its notices. Training is about exercising the instrument, holistically and completely."

Montano has his own unique approach to acting instruction.

"In my school, we don't even work on scripted material for at least three months," he says. "We get the person comfortable with expressing themselves in public, to be in a state of being watched while doing the things they do. It's easy for me to make breakfast in my kitchen, but if I'm making breakfast in front of 30 people, and I don't know they're there, I'm a different guy. We try to get rid of the self-consciousness that we have when we're in front of people, so that we can be true to the craft.

"First thing that I do is see the talent that is present. Everybody has a certain amount of talent, and I check to see where their talent is in relation to their body. That is where we begin the process."

Much of an actor's talent lies within him- or herself, and how much of it comes out to show – if any at all – depends on the individual, Montano says. It's about becoming an imaginary person who might not be very different from the actor or actress.

"A lot of the process is getting in touch with your feelings, expressing your feelings, being able to connect to an emotional life, being able to prepare something based on a true suggestion in an imaginary circumstance. We work on creating the character and the craft based on what's inside that person.

"If you go to college to study acting, you'll get an academic study of it and an academic teaching. You'll get Acting 102, Acting 103. At my school, it tends to be more about asking 'Who are you as an actor? What is your voice? What is your expression? Where is your power?' We do that by getting in touch with their essence."

And so on and so on.

A Few Extra Drills

Acting is much more than stepping on a stage or in front of a camera and going to town; there are many more aspects of the profession.

Improvisation

Try this for a minute. Imagine that someone asked you one of the following questions, and then put the book down and try to answer them out loud:

"Is there any value to watching television?"

"At what age should a person be allowed to drink alcohol?"

"If you won the lottery, what would you do?"

"What do you think would make the perfect wedding?" (It would be interesting to compare male and female answers to that one!)

How long did you spend elaborating on your answer? Congratulations: you've just completed your first improvisation exercise! Like many other aspects of acting, we improvise every day. It's just that we don't have predetermined tasks, like many improv activities do.

"Improv is very important," explained late Emmy-winner Kathryn Joosten. "It makes you think on your feet. It shows the audience that you're thinking, not just waiting for the next line."

In a nutshell, improvisation is basically dialogue without a script. It's a scene that's made up as the performers go along. It forces us to think off the top of our head, to develop ideas on our feet, on the spur of the moment.

"It's not about seeing how funny you can be or how clever you can be," says longtime character actor Kurt Fuller (*Ray* [2004], *Wayne's World* [1992]), "but when you're acting and don't realize you're acting, that feeling you get is what you're always looking for. When you start talking with somebody else's voice, that's what you're going for."

As he and many other actors and actresses will tell you – and told me during our interviews – very few films and plays stick solidly to the script. Far more often than not, a line will be changed here, a scene added or subtracted from there, to make the film better and stronger, and to make the characters more real, more distinguished, more well-established.

That's why improvisation is so important – it allows us to help ourselves get a stronger hold on our characters as the production creation goes along.

Ever come across a situation that seemed hysterically funny at the time, but when we try to describe it to someone else, it doesn't seem as humorous to them? Ever said something like, "It was hilarious, but you had to be there to really GET it"? The same issues apply with improvisation, and it offers the same advantages. Things that may appear to work while reading about them may not come across as well in action. Spontaneity is an essential part of the performance.

"Every actor should take an improv class, because it teaches that you have to trust your character," says Fia Perera, who utilized the technique a great deal while filming the script-less 2008 horror flick *Paranormal Entity*. "It helps you trust that everything that comes out of your mouth, you can do. Everything will lead into the story if you're really in the moment." *Entity*'s predecessor, the box-office atomic-blast-esque *Paranormal Activity* (2007), was also filmed without a direct script.

Improvisation is a wonderful world of learning for actors, a place where we can be in any situation, always adapting, always changing – in other words, living the life of an actor.

"Improvising actors often surprise themselves with an impulse action," says longtime coach Bill Howey. "Impulse action creates an incredibly powerful life for the character and the audience. Improvisation is using what you already possess to deal with the moment... Good acting is to act what is not known, rather than what is known while telling the story of the script."

Put yourself exactly where you *don't* want to be – because every actor does so at some point. Make yourself someone you'd never in a million years want to be anywhere near; that's going to happen at some point in your career.

Imagine you're a new convict, with a judge asking if you've got anything to say before she pronounces sentencing. A preacher, calling his flock to open up the doors of their hearts and let that higher power find a new home. A spouse being told that they're being walked out on, or the one doing the strolling. A single mother trying to conjure up her own "birds and bees" story for her newly teenaged son. A parent trying to keep his composure during a television interview, asking the public for help to find his kidnapped baby daughter. A coach used to getting his own way, letting the athletic director know that a few low grade points won't keep his star player on the bench. A patient hearing that something new and negatively surprising was found during a routine checkup – or the doctor delivering that news.

We can't always rely on the directors and the writers to fix everything as we go along; sometimes, performers will have to do it themselves. Practicing by putting ourselves in this sort of situation is a good way to do this. Remember that these things are exercises, not actual shows. There's no judges or audiences to gauge our work. We are simply trying to help ourselves, and each other, with our comfort level in action.

Group exercises:

The Present. I learned this one from a drama teacher during my college years. It's best put on with a group, but can be performed with a partner as well.

It's Christmas time, and people are exchanging gifts. One person hands another person a present, and wishes them a happy holiday season.

There's just one problem – the gift is invisible to the receiver. Only the person giving the gift knows exactly what it is. Now, the giver has to give some clues as to the present's identity, and the "lucky" person has to ask a few questions to find out what it is they've been given.

Try to avoid "yes or no" questions. They don't really develop a person's thinking, and they tend to bog the flow of the exercise. If you're the giver, try to think up some clues about the gift. Is it something that they might want on a personal level, or something they may need out of a point of necessity? Is it something that you like, so you hoped that they would feel the same way?

If you're the receiver, pay close attention to the clues that your partner is giving, and try to build off of them. If he or she infers that they're handing you a cleaning project, you might want to say something like, "Oh, I'll put it to good use in the bathroom!" If they say, "Oh no, it's for something else," you can narrow down the field a bit.

If you get the impression that it might be a toy, you might say, "Thanks, my baby daughter will really love it." Then your partner might say, "Well, maybe someday, but she's a bit young for this sort of thing right now." That's when you know it's probably not a doll or a Pop-Up book. It might be a video game, a pair of Rollerblades, or a book for young adults.

It's important to remember that improvisation has no script, so this conversation may veer off into other subjects. I've seen people go for over 10 minutes with no warmup whatsoever. At the start of your acting career, that's OK; the last thing you want is to limit your exercises. Tryouts like this are about learning to build off points of a conversation, and it's OK to let that conversation go where it needs to at this point in the game.

Silent Practice. Like the first exercise, this one doesn't involve props. However, it doesn't allow voice work either. Silent improvisation is integral in acting. Remember the play *Our Town*, one of the longest-lasting shows in theater history? Yes, it's a gorgeous, moving story, a landmark in American stage production, but that, sadly, is not the only reason why it's so popular in high schools and community theater.

Another, perhaps the main one, is because it's so inexpensive. It's full of invisible props. Just about every small object, from George's watch and baseball to Emily's mother's silverware, exists only in the mind of the performers, and through them, the audience.

This exercise goes a step further, and requires quite a few people, probably at least four or five. One person stands up in front of the group, and begins to pantomime an activity. He or she might be making a bed, working on a car, cleaning up a kitchen overrun by a child's birthday party, or whatever else the person wishes.

As the first person's partners realize what he or she is doing, they get up and perform similar tasks. If the first person is mopping, the second might get up and start spraying. The third might wash a few dishes. The fourth might repaint the ceiling, and so on and so forth. Once we start doing something like this, it's amazing how easy it can be for us to forget that we're only pretending. It's easy to quickly get so lost in a character that it might require everything but an alarm clock to get us back in the real world.

The Story. A group of people sit in a circle, and one person begins to tell a story, usually with an enticement beforehand. Perhaps they were walking through the park when something floated above them and blocked out the sun. Maybe they were at a sporting event, and something very strange occurred. Maybe anything.

The first person speaks for awhile, and, like all other such activities, isn't concerned with grammatical correctness or story structure. Talking in such a way is a wonderful stimulus for the mind, and helps our independent thought process start moving at high speed.

After the first person has laid the groundwork for the story, it's the next person's turn (this can be done at predetermined points, or rely on spontaneity). The next person continues where the first one left off, and puts their own spin on the story. What happened next? Did the characters come up with new ideas? Did the story take a new twist? Did something unexpected happen, or did everything continue in a vein similar to the one laid by the original talker? Again, the story doesn't have to make sense: that comes later, in actual auditions and other work.

Eventually, the story makes it way around the circle, until it's the last person's job to end it. Maybe he or she will put a happy spin on it. Maybe the bad guys will win in the end. Maybe (but hopefully not, as this is the grandpappy of all cop-outs), the last words of the tome will be, "and then he/she/everyone woke up, and realized the whole thing had been a dream."

The Autobiography. Here's one that can be done alone.

Find a magazine, a book, preferably a publication you haven't seen before, with lots of photos in it, preferably of people.

Close your eyes or put the book behind your back, and turn to a random spot, a photo in the book.

Quickly glance over the photo. If it's of just one person, that makes this easier. If it's of a group, hurriedly choose one.

Now put yourself in that person's shoes, and tell their life story as if you lived it. Who are they? What are their likes, dislikes? What was in their past? What is their future going to be?

Try to quickly ascertain as much as you can from the photo. Pay attention to the person's physical look, their facial expression, their age, their gender, and their atmosphere. What might you try to guess about the life this person has lived?

Speak in the first person. Give the person a name, a realistic one determined by age, atmosphere, gender, etc. Try to think of this person's hopes and dreams, and compare and contrast them with their reality. What's their current life like? Are they happy? Are they satisfied? Would they like to see their situation changed, and are they doing anything to make it happen?

Try to put yourself in the position of someone much different from yourself. If you're a grown American woman, become an old man from another country. If you're a bit on the other side of the hill, try to imagine what it would be like to be a child in today's world. Acting is about becoming other people, taking on their characteristics, their wants, their personality. This will help us prepare to do so if (probably when) we have to in our actual performances.

Fran Montano's dinner improv: "They go out to dinner, and one person bounces the check," he explains. "They can, without a script, kind of organically connect to what that does to them. It's not comedic improvisation; it's working without a script, and making them ask, 'What am I doing here? What are you doing? How am I feeling about this?' Then after that, we introduce scripts. I find that the people that take this class are incredibly grateful. I have had advanced people take it just to become refreshed, as well as people who came to L.A. with theater degrees and 10 years of experience. It just adds to their package."

Writing a biography of a person you've only seen in photo form can help you generate a background for the next character your acting career will transform you into. Don't be afraid to step inside the mind and body of someone far from yourself!

Forming your character's backstory

Quite often, acting is about putting oneself in an unthinkable position, a time and space that no one could ever truly prepare for.

But there's a special way to get into the character that's going through something that the performer never will, and it's called the backstory.

A backstory is, in a nutshell, the biography of the life your character led up until the point that the film's storyline kicked in.

Ask yourself – why is this character the way they are? What happened in their past to make them as such? Even if the character appears completely normal – social, friendly, outgoing, the like – there was probably something, or some things, from their upbringing that helped them become so. We as people can look back at our pasts and find some experiences that made us how we are; now it's a question of asking and answering those same questions for a person we must now become.

Emotions ring truest when there's substance behind them; people need reasons to behave the way they do. Even if these reasons aren't stated directly in the screenplay and to the audience, they can be invaluable if only existing in the minds of the performers.

When you're trying to define a character, check over the screenplay and think about how they speak, how they act, the gist of their personality. Then try to take your own journey down their memory lane.

Sometimes this can be as simple as finding a small detail about the character and making it mean so much more than met the senses. Look at how they dress. Check out any marks on them. Why did they decide to get that tattoo, those piercings? Is there a small scar that is the sign of a small injury from the past, an incident that eventually came to mean so much more than we thought at the time?

Check out how the person reacts to others. A female who prefers the company of men might have grown up in a male-dominated family, or had to be a big sister who protected her small siblings and other family members from bullies. A socially awkward male might have been yelled at in his youth too often by a teacher, a parent, or someone else – again, something that might not have seemed like a big deal in the past, but turned into one.

Someone with authority issues might have had a run-in with a teacher or a police officer. A teacher or police officer who overreacts to something might be getting revenge for something that happened to them in the past. An adult with a sense of humor probably pulled some mischievous, but mostly harmless pranks as a child; someone who appears to be wound a bit tight might have had a fight with the class clown.

Very well, though par for the course from them. Indeed, a great deal of this comes from the ability that we're born with, and that we develop from coaches and classes. But backstories can be a jumping-off point – as so many people told me throughout the course of this book, we can get a tremendous amount done when we just sit down and think about the why's of the situation. Just showing up and trying to snap into character won't get us to our full potential. We need to understand the reasons why our characters do what they do, even if we're the only ones with such knowledge.

When I got ready to become Hawkeye Pierce in *M*A*S*H* back in high school, I had some tough competition already. Donald Sutherland had had the role in the 1970 film, while Alan Alda helped the TV show (1972) become one of the most famous in American history. So trying to compare yourself to others in the acting sense probably isn't the best idea when you're heading for a role.

So, after checking out some of the past performances, I decided to create a backstory for Pierce the man. I saw him as someone who'd never put much time into academics, but found that they came to him easily. He was a free spirit, but not much of one – I could see him attending a protest rally, but leaving as soon as the cops showed up. Forget about marches; they'd bring too much attention to such a person.

He had a multitude of reasons for attending medical school; I suspected that becoming a doctor wasn't about helping people, or at least that wasn't the top priority. I felt that he went for the social aspect; being in the field meant that he'd always be around people, and being a loner would have driven the guy crazy. But he also secretly liked having someone's life in his hands; yes, it would be tough if they died, but hearing someone say, "You saved my life!" was this man's ego boost.

Authority wasn't a big thing for him; he was probably the student that didn't say much in class and typically sat with his feet up and wearing sunglasses, then drove the professors crazy with some of the class's highest grades. Studying? Yes, it happened, and there was a set schedule, but never anything past the original plans – that was for hanging out with his buddies at the bar.

When he went home, however, and had a few moments to think about his life, he might not have enjoyed what he thought. He couldn't help but wonder if he'd be able to make his mark in the medical world, perhaps the most competitive field out there. He wondered what it would be like to make a fatal mistake on a patient, and whether he could live with himself. Perhaps in his youth, he'd suffered some kind of setback – finishing second in the science fair, falling a few points shy of salutatorian, watching his baseball team give away a big lead and lose to a team they should have stomped. These are the sort of things that can stay with people, and they may well have stayed with him – or at least the him that I became.

If we know why our characters' actions make sense, it makes it easier for us to make it realistic to the audience. Films don't always have the time to spoon-feed their audiences the reasons why everyone does what they do – sometimes these things need to be thought of far ahead of time. Throughout this book, you'll find more, and probably markedly better, such stories.

Backstories can help this sort of thing. Sometimes we just need a few small details and an abundance of independent thought to make our characters who they are, to give them some sort of personality, no matter how much or little of it they get to show in a film.

Some more ideas...

An audition stage isn't the only place to get started in the business! There's other ways to show our skills to those who make the casting decisions, and show off quite a bit of diversity at the same time; always a huge benefit. It's far too easy to get lost in the shuffle of those crowing through the main entrance of performing; here are a few side doors that have led many to stardom!

Voice work

They must have known there was something special to find.

The speech teacher at the University of Michigan. The man who'd one day become one of the most recognizable faces to children across the country.

They knew that their new pupil could be something special. They hadn't heard much of his voice, but the spoken word, like every asset of an actor, only works well when it's used properly and in abundance.

The teacher thought back to her own times of study. One of her colleagues had taught her that actors' tones must be cleared of any cultural or geographic affectations, and, working with a young man who'd grown up in the south and battled a lifelong stuttering problem, there might have been at least one strike against her already.

With one tough lesson after another, the lady worked with her student on lucid speech – just as any teacher would, she walked her student through the drills step by step by step, then made him retake the journey a few more times.

A strong believer that acting comes from within, her acting colleague taught the same student to recognize and face the muteness and rapid-fire speech that dogged him in stressful situations in real life – to use his emotion as a stepping stone to acting success, rather than suppress and fight it.

The performer's name was Will Lee, who'd spend years of national stardom as *Sesame Street*'s (1969) Mr. Hooper. The student was James Earl Jones.

"I do not believe that speech is a natural function for the human species," says Jones, calling to mind the manner in which humans communicated before the first languages were written, as well as the Earth's many species who converse without a syllable. "Therefore, any barrier to speech – stuttering, for instance – only intensifies the difficulty of an essentially unnatural process, the futility of words. . . I came to believe that what is valid about a character is not his intellect, but the sounds he makes."

He'd never stop displaying the intellect or the sounds, hand in hand. While Jones has done more than enough work to fill books bigger than this one, let's just focus on the voice that just about everyone who's spent time in front of a screen over the past few generations can recognize.

Starting, of course, with accenting a lord named Vader.

"I used to tell people that the film's producers first called up Orson Welles," Jones recalls, "and he was busy, so they called up Victor Jory (Jory played Jonas Wilkerson in *Gone With the Wind* [1939] and the eerily-voiced Lamont Cranston in *The Shadow* [1940]), and he was busy, so they called me. For a long time, I denied that I was Darth Vader's voice because it was fun to deny it." Still, it kicked off a career in voice-overs and commercials that's never stopped.

Can't find stage work nearby? Look around for auditory auditions! Go through advertisements for television commercials and radio shows. Nearly every fine actor or actress has done some voice work at one point in time or another, be it before their career started or in the latest Disney or Pixar blockbuster.

Nancy Cartwright might still be able to walk through airports and malls without getting mobbed, but only as long as she stays silent – speaking might reveal the woman that elevated Bart Simpson into a pop culture icon a few decades ago.

After getting her vocalities down pat in high school speech classes, Cartwright stayed in front of the camera for a while, playing a tormented older sister who, ironically enough, gets eaten by an evil cartoon in *Twilight Zone: The Movie* (1983). A short role on *Cheers* and some more voice work followed (she voiced the cartoon shoe that Judge Doom drowns in 1989's *Who Framed Roger Rabbit*), and soon came March 13, 1987. Fox's *Tracey Ullman Show* was putting together some animated "bumpers" to show up for some quick laughs between commercial breaks, and the Simpsons were about to launch.

Actually prepared to read for Bart's sister Lisa, Cartwright headed to the studio with the tunes of "Superfreak" running through her ears. But when she arrived, Cartwright noticed a mini-biography of Homer and Marge's oldest spawn (demon spawn? Some would argue), and saw herself.

"Personality," the description read. "Devious, underachieving, school-hating, irreverent, clever." Basically, an evil genius who could have been valedictorian if he'd just use his powers for good.

"This was right up my alley and next to the Dumpster behind the greasy spoon," Cartwright recalls. "'Clever' and 'devious' rise up in the heart of any actor who sees a description like that... Typically, when auditioning for a part, I will give the producer or casting director a number of choices; our ideas may not match on the first try. But not with Bart. I knew him. There was no second-guessing it."

She met a fellow named Matt Groening, who'd created the healthiest dysfunctional family in TV history, and zipped through Bart's monologue ("most likely it had something to do with terrorizing Lisa and being choked by Homer."). On the spot, she became the voice of an elementary school-age boy. Over a quarter-century later, the *Simpsons* train continued to roll through Springfield all the way through modern America, with everyone from Paul McCartney to Michael Jackson to Lady Gaga taking a quick step onto the ride.

"It wasn't about money or the cushiness of the gig," explains Cartwright, who mentions that doing a full episode of the show takes a grand total of about six hours a week – thereby making her work the envy of sitcom stars who get a few days off a month during filming. "It was about years of classes, studying tapes, working on characters, developing new ones, and enduring many auditions and rejections. Being any kind of actor is not an easy task, the cash one gets doing an animated character, at least a regular one, for the amount spent is, well, enviable."

Doing voice work achieves several goals. First of all, it develops the speaking prowess needed when you finally get that on-stage or on-camera role – few things will turn off a casting director faster than an audition he or she can't understand. By doing work without a camera, or even a visual audience, you'll learn more about voice projection, tone of voice, even non-spoken sound effects, like coughing, laughing, shouting in agony or ecstasy, etc.

That's a very important part of acting, attests acting coach Eric Stone.

"With today's technology," Stone says, "you need to get yourself a program of how to have command of the English language, a program that can teach you how to speak. This is assuming you're an American, or you want to sound like you're an American. We're talking about a Midwestern white guy or white girl. When I say white, I don't necessarily mean the color of our skin, but that kind of American view. You want to have command of your language. It's not just how to speak English; it's how to speak and be understood as Americans speak and understand." Jazwinski recommends checking out the anchors on national news shows to get a strong idea of what it means to speak "American English."

That's why, if you have a natural non-American accent, adapting to your vocal surroundings is a necessity for a budding actor. Learning English is just like learning any other language (I've often heard it's much harder than most), and learning "common" American English is just like learning any other dialect from any other country or culture; it's not something you need to adapt to permanently, just something to keep handy if an audition comes up. Heath Ledger was one of the most underrated performers at this sort of thing; watch an interview with him in his normal voice, and you'll be amazed at how different he sounded away from the camera. From *The Patriot* (2000) to *Brokeback Mountain* (2005) to even winning an Oscar as the diabolical Joker in *The Dark Knight* (2008), Ledger's voice box was a cavalcade.

Dialect is very important when working in voice work – a person from New York isn't going to sound the same as someone from South Carolina, just as an Irishman, an Englishman, and an Australian could speak the same language for hours without understanding each other. Acting coach Roger Ellis recommends that actors should be able to practice at least five dialects before hitting the stage or screen, hence the reason why voice work is one of the first things his new students partake.

"They empower themselves by working on their speech ability," Ellis says, "being able to say things like, 'United auto workers can be caterpillar inc. in their bitter contract battle before placing your bets talk to Paul Brandon, who can't wait to cross the picket line that caterpillars factory needs Peoria Brandon recently laid off our rubber parts plant where our base pay was $6.30 an hour. It's one block from the heavenly gate at the cat complex. Our supplies came from 12,600 works who have been on strike for the past six months. Seventeen dollars an hour, they don't want to work, asked Brandon. I don't want to take another guy's job, but I'm hurting too.'"

Try saying that a few times, enunciating all the parts correctly, and you get an idea of how difficult voice work is – it's so much more than reading words from a page. Jones didn't become a Hollywood legend just because he had a distinguishable voice; knowing how to use it correctly made his one of the most familiar sounds in film history.

"What's incorporated in that is that you will learn that speech music breaks down into three components: pronunciation, liaisons (how words group together and connect), and pitch," Stone said. "You learn how to identify the way these things work. It's what creates things like a well-spoken question, like "What would you like?" instead of a monotone that comes out, "What. Would. You. Like." That way, when you get to Hollywood and come work with me, we bypass a whole lot of what actors do, which is learn their dialogue as speaking in print."

"First off, you drop the 't' on 'What,'" Stone says of his actors' voice practices. "It's not, 'Would you,' it's 'wouldju.' That's the liaison, and 'like' is the stressed word. If I was a waiter in that situation, I would put the stress on 'You.' If I got frustrated because they couldn't decide what they wanted from the menu, I'd stress, 'What WOULD you like?' If they asked for something absurd, I'd stress, "WHAT would you like?"

Like everything else in acting, it's a step-by-step (or, in this case, a syllable-by-syllable) process. Start by picking up some Books on Tape, and listening to them while driving home, sitting around in the living room, or even with headphones while out for a luxurious hike. The people who do these things are chosen because they know how to use the English language to the finest of its offerings.

Voice tapes from professional coaches, and recordings of plays, poetry, even novels and short stories are available, read by people who know the basics of voice work. Pay attention to the tools they use in reading and speaking — and you can learn from them.

Also, you might want to read some selections from a book or play, and tape-record yourself doing them. Imagine that you're playing the character, trying to capture all of his or her feelings and emotions within your spoken word. Pretend you're on a radio play, and it's your job to help your audience know your character through your voice.

Then sit back and listen to yourself. If you sound hokey to yourself, if things don't sound right to you, chances are the audience is going to feel the same way.

"Once you start listening to your own voice," cautions Jones, "you risk becoming trapped into affectation. The listener, not the speaker, should be aware of how the voice sounds. The speaker should be concerned with what he seeks to communicate by the sound of his voice."

Body doubling

Billions of people have seen Shelley Michelle on the screen. But if her name doesn't immediately get the memory bells clanging, it's because, well, they may have only seen *some* of her.

She was Julia Roberts' back and legs in *Pretty Woman* (1990). She played Kim Basinger's legs in *My Stepmother is an Alien* (1988), and Barbra Streisand's lower half in *Prince of Tides* (1991). She even got to sub in for Anne Archer to make love to Dennis Hopper in the TV flick *Nails* (1992), and became one of the most famous forms in American history, portraying Madonna in a TV documentary.

No matter how big a budget a director has to work with, she doesn't want to spend money she can save, or put elsewhere. That's where body doubles come in.

Remember the last time you saw a scene where only *part* of a main character was shown? A close-up of their feet (running, walking) or hands (driving a car, writing, dealing cards), or just seeing them from behind, their face unseen?

Chances are, it wasn't actually the performer. The big-time actors, like many Michelle and her colleagues have stood in for, cost serious green for their time, and the longer they're on set, the larger their checks get. That's fine for them, but not for the crew and the investors – in other words, the ones that upcoming performers should really focus on impressing.

Shots like this are where body doubles come to do their jobs; a great way to get into the business is to become someone's arms, hand, legs, whatever – eventually, we might get to add talent to physicality!

That's where the doubles come in. Just donating someone's limbs, hair, or whatever else for a few minutes can make things much easier and cheaper for a film crew. With the main performers off earning their salaries, double-involved shots are quick and easy.

Now, let's make sure we know what we're talking about here, and what we aren't. Body doubles are not *stunt* doubles – those are the people that act out action scenes, like car crashes and building plunges. That's a different and *much* more difficult job. And we're not talking about stand-ins; that refers to people used to do just that: stand in for the actors while lighting and shot angles are worked out.

In the oft-overlooked art, Michelle's something of an authority in Hollywood. It's because of her – and others, of course – that doubles get Screen Actor's Guild credit, something that didn't happen until the 1990s. Since 1997, her company, aptly titled Body Doubles and Parts, has been assisting others in pursuit of one of the most physical types of performing.

And, as Michelle's career has shown, being parts of someone else can launch us towards a shot at showing off our full selves, not just a hand here and a leg there.

In a vain started by Betty Grable, whose legs kept up the spirits and hormones of thousands of World War II soldiers, and continued by Tina Turner and many others, Michelle's bottom limbs vaulted her into stardom. A ballet dancer almost since she could walk, Michelle tossed her name, and her body, into the Basinger Sweepstakes when casting came calling in the late 80s for *Stepmother*.

So did about 5000 other ladies.

"I was putting on nylons to audition," she recalls. "The directors were looking for something as close to the actress as possible to make it look real."

The auditioning numbers fell to 500, then to 200. Then Basinger herself picked Michelle's pair.

A year later, she doubled for Catherine Oxenberg in the thriller *Overexposed* (1992).

Oxenberg, she says, "was from a big family, and felt that it was not morally correct for her to do nudity." It's one of several reasons why people would want such a double, she continues.

"Some actresses are not comfortable showing body to whole crew if she's the star," Michelle says. "Maybe she's just had a baby, and not in the shape she wants to be. Maybe she's just uncomfortable with nudity."

Her next film, however, jump-started one of the biggest careers in Hollywood history. As Vivian Ward, the title character in *Pretty Woman* (1990), dragged herself out of bed and got ready for another tiresome day with customers, people saw Roberts' face (always a treat). But they saw Michelle's back and legs.

"Julia was very nice," says Michelle, who also doubled for Roberts on the film poster. "A lot of people still call me '*Pretty Woman* legs.'"

She doubled for Streisand as the actress lay across a psychiatrist's couch in *Tides*, and became Basinger again for a scene with Eric Roberts in *Final Analysis* (1992).

"The beauty of being a body double is that your face isn't in it," Michelle explains. "The movies are an illusion; in a way, you're the best kept secret in Hollywood. It's a little less intimidating. The actors are happy that they don't have to do the nudity, and the body doubles are happy because their heads are kept out of it. You can walk off the set, and no one knows."

Of course, Michelle's picked her own spots in the spotlight as well. There was a small role as a student in the Jean-Claude Van Damme action flick *Double Impact* (1991), and a starring role in *Married People, Single Sex* (1994). She and another gorgeous woman went in the altogether in a three-way party scene in *Rising Sun* (1993) that automatically made Cary-Hiroyuki Tagawa the envy of millions of men, playing his sexual submissive misses before protecting him from a rush on oncoming cops.

Some of the best types of employment for actors looking for the big break are aerobics instructing and personal training – they can get you in shape between jobs and auditions. As we'll hear throughout this book, physical fitness is almost always a boon when it comes to those in the upcoming acting sense. That's the last benefit of being a body double, Michelle says.

"It's our job to be in shape, so I'm constantly in the gym, training, doing ballet, yoga, martial arts," says Michelle, who put out a fitness DVD. "We exercise anytime, anyplace, wearing anything, working on the buttocks, the thighs, all that stuff! Body doubling is a really good way to get your feet wet in the business, and I got my leg in the door of the acting world!"

Chapter Three:
One-Scene Wonders

*L*et's say that you've got a step in the door, in a small role. You might not have a line, a name, or even a spot in the credits. But even if all you do is take a few small steps past the camera, you've still got a job to do, and a character to play. Many characters, especially early in their career, start off with nine-nanosecond appearances as an usher who tears a ticket, a bartender that sells a drink, or someone sitting on the jury in the background of a legal thriller.

In times such as this, it may be difficult not to overact. It's easy to think, "I've only got a few seconds to work with here, so I'd better find some way to stand out!" and do something that draws attention straight to oneself. Perhaps speak unusually loud, make exaggerated gestures, or do something else that will distinguish us in some way, no matter how small.

But that's not the way to go about it. For one thing, it's unrealistic, and realism is key in acting. We don't overact in life – and if we do, we often end up in all kinds of trouble! – so to do so in a short scene would give us all the way away as people who are clearly *acting*, rather than the *being* that true performers entail.

Also, it confuses the audience. It might make them lose focus. They might think, "Wait a second – what's happening here? Is it about the main character, or is it about this new person? Will they become a focal point for the show in a few scenes?" When they find out that the answer is no, chances are they'll be disappointed and confused: two of the last states we ever want an audience to enter. Beyond that, they'll see straight through the overacting and know that the person was trying to take – perhaps even steal or hog – the spotlight, which doesn't bode well for actors in the early stages. This is not the time to be a standout, at least not in that way.

Getting ready for such a role, it's a good idea to plot out the character's entire life beforehand and afterward; if we were in such a setting, how would we act in this type of environment, particularly if we're acting out a common occurrence?

"You have to remember that you're living the character's life," says longtime character actor Kurt Fuller, who had such roles in *Ray* (2004) and *The Pursuit of Happyness* (2006), among other films and

TV shows. "You have to imagine your character all the way before the moment you see him, and everything after, so when you get to that moment, it's not like, 'OK, I'm acting now, and I want to make my mark!' It's the five minutes in my life that you get to see, and if you're confident and know the character, if you don't overdo it or push it, and you're incredibly comfortable, it's much deeper and resonates more. Less is more – it's only taken me thirty years to realize that's true."

Trying to stand out in one film or show (in this chapter, we'll meet standouts from both sized screens) might cost you a good shot at others later on. Showing that you know how to handle yourself in small parts and working well within the confines of the role will eventually show others that you've gotten hold of one important step in the acting business, and might just be ready to take the next step – and maybe see your name in the credits.

When we first meet Carl, Shermer High School's top janitor, he's, well, doing exactly what a master of the custodial arts should. Strolling into the library, he stops to empty a trash can, and then... wait for it... empties another.

For the impromptu members of the Breakfast Club, a Saturday in school is roughly the 27th ring of hell. But for the man and his trashcan, it's just another day in a former paradise.

Just pretending like it's another day, even another few moments, on the job – that's the responsibility of those handed the job of showing up and leaving fast in a film, oftentimes if only for a few moments.

"You try to give the character a life before and after, so when you appear on the screen, you don't appear as a blip," explain John Kapelos, whose role as Carl will be discussed further in this chapter. "You try to give a sense of where you came from and where you're going. For example, in *Breakfast Club* (1985), I had a specific place in my mind when I came on screen. I wasn't just an actor walking on set; I was a janitor who'd just come from taking a few-minute break in the basement, and now had to clean up some crap. What the audience is seeing is a continuum of the character, rather than something new."

The title of this chapter might be a bit misleading; in the music world, being a one-hit wonder is hardly a term of endearment. Can you name a Calloway song other than "I Wanna Be Rich," or something by the Sugar Hill Gang except for "Rapper's Delight"? If you can, you're the exception.

But in the film world, things can change a bit. In movies, the ability to stand out in one scene – the right way – can make a strong impression on the audience, and kick-start some strong careers. You might prepare for weeks, then wind up with only moments of screen time – but if done right, it can be enough, and now we'll see some instances therein.

In some cases, it's only a few steps away from the biggest screen of them all. Anthony Quinn only had to play Paul Gauguin for eight minutes of *Lust For Life* to take home 1956's Best Supporting Actor, while Judi Dench was Queen Elizabeth for about the same amount of time in 1999's *Shakespeare in Love* – long enough to be the Best Supporting Actress.

And let's not forget that one of the most overlooked facts of *Silence of the Lambs* (1991), thereby making it just one more testament to his immeasurable talent, is the fact that Anthony Hopkins' Hannibal Lecter is only there for *sixteen minutes*, less than *one-sixth* of the flick – and he snared Best Actor for less onscreen time than many Supporting winners!

Now let's meet some who have crammed a great deal of strong acting into miniscule screen time, some that did all the right things in the time they had to work with...

Otoja Abit: *Stonewall*

It was ironic. No, appropriate. Hell, it was required, for crying out loud.

A place where a group of people that everyone saw as passive, scared, submissive, and every other adjective for the bullied finally joined and stood up wasn't just *supposed* to happen at a place called Stonewall. It was the only venue where it could have.

Nearly half a century after the first solid steps towards equality for homosexuals were taken, and just a year *before* the landmark decision allowing them to wed, Roland Emmerich and the rest of his crew arrived in Montreal to tell the story of an American landmark. Far from the story's actual stomping grounds of New York, and even farther from the directing lands he'd conquered in *Independence Day* (1996), *Godzilla* (1998), and *The Day After Tomorrow* (2004), Emmerich was now stepping towards the epics of history, on a much more watered-down scale than *The Patriot* (2000). As prevalent as gay rights have been in the public eye over the past few decades, not many are aware of the significance of Stonewall and what happened there – aside, of course, from those lucky enough to wander through the Big Apple in the midst of summertime.

The people that made it happen are even more underrated. Like a lady named Marsha P. Johnson.

To be fair, the term of lady might fall a bit short. One of the most well-known and wide open drag queens of the 1960s, Johnson campaigned and hit activism as hard as anyone for gay, transgenders, transvestites, and anyone else she felt was under injustice's thumb.

Clearly, she deserved a place in the *Stonewall* (2015) story, as much as anyone else on that June night of 1969. But who could tell it, and how?

"It was an opportunity to tell an important story with people you trust," remembers Otoja Abit, "to explore the reality of Stonewall and civil rights and its part in history. At this point in my career, I'm trying to learn about life through experiences, and this was a perfect opportunity I could relate to."

Many could, and too many still can. Gay people, minorities, women, men, young people, the elderly, most of us have felt this sort of thing at more than one time or another.

"It's as prevalent right now as was happening in this world back in 1969," Abit says. "Gay rights was a thing worth fighting for back in 1969, and the racial movement was also happening. But this was more about fighting for what you believe is unjust. It was about fighting for what you believe should be an OK thing, even when people or society tell you you're wrong."

Marsha P. Johnson was a landmark in the first real gay civil right moment in the 1970s; Otoja Abit (left) got to step back in time to play Johnson in *Stonewall*.

Since its inception (by the mafia!) three years before, the Stonewall Inn had become America's premier gay bar, but police raids — which "randomly" occurred about every month — did their best to disrupt things, lining visitors up against the walls, searching for IDs, ejecting who they pleased, anything to stop people from coming back. In the early hours of June 28, 1969, a crowded night was interrupted by another such invasion. But things didn't go as hoped.

To become a transgender woman, the first "real person" role of his career, Abit visited the same sort of places Marsha often frequented.

"You have to see what it's like to see drag queens in action," he explains, "whether it's what you see in your imagination or what you see on TV, but you have to be there and see for yourself what it really is to experience a drag queen. I was able to go to different clubs and explore who drag queens are. Drag queens are almost regal stars." He also looked over a 2012 documentary on the activist entitled *Pay it No Mind* (Johnson often snidely claimed this as the representation for the P. in her name!).

"I met a drag queen that knew Marsha," Abit says. "I learned about her character, her essence, her voice on speaking about things." One day, he ran into Jon Robin Baitz, who'd scripted *Stonewall* and nearly won a Pulitzer for his playwriting.

"When I got cast, I was very nervous," Abit says. "Bringing a person to life would be very difficult. (Baitz said,) 'Don't let your fear debilitate you. You're going to be the first person to portray Marsha P. Johnson.' Once he said that, I realized I was in good hands."

But Marsha wasn't, quite often. We're not there yet.

None of the soundstage stuff here; Emmerich had an entire replica of the Greenwich Villiage neighborhood built. Abit and the rest of the cast strolled around the makeshift place and felt themselves walking into the past.

"I felt like I was there in the 60s," he says. "It helped me immensely internally. Being in the world and believing I am in the 60s, rather than in front of a green screen."

Back in 1969, a group of locals gathered outside Stonewall. Some were kicked out of the Inn, but still waited nearby. As a woman was pulled out of the bar and brawled with some cops, one of them whacked her with a baton. That's when people had had enough of this.

Before the film's riot, Abit's Marsha was cuffed to Inn owner Ed Murphy. And if *Stonewall* had been a switch for Emmerich, one of his main performers had jumped even farther: after two rounds of *Hellboy* (2004, 2008), Ron Perlman's morph to Murphy was cross-continental.

That, and being cuffed to Marsha made Perlman look like the small guy for one of the first times in his career!

"Ron Perlman was a delight," Abit says. "We had to film a scene when Marsha punches Ed. We rehearsed it, but we never discussed whether I really hit him. Would he beat me up? I didn't hit him."

They are two of the first to be escorted to a paddywagon. But the cops suddenly have a few (thousand) other distractions outside.

Calls for backup fell short, and people start pelting the police with coins, garbage cans, rocks, anything they could find. Cops hid inside the bar, but the crowd kept attacking. Gay people, so often stereotyped as scared and submissive, were on the offensive for the biggest time in American history.

Meanwhile, Ed managed to uncuff himself and escape, leaving Marsha behind. Not that she minded – Marsha went outside and stood as tall as she ever had, standing with a large group of her friends who were fighting the fight she'd been hoping for.

All the way, Abit kept Marsha in his mind. At a director's word, everything could stop and the cast could go back for a redo. Marsha hadn't had such a luxury.

"Marsha was arrested so many times," he says, "and she just accepted it, like Malcolm X and Martin Luther King Jr. (King had been murdered just a year before.)

About four years before, "I was living in Huntington Beach, I realized what it was like," he continues of Marsha's life. "You're having a good time and the cops come in, basically coming into your home, and arrest you. Each take, I was able to take off the handcuffs, but that's easy compared to what Marsha went through. She had no cuts, no time-outs. They took her from one place to another, dragging her there, because she was gay, because she was black, because she was a drag queen. I realized this was what it was like, being arrested for being something you're proud to be."

Marsha and her colleagues go to battle, revving up the crowd as the police, realizing that this isn't going to be a regular night, flee.

In real life, the same thing occurred the next night. Gays rioted, attacked cops, tore up buildings, unleashed a wave of aggression that had been building up for decades. A message was sent to gays across America and around the world that they didn't have to take it anymore.

The action started not a war, but a movement. A year later, Gay Pride marches popped up all over America. Today, the world celebrates the riots' anniversary as an unofficial gay holiday.

For maybe the first time in American history, the public realized that, hey, gay people could fight. And they *would* fight. And they haven't stopped. They fought for equality. They fought to make the government give a damn when thousands of them starting dying from what people desperately tried to label the "Gay Plague." They kept fighting against generations who tried to stop them from something as simple as marriage equality.

"*Stonewall* may have been ahead of its time," Abit says. "It was a treat for people who weren't gay, and it gave the young LGBT community a glimpse of what it was like at that time." But Marsha P. Johnson's story wouldn't have such an ending.

Just after the annual Pride March in July 1992, her body was found floating in the Hudson River. Cops called it intentional; her friends disagreed. A final verdict has yet to be announced. Today, she's considered a martyr of the gay movement.

"People were aware and people that didn't know her could see her on the screen," Abit explains. "I realized that getting down to her core, there were three strikes against her – being black, being gay, being transgender – and she held her head high with pride. She just wanted to be free. She was very much a regal person."

Kristen Adolfi: *Whip It*

What exactly WAS roller derby? The young woman couldn't figure it out.

It wasn't that she wasn't physically fit; it was just that there was a whole new game in town, a foreign language of sports. But hey, if it meant making a few fresh friends, it was worth it all.

She got off to a rough start, even a painful one. But being a true champ, she stuck with it, and ended up snaring more from the game than she ever thought – benefits that extended far off the track.

Sounds like the main plot of Drew Barrymore's incredibly underrated 2009 directorial debut *Whip It*, doesn't it? You got me.

But it's also a mini-biography of one of its supporting cast constituents.

About four years ago, "I was living in Huntington Beach, looking for a way to meet people and make friends," recalls Kristen Adolfi. "Then I saw something on TV about roller derby, and I was like, 'What is that?'"

Sports were nothing new to her; she'd been stopping shots in soccer goals for over a decade, bossing around ski slopes for a while, and even dabbled in barroom boxing (the practice of gorgeous gals battering one another with ridiculously oversized gloves). But here was something new.

Kristen Adolfi (right) and Rachel Piplica (left) played an underrated sport in an underrated film in 2009's _Whip It_, the directing debut of one Drew Barrymore.

Perusing the Internet, Adolfi learned of a team in nearby Orange County. For the first time in a decade, she'd be on roller skates.

At least, for a few milliseconds.

"I fell flat on my ass!" she laughs. "It took me a couple of weeks to go from one of the slower girls on the team to one of the fastest. But I fell in love with (derby)." On the track, Adolfi became Krissy Krash, actually quite mild when compared to some of the monikers her colleagues use.

Eventually, she headed over to Los Angeles, and continued her career with the L.A. Derby Dolls. Soon after, Adofi glanced into the stands during an event, and noticed a familiar face.

It was one she'd seen for years – but this was the first time in living color.

"Drew Barrymore started coming to watch us," remembers Adolfi, who called _50 First Dates_, Barrymore's 2004 amnesia-charged romantic romp with Adam Sandler, one of her all-time favorite films. "We heard about a movie, and word started spreading that they were looking to cast a couple of girls from L.A."

Eventually, Adolfi, who'd done a bit of modeling, and several of her fellow derby divas were called to audition for the film, written by Shauna Cross, herself a veteran of the roller sports (the film's based on Cross' 2007 book _Derby Girl_).

"It was kind of scary," Adolfi says. "They were so nice to us, because we clearly were all terrified." The girls hung out and assured each other and themselves that they'd done just fine.

A few weeks later, Adolfi and her teammate Rachel Piplica got callbacks. Heading into a warehouse, they saw Barrymore and Ellen Page – fresh off 2007's _Juno_ and now heading up a new cast – sharpening their skating skills.

Film officials explained that they wanted Adolfi and Piplica to do a few scenes – without words.

"They told us that the characters were deaf," Adolfi says. "We ran a couple of scenarios without any words. They had us pretend to sign some stuff. We didn't really know what we were doing at all."

For a while, it was back to basics — skating, life, and Surf Camp, Adolfi's Santa Monica summer program to teach kids about the beach. Then, over a month after her second tryout, the call came.

She and Piplica would be heading to Detroit. Alongside Barrymore, Page, Juliette Lewis, Oscar-winner Marcia Gay Harden, *Saturday Night Live* (1975) mainstays Kristen Wiig and Jimmy Fallon and others, they'd be becoming the Manson sisters, a pair who'd overcome hearing problems to make it to the annals of derby-ing.

"The feeling was unreal," Adolfi says. "It was like winning a lottery."

To get in character, she and Piplica spent time together with little much voice usage.

"We'd go to dinner and try to communicate without talking," she says. "The hardest part was learning how to listen to what was going on without making it apparent that I was listening. When someone walks into a room, you think to turn and look at them, and you have to think, 'Would I have noticed, or would I have waited for everyone else to look, and then looked too?'"

The experience even showed the pair an innovation to their old sport, she continues.

"We skated with earplugs in," Adolfi says. "There's so much communication that comes out on the track. You're so used to hearing someone come up behind you and tell you, 'Hey, go high, go low!' It was very strange. We were so used to that communication, and not having it was a trip."

Halfway across the country, the two embarked on an original innovation, and even got to teach a little in the bargain.

"(Barrymore) was so positive," Adolfi says. "Everyone really understood that we had no idea what we were doing, but at the same time, everyone was very open to learning. Acting was their deal, and roller derby was our deal, so we learned a lot from each other."

Trainers from Adolfi and Piplica's league helped Page become Bliss Cavender, a reluctant Texas beauty queen who finds a sense of aggression and rebellion in the circular game, becoming a member of the Hurl Scouts, the laughingstock of the local roller derby league. In true Hollywood fashion, the renamed Babe Ruthless instills a sense of drive and camaraderie in the squad (Barrymore has a small role as smartmouthed Scout Smashley Simpson, whose nose is broken by Adolfi's character early on) pushing them to the top of the league standings and a battle with perennial powerhouse Holly Rollers.

"Some of the big hits were done a couple of times," remembers Adolfi. "There's a scene where (the Scout coach) gives our play to the other team, and they go out and just stomp us. That scene was cool because it looked really awesome, but we had to do the falls about 30 times. We'd speed up, and then, *bam*, right on our butts."

Unlike the typical Hollywood fare, however, the team doesn't quite reach the pinnacle of success, as Lewis' Iron Maven (Piplica's real-life track mark is Iron Maiven) leads her Rollers to another victory. But here's where Barrymore and Cross truly show their off-camera skills, as the squad still comes out as true winners, finding more than enough to celebrate with their silver medal and a new respect from their opponents, fans, and everyone else.

"(Winning) didn't really matter, because we all appreciated the hard work that everyone put into it," Adolfi says. "The biggest fear for people of derby was that it was going to look fake. But with the camera work and a lot of the choreographing, they did a great job with keeping that balance fun between fantasy and real derby. It was just like being with my own team."

Tracy Ashton: *My Name is Earl*

Tracy Ashton is hardly at the bottom of the acting world; she's been around for a few years. But she's part of a large group of people that are still looking up at a higher, more successful selection of the acting population – and pounding away to get through.

Hammering, that is, on the glass ceiling (made up of ignorance, stereotypes, and a refusal to look beneath the superficial) that keeps Ashton, and others in her plight, from making it to the bigtime mainstream in Hollywood.

"It's a challenge to be an actor with a disability because there are not many roles available," says Ashton, who lost a leg to cancer in her mid-30's. "Even if a role isn't written specifically for a person with a disability, it doesn't mean that a person with a disability can't play that role. Hopefully down the road, we'll see more people with disabilities represented in the movies, on television, on stage, and in every walk of life, because in every part of life, there is a person with a disability."

Ashton started out much like any other upcoming performer, studying acting and dance at Southern Illinois University and embarking on a stage career. Then, in her 20's, doctors found a tumor in her left leg. It turned out to be myxoid liposarcoma, dangerous not just because of its infrequency, but because it often shows up as benign until it's too late.

She battled the disease for over eight years, undergoing radiation and a surgery that took over 13 pounds from her leg. But the tumors kept coming back, and brought a high risk of spreading along with them.

The mother of a four-year-old, Ashton decided not to take the risk, and gave up everything below her left hip socket.

"I wanted to raise my son," she says. "I knew it was time to let it go. I was lucky in many ways.

"I wasn't even thinking of a career in acting," she says of her immediate post-operation mindset. "I quit everything so I could focus on getting well. I really had no intention of acting again. After I recovered from the amputation though, I wanted to do something creative again, so I decided to take an improv class."

That led to sketch comedy down the road, and more theater work. One day, at a Los Angeles function, Ashton met Peter Farrelly. He and his brother (and filmmaking partner) Bobby have long been known for their support of the disabled.

Ashton auditioned for *Stuck on You*, the 2003 story of Siamese twins that move to Hollywood to pursue an acting career. The Farrelly brothers believed the film might be a good way for members of the handicapped community to show what they could do.

Tracy Ashton, who lost a leg to cancer, stole several episodes as she stalked, taunted, and slandered Jason Lee on *My Name is Earl* (2005).

In the end, 11 disabled performers made it to the screen (not counting, of course, the main two characters, played by Matt Damon and Greg Kinnear). Ashton got a small role as a casting agent.

"Many types of disabilities were represented," she says. "That was great. I see a lot of the same people at auditions."

As *My Name is Earl* kicked off in 2005, Jason Lee's title character became an American everyman, a ne'er-do-well (at least, until now) with a shaded – OK, pitch black – past, trying to right a few wrongs, and usually failing, much to audiences' comedic delight.

As would be a recurring theme for Earl throughout the series' four-year run, his past kept coming back to haunt him; in the second episode, it was in the form of Didi, a one-legged shotgun-wielding babe who'd seen the slacker make off with her car – and hadn't forgotten.

"There were three or four women who came in to audition for the role," she said. "Usually whenever there's a 'disabled' role, everyone with a disability comes in to audition, but this show was looking for a specific disability."

Two days after trying out for the role, she was heading onto the set, ready to catch Earl in an alley and plant him straight in the crosshairs.

"It wasn't anything that took a lot of preparation," she said, "other than my entire life leading up to that point."

But it wouldn't be Didi's only appearance; she'd show up here and there for the series' entire run, sometimes fawning over Earl, other times out for his windpipe. Her eleventh and farewell appearance came on the show's third-to-last episode in 2009.

"You get your script, you memorize your lines, and you show up on time," she says regarding what to do when one snares a job. "I stay in an acting class, so I work on my craft outside of the jobs that I get, so whatever role I get, I feel like I can jump in and do it."

As one of the founding members of *Attention Deficit Disorder*, an improv comedy group, Ashton can be seen on stages around LA and on the web. "We're shooting a pilot called *Urgunt Care* and it's great fun to do. It's so nice to be able to create a show with people who are talented and committed to doing the work."

By the way, that glass ceiling we discussed earlier? It's not safe up there, as long as many join Ashton in her pursuit and keep pummeling. Acting on the big screen, the small screen, singing, theater work, writing... no matter what, the entertainment industry is there for the taking... by storm.

"I think the entertainment industry needs to use this vast pool of resources that it has, to reflect what the real world actually looks like," she says. "I'm hoping that there will be more opportunities that will come my way, and for other people with disabilities. But I also hope that people with disabilities take their craft very seriously and learn how to be an actor, a writer, a singer, or whatever avenue in the industry they choose."

Mary Badham: *To Kill A Mockingbird*

After Mary Badham finished tying together a film that would make nearly the impact on the screen that it had made in the literary world (both as a blow against racism and one for female equality in writing), she'd hear for the rest of her life about the wonderful job she'd done on the screen. Badham was the child star who managed to steal scenes from Oscar winner Gregory Peck and later-Oscar winner Robert Duvall in *To Kill A Mockingbird*, the 1962 adaptation of the Harper Lee book from two years earlier, a tale of a black man unfairly accused of rape and the man named Finch who puts everything on the line — even, inadvertently, the safety of his little girl Scout (Badham) — to save him. Scout becomes the unexpected spotlight of the piece, part narrator and participant, who saves her dad from an angry mob, and gets herself saved a bit later (Oscar nominee Kim Stanley did the voice work for the adult Scout).

Scout Finch (Mary Badham) and her dad Atticus (Gregory Peck) have a deep discussion over life's mysteries in *To Kill A Mockingbird* (1962).

For decades, Badham saw the film, and her performance, analyzed and praised from all corners of the country as generations used it to learn about writing, law, and history. For American women of all ages, it was a message of their equality — even as a little girl, Badham could help her own gender take the first small steps toward fairness.

But through it all, there was one thing she could never seem to locate: the kids' treasure box seen in the film's opening credits.

"I looked for that box for 30 years," Badham recalls. "Literally. I went to the studio, I called Atticus (after the film, she and Peck remained in close contact, keeping their cinematic monikers), I talked with people on the backlot. Anybody who would listen to me, I was asking 'em about this box. And nobody knew anything about the box."

Perhaps not — but before Badham was a teenager, women across the world knew exactly who she and Scout were. And beyond that, she was an inspiration to women far older than her; handicapped by the prejudices that women of the time faced (far too many such mindsets are still around, even in the 2010s), women saw in the young fictional character what they wanted their own lives, and themselves, to be.

It all started with a cattle call at her local theater.

"They had actually interviewed about 4000 other children before coming to Birmingham," Badham recalls. "They wanted a child who looked like she could be Gregory Peck's child."

After a quick meeting with the crew, it was off to New York for a screen test, and all the way to Scout-hood.

"We went to a theater," Badham recalls. "Some of the kids had monologues or little skits. One of my girlfriends and I got up on stage, and we made stuff up on the spot. That's what they were looking for; they wanted real children with real imaginations who could just go with this flow.

"(Scout) was allowed to just be herself," explains Badham. "Miss Dubose (a curmudgeonly Finch neighbor) fussed at Atticus because he allowed her to wear the clothes that her brother had outgrown. But it was the Depression; a dress at that point would have been very expensive and money was in tight supply."

At the time, education — in the school, the home, or the social setting — also wasn't very open to ladies.

"Atticus let (Scout) read and had real conversations with her. That's the main role of a parent — to engage their children in conversation and teach them basically how to function in an adult world. Scout took to that tooth and nail. She wasn't cut in the same mold as the little proper Southern young lady who had to wear dresses and not discuss anything important."

Like Lee herself, who based the storyline on a case of an Alabama black man accused of rape and convicted and sentenced to die by an all-white jury (the man's sentence was commuted, but he suffered a nervous breakdown and soon died of tuberculosis), Scout was not only the daughter of a lawyer, but an outspoken, energetic child, qualities that Badham quickly showed in herself long before filming began. When a reporter commented on her small size, Badham fired, "You'd be little too, if you drank as much coffee as I did."

Sadly, Badham had had some unwilling preparation for her role in her own Southern-based upbringing.

"It was that way even when I was growing up," she unhappily recalls. "Women were to be seen, but not heard. They were not engaged intellectually much. So for Scout to be able to put her ideas out there, to see her think through situations is really important because you don't see that very often. Even in 1960-something, Alabama had not changed that much: the social codes, the racial codes, and the parental codes were all still in place."

During filming, it appears that the childhood codes were as well — especially the unwritten rule requiring brothers and sisters, particularly those close in age, to torment one another relentlessly (Like her fictional creation, Lee had an older brother who did everything in his power to make her adolescence a journey through hell, and Finch had been her mother's maiden name).

"Here were John (Megna, who played the Finchs' cousin Dill) and Phillip (Alford, Scout's brother Jem), and John just idolized Phillip and followed him around like a puppy dog," says Badham, who also befriended Peck's son and daughter during filming, "and here was this ratty little girl who wanted to get in the middle of whatever they were doing. I just wanted somebody else to play with. Evidently we would have these big fights; I don't remember any of it, but Phillip seems to think we fought all the time."

Fortunately, director Robert Mulligan and other crew members understood just what rivals siblings can become, and allowed the children — and through them, the film — to revel in it.

"During that period of time, I'm not even sure that we got complete scripts," Badham says. "During that time period, there were subjects and words that were not deemed suitable for women and children, so I probably was not briefed on that at the time. I was only nine when I was hired, so they gave me just what I needed."

Although they appear to be present during the climactic trial, the children were not permitted to watch the scene's filming.

"Basically (Mulligan) would let us just play, and he would set it up as play," Badham says (ironically, Alford lived just four blocks from her in Birmingham). "When they first started with us, they started with the cameras far away because we hadn't done anything, we had never been in front of a camera before. So they had placed all the equipment far away from us, and then they would gradually move it up. So by the time they got ready to shoot it, we were done with rehearsal, the camera's right there, the lights are here, and everybody's ready to go, and we're all relaxed."

Only as long as Mulligan wanted them to be, of course; in the scene where Scout counts to 10 while waiting for her brother to come back, there's a gunshot — and her shocked effect is authentic; Mulligan didn't tell his youngest stars about it. The unexpected arrival of the father of town crazy Boo Radley (Duvall) sparked a similar response.

"When Boo's daddy came around the tree, (Mulligan) didn't tell us this guy's going to pop out around the tree," says Badham, whose character is saved by Boo from a fight in the film's last reels. "That scared us to death! Those reactions, they were for real because it scared us to death."

The culture shock that the young Alabama native received upon heading across the country to California to film the flick caused only a slighter reaction. To the youth, places with things like racial integration, let alone interracial *marriage*, and other such diversity, were foreign lands.

"Out in California, my nearest neighbor was this black man who had this beautiful blonde bombshell, six-foot-tall wife and two beautiful children," she recalls. "We'd go to their house for dinner and they'd come to ours. There was an Oriental family, and we'd play with their kids and everything was fine. Then I'd have to go back to Alabama, where if a black man so much as looked my mother in the face, he could be beaten to death and no one would say anything about it."

She'd shot to stardom like a rocket, becoming then the youngest person ever to receive an Oscar nomination: Badham would lose the Best Supporting Actress honor to Patty Duke — herself just six years older — in *The Miracle Worker*, and fame can be a powerful magnet for new friends (who wouldn't want to hang out with a famous movie star?). Sadly some might let it go to their heads — an unfairly negative stereotype caused by both a few embarrassments to the majority and humanity's nature to remember the bad over the good. Back home, America's newest starlet experienced both sides of the equation.

"My experience was everything from people wanting to be my friends who had not been my friends before to people who I had been friends with before not wanting to have anything to do with me," she says. "It was a strange kind of push-pull thing, and what's most important to you as a child is your friendships. I never knew whether somebody wanted to be friends with me because of me or because of who I was. That's a very difficult place to be as a child."

But it wasn't the only difficulty that her newfound fame and experiences would cause; when she got back, Badham realized that she couldn't fully leave her character, her new lifestyle behind, and maybe she didn't really want to.

The uncertainty that her new knowledge, her new experiences, had instilled in Badham, showed her that Alabama might have been the place she began, but it wasn't where she wanted to finish. The fake lifestyle that she'd enjoyed as Scout was a bit too enticing not to learn more about what the evolving miscellany of America's racial and gender worlds had to teach her. "It was like putting a square peg into a round hole," she says of her return. "It became increasingly difficult as I got older and especially as my awareness level came up, how different things were. So, it was hard. I ended up having to leave."

Still, the connections that she'd made with her cast-mates would remain forever. Peck, who subbed as a father figure to Badham during filming when her own father had to stay in Alabama for his job (tragically, both Badham's parents died when she was young), kept in contact with the girl he'd always call Scout, and who would always refer to him as Atticus. It's why Badham called the bedroom scene where Scout reads to her daddy to be one of her favorites.

"It's something that I had always wished that my father would do with me, so I got to play that out, and it was a warm, wonderful scene to do," she says. "Atticus read to them and encouraged their education. Scout was not the little girl type. She was out there, not the demure southern creature that everyone wanted her to be, fire and brimstone. Atticus was willing to let her be the little girl that she really wanted to be."

Long after the last cut was called, far after the final credit rolled, decades after the final scene was filmed, the two never let go of the bond until Peck's death in 2003.

"It would be nothing for me to pick up the phone, and (Peck) would be on the other end: 'What are you doing, kiddo?'" she says. "It was just marvelous. And after I lost my parents, I really can't thank him enough for calling me every once in awhile and checking up on me and just being there for that psychological support line." Note: Lee made it to age 89 before passing in Feb. 2016, just weeks before this book was sent to press.

After *Mockingbird*, Badham didn't do much more acting, though she did appear in a popular 1964 *Twilight Zone* episode "The Bewitchin' Pool," the story of a young sister and brother who discover that their family swimming pool is a passage to a magical children's playland (she had a small role in the low-budget 2005 flick *Our Very Own*). But no one who was a part of the landmark film – including the viewers – would ever forget it, and no one's ever stopped thanking Scout for showing them how to be just a little bit better.

"This book and this film have put families back together again," she exclaims. "It's done miracle stuff, major stuff. I've had a letter from South Africa about how it has really helped this family, and one from Northern Ireland. It made such an impact on these people and helped them get through some of the stuff that they're going through."

Perhaps that's because *Mockingbird* is, at its core, the story of a truth that needed to become reality. Many see the movie world a place to find stories of lives they can only dream of living, and there was a time in America – not nearly as long ago as we wish – that bigotry was rampant, that innocent people's lives were ruined just because someone didn't like the color of their skin, and that racial integration wasn't a pipe dream. *Mockingbird* probably couldn't have come out any sooner than it did, but its timing was the perfect spot for a film forecasting a hopeful future that America's still entering.

"It teaches us so many of life's lessons that we haven't learned yet," Badham says, almost wistfully. "These are world issues that we're still dealing with, and for the most part, they're based on ignorance. I truly feel that ignorance is the root of all evil, and education is the key to freedom.

"But I think the main thing is that it hearkens back to what we feel is a more innocent time. When children could go out and run around in the streets at night and play. It's a different world we live in today, and it's fun because it's from a child's point of view. I have a lot of parents tell me, 'I don't want my child seeing this. I don't think they're old enough.' I think, 'You don't get it.'"

But the lessons that Badham, Peck, Mulligan, and all the rest set out to teach go far beyond the outside world, she continues.

"I see it today with parents working and being tight on time," she says. "Parents will be short with their kids… not wanting to engage the kids in conversation because they're tired and they don't have time. But that's so critically important. I think that's what we see with Atticus. He does engage his children in conversation, and he does try and let them think through situations and expand on them."

Still, as hard as she looked, as long as she searched, as many people as she "interrogated," Badham could never find that elusive box of valuables. Then, a few years ago, she went to Prince William County, near Washington, DC, to give a speech.

"I said… wouldn't it be great if we could do a *Mockingbird* reunion and get as much of the cast and crew as possible and hook up all the schools and have this for historical reference in the future?" Badham recalls. "They thought it was a great idea… and we made it happen."

During the program, Badham was seated on a stage. Then a fellow came out, and announced that he had a surprise.

"I'm going to make a grown woman cry!" he announced cheerfully to the crowd. Then he placed the obscure object in her lap.

"Cry I did," she recalls. "He put this box in my lap, and I opened it up and there are the treasures, plus a lot more that I didn't know about." It turned out that the fellow who created the credit had owned the box since his own childhood, and let his children and grandchildren play with it, and add their own toys to it.

"I feel like the box belongs in the Smithsonian," Badham says. "I want it protected because it's a national treasure. I'm just thankful to know that it's safe and sound and being loved."

No matter what, she can know that that's how generations of viewers will feel about Scout – and the lady she became.

Dana Barron: *Vacation*

Someday, it just might happen.

A large family will go on a long vacation, perhaps across the country, or even the world – and absolutely *nothing* will go wrong. Departures and arrivals, by car or plane, will demonstrate the epitome of punctuality. All attractions will live up to anticipation. No arguments amongst the kids. Nothing will be lost or left behind, even for a second.

Yes, that just might occur – and at right about that same time, an atheist will be elected pope, Neptune will be colonized, and the Loch Ness Monster will swim to shore and hold a worldwide press conference about how she managed to stay out of our sights for all these centuries.

Yes, family vacations tend to go wrong; it's practically illegal to even expect otherwise. Still, when she got a shot at the films that would hilariously demonstrate all these misfortunes to the nth degree, Dana Barron, along with everyone else involved, just saw things as one new shot at the acting marks.

"If you get some sort of television or film experience behind you at a young age, people will pay attention to you," says Barron, who caught her first acting bug before she finished elementary school. She'd done Broadway, then made her film debut in the 1980 slasher flick *He Knows You're Alone*, alongside another struggling star named Tom Hanks.

The only gal to play Audrey Griswold twice, Dana Barron set off on the family's first *Vacation* in 1983, then came back two decades later in 2002's *Christmas Vacation 2.*

Looking for the stars for his latest comedy, Harold Ramis had visited New York. His pal Chevy Chase, still trying to break all the way into films from *Saturday Night Live* (1975), had snared the father role of Clark Griswold, with Beverly D'Angelo as his tough loving wife Ellen. Ramis picked Anthony Michael Hall as their son, but he needed a daughter for Hall's Rusty to exchange torture with. Hall and Barron staged a makeshift car trip sibling rivalry war, and Ramis saw the connection.

"Michael and I had a good sibling kind of relationship, with chemistry," Barron says. "I had an older sister that I would bicker with naturally, and it was good chemistry from the start."

Before the Griswolds even start their *Vacation* (1983) to Los Angeles to visit the legendary amusement park Walley World, their first downfall hits, as Clark's car order falls short, forcing everyone to pile into a station wagon slightly smaller than the plane that Ellen wanted to take. Still, things eventually get going, and it's on to Los Angeles. But not really.

"It wasn't Shakespeare," Barron says. "If you read your lines and you know your lines and you understand being that age, or not far from that age, you just slip right into the role. It wasn't a period piece. I was reading lines and getting directions from Harold and Chevy, just making a character."

After being liberated of their hubcaps by a gang in St. Louis, the family stops over in Kansas, where we meet Randy Quaid's legendary Cousin Eddie, whose kids introduce the Griswold kin to the mental state of baking (Audrey even carries off some for later). Forced to transport the curmudgeonly Aunt Edna to Phoenix, the group drives off, forgetting that Clark tied her evil dog to the bumper of the car – a situation that has undoubtedly befallen several in his position in reality.

"By being real, it became funny, because it's tough to believe that all that stuff could happen to this poor family that's just trying to have a vacation and be a normal family," Barron says. "You just have to believe as much as you can for the audience to believe you. It's much easier to do a good scene when the writing is fantastic."

The dog's death is too much for Edna to take, and Audrey and Rusty are forced to ride next to a corpse for a while until the resourceful Clark decides to strap her to the roof before dropping her off at a family member's house in the midst of a downpour.

"We had to wear wetsuits under our regular clothes for that scene," Barron recalls. "It helped the scene, because we're supposed to care about her. It wasn't something we were head over heels for, and you're stuck between trying to care and saying, 'Let's get the heck out of here and go to Walley World.' We were all caught in this horrible thing, but let's move on."

At this point, everyone's about ready to turn around and leave this nightmare in the desert, but it's personal for the patriarch; Clark's family started this journey to hit the park hard, and no one's giving up on him, no matter how much they'd love to.

They finally arrive, and a collective breath is taken amongst the Griswold family.

Then they see a sign outside: it's closed for repairs. All this time and effort for naught.

It's more than Clark can handle. With the help of a realistic-looking gun than actually holds BBs, he convinces awkward security guard Russ Lasky (John Candy, himself still trying to make it big) to open things up for the family alone.

Getting to ride roller coasters and other such rides for hours on end, even if for filming, might seem a dream for many, but it brought a new challenge for Barron.

"I get seasickness and car sickness," she says. "I had to take Dramamine, and it makes you tired. I fell asleep on a bench, and they had to film around me for a while." Hence why Audrey's missing from some of the park scenes.

Once her meds – much more helpful than the ones from Eddie's kids! – kicked in, Barron says, "I rode it so much that I'm not afraid of roller coasters anymore."

A SWAT team and park owner Roy Walley arrive, but Clark manages to get the owner to see his plight as a fellow family man, and everyone's allowed to stay. Interestingly, that's not how things were supposed to end for *Vacation*; Candy wasn't even there at the start. The first conclusion had the Griswolds going to Roy's house and forcing him to act out the World's musical themes. Then they got on a plane home, only to find out it's the wrong plane and forcing Clark into an impromptu hijacking.

That didn't work; months after Barron and everyone else thought they'd heard the final "Cut!" everyone was back at the World (notice that Hall, who hit a spurt in the midst, is a few inches taller at the park than in the rest of the film) during a California winter.

"People enjoy comedies they trust," Barron says. "It touched people's hearts because everyone understands the family's strife, and loving each other in spite of what's going on. In life, when things work and go smoothly between the director and the writer, to the props people and everybody, it just works. There's a magic to the set."

Whatever happened, it worked – the film not only made it to the top-five-grossing comedy list in the history of American film, it kicked off a series that's become a landmark in cinematic humor.

One of the series' great running gags become that the Griswold kids keep switching back and forth in age – Audrey and Rusty seem to take turns being older and younger as the films move around. It's probably due to Clark's humorous negligence towards, well, basically everything. But it might not have happened if one decision had been different.

As *European Vacation* rolled towards filming in 1985, Hall got a shot at an even bigger role, and took it, snaring one of the male leads in 1985's *Weird Science* (and hey, who wouldn't pass up the chance to hang out with Kelly LeBrock for a few months?). With one Griswold kid gone, it was decided that someone else should be Audrey as well, and Dana Hill got the nod, with Jason Lively as the new Rusty (tragically, Hill would die at just 32 in August 1996, stricken by diabetic complications).

The Griswolds' large Chicago home became the centerpiece for 1989's *Christmas Vacation*, as both Clark's and Ellen's families visited all kinds of dysfunction upon them. This time, Juliette Lewis and Johnny Galecki played the kids. Five years later, Lewis would venture into a slightly different genre as the lady lead in *Natural Born Killers*, while, decades later, Galecki hit things uber-large on TV, first on *Roseanne* (1988), then as Leonard Hofstadter on *The Big Bang Theory* (2007). Ethan Embry and Marisol Nichols were the kids when the family hit the city that never sleeps in 1997's *Vegas Vacation*.

Then, in 2003, after playing support for the main group in three of the first four films (he didn't follow them to Europe, though that's an interesting consideration), Cousin Eddie got his own spotlight in 2003's *Christmas Vacation 2*. After losing his nuclear facility job (to a monkey, par for the course with him), the cousin takes his family on a holiday trip through the south Pacific, where sharks and shipwrecks show up to cause havoc.

And Barron's Audrey was back for the ride, this time with no brother or parents. Twenty years after kicking off the character, Barron became the first to get another shot at her.

"I think that's a record for reprisal of a role after twenty years," jokes Barron, who won a 1989 Emmy for her work in a CBS *Schoolbreak Special* about sexual assault. "It was just Audrey being Audrey. I was trying to be her, just a little older. I was just working off my character. It was different without the whole family."

Michael Bentt: *Ali*

They knew he could fight. He'd done it for decades. They knew he could bounce back. He'd done it before. They knew he'd been hurt; his story had come far too close to tragedy, the same sad legacy of the man they wanted him to become.

Then maybe it wasn't a coincidence that Damon Bingham just *happened* to be standing there on that Manhattan street that fateful day.

"I bumped into Damon, and he recognized me," remembers Michael Bentt. Damon's dad was Howard Bingham, who'd photographed Muhammad Ali for years (the younger Bingham would eventually manage Muhammad's daughter Laila). That was probably pretty common for Bentt; millions had seen him score one title and honor after another through years of amateur boxing throughout the 80s, then a *slightly* more renowned belt in 1993.

His boxing career – and nearly much more – had ended the next year, and now Bentt was trying out in Hollywood, like gloved predecessor Jake LaMotta and others already had. He'd stood behind Michelle Rodriguez in the underrated flick *Girlfight* (2000), and was in the midst of training a young relative of a *Law & Order* (1990) producer.

Ron Shelton, who'd helmed more sports movies than just about any director in Hollywood, had seen a tome Bentt had knocked out about boxing, and started spreading Bentt's words. Now a new biopic was in the works, and Damon coincidentally was at the right time and place to spread the word.

"It was serendipity," Bentt remembers. Soon enough, he was on the other side of the country, trying out for *Ali*.

Not for the title role; that had long since been assigned. The crew wanted Bentt to be the man that inadvertently helped launch Ali's star as a public figure, stepped far past the ropes of the squared circle. Going for name recognition, they'd originally handed the role to Ving Rhames. Now they were thinking more about experience, in boxing if not so much in acting. Two years after almost winning an Oscar for *The Insider*, and six years past *Heat*, Michael Mann was working on his first real-life tale.

"When I walked into Michael Mann's office," Bentt explains, "I wanted him to see Sonny Liston, not Michael Bentt. I got my hair cut and moustache done like (Liston). But we didn't talk about Sonny Liston at all. We talked about England. He'd gone to school there, and I was born there." But Bentt hadn't stayed in his homeland; switching to the Big Apple, he'd racked up numerous local, state, and eventually even national and international titles with the gloves.

The meeting over, Bentt went back to New York. As his plane hit the runway at JFK International Airport, his cell phone rang. Mann wanted him back on the Pacific Coast.

Meeting with the director, Bentt heard a voice in the hallway. The main star walked in.

"Will (Smith) saw me, and started to go off in improv," Bentt says. "I went after him as Sonny Liston. That's when I had the part."

Sonny Liston could have been an American hero. His story had the makings: emerging from a poverty-stricken childhood peppered with legal trouble, all the way to international acclaim in the ring, a superhuman creature with strength inside and out that everyone envied. Roaring to victory in all but one of his first thirty-four fights (in just over eight years!) before crushing heavyweight champ Floyd Patterson in consecutive one-round knockouts, Liston could and almost did have it all.

The scared, confused look on Mike Bentt's face is the same one Sonny Liston wore in his second loss to Muhammed Ali, whom Will Smith almost won an Oscar for playing in the 2001 biopic.

It *should* have been a Cinderella story, although it's tough to equate a man like Liston with fairytales.

A sport like boxing, a violent brawl, one against another, has always had a need for villains. People who we want to see get beaten up. We want to see lose. We *pay* to see them lose. As long as we pay, the sport doesn't give a damn. Muhammad Ali was one of the first to put a sportsman's spin, a personality, on a public figure's face, and he needed an Abel to be his self-proclaimed Cain. It was OK with Ali, and others, if he wasn't the most popular fellow on the block, as long as people came to see him try to put actions behind words.

Liston never had that. He was known, but certainly not loved. Of course part of that had to do with being a successful black man in the late 50s and early 60s, but there was more to it. Angry, uneducated, an ex-con, there were enough strikes against him to make people not just dislike him, but not give a damn. It's why when he destroyed Patterson for the heavyweight title in Sept. 1962, a bout that everyone all the way up to President JFK tried to halt, a mere smattering of press appeared for his arrival in Philadelphia. Public imagery wasn't considered as big a deal in the olden days of three-channel TVs and paper newspapers, but Ali had it down. Liston didn't.

"Sonny Liston was painted as monster, and you don't get to be a monster like that if you weren't victimized," Bentt says. "Most fighters fight because they've been victimized by something. That was essentially where I had to come from, as a survivor. I used to be a fighter, I've experienced triumph, I've experienced failure, similar circumstances to Sonny Liston, so it was easy for me to plug into."

Unlike his role model, Bentt's pro career had sputtered in Feb. 1989, his debut ending in the opening round and taking him away from the sport for nearly two years. Then he came back.

Aided by sparring with a boxing legend named Holyfield, Bentt caught fire, knocking back ten straight men. But few took him too seriously, expecting him to be sent to Stepping-Stone Land by flashy Tommy Morrison in October 1993.

Wrong. In the biggest upset since Douglas creamed Tyson, Bentt hammered Morrison out in less than two minutes (much quicker than Rocky Balboa needed!). But it wouldn't last.

As tough as it was for Bentt to get back in boxing shape to become Liston, Smith was heading there for the first time. Bentt was right there with him.

"Training Will was fantastic on that kind of big stage," he says. "I couldn't go in there and make Will Smith look bad. Michael Mann hired me because of my temperament. If (Smith) made a mistake as Muhammad Ali, I made him pay as Sonny Liston." Many of the film's extras, some of whom ended up not even appearing in the finished film, were ex-boxers themselves; Mann's always been known for authenticity. Now Bentt had to find some of his own – or, perhaps, find Liston's.

"On a spiritual level, an emotional level, even a sexual level, as actor has to explore all of those things," he explains. "Where is the character spiritually? Is he an atheist? Is he a Muslim? Is he afraid of Muslims? Where is he intellectually? A high school dropout or really smart? It challenges you. One thing that I found really interesting is that Liston was illiterate, and people who are illiterate only have two modes of expression: silence and rage."

As we found out early in Ali's career, he certainly wasn't concerned with the first option. Early in the flick, just after Liston destroys an opponent, the man then known as Cassius Clay grabs hold of a press conference, yammering about why exactly he knows he'll take the title. His opponent has nothing to say (all but blasting ice rays from his eyes), although in sad hindsight, he probably wished he had the words.

"When Liston is being lambasted by Clay in first weigh-in, the guy is seething," Bentt recalls. "Maybe he was called stupid or an ugly nigger, and he's hearing those voices. Then there's this cool cat, handsome, that he just wanted to smack. (Liston) has to put this face on, but then he snaps."

"I'm 'aw fuck you up!" he fires in response to Clay's taunts. That's what he says, right in public, in front of a crowd of reporters and people he doesn't know, in the closest thing that existed back then to up-to-the-minute reporting. No poems, no quips, not even much of an insult. Just "fuck you up!" It's all he knows, and it's the sad side of reality.

Ali's poetic insults and predictions got people in the seats and his name in papers. A simple, "I'll kick your ass!" doesn't get it done – hell, anyone can say that. But if Liston had done so on that Feb. 1964 night, come through on his promise, done what many fully expected him to do, sports as we know it might be very different today.

And if something else had been any worse for Bentt, he might not have been around at all.

In his first brawl after shocking Morrison, Bentt stepped back to his English homeland and into the ring with Herbie Hide on March 19, 1994. Seven rounds and one ten-count later, his reign ended. Shortly thereafter, he almost lost even more.

Rushed to the hospital, he spent nearly four days in a coma. He eventually came to, and doctors didn't see any lasting damage, but Bentt's retirement had been shoved upon him. One day in training, though, Smith inadvertently cracked him as hard as Ali ever hit anyone.

"I'm not supposed to get hit, and Will was nailing us with those shots," Bentt says. "But if something happened, and I got injured, it was worth it. Going from amateur to a heavyweight championship to being in a film directed by Michael Mann, if I have to take one for the team, I'll do it. Mann is a maniacal director, and I get off on that. You push me the right way, I'll jump off a building without a parachute. Michael does that for me." *Ali* would mark the first of five collaborations between the two.

Rhames, long rated high amongst the ranks of Hollywood professionalism, helped Bentt through his first factual role. Several times during filming, Bentt followed his assistance to Vegas, but certainly not to the crap tables (and Rhames, who'd already won a Golden Globe for a Don King bio, got his own Liston turn seven years later with the underrated full-length biopic *Phantom Punch*).

And it finally came time to call "Cut!" on rehearsals. Nearly half a century before, Liston and Ali had battled it out in Miami Beach. Now Bentt and Smith were in the act of reenactment.

The fight swung back and forth for the first few rounds, a length many hadn't expected it to reach. Ali nearly quit, blinded by something on Liston's glove (what it was and how it got there are still conspiracy gold). But in the sixth round, he comes to life, blasting away at an opponent who's never seen anything like this.

On his stool, Liston's done. The film makes a big deal of him spitting out his mouthpiece, a symbolic display that he's not coming back.

"Sonny spits out his mouthpiece, and I never did that," Bentt says. "I had to find out what would make someone do that physically. Trust me: there were plenty of times when I was fighting and I wanted to quit, but I never did. I had to find something in me that said, essentially, 'Fuck it.' Some guy has my number, I've been there. I've been knocked out, and when you have that kind of background, getting knocked out in a high-profile fight, it never leaves you. I could very easily dig into that." For a short while, his mind was back in the ring for his first loss.

"I was sourcing the time I got knocked out in my first pro fight," he explains. "As an actor, your life is your material. It's your body and your experiences. It gives you permission to access them."

When Ali and Liston stepped back into the ring in May of 1965, quite a bit had changed. Liston had trained hard, but reports of his ever-present boozing still ran around. Sad and hardened over the violent death of his friend Malcolm X the previous February, Ali was missing his bravado. But no one could have guessed what would occur.

A fast, but seemingly glancing, right from Ali put Liston down. As Ali gestured for him to get up in perhaps sport's most famous image, the audience went insane, as most had missed the shot. Liston wobbled up, but the referee ruled he couldn't continue, and the fight ended.

Some say it was a legit hit that just happened to land right, always a tough call in boxing. Others say Liston, often accused of being tied to organized crime, threw the fight so his gambling pals could have a payoff. Then there are those who think he was just scared and frustrated, and used a good whack as an excuse to quit early. That's where Bentt falls.

"When Liston takes a dive, I think he did chuck the fight," he says. "I don't think that one punch hurt him. I think he was like, 'Fuck it, I can't beat this kid!'" Too many people, however, assume that the fight ended Liston's career. Hardly – he turned around and won fourteen straight fights and nearly took the North American Boxing Federation title before being knocked out in a fluke blow from Leotis Martin on Dec. 6, 1969. The next June, Liston took out Chuck Wepner, whose March 1975 brawl with Ali would form the basis for a certain film series about a Philadelphia club fighter.

But he wouldn't see the next year; Liston died just before the start of 1971. How he died is another matter for conspiratorial debate.

On the way to his first Oscar nomination, Smith went on to act out Ali's legendary battle with George Foreman (Charles Shufford) in the Rumble in the Jungle down in Zaire (Jeffrey Wright played Howard in the film); Bentt finally finished taking Rhames' advice with one more trip to Vegas.

Again, it wasn't for the casinos. In Paradise Memorial Gardens, there's a headstone reading, very simply, "A Man."

It's Liston's final resting place. It had been Bentt's inspiration.

"Every couple of weeks, I just sat with the guy," he remembers. "It was powerful energy. I walked on the beach and went in the water. It was like he was saying, 'You can go back now. I'm good.'"

Editor's note: Muhammad Ali passed away on June 3, 2016, literally days before this book went to press. A sad day for America in every area.

Elisa Bocanegra: *White Oleander/Girlfight*

"Hi, this is Elisa Bocanegra," comes the bubbly voice across the phone line. "It's nice to talk to you. How are you doing?"

She's quick to discuss a project that might have seen the light of film by the time this book hits the shelves.

"I'm writing a kids' movie screenplay!" Bocanegra proudly proclaims, though she superstitiously won't give away the title. "I'm obsessed with that genre. It's a musical, and I hope to be in it." Before she hit the big screens, Bocanegra's sing-tones rang across tons of church pews.

All in all, it's tough to believe that this friendliness, this openness, this optimism, could be coming from someone whose most-seen moment – though not her best, not by any means – was as someone who personified every teacher and introverted schoolchild's worst nightmare.

It's about halfway through 2002's *White Oleander*, and Astrid Magnusson (Allison Lohman, who for some insane reason didn't get an Oscar nomination for this) has gone through more by her teenage years than any of us should in our whole lives. Barely into her teenage years, years she spent without a father, her domineering mother Ingrid (Michelle Pfeiffer, in the full-blown evil role that all gorgeous Hollywood women usually try at least once) is in jail for a long time for killing Ingrid's boyfriend.

The confused Astrid is sent off to a foster home run by a recovering addict (Robin Wright Penn, following the same rules as Pfeiffer in this). But showing that the battle with substance abuse is one that few ever win, the woman falls back under its influence and nearly murders the young girl.

Fortunately, Astrid has seemed to find some stability (which doesn't say much, considering her past) at a home for abandoned kids, full of chances to re-embark on her own aspiring artistic career.

One scene later, her world has been flipped at least 540 degrees yet again. Astrid stumbles toward the back of a room, while one of the home's forces of young evil is restrained from working her over.

Two years after helping someone else fight in 2000's *Girlfight*,
Elisa Bocanegra tried to start one in *White Oleander* (2002).

"Don't ever look at my boyfriend again!" roars the young woman, guilty of both a penchant to violence and a serious overestimation of the value of boyfriends (we are NOT that important!). "You look at my boyfriend again, you're dead!"

That's Bocanegra.

"Allison Lohman was such a dream to work with," she says. "She was very open. It was a scary, violent scene. It made both of us uncomfortable, but we just went for it, because it was our job."

In a scene that follows shortly afterwards, Astrid finally starts to rediscover the solid ground that's been yanked out from beneath her since her mom's departure, and locate her spine in the process. Armed with a knife that she can't seem to figure out how to wield, she sneaks up to her tormentor, arisen from a deep sleep with a look of fear on her face that seemed unthinkable literally seconds before.

"If you and your friends even jump me again," says Astrid in a shaky tone that shows that her transition to adulthood is still in the making, "I'll cut your throat while you sleep." Her troubles don't end – more death and heartbreak lie in Astrid's path as the film continues – but it's the first sign to the audience that she's assuming some semblance of control within.

"I think that my character symbolized the danger of what (Astrid) was going through by going into foster homes and foster schools," explains Bocanegra. "Growing up myself in inner-city neighborhoods and rough schools, I understood what the character was going through, losing her innocence by going through foster systems, being exposed to really tough kids. I felt like I could bring a truthfulness to the violence of the impoverished world that these girls grew up in."

It was a time from which she wanted to re-escape quickly.

"I was only able to see it once, at least my part," she recalls of the flick, suddenly sounding wistful. "Seeing that violence in myself was very disturbing."

Again, unfortunately, she'd seen it before, without directors to yell, "Cut!"

"I went to very rough schools when I was young," remembers Bocanegra, who spent her youth in Newark and the South Bronx, neither of which are known as diplomatic paradises, "and, like the character in the film, I was afraid a lot of times, but I had to stand up for myself. There comes a time when you meet a bully and you do what you have to to stand up for yourself physically. It's scary, but necessary at the same time."

Working with some of the biggest names in Hollywood gave Bocanegra some of the same feelings.

"I'll never forget the day I went to read for (the part)," she recalls gleefully. "It was Michelle Pfeiffer, Robin Wright-Penn, Renee Zellweger. The film was my first foray into big-budget projects. I really did live in Los Angeles at that point."

Still, her first strong mark on the world of cinema came a bit closer to home. As Bocanegra honed her skills in New York theaters while the world proceeded to switch millenniums, her agent told her about a group of independent workers putting together a flick about female boxing.

Not 2004's *Million Dollar Baby*; that was years in the future. This one had a smaller budget, a first-time director in Karyn Kusama, and no A+-list stars.

In other words, *Girlfight* would be a great place for everyone to get started.

Still, Bocanegra almost dropped off the card before the first bell rang – her agent told her she might have to strap on the gloves herself.

"I said, 'I'm not a boxer. I look too sweet to be a boxer! Nobody's going to believe it!'" she says. "But I'm glad I went." That's because she ended up as Marisol, the best friend of main character Diana (Michelle Rodriguez, who springboarded the role to a few *Fast and the Furious* films, as well as 2004's *Lost* and *Avatar* of 2009).

"I thought Marisol was full of heart and open, somewhat of an outcast," Bocanegra says. "Diana is an outsider herself, and they became friends because they have that in common. I met Michelle, and we had incredible chemistry."

For her audition, Bocanegra looked to her past – and her wardrobe.

"About 90 percent of what I wear in the film comes from my own closet," she says. "The thing about Marisol was I thought that she was the girl who was a unique dresser in school. I planned an outfit really carefully. I thought since she would be friends with a girl who was a fighter, that she would be eccentric in her own way. I gave her a pretty colorful, wacky outfit which we wound up using in the film."

Like *Rocky* (1976), *Million Dollar Baby* (2004), and any other great boxing film – and just about all great sports films in particular -- *Girlfight*'s (2000) main subject is the people that take part, not only the game they play.

"The reason *Girlfight* appealed so much to the indie crowd was because it was a film about teenagers, but about their humanity," Bocanegra says. "I think that that was very intriguing, and still is intriguing for those who see the movie for the first time. It has a different edge than most teenage films. We really see what's going on with the kids."

As 2001 kicked off, independent film festivals around the world started handing out their awards for the previous year's flicks. *Girlfight* took top honors at the Sundance Festival, one of America's top festivals of its kind, and in France at the Cannes and Deauville events. Like *Pulp Fiction* (1994), *American Beauty* (1999), *The Blair Witch Project* (1999), and other films, *Girlfight* had emerged from the independent list to hit the film mainstream.

"As a performer," Bocanegra says to upcoming performers, "if you limit yourself to just doing things that give you a lot of visibility and money, then you cheat yourself of the chance to work on projects that could make you a great artist, like *Girlfight*. That kind of work can change your life." Kusama went on to direct Charlize Theron in the 2005 action flick *Æon Flux* and Megan Fox in 2009's thriller *Jennifer's Body*.

As the actress headed back to the Big Apple stages, her phone rang again, and didn't stop. Because this time, it wasn't just her agent with one offer.

"Hollywood called," she remembers. "I knew that you didn't get many opportunities like this. I was flooded with phone calls. I was very fortunate. That's the miraculous thing about *Girlfight*; we did it about 10 years ago, and it's still so much in people's minds that I still get auditions from it."

Over the next few years, she started showing up in one-shot deals on *NYPD Blue* (1993), *Gilmore Girls* (2000), *Judging Amy* (1999), and other shows. Around the time she was getting ready for *Oleander*, Bocanegra joined her *Oleander* co-star Patrick Fugit, along with Mickey Rourke, Mena Suvari, Jason Schwartzman, and others in *Spun* (2002). She was Giggles, the friend of a group embarking on a three-day crystal meth binge.

"(Giggles) was a homegirl, a Mexican, blue-collar gal," Bocanegra says. "I'm Puerto Rican, but I had to use a Chicano accent and adopt a chula accent. I hung out in East L.A. a whole bunch, having good food and talking to the folks. I took my tape recorder with me and recorded conversations. I'm a singer, so I pick up on accents pretty quickly."

Like many of her stage/TV/film colleagues, Bocanegra blends fact and fiction when getting ready for her roles. It's part fiction because she has to imagine a life that wasn't actually lived. But some of it, a good part of it, is still real because she now has to continue the life, and to use the "experiences" to learn how her character should function in the situation, in order to become them. Acting isn't about impersonating others – that's reserved for the spoofs that Leslie Nielsen and the Wayans family have shown us so many times. Acting is about *becoming* another person, for no matter how long.

"My acting coach talks about trying to discover what the character's dream is," Bocanegra says. "What is their dream? What is their intention? How are they going about getting the dream? It's important to understand your character's objective, and go for it."

Wolfgang Bodison: *A Few Good Men*

Remember the line, "You can't *handle* the truth!"?

If you're a fan of 1990s films, you'll probably be able to name the film, the speaker, and even the setting in about fourteen nanoseconds.

Many *A Few Good Men* (1992) patrons have heard the line quite a few times over the past few decades. Wolfgang Bodison, however, got to hear it before most others – and in living color.

"When you saw (Jack) Nicholson do, 'You can't handle the truth!' whether he was on camera doing it, or he was off camera," recalls Bodison, "doing the same act for Tom (Cruise), he did that speech with the same fervor every time he did it, which you don't always see. So that was exemplary of the kind of work you saw done."

Bodison played Lance Corporal Harold Dawson, a marine on trial for the murder of a colleague. Sharing screen time with Nicholson, Cruise, Kevin Bacon, Demi Moore, Kevin Pollack, and others in one of the most star-studded films of the decade, the actor found himself in an only slightly less stressful position.

"It was a matter of keeping up and making sure I carried my own," Bodison remembers. "Everybody was fantastic to work with. It was just the experience of working with them, more a matter of learning from them and their professionalism. Everybody brought their 'A' game and everybody was there to do their job. There was no conflict of egos; the professionalism was outstanding."

Professionalism. That's a word, a technique, that marines practice every day – maybe Nicholson's Colonel Jessup had it right when he said, "We use words like honor, code, loyalty. We use them as the backbone of a life spent defending something." Bodison had to learn them in record time.

"(Dawson's) job was to protect those who couldn't stand up for themselves," says Bodison, echoing his character's final scene. "He was a character that intrigued me. I guess it was that sense of integrity and honor that he had. He was all about protecting the people."

Two years after working as Rob Reiner's assistant on *Misery*, Bodison was actually chosen to become Dawson while helping Reiner find shooting locations for *A Few Good Men* simply because of Bodison's physical resemblance to a marine. Never having been in the service himself, Bodison did his own "basic training" with a visit to California's Marine Corps Base Camp Pendleton, a 125,000-plus-acre training facility, the largest of its kind on the West Coast.

Like every person who ever starts out to become a marine, Harold Dawson (Wolfgang Bodison) dreamt of becoming one of *A Few Good Men* (1992).

"I visited the brig down there," he says. "I just went around the facility a little bit. I also went down to the Marine Corps Recruit Depot down in San Diego and watched the recruiting class.

"I worked with an acting coach to connect with the character and kind of understand the journey that he was going through. I found things in my life and found things about myself that could connect with him."

He kept doing so after the first stage of filming ended; six months afterward, the actors re-gathered in the courtroom to re-shoot the participants' reaction to the verdict. After the two marines are found guilty of conduct unbecoming a marine and dishonorably discharged, a shocked Dawson stares into space, while his co-defendant Loundon Downey (James Marshall) wonders what happened.

"What did we do wrong?" he cries. "We did nothing wrong!"

"Yeah we did," says a resigned Dawson. "We were supposed to stand up for people who couldn't stand up for themselves."

"That was the idea for (Dawson)," Bodison says. "Even though I did what I did, even though I was following orders, I realized that it was wrong. I should have been looking out for others."

Making it up through the acting world can be about as stressful as trying to go from corporal to captain in the marines — but Bodison knows it can be done.

"You can do it!" he says to potentials. "You're going to have your naysayers; like any dream, it's not going to be easy. The thing about acting and the film business is that there's no sort of linear path to them; it's not like you can go from 'A' and get to 'B.' Everybody has a different journey. We can go from 'A' to 'Z' to 'D,' and then to 'L.' It can be very stressful, and also very exciting.

"Study the craft. Get into practice, try to do some theater. Try to meet some casting directors.

There's so many different ways to try to break in; there's no one way to do it, other than to throw your-selves into it and find your way. I'm still finding my way, every single day."

Dwier Brown: *Field of Dreams*

What is there to write about the final scene of *Field of Dreams* (1989) that hasn't been said, written, discussed, and quite often, cried over by millions of people around the world for over two decades? The closing scene where Ray Kinsella (Kevin Costner, like anyone could forget) plays the game of catch with his long-passed father John that the two never got to share during John's life would make the Mona Lisa lose her legendary smile and try to stop it from dissolving behind some tears.

But the scene would never have worked as well without the two hours of buildup that come be-fore it, and that's truly what makes arguably the best sports film of the 1980s stand taller than Fenway Park's Green Monster.

One of the most touching moments in sports film history was John Kinsella (Dwier Brown) playing catch with his son Ray (Kevin Costner) in *Field of Dreams* (1989).

Because *Field of Dreams* is a sports film that's not really about sports. It's a story about losing one's dreams and finding them again, just in time. It's a story about seeing a chance slip away, then snaring it back, even after all the shots appear to be gone. Most of all, it's an unusual story that blends the love of a game with the love of a family. The baseball aspect? It's there, but secondary nearly to the point of irrelevance.

And for Dwier Brown, the final scene, as well as the entire flick, carries more than one special meaning.

"When I read *Field of Dreams*," recalls the man who has the catch with Costner in that scene, "I thought (John) was a tiny little part. It wasn't until the cast and crew screening that I saw how much the movie moved toward the revelation of my character in the end."

Like Ray himself, filmgoers might have been fooled early on by the so-oft-quoted line, "If you build it, he will come." (Conflicting reports have either Coster or Ray Liotta, who played Shoeless Joe Jackson in the flick, actually performing the voice.) But it's not until just before the end that he, and we the viewers, learn the full meaning of the words, and the film.

"*Field of Dreams* is a very subtle sort of film that requires the audience to go on this journey to figure out what Ray has to figure out, and when they see the end result, we get to see the intricacies. We're kind of dependent on each other, and it's hard to imagine that momentum when you're reading it."

Less than two months before shooting got started, Brown snared the role and went to work. Just before "game" time, however, he got a source of preparation he'd never wanted.

"I prepared for it the same way that I usually do; I try to find the emotional state of mind of the character in regards to the story," he says. "It was easy for me to be in a perfect place with everything I've ever wanted, and that my son made possible. I was really able to identify with that. John Kinsella was a character who had his dreams put on hold by his life happening, and it appealed to me because, for many of us, dreams sometimes get put off."

As a youngster in midwest Ohio, Brown saw his own baseball career end as a high school freshman, and turned instead to track and field.

"I always though it was funny that my picture from *Field of Dreams* is in the baseball Hall of Fame and the guys who made the team aren't," he says. "Once you get a part, almost everything you do turns into (the role). You become the role. I brought my dad's old split-fingered baseball glove, but they have me using an old catcher's mitt for filming. I caught with it, just like when I was a kid. I wanted to make sure that when the cameras were rolling, I wasn't going to cough up the ball.

"A week or two was pretty intense, studying of the script and getting in touch with it, but a lot of it was pretty intuitive; some of it happens to us when we're not intending it to."

Or sometimes, as he found, when we never want it to; just before filming began, Brown's father Walter passed away.

"That was also a moment that made (the role) a fresh issue for me," he says. "I was at my father's deathbed when he was dying, and he had a lot of concerns and regrets that were difficult for me to hear. As you get older, those things happen; sometimes you wish you'd have gotten the chance to do something different."

He's one of many who wishes baseball would do something different about the infamous Black Sox scandal, in which Jackson and seven others were banned for admitting they took money to throw the 1919 World Series. The players were acquitted in criminal court, but Kenesaw Mountain Landis, baseball's first commissioner, blacklisted them from ever again competing, or getting into the Hall of Fame, which Jackson certainly would have.

"If (Jackson) threw it," Ray rages in tongue-in-cheek mode early on to his daughter Karin (scene stealer Gaby Hoffman), "how do you explain that he hit .375 for the series and didn't commit one error? Twelve hits, including the series' only home run — and they say he's trying to lose?!"

"It's ridiculous," she acquiesces, with a shrug that combines both childhood innocence and outright hilarity. Again, remember, the film glosses over the fact that Jackson *admitted* he took money.

"Shoeless Joe was never proven guilty," Brown says. "In the sport, in those days, the players barely got anything (financially) and there were certainly temptations to do what they were accused of. It would be nice if we could know what actually happened. I know that Shoeless Joe played a great series, and you'd be hard-pressed to find anything he did to cost the team a championship. It would be nice if we could be judged by what we do on the field."

Generations of filmgoers have judged the film for doing quite a bit right on the field that Ray builds.

"The idea of meeting your father as a young man before he had children seems kind of logical," Brown says. "Would you get along with your dad? Would you be friends if you were the same age and didn't know his?"

That's part of the reason that it was easy for Brown to play Costner's father, despite being four years younger than Costner in real life.

"I didn't know Kevin particularly well, but I certainly admired him, and I think that was appropriate for the movie," Brown says. "If I was John Kinsella, and I got to come back from another world to play baseball, and it was made possible by my son, I thought about how glad I would feel, and how grateful. Kevin made that easy for me."

And together, the two made it easy for millions, even those not into the diamond game, to make the "Dreams" come true.

"That moment got me at the cast and crew screening, and every time since, I tear up," Brown says of his scene. "It's not so much about my father and I, but about how the scene was written and captured.

"I think that, no matter how good your relationship was with your dad, many of us would take another fifteen minutes, or another inning of a baseball game, or an opportunity to play catch if the chance presented. All of us can feel that; I think it has to do with fathers and children, and that's a concept for everyone."

Vivien Cardone: *A Beautiful Mind*

Even after a decade of time, oceans of critical acclaim and tickets sold, and a Best Picture statuette, it's still tough for her to believe.

"When I auditioned for *A Beautiful Mind*, I was about seven years old," Vivien Cardone remembers of the 2001's top pic. "I was really just having fun playing make believe, meeting new people, and doing what I loved. Really, when I look back on my experience, it felt as if I was in a dream. Even now I occasionally have to remind myself that I actually played Marcee, that I didn't make it all up in my mind."

It's still almost like a dream to her, like the character she played might have been just a figment of Cardone's imagination. And in a weird sort of way, that's almost appropriate.

Early on in *Mind*, Russell Crowe's John Nash is doing better than most, at least from the outset. He's got a stronghold on one of academia's most gleeful torturers in mathematics, about to finish up at Princeton University. Nash is starting to feel the pressure to put his words into published paper, although it's stronger than anyone could have guessed.

Aided by his new pal Charles Herman (Paul Bettany), Nash stumbles onto the theory that, in the simplest form, determines that cooperative approaches are more successful than going it alone (all for one, indeed!).

It doesn't work when used to win a lady's heart in a bar – the fellow who finds a concrete solution to *that* problem will become a quadri-trillionaire – but Nash's creations nab him a shot at teaching at MIT, not to mention the heart and hand of gorgeous student Alicia Larde (Jennifer Connelly). It's a union encouraged by Charles – something else that would become ironic in real life.

But even that's not big enough to contain his brain; the Department of Defense eventually hauls Nash to the Pentagon to knock hell out of the codes that Russia keeps hiding inside innocent-looking letters and magazines. The Cold War is starting to freeze and it's up to him to shut down those Commie bastards!

One night back at Princeton, Nash happens to run into his old friend, and there's someone new with Charles: his young niece Marcee. Fatherhood hasn't really been on Nash's mind of yet, but this little girl might be the type of daughter he and Alicia would love to have someday.

That's where Cardone strolled in. Still, Marcee – so we thought – was just an average girl, so being one herself would make the transition pretty simple for Cardone.

"I believe the casting directors and (director) Ron (Howard) were looking for a specific type of personality trait that was natural and authentic in the girls who auditioned," she says. "So when the audience watches Marcee on the screen, what they are really seeing is Vivien."

Still, one thing stands out, although only if you're looking for it. With her uncle and new friend catching up on things, we see the youngster joyfully prancing through a field, full of feathered friends. Despite birds' tendency to overreact in group formation at the sight of even a single small homosapien, none of them even respond to Marcee. No flying away, no glances, even subtle, toward the child so nearby.

Is something going on? No matter; Nash's world gets real and difficult very fast. Some strange men start to follow him, perhaps Soviets themselves or those turncoat Americans that Joe McCarthy convinced so many were plotting against Old Glory. Then they attack, nearly blasting him away in a wild car chase.

For a character who only existed in the main character's imagination, young Marcee (Vivien Cardone) made quite a difference in *A Beautiful Mind* (2001).

He still manages to stay on the code-smashing, and even sees Charles and Marcee from time to time. However, he, and to this point we the audience, don't notice that the two never react, nor are they reacted to by anyone else. Also, they still look the same after a few years.

Indeed, it's something of a dream, and Nash is about to get the most painful of wakeup calls. In the midst of showing off his skills to Harvard, some ominous looking men arrive, and he won't be lucky enough for them to be Commies.

No, involuntarily restrained at a hospital, Nash learns the true heartbreak. The pressure becomes too much and shoves him straight out of sanity. The traitorous mental thief of schizophrenia is causing him to believe he has so much more. It's the disorder that forces the mind to create representations, often in human form, of what we wish we had, or could accomplish.

The invaluable government-saving work? All a formation so Nash could convince himself of his own worth. Charles' friendliness? He never experienced it in real life. Even Marcee? All in his mind, there to represent the family Nash wasn't so sure he wanted.

"During his journey through his illness," Cardone says, "he creates relatively harmless figments as well as very dangerous ones. Because of the paranoia that results from such dangerous imaginations, he needs a way to counteract it, hence the fabrication of Marcee. Through her innocence and purity, she becomes a balance between the chaos, a comfort through all of Mr. Nash's struggles. I think she also becomes, in a sense, his guide through the awareness of his illness. He only discovers he's sick when he realizes that Marcee never grows up."

That must have been difficult enough for Crowe, even after eons of performing and just a single year from his Best Actor-winning turn in *Gladiator* (many thought Nash would bring him another statuette, but Crowe was edged by Denzel Washington's villainous turn in *Training Day*). For someone who'd been *living* for less time that Crowe had been *acting*, however, things got very tough, even having to leave some of Marcee's natural naiveté behind for some sinister showings.

"There were several emotionally charged scenes that required a certain reaction to that situation," Cardone says. "Because I was so young, and I think this can be considered true for many child actors, it was difficult for me to draw out those emotions, because I hadn't yet learned how to associate the emotions I had felt in past experiences with the emotions I needed for that scene."

To her rescue came a colleague, both past and current.

"Thankfully, I had the help of both (director) Ron (Howard), who had his own experience as a child actor and knew how to speak to children to elicit the response he needed, and my mother, who knew what memories would trigger those emotions. It is very important for any child actor to have someone who can help guide them through their emotions until they are old enough to understand how to control them."

Perhaps the scariest aspect of mental illness is the lack of control we have upon it. No medicine is sure to cure it. No amount of therapy is certain to rid our minds of it. All too often, we're forced to adapt to it, to accept that it will always be there to toss obstacles in our way, obstacles that we can't remove, but can only go around.

Even after years of help from Alicia and his therapists, Charles and Marcee still show up in Nash's world, usually appearing as friendly and welcoming as ever. But to reciprocate or even to acknowledge them would be to relinquish what little progress Nash will ever make against his ailment.

"When I'm confronted by fans who've seen *A Beautiful Mind*," Cardone says, "the most common scene they mention is the Princeton steps scene, where John Nash ignores Marcee as she stands with outstretched arms, waiting to be embraced. Even though it's such a short scene without any dialogue, it's an incredibly difficult moment in the film for John. Even though Marcee is just a figment of his imagination, the love he has for her is real, and it's breaking his heart that he has to abandon her. It's really a very sad moment for both the characters and the audience."

Fortunately, by the time it came time to check out the final product, she and legions of others felt the opposite way.

"Watching it on the big screen for the first time was amazing!" Cardone says. "I think I really fell in love with acting at that moment. I realized that I was part of something so magical, something that would touch the hearts of millions of people all around the world. And I also realized that I had just been immortalized. It was very overwhelming." Connelly's turn as Alicia nabbed the Supporting Actress honor, and she and Bettany married soon afterward.

A year after becoming Marcee, Cardone became the daughter of Treat William's Dr. Andy Brown as their family arrived in the title Colorado town of 2002's *Everwood*, there to recover from the passing of Brown's wife.

"I was a little older when I did *Everwood*, so I was beginning to understand the importance of a good role," Cardone says. "I also was intrigued by the idea of playing a tomboy. I was a complete girly girl when I was little, and it was the first time I was going to play a character that was completely different from myself. I was really excited for the challenge."

As those stuck as the only (and youngest) women in a family have a tendency to do, Delia just tried to become one of the boys.

"In the beginning of the show, my preparation was mainly for acting more boyish," she recalls. "I deepened my speaking voice, which took a good amount of practice to get the hang of, and I tried not to gesture in my typical feminine manner."

Feminine or otherwise, gesturing in any sense comes across quite differently when the screen changes size, she continues.

"Acting on television is very different from acting on film," Cardone explains. "When you're in a film, your emotions are displayed on a seventy-foot screen. Even the smallest smirk or raise of an eyebrow becomes dramatically enhanced, so I make sure to be attuned to the subtlety in my performance. With television, you actually have to be more animated with your performance, because the screen it will be projected on is much smaller. So I practice going a little bigger with my emotions when my performance is for television."

Over the next few years, Delia watched father and her older brother Ephram (Greg Smith) and deal with one female issue after another (future *Desperate Housewives* [2004] star Marcia Cross became Andy's galpal for one season), not to mention the business and academic issues that so many of us can quickly, if not joyfully, find ourselves re-lost inside.

"As Delia got older, the role became more complex," she says. One of the WB network's top-rated shows, *Everwood* ran until WB merged with UPN to form the CW in 2006. "Situations became more emotionally demanding. At that time I was given an acting coach to assist me in the transition, which was very beneficial for me. I learned how to use different situations from my past towards my performances. I didn't realize until my training that even though the memories and the scene didn't match in their content, they both emulated the same emotional response."

About a decade after *Mind*, Cardone got her own shot at challenging the human mentality, bringing *Fatal Attraction* (1987) to the college years as an obsessive woman scorned in a 2010 episode of *Law and Order: Criminal Intent*.

"(She) was a very complex character and went through an emotional rollercoaster throughout the episode," says Cardone, who got ready with her acting coach, along with checking out the darkly true tale of 1994's *Heavenly Creatures*. Still knocking on the door to success in America, Peter Jackson directed Melanie Lynskey and Kate Winslet as a young mentally ill couple who brutally kill one of the girls' mothers. "I did my best to immerse myself into (the character's) world, and being on the sets working with all of my talented co-stars really aided with my transition into (her). I find that the best way I can become the character is to put on the costumes, walk on set, and let the moment guide my emotions."

Darlene Cates: *What's Eating Gilbert Grape*

What happened later? What's happening now?

Throughout this book, we'll focus mainly on what our on-screen friends did to get ready to entertain us ahead of time – as in, ahead of the first cry to film. But what about the aftermath, of the performers, if not the pretend persona?

We tend to see the people on screen as *only* their characters, not really thinking much about what the people behind them have gone through, or will continue to do so after the credits roll. We don't always worry about what they've undertaken long – years, even decades – before the film and character were even developed, and what they may face in the future – again, years, even decades. Film fans don't have the longest of memories, nor do they consider much about whatever happened to the performers that entertained them, just about the people portrayed.

But now we will. Now we'll hear the story of someone whose life truly did become the basis for a scenes-stealing (plural intentional!) work, but hardly in Hollywood fashion. Someone who didn't obtain the "happily ever after" ending, albeit still in a much brighter way than her character!

Looking at the mother of the title character in 1993's *What's Eating Gilbert Grape*, we're left to wonder. How can things get that far out of control? Being overweight is one thing; obese to the point of hardly being able to move, let alone walk, is another matter. How can someone get so far past the point when she or someone else decided that a change needed making?

Darlene Cates knows, although there's definitely more than one answer, even for herself.

"When I married and left home," says the Texas native, wed before adulthood, "food became a substitute for my friends. When my husband left home (for the military), I went back to live with my mother, who was married to an abusive alcoholic." Like so many whose weight becomes a heavier burden than it ever should, literally, Cates found solace in the culinary offerings – and people with this habit tend not to indulge in the healthiest of grubbings either (ever hear someone say, "When I'm frustrated, I eat salads!"?).

Two pregnancies in less than three years left behind some weight that never really went away as well.

"Food was a comfort," she recalls. "I put on more weight with my pregnancies and never lost it. It just started creeping up on me, with slow metabolism and overeating."

She went under the knife in 1981, and it sadly wouldn't be the last time by far. But stomach stapling only temporarily cut some weight off her body: Cates lost over 100 pounds, but they came back and brought some unwelcome partners.

"The feeling that you had before that caused you to use food to satisfy every frustrated desire to build yourself up is still there, and surgery doesn't affect that," she says. "You need to find out why you got that way in the first place."

Living in a small town, it was tough not to stand out, something that, along with her weight itself, became her first unplanned preparation for *Grape*.

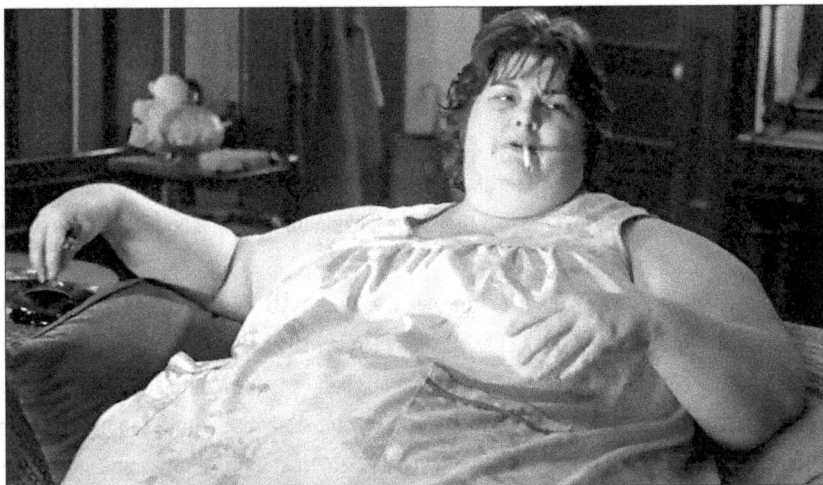

The weight trouble that plagued Darlene Cates in character in
What's Eating Gilbert Grape **got even worse after the 1993 film.**

"I did my grocery shopping at midnight," she remembers. "I was ashamed. I didn't like the way people looked at me, and didn't like the things that teenagers and kids said to me when I tried to go to the mall. I was not a total recluse, but I wasn't living my life the way I should have been and wanted to be. There were a lot of things I did not do and places I did not go. Even going to my mother's funeral was difficult for me."

Even with just a few thousand others in her village, Cates started to reach out to others like her, starting one of the area's first weight support groups. One day, the group got a call from Sally Jessy Raphael's talk show producers, asking if they could help find participants for a show about overweight people averse to social contact. The reluctant lady headed east to the Big Apple.

She had a blast, and came home ready to break her introversion and get back out into a society she only mainly learned of through her family (as of this writing, Cates has been married for over half a century). Cates couldn't know that she'd be doing the same thing shortly after, the same role in a different scale.

As Cates told her story to Raphael and her viewers, a fellow named Peter Hedges was watching. Fresh off writing a book called *What's Eating Gilbert Grape*, Hedges saw someone he wanted to meet.

His was the story of a young fellow in a small, uneventful town. Forced with being the man of the family after the death of his father, the title character contends with a mentally challenged brother, two bratty sisters, and an obese mom who hasn't been outside in years.

Hedges wanted to see his story on the big screen, and he didn't have many options for the maternal role; few performers would enter so far into dangerous territory for a role in a film that, for all anyone knew at the time, could have been a box-office bust, assuming it was made at all. But for one of the first times in her life, Cates' size became an asset.

One of Raphael's producers called, and told her to expect a similar notification from the *Grape* casting group. Cates thought the joke not the slightest bit practical.

"At the time, I didn't know anything about acting," she says. "They told me they had people who could teach us how to act. That told me that they were looking for more of a body type than somebody who could act."

Still, adjusting to set life was tough for someone who'd never acted before; Cates was surrounded by Johnny Depp in the top role, a young John Reilly, Juliette Lewis, Mary Steenburgen . . . and, in the role that really gave him a spot on Hollywood's map, a kid named DiCaprio, playing Momma's youngest son Arnie.

Cates worked with a speech therapist to develop Momma's typically soft, sad natural tone. But the majority of her "preparation" had been her own past. Cates had some things, some life experiences to rely on, that none of her new colleagues could ever truly understand or feel. In a far cry from her beauty queen days, Momma's a prisoner in her own home, too sad and tired to venture out onto the front porch, or even go upstairs for the luxury of sleeping in a bed. She's also a mysterious laughingstock around town; few even know what the former headliner looks like, and youngsters dare each other to venture by the house to get a sneak peek, sometimes with Gilbert's help.

Creating a character backstory can be a wonderful stepping stone to a strong portrayal; Cates just had to look back at her impromptu autobiography. Many actors will tell you about "losing themselves in the character," but she was already there, and had been for quite some time. In this case, that wasn't a good thing.

"It was so much of my life," she says. "There were things in there that I could relate to. There were things that promoted the stereotypes that I didn't like. After I got to Austin, we spent a lot of time in a room talking about the project. They made me feel very respected and very loved and very accepted."

Still, she was the new gal in town, and that can be intimidating as all hell for *any* inexperienced performer, regardless of the circumstances. Early in filming, Cates says, the original actor playing Gilbert's grocery store boss Mr. Lamson was removed, and Tim Green showed up to finish out the role. Cates was horrified a similar fate awaited her.

"When I asked about it, I was told that he just wasn't right for the part," she remembers. "I was waiting for them to tell me to go home."

"There were times when I didn't know what I was doing and why," she says. "I thought I knew until I got there. I told my son to take me home.

"He said 'Mom, they think you can do this or you wouldn't be here. Just give yourself a chance. After we've done one day, if you still don't feel like you want to be here, I'll come pick you up.'"

Cates filmed a scene in which the family discusses Arnie's upcoming birthday party. That's when she realized that this sort of thing was for her.

"Once I'd done it, I loved it," she says.

Arnie's personal safety net, Momma, like the rest of her family and probably the rest of the town (Gilbert refers to the area early on as "like dancing to no music"), seems content to just sit around and wait for life to pass her by, occasionally glancing enviously at the trailers that drive by outside (the highlight of Arnie's life), filled with people that want just a little bit more. Her family's not quite dysfunctional, per se; there's hardly any function at all.

But then, the rambunctious Arnie makes the local water tower his personal playground one too many times, and the cops haul the youngster off to jail. That's when Momma's had just about enough of this self-sequestration mess, and one of the film's most memorable scenes hits.

Even before that part, Cates says, "It was so easy to draw on experiences from my own life. I have a brother that is developmentally challenged, so it wasn't a reach to think about how I would feel if they had taken him, and I had to go get him."

Storming determinedly out of her house, to the amazement of her children, Momma forces herself into the car. With Gilbert at the wheel and everyone else on the other side to balance out her weight, the family rolls toward the courthouse, and we see them put on a unified front for the first time in the film.

Upon arrival, Momma immediately becomes the center of unwelcome attention; she's the biggest many youths have ever seen, and there's some that knew her, but can't believe how much she's changed. The cops that took Arnie can hardly utter her name.

"It was very difficult, because it was symbolic of all the fear and embarrassment that I had about going anyplace," says Cates, whose family members were extras in the scene. "That was my worst nightmare, to go out someplace and just have people staring at me and judging me. When we did that scene, it became very real to me and I broke down after the first take. I had to sit down and cry for a little bit, and fortunately, we didn't have to do too many takes – I think we only did two."

Shock gives way to intimidation for the cops, who hurriedly let Arnie go. But there's suddenly a crowd outside (this happens several times during the film, showing that there was indeed little to do in Endora), and no one can stop staring. One moron takes a photo of her, and it's tough not to want to jump straight through the screen and jam the camera south of his Adam's apple.

"The guy stepping out to take the picture was so pivotal in the whole storyline. Up until that point, it was so easy to judge Momma, to not be very sympathetic for her situation. But that particular scene when the audience saw the emotional pain she was going through, and for that man to just step out and take that picture, that changed the whole attitude toward Momma. People became more sympathetic toward her situation." But, tragically, they won't get to stay on Momma's side for long.

Shortly thereafter, the family celebrates Arnie's eighteenth birthday, and she and Gilbert finally reconcile their simmering feud, Momma heads upstairs in her bed for the first time in years (herself unable to walk, Cates had a stunt double for the stair-climbing filming.

"I never meant to be like this," she says to Gilbert. "I never meant to be a joke." Just remembering the scene makes Cates emotional.

"That was hauntingly surreal because I had been in somewhat of the same position, talking to my son, telling him that I didn't want to be a burden, didn't want him to be ashamed of me," she says. "I can't really describe the exact feeling that that invoked; it was just art imitating life. It just seemed so strange to me that here I was on that movie set, telling somebody else's story, and it was so similar to my own. The uniqueness of it wasn't lost on me. Those were things that I had struggled with, so similar to my own life. I drew on what I had from my own life, and fortunately, it seemed to work."

Arnie comes upstairs to say goodnight to his mother, and finds that her heart has given out for the last time.

"I was just trying not to breathe," Cates says of Momma's passing. "The camera couldn't see me take a breath. The first time that Leo screamed in my ear, I thought they would have to peel me off the ceiling. They got me earplugs to finish the scene." Realizing that removing her from the home would require a crane, and draw another crowd of jeering mental midgets, the kids finally find their footing on the same level. They take all their possessions outside, then burn the house down. The girls move away, and Gilbert and Arnie run off together. It's sad, but it's also an uplifting ending, showing that the unity Momma always wanted in her family finally came together.

Watching it from the audience, she recalls, had a much different effect.

"A lot of my friends and family were bothered by that," she says. "It was sad. I cried. I was able to disassociate myself from the character in this movie."

And afterwards? Well, let's focus on that.

First off, Cates is, indeed, alive (she's lost roles over false rumors of her death). Secondly, the stomach stapling decades ago has been her only such technique; even with the advancements in gastric bypass, she's never gone that route.

But still, with her weight fluctuating, Cates' health has taken nearly the worst of turns, and more than once. Severe stomach problems sent her to the hospital around Christmas 2010.

"The doctor told me to tell my family goodbye," she says. "He said he didn't know. I told them I would either see them when I woke up, or see them on the other side." Over six feet of near-dead intestine was removed.

Her sutures didn't always hold. Wounds didn't heal correctly. An infection nearly ate her body from the inside out.

After three more surgeries, Cates spent months in the hospital. She lost some more weight, to the point that malnourishment set in by the time she was healthy enough to go home.

But she did. And years later, those catcalls and smart comments that she's heard both before and after Momma just don't happen anymore – much.

"When I go out and people look at me," she says, "I don't know if it's because I'm fat, or if I've been in a movie. I'm able to go out a little bit more."

Just maybe, she's getting to experience the same newfound sympathy, the respect that Momma didn't get to feel for long enough. Let's just hope that this sort of art keeps imitating in her life.

Mark Lindsay Chapman: *Titanic/Chapter 27*

One moment that helped make Mark Lindsay Chapman's acting career came when he *didn't* get a role.

A budding star with a few TV appearances on his resume, Chapman (then known as Mark Lindsay; another Mark Chapman was already quite a theater star in Britain) went to read for a small role in the 1985 TV movie *John and Yoko*, based on one of the music world's most well-known couples.

Like any acting mainstay, Chapman went full force with his tryout. But things weren't mutual; going through his lines, Chapman could feel the casting crew's attention moving elsewhere.

"I was in a bit of a hurry," he says. "I had to get to another audition. I said, 'Excuse me, would you mind to start paying attention?'"

In a move reminiscent of the *Seinfeld* (1989) episode where George Costanza tells off Yankee head honcho George Steinbrenner and gets offered a job, they threw him a new script. This time, he'd be reading for the male title character.

Chapman flew to New York, and auditioned for Yoko herself. He visited the building where Lennon was murdered. He read some poetry that Lennon had written.

Perhaps he was on his way. Maybe his name would soon be a household word. Maybe he'd stumbled onto the key to a strong career.

Then, one fateful day, Chapman was called into the studio.

"They said, 'We told Yoko what your last name was,'" Chapman says. "They said they had to fire me." They couldn't have Lennon being played by someone named after the man who'd murdered him (well, close: Lennon's killer was Mark DAVID Chapman).

But almost overnight, Chapman's name went to the spotlight. *Rolling Stone* gave him a call. He got invited for an evening on Johnny Carson's show. Everyone wanted to hear the story of a man who missed a role because he had the wrong moniker.

"I had more publicity than I'd ever had in my life," Chapman says. "To this day, I get asked about it." The attention worked; he landed recurring roles on *Dallas* and *Falcon Crest*, among other shows, and has worked steadily since.

Of course, nearly two decades later, the irony would come full circle…

Having just finished up the 1995 thriller *Separate Lives*, Chapman's flick co-star Linda Hamilton was hanging out with the actor and his family.

Mark Lindsay Chapman acted out one American tragedy in *Titanic* (1997), then become another as John Lennon in *Chapter 27* (2007).

"My daughter and ex-wife started talking about *Terminator* (1984)," he recalls. "Linda told me about how (her then-husband) James Cameron was afraid of water; he'd almost drowned as a kid. It made him want to do a water movie."

For those who haven't put this one together yet, it would end up... *TITANIC!*

"Jim knew that I'd lived on a boat in England in my life," Chapman recalls. "He knew I'd sailed a lot."

However, there was one little thing they were concerned about, while casting the role of Chief Officer Wilde, a guard who, like many in the film, eventually adapts into the "every man for himself" attitude.

"They said, 'We really need an asshole to play Wilde, and we don't think you're that kind of guy."

A native of Liverpool, Henry Tingle Wilde moved quickly through the ranks of seamanship, serving as second-in-command on the *Olympia*, then the world's largest ship, in 1911. The next year, he helped *Titanic* through the water for the first time.

Wilde spent the opening hours of the voyage supervising the deckhands. Since he was off-duty when the iceberg got too close, it's unclear what happened next, other than that his body was never found.

Chapman asked his father to do some research at British museums. His findings surprised everyone.

"The Chief Officer was always thought of as the hero, but he was actually not," he remembers. "He was a real asshole who light-loaded the lifeboat." Knowing that, making this guy a jerk would be a piece of cake.

Even with three hours of the finished project that the film would end up becoming, "There must be another 50 or 100 feet of improvisation, me with the whistle or launching the boat.

"That stuff went on for three months of nights," he says of filming. "We worked from about four in the afternoon, at Rosarito Beach (near Baja, Mexico), to six in the morning when the sun came off."

The cast, including hundreds of extras, stunt people from across the globe, and, of course, two youngsters named Leo and Kate, got a few weeks off in the middle of filming, which wouldn't nearly be enough.

"We were getting various water-related illnesses," Chapman says, "chest illnesses from water that wasn't terribly clean."

Still, he became the jerk, holding people back from escaping on the boats because they were from the wrong gender or social class. However, when a rich man grabs a strange child and "pleads" for Wilde to make them an exception, he acquiesces.

However, Wilde, as the filmmakers play the "creative license" card (you **DID** know the term for their *totally* rare bending of the truth for dramatic purposes, right?), makes one more appearance and becomes an inadvertent savior.

Having said her sad goodbye to her new love, Rose Dawson (Kate Winslet) desperately searches the water for signs of life. A boat just came by looking for them, and she knows it may not come back.

Calling out doesn't help, and she's surrounded by death, with bodies floating around like a party from hell.

Then she sees the corpse of Wilde. But his health isn't her concern. That whistle of his, however, might be her only chance.

She swims over, and blows it with what little wind she has. But it's enough – the people on the boat hear, come back, and pick her up, and she's safe for now.

Things didn't work out too well for Wilde. But Chapman could brag that he was in a film that brought in more domestic gross than any film in history (to that point, as Cameron eventually beat his own mark with 2009's *Avatar*), and took a Best Picture award. Cameron, who also won Best Director, once came down to the set during filming, put on a corset, and jumped in the water, asking who had a problem! Apparently, his phobia was in the past.

Chapman spent much of the next decade on TV, with recurring roles on *Days of our Lives* (1965) and *Young and the Restless* (1973).

"The best advice that I can give is to learn the lines," he says to upcoming actors. "If you have talent and you've done theater, you're used to making a character come to life from the pages. If you've got a good director, he'll help you out. Mostly you hope for rehearsal time. When you're doing TV, you're basically at a factory. They put you in a trailer, call you out, and you'd better have your lines down. The director may have a couple of words with you, and then you'll shoot it. You best hope you get it right the first time, because they don't like reshoots."

In 2006, two decades after his name cost him a role, his phone rang. Chapman learned of an upcoming flick called *Chapter 27*, a mini-biopic of Lennon's killer.

This time, they wanted Chapman to become Chapman's victim.

"I said, oh, fuck off,'" he recalls. "They said they wanted me to read for John Lennon. It's a small part. I said, 'What are we going to do about the name? I'm not going through all that shit again.'"

But then he remembered his own days as a Beatles fan. He remembered the shock waves that washed over America that dark December night, a moment that far too many can recall as to exactly where they were and what they were doing when the announcement came. Howard Cosell announcing Lennon's murder on *Monday Night Football* is still considered one of the darkest moments in sports history.

For his part, Chapman was on his way to perform in a theatrical production of *Godspell*, and had to pull his car over when he heard the news. So he went for the short role.

As Lennon, he got to become one of the most famous folks in America, with Mariko Takai playing Ono. He was watched by a multitude of fans as he headed into his building. He acted out the infamous photo of Lennon signing an autograph for his killer. He even felt what the man went through in his last moments (although on a slightly safer scale).

Once again, the film's meant to be a short biopic of the killer. Jared Leto, who'd put on some serious poundage for the role, would be the "other" Mark Chapman, and he avoided the man playing Lennon during filming. Lindsay Lohan had a small role as Jude (inside joke on the name!), who develops a weird relationship with the assassin.

"It had been 20 years," Chapman says, "and I enjoyed being there." Finally, he'd come full circle with the role – and it's a place many others can reach.

"Take the roles," he says to actors in training. Don't get married until you've made it as an actor. Your acting career is what you make it. Tie a second string to your bow. Go to film school. Learn some camera work. Use your lenses."

Richard D'Alessandro: *Forrest Gump*

Just after the Best Picture of 1994 hit screens nationwide, Richard D'Alessandro was shopping at the supermarket.

Suddenly someone walked up to the actor and pointed at him.

"Viet-fuckin'-Nam!" the fellow quipped.

D'Alessandro grinned and nodded. After over a decade in the acting business, he'd finally become synonymous with a line.

"People would say, 'Viet-fuckin'-Nam!' and then they'd say I was great," recalls D'Alessandro, who howled the line as legendary radical Abbie Hoffman during the Washington, D.C. rally scene in *Forrest Gump*. "Then it happened again and again and again, and every time somebody saw me, they'd say, 'Viet-fuckin'-Nam!' If I drop dead tomorrow, I'll be known for 'Viet-fuckin' Nam!' It was the first time I'd ever gotten recognition for work."

Richard D'Alessandro (right) stepped in as legendary war radical Abbie Hoffman in 1994's *Forrest Gump*, which took Best Picture and won Tom Hanks (left) his second lead acting Oscar.

After working sporadically on films and television throughout the 80s and early 90s, the Long Island native decided to try out for one of history's most (in)famous faces. A lifelong political activist, Hoffman spent much of the 60s and 70s protesting the Vietnam War (even playing himself in a cameo in Oliver Stone's 1989 Oscar-winning *Born on the Fourth of July*), hung out in hiding while a fugitive on drug charges for which he eventually did four months in jail, and protested the CIA's actions throughout the 80s. Today, two decades after his suicide, Hoffman is still seen as a revolutionary, a face in the political activism world.

During his research on Hoffman's background, D'Alessandro called several news stations, looking for those who might have known the man. Eventually, he met with longtime Hoffman friend and fellow activist Jerry Rubin, who stood trial with Hoffman as two of the "Chicago Seven" defendants, accused of conspiracy and inciting a riot during the 1968 Democratic National Convention in Chicago (the seven were found guilty of inciting, but their conviction was overturned on appeal). D'Alessandro also met former Hoffman friend Tom Hayden, another member of the "Seven," who'd later served as a California senator. He talked with Bobby Seale, one of the original members of the Black Panthers, who had known Hoffman.

Along the way, D'Alessandro even contacted Johanna Lawrenson, with whom Hoffman had lived while on the lam.

"She showed me some never-before-seen footage of (Hoffman) at rallies," D'Alessandro recalls. "I got a lot of insight from a lot of people." Including, it would turn out, himself.

Though Hoffman reached his heights in the public eye a bit before D'Alessandro, born in 1960, was old enough to really understand him, "I found a lot of myself in him: his need for conflict, and his need to not let the government have so much control over us. The guts he had, he didn't have censors. He was outspoken and said what he had to say. I'm the same way."

For his audition, D'Alessandro put together a long speech against Vietnam, much like his "role model" would do. He sewed together several American flags into a shirt, much like Hoffman was wont to do, and put on some army greens.

Then he strolled into the room and met the men behind the movie, including director Robert Zemeckis.

D'Alessandro launched into his verbal discourse, becoming Hoffman for a few minutes. When he finished, the fellows at the table looked at each other.

"Well," Zemeckis said, "you certainly did your homework." A few months later, D'Alessandro was giving Hoffman's speech at the Lincoln Memorial Reflecting Pool, just before the Washington Monument (his actual speech in the film is taken from talks he gave in the nation's capital, although not at the Pool itself).

Population-wise, it's the biggest scene in the film, with 3000 extras and about 1000 more onlookers, not to mention a film crew of roughly 200. For the eight days it took to film the scene, extras had to get up before dawn and visit the crew's warehouse of 60s memorabilia, strapping on fake afro wigs and long-haired gimmicks, putting on clothes, beads, chains, and other attire from the time.

Standing before such a huge crowd, D'Alessandro felt closer to Hoffman than ever.

"That was invigorating," he recalls. "There were some cold days, but I could feel the energy. That energy helps you go over the top. It puts you really there."

As was his inadvertent practice for the entire film, the title character (Tom Hanks, in his second consecutive Best Actor performance) happens to find himself in the right place at the right time; just back from earning a Congressional Medal of Honor in Vietnam, he's still in his military garb, wandering through the crowd, wondering why the man at the microphone can't stop saying, "F-this! and F-that!"

Noticing the soldier, Hoffman asks Gump to say a few words as someone who's been there and seen it all. Gump knows exactly how to put it into words: "There was only one thing I could say about Vietnam."

But just as he starts to speak, there's a problem; a sneaky fellow from the government doesn't want the public to hear the speech, so he yanks the cords out of the speaker. Forrest is giving a fine speech, but no one can hear it. Just as the sound system's back on, he ends with one of the film's lines that would find its way into cinematic lore: "and that's all I have to say about that."

Though Hoffman's the only one to hear Gump's actual words, he congratulates his new friend, and the crowd cheers him on.

Now, for the first time for many, it's time to hear – or read – the long-wondered about words.

"Forrest was saying that everybody lost somebody," D'Alessandro says. "People lost brothers, sisters. Some lost fathers, mothers, uncles, and aunts. Forrest was speaking up."

Julienne Davis: *Eyes Wide Shut*

She knew the character would be important; she just didn't know how much or how so.

She knew she'd be alongside some awfully big names in the cast; she just didn't know what everyone would be doing.

But what Julienne Davis knew for sure about 1999's *Eyes Wide Shut* was the fellow in the directing chair – and, just with, well, about everyone who'd so much as walk past the camera in one of his flicks, that name was plenty.

"At the time, I was a working model," she remembers, "living in London, give or take, since 1989." She'd studied acting some years before, but modeling had paid better and allowed her to travel across the globe.

So when a casting call came about for the flick, Davis was a bit hesitant about the character she'd be going in for: the request was for models in g-strings and high heels... wearing masks.

It might have sounded like the makings for some cheap horror flick: mysterious scantily clad women wandering around in *masks*?

"I said, 'Who's the director?'" Davis recalls. "They said it was Stanley Kubrick. I was like 'OH?!'"

Her thoughts immediately rushed back to high school, where she and her classmates had done some film critiquing.

"Everybody wanted to be in that class," she remembers. "We did a whole focus on Kubrick."

Far from the modeling world's runways, she strolled into the audition. Whereas most models do their thing in front of a large audience, with few colleagues, this one went the other way at high speed – she'd be up against hundreds of other women, as casting had raged through America before crossing over to England. Those who made the decision cut were few, and many that did make it would end up as extras, just walking through the background while the main characters played. Only a few would get a real shot at the true role.

Still, soon after, her agent called. The director himself wanted to meet her.

Kubrick, she recalls, "was asking me about things you wouldn't expect. He asked me why I was in London, what I was doing there, what my parents did."

Then he asked for a few more screen tests.

"I waited for an agonizing two weeks," she says wistfully. "Then I got the part."

Still, displaying his trademark uber-secrecy, Kubrick didn't tell anyone much about the film, even those who were performing in it, aside from the headliners.

"It was in (Stanley's) interest to not say too much to someone he didn't know," she says. "I didn't see the script – all I saw was the pages I was in. I knew that Tom's character was a doctor, but not what kind of doctor he was."

Her character didn't survive 1999's *Eyes Wide Shut*, but Julianne Davis (right) was a strong part of Stanley Kubrick's farewell film.

Oh, those big names we mentioned earlier? That Tom fellow was one – it was followed by Cruise. He and Nicole Kidman, then still one of Hollywood's hottest couples, carried the leads in the story of a lost soul named Bill, a doctor caught in a sexually deviant weekend, driven to near-adultery after his wife Alice admits an imagined affair of her own.

But before any of that happens, the two enjoy themselves at a party for the local rich and snobbish. Suddenly, the host (Sidney Pollack) calls Bill upstairs for some impromptu medical care.

Mandy, the host's lovely and paid date for the night, collapses on a chair, the victim of too much partying in powder form. Davis had been getting ready to become the unlucky lady.

"I'd smoked pot when I was younger, and I knew what it was like to be wasted or drunk," says Davis, whose modeling career had included nude – but not pornographic – work. "I'd watched some things about characters that had been drug addicts, like the scene from *Pulp Fiction* where (Uma Thurman) overdoses. By the time I got on set, I knew what I was ready for." Roused back to coherence by Bill, Mandy discusses something about rehab.

Disheartened by his wife's fantasies, Bill soon learns of a secret mansion not too far off, the home of a massive orgy, everyone's identity hidden behind a Halloween trademark. Everywhere he looks, however, he can't help but see Alice's heavenly form.

Including in the frightened woman who approaches him, warning him that he doesn't belong. We don't see her face (unfortunately!) but it's clearly Mandy.

"I felt like Tom looked at Mandy like she had been Nicole if Nicole had turned out differently in her life," Davis explains. "All the girls had a little bit of an essence of Nicole's character, like reddish-auburn hair. She was a different version of her, if she had gone a different way. She was trying to save him because he had saved her."

It doesn't work, as he's quickly escorted to appear before the master of, ahem, ceremonies and the participants. His attempted savior is led away, and Bill is forced to reveal his identity, then leave.

Davis didn't work in the orgy scenes – her choice as a person, an actress, and, tragically, a victim.

"A year before (filming)," she remembers, "I had been sexually assaulted on the streets of London. I was not raped, but it really did my head in. When they said 'Cut,' I said 'Robe, please.'"

As the film world – still mostly in print form, as the Internet wasn't really in high gear just yet – started to buzz about Kubrick's next creation, rumors ran rampant: a popular one was that Cruise's character would show up in women's garb, which was ludicrously off kilter, as transvestitism wasn't even mentioned in the storyline. But more than anything else, everyone wondered just when they'd get to see the flick. Dragging on for over a year, *Eyes Wide Shut* became one of the longest shoots in American cinema history. Davis was on and off the set from February to November 1998.

"(Kubrick) did quite a few takes," Davis says, "but the reason he did so many takes was to get the timing correct with the camera movement in relation to what was happening in the scene. It wasn't like he was saying, 'That wasn't good enough, do it again, do it again, do it again.'

"It was sometimes enjoyable," she continues of working for Kubrick, "sometimes frustrating. To me, it seemed like there was a level of disorganization in the order in which he addressed things. They were painting and repainting the masks up until the last minute; the paint was wet on my character's face. After they changed the masks on the actors' faces and had the music playing, he would say, 'I'm not sure about the masks.' This was after we'd been rehearsing for three weeks." Still, being in a Kubrick film handed out some rough challenges far from the cameras, as she'd find out soon enough.

But first, the *Eyes* had to let everyone know what happened to Mandy – sort of. A newspaper informs Bill that a former beauty queen has died of another overdose. This time, he wasn't there to save her.

His old friend from the party informs him that shutting up and walking away is the best course of action. He agrees. Like so many other storylines in Kubrick's world, the director decided to leave it a sentence fragment, leaving the audience to fill in the end punctuation. Kubrick never let his viewers forget that we were guests in his world; he saw the world his way, and dared anyone to even ask him to compromise on it. Never happened.

"I wrote Mandy's backstory as a beauty queen who'd gone down the wrong road," Davis explains. "For me, being an actor is really convincing yourself that you are that person, in that place, saying those things, with that history. If you as the actor don't believe you, then who else is going to believe you?"

As she pulled up to the premiere in the summer of 1999, Davis tried to stay upbeat about her film debut. But she and so many others had a very good reason for wistfulness.

Kubrick's sudden death on March 7, 1999, allegedly hours after finishing the final *Shut* cut, shocked and saddened the film world.

"He wasn't ready," she remembers. "We had talked, and he had said how excited he was about making *A.I.*, so I know he wasn't ready." Steven Spielberg, a longtime friend of Kubrick, finished *A.I. Artificial Intelligence* in 2001.

Stepping out of the limousine to the premiere's carpet, however, Davis got a taste of stardom that no auditions, no rehearsals, no backstory could have ever prepared her for.

"There were 300 flashbulbs going off," she says. "It was overwhelming. I got plucked out of obscurity and I felt a bit like a rabbit caught in the headlights. I was getting interviewed by the press for an hour and 25 minutes." Cruise and Kidman might have been used to this sort of thing; the pair was tabloid fodder from before their marriage to long past their subsequent divorce. Davis was in a new universe – and it didn't stop or even slow for a while.

"A lot of people came out of the woodwork," she remembers. "I got gifts, dresses, diamonds, invited to parties, everything."

Then fame's rougher sides started to step in. Stories with much more sensationalism than truth started popping up in tabloids, handing Davis the unfair "party girl" label that such publications love to proclaim. She was used to being photographed at model shoots; the paparazzi barrage was a separate matter.

"It makes you a little paranoid, I guess," she says. "Newspapers and magazines were taping everything I said. Journalists will say whatever they need to as long as there's a *little* bit of truth. The paparazzi was taking pictures of me, but it doesn't mean anything after a while. Fame is empty. Fame is fleeting."

It's taught her some tough lessons as her career goes on.

"Don't ever feel safe," she says to fellow upcomers. "Don't feel that once you've made it, you can relax and let your hair down. Be gracious to everybody. Rely on yourself, keep your head down, and work hard. Be great at what you do. Be kind, and be true to your word. If you say anything bad about someone, it gets back to them very quickly, and comes back on you two-hundred-fold. If word gets out that you're a nightmare, word travels quickly. Be neutral always."

Dayni Deats: *River's Edge*

She stepped away from her character. She moved away from herself. She tried to get as far from reality as humanly possible. Right in the midst of the most prominent acting role of her life – to that point – Dayni Deats tried to take her mind and get it elsewhere.

"There's a practice called the fourth wall," Deats explains. "I had talked to an acting coach about it. The set is three walls, and the camera is where the fourth wall would be in the room, and as long as that fourth wall is there, you're exposed."

In acting jargon, "breaking the fourth wall" is associated with a scene where a character directly addresses the audience by speaking straight into the camera. Deats' character wouldn't have that kind of opportunity.

"The fourth wall is like making an imaginary wall between you and the camera, and you kind of pretend that you're alone," she says. "You do that if you're acting with a friend, if you're acting with yourself, or whatever, you put that fourth wall up. That was what I thought of most of the time: that (no one else is) there, that I'm in my room by myself. It's meditation or something. I was like, how do I *not* be here?"

Charging as far as possible from John Hughes' barrage of Brat Pack rom-dramedies that had charged through the first few years of the 1980s in American film, 1986's *River's Edge* put its group of youths in a far more sinister position.

"It was really risky for that time," Deats says. "Had it come out now, it could have gone further, because people are further (along). That was still the 80s, and they thought kids were still like *The Breakfast Club* [1985]."

Not quite. Like *Club* and other popular Pack films, *Edge* did examine the crazy world of the teenage years, full of identity issues, battles with the society that so many of said age felt was made to prosecute them, and the bounds of friending. But this film also went in a far darker and sadder direction, taking its young cast and surroundings down into the worlds of drugs, poverty, violence, and, ultimately, murder.

"I got the role accidentally," Deats recalls. "I didn't plan to be in that. My roommate at the time was an actress, always auditioning. We'd go to the auditions together and I'd sit and wait for her." As her friend tried out for a role, a crew member walked by and noticed Deats.

The *Edge* people had already gone through a huge search for their victim, and, one way or another, had found reason to thin out the herd all the way down to zero over and over, a quest that had taken so long they'd been forced to start filming other scenes with an incomplete cast.

Still, something or other told this fellow that his new find might have what it took to play someone who'd spend ninety percent of her screen time acting out rigor mortis in the nude. And after they'd checked out hundreds of possibilities, Deats showed the *Edge* crew they'd found just what they were looking for, all in a matter of hours.

"They hadn't found a match, because everyone was afraid to get naked," Deats remembered. "It went fast. After I read, I went to the set later that afternoon. I said yes, and that opened up the door, and I didn't really know what I was saying yes to."

Moments into *Edge*, viewers get quite the unsanitary taste of what they're in for, and it's about as subtle as can be done for this sort of tale. One of the first scenes is of a fellow named John (Daniel Roebuck), sitting off by himself, smoking on a riverbank.

His girlfriend Jamie's there too, laying back, naked, staring off into space.

Because he killed her before the film's timeline began. But the fact that he's alone, and pretty calm for a first-time killer, keeps us from freaking out as well.

"I grew up in a film family. I was raised on the sets," Deats says. "I just thought I could (play Jamie). It was a very cavalier thought, but that's what I thought. I never considered any of the ramifications, like how horrified my family would be, or to have a theater full of people to see me naked at nineteen. But that's the beauty of being nineteen: that you don't look ahead."

Looking for every excuse to leave his dysfunctional household, John's friend Matt (Keanu Reeves) and their loner pothead pal Layne (Crispin Glover, who really chews up the scenery in this flick) head out to get some green goodies from local dealer Feck (Dennis Hopper, galaxies from the interaction he and Reeves would have eight years later in *Speed*!). Feck's only companion is an inflatable doll, there to replace the woman he found himself forced to kill years before.

Eventually, John shows up. He, Layne, Matt, and their galpals, including Ione Skye's lovely Clarissa, the object of Matt's fantasies, head over to visit Jamie.

Still, there's a certain stoicism running through the group, although for some, it's more about doing nothing from being too scared to make a choice. Layne's thinking about how to solidify a false alibi and get rid of the body, but he's much more enthusiastic about the idea than even John, who, while not showing much remorse, seems to think he deserves to get in trouble.

Deats had been checking over the facts that *Edge* used as a cinematic springboard, the 1981 murder of fourteen-year-old Californian Marcy Conrad by her teenage boyfriend Anthony Broussard, who showed off Conrad's corpse to his friend before dumping it into a ravine. It took days before anyone grew the guts to call the cops, but Broussard pleaded guilty to the crime and got a twenty-five-to-life sentence.

"Back then, there wasn't the Internet, so I had to look all that stuff up," she says. "I read all of the newspaper articles and stuff like that, stuff related to the killing. I think every actor has to prepare for their role by studying their lines or reading the story about their character, or trying to get all that information."

As is almost always the case in the acting business, the storyline switched around as the flick moved from screenplay to screen, and even during the editing process. Earlier versions had Jamie alive for at least part of the film.

"The character was alive in the shooting and the script," Deats says. "There was a little set up while she's alive, with her boyfriend in this relationship. She was in the morgue when her mom came to see her. When you saw Jamie alive, you gathered an opinion of her and the situation, and it changed how you felt about the movie. Without seeing her die, you had to decide, well, did she deserve to die, or did she do something? Was she innocent? Was she an asshole? How did all of these people play the part?"

As it turned out, all viewers saw of Jamie's livelihood would be a very short scene near the end, and then only for a silent close-up of John's hands going around her neck to take her breath away. That's truly one of the deep features that sets *Edge* apart from most other flicks of the sort. It doesn't totally vilify John, turning him into some kind of cold, conniving jerk ready to backstab anyone to get away with what he did (his only explanation for the murders is "She was talking shit.") It takes something as horrible as the violent theft of human life and manages to *not* make it the storyline's focal point. It's not about the crime or why the murder occurred. It's about how people in a situation like that react, and while the situation is certainly unthinkable to most, it would be a stretch to call it unrealistic.

Preparing for and even during filming, Deats felt the same way at times.

"Especially with actors working around me, I didn't realize what it was going to take," she says. "I thought, I've been on sets a million times, I can do this. In the end, I could, but at the time, I was like, whoa!" Her family had indeed been in the business since before Deats herself was around; her grandfather Rufus worked as a key grip (the people who decide what electronic toys will be needed for the film, then work out the cameras and lighting during filming) and her father and brothers followed in Rufus' work steps.

Deats' dad Richard won an Oscar for technical achievement in 1984 for designing a portable camera crane, and her brother Jerry helped in the cinematography that brought *The Social Network* an Oscar nomination in 2010. Her mother Emmy worked for decades in the legal department at Universal Studios.

"I couldn't see (*Edge*) for years, and it was really hard on my family," Deats says. "It caused a lot of drama and fighting, and stupid stuff that I didn't expect it to cause. No one wants to see themselves playing dead and it was depressing, even when I was sitting on the set in my bathrobe, if I would catch a look at myself. I'm walking around like a corpse. I didn't recognize that person. I cried when they made my hair short and blonde – I thought it looked so ugly."

But death, particularly the violent murder of someone who had so much time and so much left to do, *should* be rough on the senses. Bringing death to acting life was much tougher than most audience members probably thought she made it look.

"If your character is living or has been living, you have to prepare for your part by studying them and deciding how you're going to portray their characteristics," Deats says. "If you're playing a corpse, you're just going to practice holding your breath and trying to think of something, to take yourself somewhere else while everyone else is working around you."

That Jamie's afterlife would begin with her eyes open was intentional, she continues.

"When we were working with prosthetics, we did a study on what happens when rigor mortis sets in and where the blood settles and everything," says Deats. "Your pupils go away, so they fit my eyes with contact lenses that took the pupil away. It was easier because then my pupils wouldn't focus on little things. I could still roughly see, but I could go to that other place and not be there. You have to do that so you don't smile or react: you have to go to another place while everyone else is talking and working."

Without being in the position ourselves, it's difficult to gauge the risks and realities of being asked for nudity in films. Some will always say absolutely not under any circumstances, others will pick and choose (and still others will do it for a few extra paycheck figures!). Still, we can't paint all such requests with the same brush – doing a nude scene for sexual purposes isn't the same as Deats' task of being in the altogether to show, in every sense, pain and death.

"I tried to not really think of it," she says. "When we do nude scenes, or any risqué scenes, anything that might be sensitive, we try to clear the set and give the talent (privacy). They give you that room to do it. As far as makeup and prosthetics, as with any actor, when you use makeup, like a hairpiece or wardrobe or whatever, you're already going into that other character. Oh, I'm this person, I happen to transfer into a corpse. But when I look down at my hands or arms or look in a mirror, I don't look like myself anymore. That's how acting works."

Dayni Deats and Kent Luttrell each played depressing dramatic dead in 1986, her in *River's Edge* and him in *Stand by Me*.

Layne rolls Jamie's body into the lake (a scene Deats claims she wasn't told of until the last minute!), and John goes to stay with Feck, a fellow stealer of life. Matt, in the midst of wooing Clarissa, calls the cops, and Jamie is quickly found.

But John's never caught: fearing that he's going over the edge in the non-physical sense, Feck sends a bullet to his brain – much less violent that Roebuck's death decades later in the *Halloween II* remake of 2009, when Michael Myers bashes in his head! Feck is caught and confesses to it all, and everyone's forced to try to move on without a few of their friends.

Like the rest of her family, Deats ended up spending the majority of her entertainment career behind the camera, soon heading into production.

"The acting thing is so much exposure, so intense," she says. "They just judge you on stuff you can't control, like how tall you are. Producing for me was like putting on your favorite jeans. I love it. I love that side of it." She and longtime director David Fincher put together some award-winning commercials for Nike, and she snared a few honors from MTV, helping Janet Jackson, Sting, and many others with their videos.

"You can't just be a pretty face, and you can't just *want* to be an actor," Deats says. "This town is full of beautiful, talented people, so you have to have those two ingredients, but you have to have one more thing, and it's different in other people. To me, it's like the combination, to have the one more thing that gets the acting thing going. Anyone who wants to be an actor that can't stand on their feet and work for twelve to fourteen hours should think of a different job. It's incomparable to everything else. This town is full of people who came from other places to try to make it happen, and the odds are less than winning the lottery. The most beautiful people, the prom king and queen from everywhere in America, everyone in the world that's beautiful thinks of coming to Hollywood and making it, that's part of the dream.

"It's a very crazy place!"

In a similar role...
Book vs. movie.

It's one of the entertainment world's eternal wars, a battle that will never have a victor. It's all about personal perception. Some of us react better to forming our own impression from the words of another, others would rather see something in living color and respond to it.

Stephen King's works have inspired this sort of argument for years, mainly because his literary creations have come to the big screen (and the small one, often in miniseries mode) more so than just about any other author.

But putting quality aside for a moment, let's look at what one medium offers that another can't. Throughout most of "The Body," a chunk of King's 1982 novella *Different Seasons*, we've been hearing on and off about the title character, a young fellow named Ray Brower. A few days before the story starts, the Maine man went out into the woods, and hasn't been seen since. Then a fellow preteen named Vern Tessio happens to hear his older brother and a friend discuss happening upon Brower's body, and what to do about this.

Vern and his pals, including resident story narrator Gordie LaChance, stroll through dozens of miles of railroad tracks, searching for the body of the boy killed by a train. The older brother and *his* friends, including story villain Ace Merrill, are on their own trek, each group thinking about the local stardom sure to be visited upon them once the discovery is made.

Still, as skilled a writer as King is, when we reach that point, it's not easy to really grasp its impact, particularly for those of us that learn better from the visual sense. Vern himself sees the body, and the rest of the group rush over to check it out. There's a strong description, but in a novella, that's all we have to feel from: words.

So when Rob Reiner moved the tale to the screen in 1986's *Stand By Me*, he had a few more tools to work from, other ways to help us feel the power of the climactic Brower encounter.

The story location was moved to Oregon for the film, and Reiner was going for realism, filming it in the state's northwestern town of Brownsville. A freshman at the University of Oregon noticed an ad in the paper, looking for some rehearsal assistance.

"They needed stand-ins for the kids who couldn't work long hours because they were minors," recalls Kent Luttrell, who'd eventually finish his college career with a degree in telecommunications. Indeed, the four main characters, including Jerry O'Connell's Vern and Wil Wheaton's Gordie, hadn't quite reached adulthood. "I had three interviews, all the way up to the director."

Over the next month, Luttrell and others worked out where everyone would be, in the physical sense, during shooting. He also picked up a copy of *Seasons* to see what he was helping act out. All the while, the crew had intended to create Brower in a prop room, rather than ask (and pay!) a true blood human to become him.

"They had a mannequin, an effigy of a kid," Luttrell recalls, "and it looked terrible."

So as the time to film the scene where the youths discover their "object" drew near, someone asked Luttrell to play dead.

"They asked me if I would mind doing it, having black beetles crawl out of my mouth," he remembers. "They needed someone who could put a beetle in their mouth and not freak out, and look dead!" The beetle detail, included in the book, didn't get to the final film.

Just as in the book, it's Vern that sees the body. But this time, as the youths happen upon Brower, there's more than reading. Sad music, a depressing atmosphere and narration, and, particularly, getting to *see* the body, and the fatal effects of the train that took his life.

Is it better to see than to imagine? Still, a matter of perception. But it's certainly different.

"They asked me about it hours before shooting," Luttrell says. "Rob said to play dead, and I did my dead face. They said that would work. I used the thousand-mile stare."

The stare, sometimes referred to as the thousand- or two-thousand-yard stare, refers to the blank, unfocused facial expression we see so often in war films, the look of a soldier whose mind has been too caught up, at least temporarily, in the horrors of battle.

Ironically, Luttrell had been one of the doubles that acted out some of the faraway scenes in the film – remember, if the main characters' faces aren't shown, it's probably not the main actors! – including the ones where the four fellows walk across the distance. Hence, the performer who'd been Ray was acting out the backtrack from his own body!

"It's cool to see yourself on the big screen, no matter what you're doing," Luttrell says of seeing the film. "I felt like a celebrity in my own mind, like I had been a part of something important."

It would be one of few character jobs in his career, but Luttrell went straight into stunt work as the 1990s arrived, eventually showing up to double in *Titanic* (1997), *Jurassic Park III* (2001), and dozens of other films.

"I doubled for Danny DeVito for ten years," says Luttrell, who sat in for the actor on both the big screens of *Man on the Moon* (1999) and *Death to Smoochy* (2002) and the small one for *It's Always Sunny in Philadelphia* (2005). "Even though there aren't a lot of stunts in his movies, when you're doubling the lead, you're not just another number. Everything's a little nicer for you: the food, the hotel. I really couldn't do anything else that gave me the free time I was used to, making the type of money I'd made. I didn't want to work fifty weeks for the same kind of money, when I make a good, decent living working four months out of the year. If you just keep focused and keep your head about you, you do fine in stunt work."

Patrick Dempsey: *Miracle*

Here's a pretty good way to gauge the effectiveness of a true-life flick, particularly a sports tale: when you know exactly what's going to happen and when and how – and yet, even with all the manufactured drama, rising music, whatever else, you can't keep the chills and rushes from waging war on your emotions. You stand up and cheer at the climactic moments and finale. You feel a sigh of relief when it's all over, that the ending you knew of far in advance was the one that occurred.

That's part of the reason why 2004's *Miracle* immediately shot straight to the top of Hollywood sports film ranks. Nearly a quarter century after a patchwork group of inexperienced ruffians iced a Russian juggernaut, even having the common decency to do it before their own countrymen, those too young to remember get as much of a rush out of the cinematically crafted version of the legend as those lucky enough to have been there and seen that.

It's also why film casters searched more for those with on-ice talent than actual acting ability, or at least experience, when putting the film together. Doing one's thing all the right ways in athletic action, for the majority of the cast, was more important than line-blaring and body language. Goals, assists, and championships overtook roles as resume highlights here.

Like many who'd eventually play for the performing Olympians, Patrick O'Brien Dempsey didn't have a dramatic background.

"I can't say that I was quite *the* hockey player, but I was a hockey player," recalls the Massachusetts native, who played for two years in college. "But growing up outside of Boston, I was a huge hockey fan.

Mike Eruzione lived near me, so I grew up hearing about him." Eruzione had captained the squad that shocked Russia — and the rest of the planet — that Feb. 1980 day on the frozen waters of Lake Placid.

Soon after finishing up at Fitchburg State College, Dempsey went to put his communications degree to scholarly work. It was tough.

Patrick Dempsey (right) played Mike Eurizione, captain of the American squad that pulled off a *Miracle* (2004) at the 1980 Olympics.

"I had a lot of energy, fidgeting all the time," he remembers. "I couldn't imagine sitting behind a desk and doing this for the rest of my life. I was slacking off in my internship, so I thought that maybe I should go to acting school."

Searching the Internet for his new educational ambition, Dempsey found *Miracle*'s chance for a pseudo-team tryout.

"I sent an e-mail," he remembers. "Within twenty-four hours, I had my first audition."

But not everything for him, or anyone else on the final team, would be as quick and easy. Thousands of young men, many of whom had just as much and maybe more talent and experience in the skating game, wanted to play just as much as Dempsey.

"The most intimidating part of me was the hockey stuff," he explains. "A lot of the guys were really good. Most of them were Division I players, AHL players, NHL players. Hockey-wise, I felt really out of my league." Remember, *Miracle* would show and tell not just of the main American squad, but of all the opposing squads as well. Basically, an entire league needed casting and full tournament acted out in a few months of time.

"I think I had nine auditions," Dempsey says. "One of them was on the ice, and for two, they actually flew me to Hollywood for screen tests. I'd grown up in a small town where people weren't movie stars. It sounded extremely farfetched."

The film crew might have thought so as well; Dempsey came far too close for casting comfort to being cut.

"I didn't know what the hell I was doing," he admits, "but (Director) Gavin O'Connor had a vision. He looked at what I brought to the table, and knew I was what he wanted. They weren't sold until the director went to bat for me."

He hadn't been the most talented as far as slapshots and body-checks. But O'Connor saw something else, something within, something that so many top leaders – like coaches and directors – have a strong knack for: a persona that gave people the confidence that they could get behind a person and find a way to victory. Decades before, team coach Herb Brooks had seen the qualities in Eruzione, and now O'Connor saw them in Dempsey.

"I wasn't supposed to be the best one," Dempsey admits. "But Eruzione was not the greatest one either. He was the one who was the heart, the locker room guy. I thought this stuff was right up my alley. I didn't have any idea of what was to come or how incredible it was."

For generations past, present, and future, our victory over Russia is the main moment, the part everyone remembers and just loves to talk about. But *Miracle* showed that there was much more to the whole story than just a game.

Like the 10-3 whomping the Soviets handed America just before the Games began. The last-second goal that preserved a tie with Sweden to open things. The three straight wins that the locals needed to reach the game (and, of course, what happened afterward, as in, the win over Finland that actually earned the medal itself!).

"There were a couple of days where we played in front of five thousand fans in a packed arena, a small arena in Vancouver," Dempsey remembers. Ironically, the same arena had housed the filming of the final fight of 1985's *Rocky IV*, the story of an only slightly less surprising victory of America over Russia!

For the main game, things got even more serious. For six weeks, sometimes over twelve hours a day, two groups of young men got ready for the second coming of the Miracle on Ice.

"It wore us down pretty good," Dempsey says. "Hockey is such a free-flowing sport, with a lot of improvisation all the time. When you begin to stage plays, they look really staged, without intensity. We had to recreate the goals the way they were scored, and they just set it up and let us play games, inserting footage between all of that to make it look more intense."

And while the acting names in the cast would get the majority of the dramatic screen time (be back in a minute!), he still had a role model to portray.

"Eruzione was coaching his kids' high school hockey team," Dempsey remembers. "I went down there and skated with them once a week for a month. I hung around Mike to get to know him. It wasn't much of a stretch. I also tried to get in shape a bit, skating-wise."

In one of his few real-life roles of a four-decade career (behind 1983's *Silkwood* and 1993's *Tombstone*), Kurt Russell became Brooks, mentoring in and out of character.

"I will always remember how professional he was," Dempsey says. "He joked around, he had a good time, he never wasted anyone's time. There was never any attitude. He was ready to do anything, to bring suggestions to the table and take suggestions. It was incredible for my first experience in Hollywood." Sadly, the film ended up as a memorial tribute to Brooks, who was killed in a car accident before its release.

It was finally time to put on the greatest show in sports history, and one considered by many to be near the top in American history itself. In true Hollywood fashion, a buzzer-beating American goal tied things at 2-2 for the game's first intermission, leading to the forever-controversial decision by Russia to bench Vladislav Tretiak, the world's best goalkeeper.

The Soviets pull ahead in the second period, but Brooks rallies his team one final time. They've been coming back all Games long. Now there's just one more time to do so.

Quickly, Mark Johnson puts in his second goal of the night. Before Russia can even comprehend this surreal experience, Eruzione breaks free and gives his guys their first lead of the game, sending the team and arena into hysterics. Dempsey called it one of his toughest tasks of filming.

"I don't have the best hands," he admits. "I got it on the third take."

Strangers in a strange, cold land, Russia goes on the attack one last time, but America's been on defense before, and these minutes just keep passing. The crowd starts to sense that history might be created here, and microphone man Al Michaels tosses impartiality out the door.

As the final minute begins, it's as if audiences are watching the game live. Michaels recreated his on-speech rant for the film. But sharp-eared viewers catch a slight change in the tone in the final seconds.

"We went into the sound studio, and Gavin told us he'd had Al Michaels do the voiceover for the movie," Dempsey recalls. "He'd had a hard time getting him to recreate it. He just didn't have the feeling. He said that, even though it was grainy, distorted, and a little bit low, he wanted to use the original recording. There was no way to recreate that."

Why mess up a perfect thing? Michaels' original classic calling was inserted straight into the film. No other way could end things so effectively.

But even after so much on-ice action, in and out of performance, Dempsey's toughest moment was yet to come.

"We had to go into the recording studio and sing the National Anthem," he reluctantly recollects. "They had the whole team sing it, minus me, and then me sing it in a booth by myself. I'm horrible at singing! They played it over the loudspeakers in the area, and it was terrible!" Ironically, but perhaps fortunately enough, it would hardly be a part of the final product.

What we saw would be much stronger. Just as Eruzione had done in the actual moment, Dempsey stands alone atop the medal platform. Then he turns around, and motions to the rest of the squad. Soon they're all up there with him, hugging and pointing skyward. If the end of the game was the Miracle's crowning moment, this one was a close silver medalist.

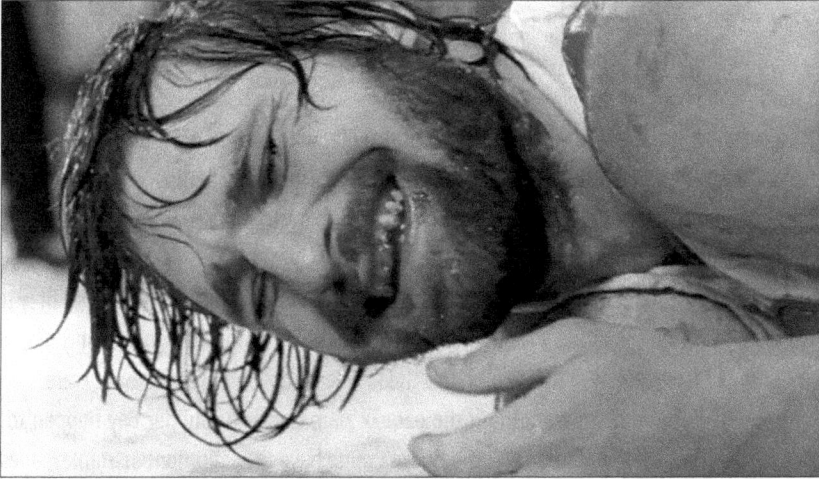

George Finn's Carl Racki comes out on the painfully wrong side of hockey fisticuff action in the climactic moments of *Youngblood* (1986).

"I got swept up in the excitement of it," Dempsey recalls. "We were nearing the end of filming, and I'd formed some credible friendships with these guys. That's something a team does. It was really so fitting to have them come up on the podium as well, not just for Eruzione when he did it, but for us when we were recreating. I wasn't comfortable by myself in the spotlight, and neither was he."

The 80s were a time of cinematic action. Filmgoers met terminators, Batman, some living lethal weapons, the second round of aliens, everything. Perhaps with 1986's *Youngblood*, someone got the idea to step over the line between sports and action and straddle it. Hockey has always been a slippery ground in the south-of-Canada land's movies, unless Disney happens to be involved, and this film showed the difficulty.

We had Patrick Swayze and Rob Lowe, doing the same sort of competitive big-little brother edge they'd shown three years before in *The Outsiders*. Lowe was in the title lead, a Big Apple boy with a shot at the pros — if he can only make it the minors in hockey's homeland.

We here in Old Glory can lay claim to baseball, football, and basketball all we want, but hockey is Canada's game, and one needn't visit Vancouver to find enough Canucks willing to fight for it. That's what Dean Youngblood, Swayze's Derek Sutton, and the rest of the Hamilton Mustangs found out, in a guy who wasn't always ready to cross the line from pain to performance.

"It was my role in hockey," remembers George Finn. "I was an enforcer, but I played the game too." By the time *Youngblood* came out, the Ontario native had spent a few years playing junior hockey in the Ontario Hockey Leagues.

"My hockey agent told me about a hockey movie coming out," Finn remembers. "I went down there and auditioned, read some parts from a script, and they signed me on." Carl Racki falls short at a Mustangs tryout early on (yes, the teams were fictional), but manages to drop on the Thunder Bay Bombers – and, legitimately or otherwise, he doesn't forget, clocking Sutton onto the injured list and scaring Youngblood back home.

"It's a movie, but there was some truth to it in real life, with an American player coming over to the Canadian side and trying out for the Canadian team," says Finn. In all fairness, Canada was demonstrating its dominance at the time, keeping the Stanley Cup up north every year from 1984 to 1990, but America's monopolized it since 1994.

"Six days a week, sixteen hours a day," says Finn, "we were suited up, doing whatever they told us to do. We would wait for the director (Peter Markle) to say, 'OK, bring this person in, bring that person in.' It was long, but it was exciting too. Sometimes the fans were down there before we were."

Ironically (feel the sarcasm wafting off the page?), Hamilton and Thunder Bay happen to meet in the deciding contest for the Memorial Cup – doesn't quite have the sentiment of Stanley, does it? – and, as *no one* ever could have predicted, Youngblood scores the winning goal! Still, Racki, as the bad guy, has to suffer a bit more, and the two square off in a brawl only slightly less impromptu than the climax of *Rocky V* (1990).

And to shock off our socks just once more, Youngblood manages to win, his fans, teammates, and family there to celebrate as Racki can only wallow in bloody despair.

"The fight took two or three days to film," says Finn. "There were certain things that Peter Markle wanted done. It was great, a once-in-a-lifetime opportunity – thirty years later, I still get recognized at the rinks!"

Karen Dotrice: *Mary Poppins*

Ever wonder how someone came up with the word "supercalifragilisticexpialidocious"? At 34 letters, it's one of the longest in any language.

The word may never have a real definition, or classification as a part of speech. It's the meaning behind it that has the true value.

Yes, it's fun to say, and it's fun to sing (though probably not to spell!). But it also plants the listener's mind directly in one of the longest-lived family films that Walt Disney managed to hand the cinematic world, from 1964.

As Jane Banks, her brother Michael, America's favorite nanny (Julie Andrews), and Mary's friend

Burt (Dick Van Dyke) the lovable chimney sweep, sang and danced with multitudes of cartoons in a number that broke ground like the San Andreas Fault in moviemaking, they appear to be having fun.

And they were. But sometimes fun can be a bit of an impediment.

"Worst of the worst was the 'Supercalifragilisticexpialidocious' scene," recalls Karen Dotrice, the young Jane. "That took weeks, because it was the big scene with the animation and the people, Julie and Dick doing flirty things, and the kids looking at the barnyard animals."

She and Matthew Garber (Michael) sat on a fence together for days at a time as the scene was filmed. Just about every day, one of them would lose a baby tooth, sending the property manager into a paroxysm.

Having to interact in the spoken and danced sense with characters that weren't real didn't make things much easier, she continues.

"We had great big hairy grips and crew members carrying around cutouts on farm animals and horses, and jiggling them around for us to react to," Dotrice laughs. "It was hard not to get the giggles."

Her journey to Jane began a few years before, as the youngest member of a family of performers was snatched up into a production of *The Caucasian Chalk Circle* that her father Roy and godfather Charles Laughton were part of.

"I didn't choose (to act)," Dotrice admits. "The director asked if anybody had a four-year-old boy to play in the piece. Everybody said no, but Dad had a four-year-old little girl. I was kind of a tomboy anyway."

Endowed in a wig, Dotrice headed to west London to go to work on stage. One night, a Disney casting director was in the audience, looking for the latest and littlest addition to a film called *The Three Lives of Thomasina* (1963).

Dotrice signed to become Mary McDhui (late acting legend Patrick McGoohan, later of 1995's *Braveheart* and *A Time to Kill* two years later, played her father Andrew), whose sickly cat Thomasina transfixes and transforms the surrounding town with her sad death and happy resurrection, all the while narrating the story.

"That film was chock-filled with animals," Dotrice says. "I was in my element on the set.

"That was tremendous fun, because they were just really nice people. The hours were strange. I had to get up early and walk around in makeup all day without getting it on my collar to stay in continuity."

Soon after, the role of Jane came calling.

"I started doing music classes to prepare for the songs, which were being re-written every five minutes, added and taken away," she says. She spent about three months in Stratford-upon-Avon, working with a Shakespeare company trainer to develop Jane's singing voice.

"She trained me for more of an opera, a classic," Dotrice says. On the first day of filming across the water in Los Angeles, that was a bit of a problem, as Jane's singing was intended to be lighter, more laid-back than the opera stage.

"The first time at rehearsal, everybody burst out laughing at my classic voice," Dotrice recalls. "They thought I was doing it as a joke."

Still, it was the first of many rough and tough encounters that the youngster would encounter during filming. For the scene where Mary and the kids slide up the Banks banister, a plaster cast had to be made of Dotrice's derriere.

"I had to stand for several hours while the thing dried!" she exclaims.

"We had dance practices every day, and I've got two left feet, but there was a lot of preparation," she says. "We spent hours and hours of trying to coordinate everything. We had the whole visual process going on. It was very technical, and none of us had any clue what we were doing."

Commonplace today, acting before a blue screen back then seemed like something out of the 22nd century.

"It was tough, being up on a merry-go-round horse 60 feet in the air," Dotrice says, "and trying to pretend you're looking at a fox and hound that aren't there. Even veterans like Julie and Dick had never seen it before. It was new technology, and we didn't know if it would work."

Still, along the way, the experienced never hesitated to give the newcomers the benefit of their knowledge, she continues. Despite Mary Poppins' strict persona, we the audience can see the twinkle in her eye that becomes a gleam through her wondrous magic and soothing singing voice as she teaches the children – and their parents – to find fun in everything.

"Julie comes off as a proper kind of person, but people have no idea that she broke character as much as she did," says Dotrice (who Andrews referred to as "a good little actress"). "I really would have been fired had Julie not come in and helped me out with signing and dancing on her days off. We worked with live orchestras; she'd come in and twirl me around and sign the songs with me and take the stress off me. If it wasn't for her, I wouldn't have made it through this."

Van Dyke, who called Dotrice and Garber's duet "The Perfect Nanny" his favorite song in the film, handed Burt a childlike persona that rubbed straight off on the actual children, she continues.

"Dick Van Dyke did nothing but curse and swear and make us giggle. It was hard to keep a straight face in anything approaching a serious scene with him. If we had the outtakes from the film, it would be a whole other movie. He was the funniest man in the whole wide world."

So was another person from far behind the scenes.

"Walt Disney was incredibly kind to my family," Dotrice says. "He appreciated the thought of sacrifice and potential damage he was doing, taking an innocent family and child and putting them in Los Angeles for such an extended time." Filming went for over six months, Dotrice says.

"Disney sent his own chauffer to take us to a nice house in Laurel Canyon with indoor heating. On weekends, we flew to Palm Springs to Disney's home or to Santa Barbara to watch cowboys and horses doing tricks." Disney had the interior of the plane turned into a makeshift candy store for Dotrice and her sister to play in.

"The whole package could have been a disaster, but Disney was down on the set almost every day," she recalls. "It was his baby. He was incredibly transfixed with his film, tweaking it and tweaking it. When you've got Julie Andrews at the helm, you're going to be fine." Even today, Dotrice says, she still sees current neighbors Andrews and Van Dyke out shopping.

Dick Van Dyke's legendary Burt (center) of *Mary Poppins* fame (1964),
shows the Banks children, Jane (Karen Dotrice) and Michael (Matthew Garber) the dark,
magical world of a chimney sweep.

During the groundbreaking "Super..." tune, she says, "We were sitting on a fence for days, trying to act confused around these things that weren't there. There would be a horse there, and a little cow there, and a little sheep. I would get swept away very easily by a scene, completely forget that we were supposed to be acting, had to poke me to get me to say anything. Julie was a like a nanny, always coming to me and helping me."

Still, child actors don't get to devote all their time to work, she learned the educational way.

"We'd get whisked off the set, and a chaperon would be standing there to teach us," she says. "It was a totally different curriculum than what we'd learned in England. We learned about what we called the New World (America), about presidents and civil wars."

Back in England a few months after filming, Dotrice finally got to see herself hard at work. The film premiered at London's Leicester Square, with all of the Royal Family in attendance.

"I was seated next to Princess Margaret," Dotrice says, "and I couldn't watch the film. I kept sneaking peeks out of the corner of my eye at these gorgeous ladies. Their tiaras and long-sleeved dresses were much more interesting than the film."

Just as they had in *Thomasina*, she and Garber would act together once more, in 1967's *The Gnome-Mobile*. While Dotrice continued to act for the time being, Garber went into music, eventually becoming part of a rock band.

"Our lives had separated," Dotrice says, "but I thought we'd be friends again when we got older. I just assumed he was in my life for keeps."

Then, in June 1977, she got the worst of news; at the far-too-young age of 21, her former co-star had died of pancreatitis.

"When he died, it was terrible, because I had all kinds of guilt for not being in touch," Dotrice remembers. "I really regretted that I didn't stay closer to him."

Between competing at equestrian events around the world, she continued to act, mostly on television, until her late 20s.

"The older I was getting, the roles were getting more racy," she says. "I was getting asked to do things I was not comfortable with. Looking at scripts, I would think, 'My god, I might have children one day. If I did this movie and my children saw it, what would they think of me?'"

She took a break from the big and small screens and went to work at a friend's Beverly Hills art gallery. Eventually, she'd marry and have three children.

"I don't like acting," she admits. "It's not me. It's not really my cup of tea. I'm very blessed and privileged to have been given the chances that I had, but I'm not a natural-born actress, but more of a private person. If I'd been born into stockbrokers, I might not have liked that either. It was the family business, but it didn't mean the world to me."

However, the Disney world never forgot about her; in 2004, Dotrice was named a Disney Legend, an award that would come to mean so much more for different reasons. While receiving the award in conjunction with Garber, Dotrice met Garber's brother, who was receiving the award on his family member's behalf.

"He didn't realize that for all these years, Matthew's residuals were being put in a trust fund that (the brother) was owed," she says. "I got to talking to him, and I said, 'You are aware of this, aren't you?' It felt like I'd been able to do something for Matthew, that his nieces and nephews would have a better life because of their uncle."

Just around that time, Dotrice's own children were chomped by the acting bug – her daughter Bella got into some occasional performing of her own.

Getting back into character, Dotrice appeared with her daughter on a 2005 episode of the TV show *Young Blades*, a youth-oriented take on the *Three Musketeers* legends.

"She was the only reason I did it," Dotrice says. "She's blessed by the Lord with a lovely exterior and even better interior and very firmly screwed-on head. I'm starting to feel like she'll do fine in whatever she does."

Perhaps that's because Bella's got a built-in coach.

"You can't just act it; acting means nothing," Dotrice says of the business. "You have to be it. You have to look at that character and find yourself. Acting has to be about truth, otherwise it's completely transparent. That ends up being the hardest work of all, because you're exposing yourself. A lot of people get into acting to hide, and with the exception of character actors, that doesn't really work, because in today's media, people want to feel that they can relate. It's a different kind of exposure, but truth is the essence."

Luke Edwards: *The Wizard*

The task had already perplexed the minds of millions of children (regardless of age!) across the nation, and would continue to do so forever more. Staring at the screen, the youngsters tried again and again, only to be victimized by one obstacle after another, the form of walking mushrooms, turtles, and members of the Koopa troop.

They'd fought the battle twice before, and maybe even won it, but *Super Mario Bros. 3*, with all its burdens to live up to, accelerated even further the tale of two mushroom-loving plumbing brothers, a princess that couldn't stay out of trouble, and a dragon/dinosaur-sort named Bowser who, even after being stomped on, dropped into fire, and so much else, kept coming back for another shot at royalty.

The kids had found their way past one level boss after another, portrayed here by Bowser's secret family, but, even with warp whistles and raccoon suits, couldn't get Mario Mario (that's got to be his name, right?) past the top bad guy.

Fortunately, they had some help. Not the latest edition of *Nintendo Power* magazine (and this was *long* before the Internet!), but right next door.

"They called me up to ask me to come over and help them beat the last level," Luke Edwards remembers. "I told them I'd never played it, but I'd give it a shot."

What?! He'd never played the game? Impossible! His neighbors, and millions of others, had sat there in the audiences and *seen* his Jimmy Woods not just play the game, but win a nationwide title! But he'd never really *played* it?

Was *The Wizard* (1989) really *that* good of an act? It certainly was.

"I didn't beat it, and they were super disappointed," recalls Edwards. "I remember feeling bad. Everyone had assumed it was me playing the game, which it wasn't. I had never played it before."

It had been the story of an era. A true depiction of what it was really like to be young at that point. If we enjoyed those times or if we didn't, it was the way it was. Few pop culture aspects have hit the nation as hard and for as long as Nintendo has, and *The Wizard* personified this. Like it or not (if you didn't, you're *clearly* mistaken and very strange), Nintendo had grabbed the nation, and most of the world, right by the attention span much harder than any other system before, and, arguably, since.

Playing Jimmy had brought Edwards a special challenge that we'll discuss soon, but nowhere near as realistically painful as becoming the title character earlier in 1989 in *I Know my First Name is Steven*. He'd been the youngster version of real-life kidnapping and molestation victim Steven Stayner, whose 1972 abduction and eventual captivity prompted several changes to California's laws toward sentences for the cretins that did this shit. Tragically, Stayner would die in his 20s in a car wreck, and his older brother Cary ended up on death row after killing (at least!) four women.

"I was sheltered from the reality of what the story was about," Edwards remembers. "I wasn't at an age where I could handle stuff like that. At the same time, kids are pretty smart and can figure things like that out, so I figured it out, although I didn't really understand it. I didn't have a real clear grasp until I watched it. It was something I would never have been allowed to watch if I hadn't been in it."

Luke Edwards epitomized the dream of millions of American kids as Jimmy Woods in
The Wizard, riding Nintendo success to nationwide fame.

Plot-wise, *The Wizard* would be a bit lighter, but there was a certain darkness as well, and not just for Edwards. In a scene that fortunately wasn't shown, Jimmy's sister had drowned right in front of him years before, and he'd been outside even society's outcasts ever since. Rarely speaking, he's only interested in getting to somewhere in the Golden State, even running away to do it.

"I have a couple of friends who are high on the Autism spectrum, and I've had long conversations with them," Edwards says. "They tell me that *everyone* is on the Autism spectrum. It's just where you fall. I've never gone through testing, but I would be somewhere in there, and as a kid, I just kind of got that."

It might have been Autism, which occurs naturally, or a form of PTSD, certainly possible after such an early tragedy. But the film doesn't spend too much time on labels and diagnosis, which was probably a good idea — subject matter like that is needlessly deep for *The Wizard*'s target audience, not the type to worry about it anyway. Jimmy had a mental affliction that caused him to be withdrawn; that was all we needed, and it was time to move forward!

"For whatever reason, I could relate to him, as a kid and even as an adult," Edwards says. "Sometimes those personality traits are things I possessed. Sometimes it can be good, and sometimes it's a liability. Being so focused or quiet is not really that great in a big, gregarious social setting. Personally, I don't do so well in those situations."

His family broken up by his sister's death, Jimmy's just too much trouble to keep at home, his mom and jerkweed stepdad tossing him into an institution. But, as is usually the case in Hollywood, it's the kids that know best, with Jimmy's brother Corey (Fred Savage, at the start of *The Wonder Years* fame) breaking him out and helping him on the trek to find out what's so special about California.

Along the way, they happen upon a convenience store that just happens to have a few Nintendo games. Distractedly giving Jimmy a shot, Corey can't believe his ludicrously high score on a pastime he'd never been aware of.

Here was about the most enjoyable part of Edwards' prep work, both before and during filming.

"I had my own NES set at home, and one of my absolute favorite things to do was to go out to the arcade," he remembers. "We were filming in a lot of arcades, and they would open the machines, so I had unlimited credits, and that was a blast!"

They also run into Jenny Lewis' Haley, much smarter on the street than any preteen should be, and a gamer herself – and finding a gal who could whup us at video games is the secret dream of boys and men everywhere, still today! Making their way across the country, using Jimmy's hustling skills on the games (and, in one hilarious scene, Haley's own crap table gifts at a casino) to fund their trip, the trio hopes to get all the way to California without a single driver's license, realizing Jimmy's dream and the nationwide Nintendo tournament that's there.

Yes, there's a guy named Lucas, a self-proclaimed national champion at Nintendo (one of the few that got into the company's ill-fated Power Glove invention!). He's the film's bad guy who Jimmy beats at the end. I'm rushing through this part of the profile because he was played by Jackey Vinson, who'd wind up on the sex offender registry. That's all the wording he deserves, although we should mention future *Spiderman* (2002) star Tobey Maguire, who plays one of his henchmen.

As Savage, along with Beau Bridges and Christian Slater as the boys' father and older brother, got the majority of the screen time, Edwards kept looking inside for Jimmy's mindset.

"With so much downtime, I would always be telling stories," he explains, "but not to anyone else. It was all internal, telling stories and acting out stories, all on my own without anybody else interacting. There was something about being in one's own world that I was already doing, so getting into that head space was really easy."

A step ahead of everyone after them, even their own family members, the group makes the tourney. Jimmy tears through the legendarily difficult *Ninja Gaiden* (GAY-den or GUY-den, depending on who is pronouncing it), and all the way to the finale.

The first *Mario Brothers* game had put Nintendo's home set on the map, the second one rocketing to stardom. Could the system outdo itself? Whispers had been running across the country for some time before *The Wizard* came out, but no one was sure if part three would emerge until it did.

Before anyone in America, including viewers, ever saw *Mario 3*, Jimmy took it on (again, in the simulated sense, as we mentioned earlier). When American gamers got their hands on it, well, those that *didn't* have one became the overwhelming exception.

Some people called *The Wizard* just an extended Nintendo commercial. Very superficial. Actually, very adult, and in this case, kids (those of us young back then) might just be a bit more credible in the source department. We saw the film as our own story. The tale of being who we wanted to be, doing exactly what we wanted. What we should do. Video games in general have always been a popular target for adult scorn, but we kids just snicker at those crones behind their backs. If only they wanted to know more. If only they would look at it from more than one set of eyes. The film's audience might have been considered limited, but those who were a part of it became members of a very special group.

And there's an unexpectedly human side as well. The least emotional of his family after his win, Jimmy finally finds his own version of California, a dinosaur-filled tourist trap that *Pee-Wee's Big Adventure* (1985) fans recognized in a second. In his own tear-jerking tribute to his sister, he leaves her photos at her favorite spot.

"In those instances, as an actor, it's so vital that your emotional life be really accessible," Edwards says, "and for me it always has been. I was a really sensitive kid, so sensitive that I couldn't handle a lot of situations. But a good side is that when I need to connect to some emotion, it's pretty accessible. I don't have to work that hard to find that emotion in me. I've observed that in so many acting friends."

Two years later, he sang and danced in Disney's *Newsies*; as *The Wizard* had launched Maguire's career, the musical showcased an up-and-comer named Christian Bale (Edwards turned down a role in *Hook* for *Newsies*). Edwards inherited the Minnesota Twins in 1994's *Little Big League*, and faced monstrous evil in the second *Jeepers Creepers* (2003). As the newest millennium rolled in, he branched out into producing, backing four films by the start of 2016.

"I got the idea in my head to start producing because it was really challenging," Edwards says. "It's different from acting. I love it because it's way more involved in all the stages of filmmaking, instead of just acting, which is compartmentalized. I always wanted to learn more."

Colleen Flynn: *ER*, "Love's Labor Lost"

Of course she would make it.

This wasn't real. This was the controlled world of TV — and the good people, the nice, happy people, the ones with everything to live for, they always win just before the credits roll, right?

The beautiful lady they saw had been through some trouble, but just for a little dramatic impact, right? She'd been thrilled to the brim earlier on, prevented from jumping for joy only by the bulge in her stomach, which, within days or even hours, would give Jodi O'Brien and her husband Sean their new addition, and for only the first time of many.

That's what millions of viewers around the world believed on that cold March night of 1995. For the past few months, they'd been yanked in and repeatedly wowed by this new show, and despite it taking place, and being named for, one of the more nerve-wracking and too often heartbreaking places one can imagine being in, *ER* was the new sensation on TV, and it wouldn't risk turning off a growing audience by breaking their hearts, would it? Especially on an episode called "Love's Labor Lost," (hereafter, "LLL") after a Shakespeare comedy – which always ends with everyone living happily (and married!) ever after!

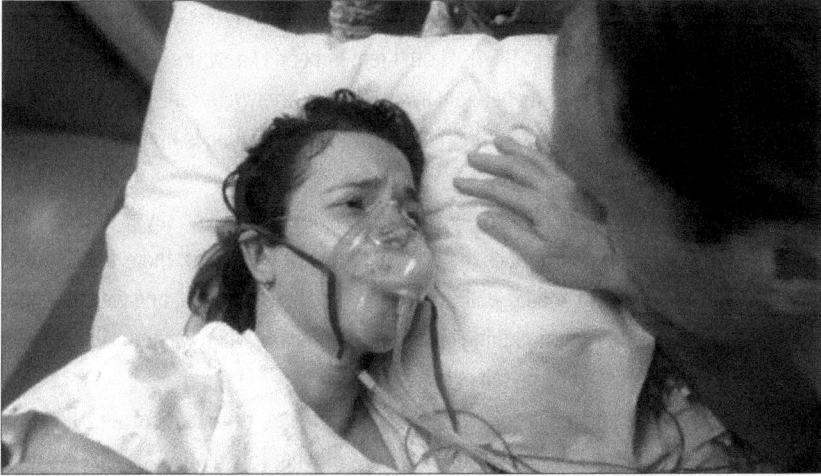

**Jodi O'Brien (Colleen Flynn) takes a terrified look at her husband Sean,
not knowing it will be a farewell in a legendary 1995 episode of *ER*.**

But Colleen Flynn knew better. Not just better than the millions across the country and much of the world. Better than her friends and family, sprawled all over her living room, watching the biggest TV role of her career.

"I have a really big couch, and everybody was sprawled all over the couch," she recalls. "I was sitting on the far end. Everybody looking at me, and I wanted to get away from them so they could watch the show. People were expecting it to get really bad, but then it would all be OK, and when (it wasn't), that just seared people's brains." Twenty years later, the episode hasn't stopped doing so.

In the midst of a tough day, Dr. Mark Greene (Anthony Edwards, probably the only one who could have pulled the role off) meets Jodi and Sean, newlyweds and soon to be new parents. Typical first-timers there, they're jumpy at about the slightest movement their upcoming addition makes. But this looks like a simple bladder infection, and the doc, a bit preoccupied by a promotion shot, gives them some simple meds and sends them home.

But he was wrong. And by the end of the day, Jodi would be gone forever because of one mistake that was too late to correct.

"When Jodi dies, (friends and family) were covering their mouths and yelling," Flynn continues, "so that was what showed me that people didn't see that coming."

Like so much of America's TV audience of the time, Flynn had been wowed by the fix few months of *ER*'s debut season. For "LLL," producer John Wells remembered a lady he'd watched pretend to practice medicine working on *China Beach* (1988) a few years before, and hoped she'd like to play the patient this time around.

"All they knew was that the woman was pregnant, and then there's a mishap," recalls Flynn, who'd also enter the medical acting field on both *Flipper* (1996) and *Nip/Tuck* (2003), along with kicking Coast Guard ass in *Clear and Present Danger* (1994). "I can't remember if I knew she was going to die or not, but the audience had to fall in love with her right away." The day after Wells called, she was already getting fitted for the expected prosthetics, with Bradley Whitford, still young in his own TV acting career, becoming Sean.

"Most of the people that I fall in love with right away love life," Flynn says. "Whenever I'm delighted by a character, it's about how much they love life, so I just went for it. There was this one scene when my husband and I walk in and he walks to the left, I walk to the right, and we bump into each other and laugh. Bradley and I were laughing in our down time, and when we got to act, there was no time to think; it was about throwing myself in there."

Flynn would never be a mom herself, but she was a veteran at the practice of aunt-hood.

"I'd seen my sisters pregnant, so I had an awareness of what (pregnancy) was like, so it was not complicated for me at all," she says. "As soon as I got the prosthetic, I got the full script." In the span of the short screen time that a guest star enjoys, even on an hour-long show, she'd have to win hearts across the world, and then break them in half and shed a wave of unexpected tears in the process.

"I tried to be as authentic and forthright as possible," Flynn explains. "I didn't see her as mysterious, but as a woman who was really excited and somewhat nervous, but mostly overjoyed. My preparation was about being very present and listening and trying to follow logic." As Jodi and Sean arrive back at the hospital, her problems haven't improved, and the arrival's just about here.

"As a guest star, you have to step up to the plate, and you get to knock it out of the park," Flynn explains, "I had an awareness that I had an amazing opportunity, a fantastic opportunity to throw myself into those scenes. All the times you're in acting class and all the times you get to audition, and then you finally get to work with these amazing professionals, all in this one room, it's what you've been preparing for." As Jodi lies there in pain, the whole staff – undermanned to begin with – joins up to make sure this one goes just as it should.

But then it comes out; an infection wasn't the problem. It's preeclampsia, a disorder that sends an expectant mom's blood pressure to the sky, and damages other organs throughout the body. It's rare, but usually easy to detect, assuming someone looks. Greene didn't.

Then things get worse. Jodi's baby comes, but her bone structure is keeping him from emerging. They have to put him back in and do some extra work for the delivery. All the while, the preeclampsia's ravaging through her. But even as the staff freaks out, screaming, yelling, dropping things (there's a long Steadicam shot that fills up a few minutes of screen time, looking over the delivery room), Greene's the calmest one there, calling everyone to attention.

"There was no time to think about throwing myself in there," Flynn says. "They were a well-oiled machine, and you felt that. You just needed to jump on the train and enjoy yourself. You can feel that as an actor. You can walk onto a set and feel how there was a one-pointed focus, and you could feel how committed they were to making that a great show."

Before her episode began, Flynn got a call from her sister, on the east side of the nation. She'd already seen what her friends and family on the western side couldn't believe was occurring.

"She was extremely upset," she remembers. "She said, 'Why didn't you tell me?'" As her episode commenced, Flynn did everything she could to let her work speak for itself.

Up in the nursery with his new son, Sean can't wait for Jodi to meet him as well. And for the last few moments, we think that she just might. Then she crashes one last time, and Greene and everyone else desperately try to pull her back.

It's too late; the preeclampsia did its work a bit too well. Blood and sweat caking Jodi's exhausted face, there's nothing left to save her. One doctor and nurse after another around the room sadly accepts it. Greene pounds her chest, hoping for a miracle. But the best doctor in the world is still just a human, and humans can't make everything happen.

And as for the episode's title, Shakespeare's version is indeed full of mischief and joy, but one of the final events is a death of one of the main characters. One of the Bard's first plays, it appears he wrote it before his technique was defined. Maybe it was a bit too accurate.

"This is the kind of difficult that is inspiring and challenging," Flynn says. "The most important thing for me is that I was full emotionally, just because of the profound energy in the room. My focus was on keeping it together because of all the work that went into the actors and their emotional lives, for me to just be still and not worry about how I looked, just so the actors could do their work. I just let it all go to these actors, because the scene is not about me, but really what happens to them." If we couldn't or wouldn't accept what we saw just yet, we see Greene stoically stride up to the nursery, sit down with Sean behind a closed door, and, with no sound, explain what happened. Some say it was the episode's saddest moment. Some called it the toughest scene in the entire series.

Back at home, Flynn's personal audience couldn't react. "They couldn't talk to me," she says. "They were gasping, upset. I understood the impact of the show through their response, very intense. The intensity of people's responses in the weeks afterward was pretty amazing." That's probably not a strong enough adjective to describe the sentiment across the ER set when the yearly Emmys arrived (NBC helped by giving the show a special airing as the awards came near).

Mimi Leder grabbed her first directing Emmy (In 2000, Flynn scored a small role in Leder's Pay it Forward), as did the script of Lance Gentile, himself a doctor. "LLL" ended up notching five awards on the night. Edwards had submitted it for the organization, but fell to Mandy Patinkin of ER competition

Chicago Hope (1994). Ironically, he'd never win an Emmy for playing Greene – he did win a Golden Globe – but took one home in 2000 for producing TV movie biopic champ *Temple Grandin*. Greene's own death from a brain tumor at the end of the show's eighth season gave us another heartbreaking moment, as he was the only original character to pass away.

Flynn was up for the guest actress in drama award (Rosemary Clooney – aunt of George – was a competitor for "Going Home," *ER*'s second-ever episode). Shirley Knight won the award for showing up on *NYPD Blue* (1993) – one of her two Emmys that night – for the episode "Large Mouth Bass," playing a lady whose daughter is killed by Mom's ex.

Twenty years later, the episode, out of the 331 that *ER* gave us over fifteen seasons, lives on, as does Flynn's work as one of the greatest one-shot appearances in TV history. "LLL" has consistently been voted one of the ten top episodes in TV history, and there's certainly a very diverse world to pick from there. *ER* even paid a certain kind of sad tribute to the episode in its own series finale, as a lady passed giving birth in the show's April 2009 farewell, "And in the End."

To give one episode too much credit for starting or maintaining a show that lasted over a decade longer would be an overstatement, but "LLL" showed that *ER* had the guts to try, and, even more sur-prisingly, to succeed, by *not* giving us a happy ending. As a person, it makes you feel like a cretin for saying this, but, when gauging the strength of a TV show, you realize that the episode wouldn't have been worth as much if Jodi had lived. Greene would have been heralded as the same miracle worker with a happy ending that we see so often in TV medical shows, off to a new quest the next week, one that would immediately replace "LLL" in our minds. Again, this sort of makes you feel like a jerk as a person, but many probably felt worse for Greene than for Sean, who'd just lost his wife. After all, Greene would be back next week; Sean wouldn't.

Happy endings don't happen often in the medical field, and perhaps "LLL" showed us that – a truth we didn't want to remember. It sent a message that it was OK to go the unusual route with this type of show, something we'd see once in a while on *Chicago Hope*, *House* (2004), and even the usually comedic *Scrubs* (2001).

"I've gone on jobs and not done well," Flynn admits, "but in this particular circumstance, that didn't happen. Maybe it was my naiveté, but I thought it was my gratitude and my awareness that this was a great opportunity. I was going to go for it."

Andrea Friedman: *Life Goes On*

Since almost the day she was born, people have been telling Andrea Friedman what she couldn't do.

Some thought that a young woman born with Down Syndrome should be institutionalized – that she could never go to college, drive a car, balance a bank account, or become a wonderful actress, seen by millions across the globe.

And for her whole life, Friedman's been proving everyone wrong.

Down Syndrome? Words like "retarded," and "disabled"? They don't exist to her – for the Los Angeles native, it's "Up Syndrome."

"I am challenged, not disabled," she says. "'Disabled' means 'cannot do,' but my challenged friends and I can do. Some things are hard for us, some things take longer to learn; but if we work hard, we can do.'"

She's been showing that for her entire life – including, since 1992, television audiences.

"I was working in a daycare center," she says. "A mother brought her daughter in, and she saw me working with some kids."

The woman knew the producers of *Life Goes On*, a series involving Corky (Chris Burke), one of mainstream television's first mentally challenged performers. She asked them to speak to Friedman about the capabilities of those with Down. She was eventually invited to the studios for a scriptwriters meeting.

"I went down to the studios, and gave them my ideas for Corky," Friedman says. "One of them was driving a car, another was having his own checking account.

"The third one was that I volunteered to be his girlfriend. He had had different girlfriends, and I thought I could be one of them."

Her proposals sounded good to the show's creators, who invited her to try out for a role.

"I came down to audition," Friedman says. "They asked if I needed a script. I said no; I knew the words by memory." Rather than having to hold and read, she'd already memorized her lines.

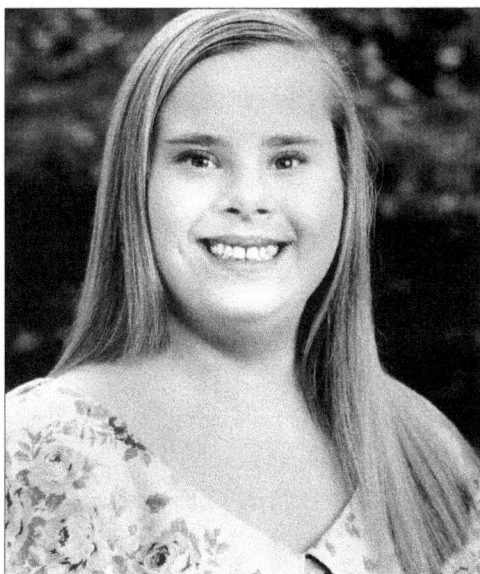

Andrea Friedman's work has set one trend after another and inspired the acting world.

For someone who's been wowing others for her entire life, making an impressing impression might be routine. But at her tryout, Friedman got one more inspiration.

"They gave me a standing ovation when I left," she said. "That felt great!"

For the next two seasons, Friedman, who worked with a multitude of acting coaches from Los Angeles to London, had a recurring role as Corky's female companion Amanda Swanson. The next year, she showed up on an episode of *Baywatch*. A few years later, she snared a starring role in the TV film *Smudge*, the story of a young woman who finds a puppy at Christmas time, and has to hide him to keep him.

Since then, Friedman's been on *Chicago Hope* (1994), *E.R.* (1994), *Walker, Texas Ranger* (1993), *Rescue Me* (2004) and other sitcoms, including a 2002 episode of *Law and Order: SVU*, when she played a rape victim.

"It was very difficult at first, but my mom helped me out," she recalls of the *SVU* role. "I had some good role models, and I wanted to continue. It was kind of a new experience, but I just went for it. I conquered my fear of doing something that I'd never done before."

That's something that she'd like to see from other mentally-challenged people who'd like to find their own place in the acting world: the guts to try something new, and the willingness to see it through until the end.

"I would say, if they want to start acting, they can study, and go for it," Friedman says. "There are acting classes out there that they can take. They can keep making their dreams come true – their goals, their priorities, and what they want in life. They just have to work hard to be stars in the future."

It's a message that she's spread to everyone from Harvard grad students of 1994 to the 2006 Down Syndrome World Congress, where she was the guest speaker.

Every morning, Friedman climbs out of bed and declares, "I love my life. I wonder how many new friends I'll make today."

The list just keeps getting longer.

Marilyn Ghigliotti: *Clerks*

If we're in a good mood, perhaps it's appreciation and friendliness. But probably disdain. Maybe some pity. But, most likely, nothing at all.

It's what we feel for the people that wait on us during those moment-long encounters we go through just about every time we walk into a convenience store. We step in, grab a pack of smokes, a six-pack of adult or non-adult beverages, maybe a half-quart of milk that costs way too much, and stroll on out, forgetting everything about the person who took our money about three seconds later, if we saw them at all.

Until, of course, we were given (gifted, his cult classic followers would say) a pass to the world of Kevin Smith and the cinematic universe he created, that's lead through stores, malls, straight to heaven and back again.

Things got started right in the midst of Smith's Garden State homeland, and not just for the fellow we'd forever know (not always like, but certainly *know*) as Silent Bob.

"I was at a change in my life, going through a divorce and was looking for something," remembers fellow Jersey native Marilyn Ghigliotti – clearly on the opposite side of the last name simplicity spectrum as the commonplace Smith! "What, I didn't really know, but first I thought after seeing some ads for some petite modeling I looked into that and did some 'go-sees,' as they say." The looking practices would eventually guide her wandering eyes to acting training, and, years later, the stage.

"While on the stage, it felt like people were actually listening to what I had to say, rather than ignoring me," she says, "which I feel many times in my life, especially being a middle child. And it's a passion that has just grown within me."

Veronica (Marilyn Ghigliotti) swoops into action to rescue her boyfriend in the opening moments of *Clerks* (1994).

Without a name of his own or enough dough to hire any stars from as far back as the C-list, or even to film in color, Smith had to make the best of a shoestring budget situation. Within the comfortable confines of the convenience store at which he himself was employed, Smith started to tell the stories of those far too often overlooked or even glanced at.

The *Clerks* themselves. The ones that stay up all night or even several days in a row, even, as his film's main character did, on their days "off." Those who days meld together into a big repetitive mess, assuming they're lucky enough to not be the next in an all-too-common string of robbery targets, an ending Smith toyed with before taking a safer way out of his flick.

And sadly enough, although this may be an unfair stereotype, the ones that grab the job intending it to be a stepping stone straight up to bigger and better things, a holdover while their real passions come to successful fruition… only to wake up one morning and realize that they waited too long for life to lead them somewhere. He's still just barely on the legal side of the drinking age, but early on in the 1994 film, we get the impression that its main man Dante Hicks (Brian O'Halloran) is headed straight to nowhere, as he stumbles out of one late shift at the local Quick Stop right into another – and he'll remind us several times over the rest of the day that he's not supposed to be there.

"When I auditioned for *Clerks*," Ghigliotti says, "I actually didn't know what I was auditioning for. (I) only heard that a local theater I had worked at was auditioning actors to be in a film. No other information."

Just about right away, Ghigliotti got a call from the director, making sure she'd be OK with the dialogue that nearly got the film an NC-17 rating.

"I took it home and the script itself had me laughing," she says. "Kevin did want to make sure that I had no problem with the dialogue I had to say, but it was just dialogue. And aside from some of the crazy and offbeat dialogue I had, there were parts of Veronica that are me and that's the nurturing and caring side of her."

But that's certainly not the first aspect of Dante's love that we see – or, maybe in a weird kind of way, it is.

Her boyfriend's day is off to a rough start – one of his first customers is a guy who keeps trying to convince others to chew gum instead of smoke, and, of course, it's *totally* because he's concerned about their health, much more so than Dante! Soon enough, he's leading an impromptu rally against those (or this one!) that are just worried about getting rich off the blackening lungs of others!

We see Veronica briefly walking through the door, but that's not really her entrance. As her boyfriend is relentlessly bombarded by those he'd (realistically or otherwise) somehow *convinced* to suck on the nicotine sticks, their emotional flames are suddenly put out, in all the phrase's senses. Perched atop a nearby counter, a determined look on her face that tells us that this is commonplace and even a little enjoyable, Veronica blasts them with a fire extinguisher used for all the new, but certainly not wrong, reasons.

Frightened, maybe angry, but certainly confused – what's a man to do to a lady a third his size, even if she did just douse him with an icy mist? – the men file out, although she's clearly just *waiting* for someone to get a little frisky.

That, and her verbal beatdown of the guy who started the whole mess (he's secretly a gum salesman, trying to get people to buy his product, screw the goodwill message), shows that she's used and probably eager to get ahead of the assumption that her size might make her easy to step on. There's a reason this gal's wearing pants instead of a skirt.

"In preparing for any role, it's about finding out who that character is as a person and making it real for me," Ghigliotti says, "and sometimes it's about merging me with that person, so that it makes it easier to find the character. Sometimes it's finding something in my own life that reflects the situation or person and that helps as well. Sometimes it's thinking about, what if I were in this situation or if I was, say, this lawyer, how would 'I' do this in real life?"

Fortunately enough, she was forced to just *imagine* the instance that, for the first time, cuts through Veronica's self-confidence. A coincidental visit from a former, ahem, *partner* of hers opens a debate about her sexual past. It will involve the practice of snowballing and the number thirty-seven, and that will be all any legit Smith fan will need to know.

"When I had to explain what snowballing was, the visual that I would have in my head really made it all that more disgusting, to be honest," she says. "But the heavy dialogue and hope that one can do it in one take was always something to have on my mind. But you do what you have to."

She's soon off to the college classes Dante should be taking alongside her, and he's left to deal with missing his street hockey game, customers who drive themselves nuts trying to find the perfect egg dozen, and a day that won't end, not to mention his friend Randal who "runs" the video store next door, and, of course, the ever-present duo of Jay and Silent Bob right outside.

Veronica will be back, and this time with lasagna. Women like this hardly ever get this amazing, even in the movies! Still, Dante's heart – more likely overridden by his libido – still belongs with Caitlyn, his adulterous ex who's now off the market forever.

But she's actually not – her mom faked an engagement announcement! – and she arrives, Dante instantly forgetting the better woman in his life.

Along the way, we'll hear and see the beginnings of tales that will run right through Smith's saga. In 1995's *Mallrats* (which, in storyline terms, takes place the day before *Clerks*), *Chasing Amy* (1997), *Jay and Silent Bob Strike Back* (2001) – itself the epitome of an inside film joke – and, of course, *Clerks 2*, (2006) we hear all about the ex-girlfriend who died in the midst of YMCA lap swimming. We see (well, just the aftermath, fortunately) of Caitlyn's inadvertent sexual encounter with an aroused corpse in the bathroom – hey, she *thought* it was Dante! – that transforms her collegiate mindset straight into undercooked oatmeal.

As would also become commonplace for the saga, it's Silent Bob's rarer-than-a-lunar-eclipse philosophy speakings that finally set Dante right.

"There's a million fine looking women in the world," he gravely informs the clerk as Caitlyn's carted off to a special place. "But they don't all bring you lasagna at work. Most of 'em just cheat on you."

Now Dante truly knows. Veronica's the one for him, and always has been. He's finally ready to be the man she always wanted him to be, the one he didn't know how to be, until now.

But it's too late. Randal's already tried to lessen the impact of Dante's dalliances with Caitlyn to Veronica, but it didn't work. She already knows where his heart and hormones wish they were.

Dishing out a worse beating than she ever has before, vowing to elevate promiscuity to an art form, she lets him know that this is over and it's not starting again. For a comedy, or at least a dramedy, this flick's going to have one painfully realistic ending.

"The thing about *Clerks* is that it's about real people," says Ghigliotti, "so you can't help but find yourself in any of those portrayed in the film, especially those that have to work in the service field. I have and those are the people that you deal with. And it will always be that way, so this movie will be around and talked about for many years to come in my opinion."

It certainly has – millions of dollars and several chapters in a saga keep telling the story. Sadly, she didn't follow O'Halloran, Smith, and the rest through Smith's remaining films.

"There's so much rejection and hard work that will go into (acting)," she explains, "and if the love isn't there, then the rejection and hard work will soon take you out of the running. Only the passion that you have for doing this will get you through the rejection and extremely hard work of working many jobs to sustain oneself until that 'big break' comes. Knowing whether you truly have the talent, what it takes, or not as well, and not being delusional about yourself and your abilities is also very important."

Karron Graves: *The Crucible*

To get ready for her role in 1996's *The Crucible*, Karron Graves had to take a few steps backward.

Back in time: she had to transport back to the 1600s, where female equality wasn't even a pipe dream and slavery – often dressed up by the more PC-sounding "indentured servitude" – was commonplace.

And backward in the area of looks as well.

After her first audition, Graves was hanging out with her grandparents. Then the film's casting director called her.

"I was told to show up really ugly," she says. "Not to shower, not to wash my face or brush my teeth." Obviously, glamour wasn't important in 1692 Massachusetts.

Not that women of the era didn't care how they looked – there was simply a different standard of beauty back then. Ladies often strolled about under layers of heavy clothes in 100-degree heat, and things like the razor weren't big at the time.

Especially for the character she was about to undergo – but more about that in a minute.

Performing has been a common practice to Graves since her elementary school years.

"I grew up singing and performing with my family," says Graves, whose sisters are also performers. "I did a lot of musical theater around the country growing up." She also did some off-Broadway work in New York.

"When I was growing up, I did more film and TV," says the actress, whose small-screen debut came as a girl scout on a 1986 episode of *Saturday Night Live*. "I was more suited to that because I was small and subtle, and had a feel for naturalistic acting. Theater always appealed to me because it's so broad and rich and full, and three-dimensional. That's exactly what I wasn't." During the single season of *Dolphin Cove* (1989), in which she played a young girl who communicates with dolphins, Graves' schooling took place in a school bus.

After that, education was the biggest part of her life.

"Some may think that the life of an actor is glamorous," she says, "and it's not, at all. The 'big things' are few and far between, and it's a lucky break if you can get something." She'd end up graduating from Princeton, snaring a Master's from Yale, and even teaching musical theater at a Connecticut college between gigs.

Still, when the legendary story of the Salem Witch Trials headed toward the big screen in the mid-1990s, Graves gave it a shot, and ended up scoring the role of Mary Warren, the indentured servant to main characters John and Elizabeth Proctor.

Before the first scene was shot, Graves' burden was there for the carrying; not only was her new role in a story that had been told so many times before – on the stage, at least – but she'd be up next to Oscar winner Daniel Day-Lewis, nominees Winona Ryder and Joan Allen (who'd gain her second straight nomination for *The Crucible*), and many other more familiar faces.

Witch fever gripped the eventual United States in the late 1600s, never more prevalent than Salem, Massachusetts, and Karron Graves (left) and Oscar-winner Paul Scofield (right, in his final American film work) brought Arthur Miller's legendary play *The Crucible* to the big screen in 1996.

So Graves went about it the best that anyone in her situation could – piles of preparation.

"I did a lot of academic research to find out what it would be like to live then," she says, "and what my mindset, mentality, and world view would be. Who am I? What do other characters say about her? What does she say about herself?"

Nothing too positive, she'd eventually decide.

"Mary was the gross, unattractive, very vulnerable, fragile, pathetic survivor," Graves says, "and she had to cover up for herself, because no one else was going to do it for her. She had to leave her parents, go work as an indentured servant. She was 18, a single female in a very Puritanical society. I loved that."

Graves engaged a whole new lifestyle – the land that America was three hundred years ago was as different from today's USA as a foreign planet.

"On set, we got our dialect lessons and learned the speech patterns, which was helpful," she says, "and the clothes, whoa, the clothes were something else. They just hung on us like sacks of burlap. They gave me a brace on my teeth that was brown and yellow and painted zits on my face. None of us were allowed to shave during filming, and we were asked not to wash our hair."

A drama coach arrived to help them create a whole new (or, in this case, centuries old) world.

"We did acting classes, workshops, movement exercises," she says. "We discussed how much physical contact we were allowed to have with each other with men in the room, what we would talk about with each other sexually, and in mixed company. I did a lot of reading books in the library. Everything centered around their religious life, so I think that was the focus. It was about figuring out how to build your life around that."

That's when the real rehearsals kicked off – and everyone drew a fine line between reality and performance, and decided when they'd venture across it.

"I was in awe of their commitment," she says. "It didn't matter if it was rehearsal, if the camera was there, if the camera was on them, they just committed fully to each rehearsal."

Still, things were different when the cut calls came, she continued.

"Between takes, Daniel joked around, helping break the tension," Graves recalls (Day-Lewis, known for his preparatory devotion, helped build the Proctor house for filming). "He was very caring, very fun. He didn't treat me like he treated Mary at all."

Proctor and Ryder's Abigail Williams set the tone for the piece, having embarked on an affair before the storyline occurs. Part of a group of young women caught gallivanting in the woods, Williams spreads the tale of witchcraft in the area, which eventually reaches Proctor's wife Elizabeth (Allen). Eventually, things spin out of control, as several innocent people are executed for their "crimes," including, in the final scene, John. Three decades after his iconic work in 1966's *A Man for All Seasons*, Paul Scofield told another historical tale with *The Crucible* as Judge Danforth, in his final American film.

Along the way, Mary starts to follow the Williams group, both out of anger toward Mr. Proctor and to out and out endure.

"It wasn't about fitting in for popularity," Graves says, "it was about fitting in for survival, and about getting a delicious taste of public recognition, public praise, even idolatry, at a time when young girls' and servants' voices weren't only not praised, they were silenced.

"Any anger would've been harbored for Mr. Proctor, and it would have been subconscious. To boot – before any of it was unleashed – she operated on the unconscious acceptance that despite the beatings, he was her bread, butter, and protection in a harsh world; it was unquestionable that she submit to his authority."

While Elizabeth, though herself subserviant to her husband, treated Mary right, Mr. Proctor's home was his own dictatorship, all too common in such times.

"When I'm talking back, (Mr. Proctor) throws me on the ground," Graves recalls. "I get beatings and whippings. It wasn't him being mean, it was just the way it was. To have a young girl defy her employer, to say, 'I cannot work tomorrow, I am needed in the court,' was huge; you're supposed to be silent. The fact that she actually speaks and defies was unheard of, unbelievable."

But as Abigail's façade starts to disintegrate, her cruelty comes forth, and, in Graves' biggest scene of the film, she accuses Mary, her supposed friend, of herself being in league with evil. A terrified Mary flees to a nearby lake, where she suddenly admits to her offenses, putting all the blame on John.

"That was a huge space, with hundreds of extras, all coming down into the water for this moment on this poor little girl who's freaking out," Graves says of the three-day scene shoot. "Is she crazy? Is she seeing the devil? Is her boss the devil? She was really an unconscious survivor – she was acting on instinct, following the pack, instead of out of anger."

However, Mary's agony wasn't entirely a performance, she continues.

"We all wore wetsuits under our smocks because of the cold," Graves says. "I was a competitive swimmer, and it was still almost impossible to move in that water with the dresses on. When we finished, my body basically collapsed, and I couldn't move my neck."

So what should be the impression of the audience toward Mary's character? Is she a coldhearted, selfish person, ready to backstab anyone to save her life? Or a tortured soul who gives her sad life and surroundings exactly what they deserve? Graves herself sees the issue from both sides.

"It was a survival scene," Graves says. "I didn't really understand until later just what a survivor (Mary) was. I didn't give her much credit at first or have a good moral impression of her, but now I think of her as being a survivor. She was alone in the world, an 18-year-old with no parents, no one to speak for her. She did what she had to do."

DeWayne Jessie: *Animal House*

One more step, and DeWayne Jessie might have strolled right out of legend.

He'd been offered a role in a film, but one far from what he'd been looking for. First off, the role was more about singing than acting, and, with a musician already in his family, Jessie wasn't really into the melodic side of performing.

Secondly, he wouldn't actually be singing at all – he certainly had the ability, but he'd never really shown it on screen, and the film crew was hedging their bets by having someone else, someone *known*, provide the lyrics, and get someone else – meaning Jessie – to just *act* out the tunes. This actor had already turned in a hell of a work without speech; re-proving himself there might not have gotten him very far.

He was right about out the door. Then a voice popped through his head.

"Why not?" Jessie thought. "Go for it. Take it anyway."

A message from someone, maybe Someone else? Who knows? But the young actor listened.

He walked back into the room – and film history would never be the same.

Long before anyone else, Jessie had heard the calling of entertainment.

"When I was three years old, I told myself I was going to be on television," he remembers. "I was a talkative baby, watching TV like crazy: '50s movies, '60s movies." One of his first forays into the performance area was the "title character" in costume at a local Chuck E. Cheese.

"I had a brother that was a singer," Jessie says in a point that will be developed *much* more, momentarily, "and a lot of those people, the singers, used to come over to my home. It made me want to get into show business, not as a singer, but as an actor. God blessed me, because I was acting as soon as I graduated from high school." That was in 1970's *Halls of Anger*, the tale of an all-black high school that's forced to integrate. Jessie stood alongside a young Jeff Bridges and Rob Reiner and the experienced Ed Asner and Calvin Lockhart.

DeWayne Jessie's Otis Day made us all want to "Shout!" in 1978, as he and the rest of the *Animal House* cast rocked the frat house and reminded America of what fraternities can all be about.

A few years later, a new screenwriter named Joel Schumacher searched for his chance to see his words on the screen, and the first two times happened in 1976, with *Sparkle* and *Car Wash*. Jessie was there for both. That same year, he stepped into one of the toughest situations for a young actor – alongside a chance to really show his talent.

Surrounded by Billy Dee Williams in the title role, his *Car Wash* co-star Richard Pryor, and a fellow named James Earl Jones, Jessie became a part of *The Bingo Long Traveling All-Stars & Motor Kings*, who attempted to break the color line in baseball a decade before Jackie Robinson. As Pryor, Jones, and a benchful of others entertain the crowd on the field, a fellow named Rainbow is there in the background, hauling their bats back to the dugout after so many extra-base whacks from the plate.

A small role next to so many growing names would be tough enough, but playing Rainbow gave Jessie an extra task to take: the character was mute.

"My family and friends told me I didn't know how to shut up!" Jessie says. "They told me, 'You can't play a mute!' I said to just watch me, and I went out and did it." A longtime fan of the Marx brothers, Jessie remembered watching Harpo be hilarious without voice.

"I used a little bit of that," he says, "but mainly I just went with my natural impulses." It worked; the performance won Jessie a special honor from the NAACP.

Now let's go back to where we started; steady work after *Bingo* kept Jessie in the public acting eye, and now he had another shot at the big screen.

College fraternity membership across America had been dropping for years. Perhaps people didn't see the need; maybe the brotherhood didn't carry the weight it once had after graduation. But while life and membership in these organizations are indeed about helping one another on the academic level, it's also about a chance to let go and have fun once in a while. Now a young director and some actors looking for a break had created a fictional school in a time of the past, and hoped that reminding America what these organizations should be about might just re-light the fire that was disappearing into kindle.

OK, enough bush beating here: we're talking about *Animal House* (1978), of course. It was time to finish out the casting of the legendary toga party scene. As D-Day, Pinto, Flounder, and, of course, John Belushi in his career-making role of Bluto Blutarsky, hit the dance floor in Greek garb alongside their ladies, Otis Day and his merry band of Knights would be rocking the Delta House stage.

Now Jessie had a shot at being Day.

Once again, as with Bingo, it wouldn't be all him; Jessie's voice would be dubbed over by that of Lloyd Williams, who'd rocked reggae stages throughout the 60s. But Jessie went for it anyway, and an iconic scene was heavy in the making.

Hanging out with cast members on the set of the made-up Faber College, Jessie remembered watching his brother Obie do his thing on music stages as he became Otis. He and the rest of the Delta men partied a bit to get into the spirit.

Finally, it was time to bring the chants of, "Toga, *toga*, TOGA, TOE-GAH, *TOE-GAH*!" to scene. In the span of the time it takes to sing a few songs, Jessie would make his own landmark.

"Shout!" One word, one title, one song, one long scene. It's rare that films would devote virtually an entire scene and several minutes of screen time to an individual tune, but it happened here. From a little bit softer now to a little bit louder now, Otis and his group let everyone know that they made him want to shout, and the scene truly personified all the extra benefits of fraternities and sororities. Taking the deserved chance to step away from books, tests, and evil administrators (like film villain Dean Wormer), and reach into a world where all our problems are temporarily wiped away with film and music. Not for the first time in the film, but probably the strongest, the Delta men show what fraternization, what brotherhood is truly all about in the most fun of ways.

Mere days after *Animal House* hit the screens, Jessie learned what an impact Otis and the Knights had made. A Rhode Island club owner asked the lead man to bring his group to a new stage. With the acting Knights quickly replaced with actual musicians (like Jessie, those in the film had been actors), a new group emerged.

Otis' voice not being Jessie's? Few would know and even fewer would care; the band sold out concert halls – and, of course, college events – for years. George Clinton helped them put out the CD *Shout*. An Oklahoma college inducted them into its own fraternity. Decades later, Jessie still becomes Otis on stage.

Along with him, the smash-hit film gets all sorts of credit for getting people re-interested in fraternity life. People found out again just why groups like Delta had been so popular before. Brotherhood – and sisterhood, as the film undoubtedly helped sororities as well – numbers went right back up, and toga parties have been a campus staple ever since.

Film audiences are about as predictable as political voters or jury members; knowing what they'll do in advance is about as plausible as flapping one's arms and flying like a bird. But just as with so many legendary films, there's all kinds of reasons to like *Animal House*. Otis' group is simply one of the more common.

"I wish I could tell you," Jessie says of its success. "People were just drawn to it. I had no idea it would do what it did. I don't think anyone did. It just happened. Once it started, it didn't stop until it was finished. That's all I can really say."

Kathryn Joosten: *West Wing/Desperate Housewives*

Sitting in the audience for the 2005 Emmy awards, Kathryn Joosten felt a cocktail of emotions.

Excitement was one; she was up for an award for her work on *Desperate Housewives* as Karen McClusky, the gleeful, wisecracking tormentor of Lynette Scavo (Felicity Huffman). Pride was there as well – after waiting until her own middle age to start her acting career, Joosten had become one of the most recognizable faces, if not names, in the TV world.

Still, memories might have been the most prevalent – and glancing nearby, Joosten could see two people who'd been there as she was forming them all.

After spending a decade as a psychiatric nurse in Chicago, Joosten became a single parent after a divorce left her alone to raise two sons. Unable to return to the medical field, she went to work for a welcome wagon, and for a painting/wallpapering business.

"Then I got the kids involved with community theater," she recalled. "Children's classes for $5 on a Saturday was cheaper than babysitting. Eventually, I became curious about it myself, began to hang around and got involved with the adult community theater."

Word on the area's newest star began to get around, and Joosten worked all over Chicago, then spent a year in a show at Disney World's MGM park.

After a bartending stint, she headed to Los Angeles and moved in with one of her sons.

"I began doing workshops and theater," she said. "It was very much about meeting the right people. Luck is when opportunity meets preparation." She made one-shot appearances on just about every show in the 1990s and 2000s, everything from *ER* to *Seinfeld* to *Buffy the Vampire Slayer*.

Late great Kathryn Joosten tormented and eventually befriended the rest of the *Desperate Housewives* as Karen McClusky during the show's seven-year run, winning two Emmys along the way.

In 1999, Joosten was called to audition as a secretary. A fired-up performance as an office manager defending her boss from someone who callously labeled him "a jerk" won her the role as Delores Landingham.

Then Joosten asked exactly what she'd be up to.

"It was called *The West Wing* and I thought it had something to do with the Air Force," she admitted. "They said, 'You're the secretary to the president.' I said, 'The president of what?' They said, 'The United States.'"

To get ready to serve under Martin Sheen's President Jed Barlet, Joosten went back to her own experiences; upon her new arrival in Los Angeles, she'd worked as a catering waitress, a fine job for someone who might have to suddenly take time off for auditions.

"I had worked with an engineering company in Pasadena that had an executive dining room," she said. She spent some time with the secretary to the president of said company.

"I watched what she did, and used her as a model," Joosten said. "She was efficient; she was proven. But she called her boss by her first name, and I couldn't do that."

Over the next few years, Joosten turned Landingham into one of the focal points of the show, calling her monologue on a Christmas show about losing a child one of her high times on the *Wing*.

"There was one time that my line to the other secretaries was, 'We work for some very important men here,'" she remembered. "That pissed me off. I sent word back up to the writers (to change it to) 'We work for important *people*,' and the writers agreed."

Right around the time that Landingham died in a tragic car accident in 2001, Joosten turned up for one of her most memorable guest appearances, helping another new show get rolling. In the fourth-ever episode of *Scrubs* (2001), titled "My Old Lady," she was Mrs. Tanner, a patient of Dr. J.D. Dorian (Zach Braff), who touchingly convinces her caretaker that life should be lived on one's own terms, and that a person can truly be ready to go.

"I had done a whole bunch of guest spots," Joosten recalled. "When you do shots like that, you feel like you're temporarily moving into someone's living room. Generally, the cast is very nice to you, but you are a stranger, and you're going to be there for the week. You're the new guy in the platoon."

Dying from renal failure and surrounded by a bickering family, the kindly lady escapes to a park for her granddaughter's birthday party, then has a heart-melting discussion with J.D.

"When was the last time you just sat around and did nothing?" she asks, just before charmingly hugging him goodbye (a gesture that, according to Joosten, was unscripted and her idea).

"I agreed with the position the woman took," she said. "She didn't want to mess around; she wanted to die her way. I agreed with that, personally and politically. I thought of my son, who was about (J.D.'s) age. It was like talking to my own kids – don't worry about me: go out and live." J.D. took a valuable lesson from Mrs. Tanner – he'd learn such things quite often as the show progressed – and spent the closing scenes stretched out at the park in the sunlight. She'd also reappear in the "first" series finale (the show was set to finish in 2009 – and damned well should have! – but continued for another year) to remind J.D. to take a breather.

As icing on the cake, Joosten's half-hour work won her a Humanitas Prize, given each year, since

1975, to promote the meaning and positive side of humanity (*The West Wing*, as a series, won the award in the past).

Sadly, just around that time, Joosten learned that she'd have to battle an enemy that was all too real: lung cancer.

"Having been a nurse, I could see that what they were looking at was small, encapsulated, not all over the place," said Joosten, who lost her mother to cancer. Though removing the tumor required surgery, she didn't need chemotherapy. However, she had trouble with the feeling in her right side, and temporarily lost her ability to sweat.

"I was on *Titus* immediately afterward," she said of the 1999 TV show, "and my only problem was that I was required to shoot a shotgun. I had to put it up to my shoulder and have a charge. I said, 'How about if I do it rifleman style, just picking it up and shooting it?'"

Joosten stretched her resume even farther, showing up on *Monk*, *Grey's Anatomy*, and many other shows. In 2004, she auditioned for what she thought would be one other quick showing, this time on *Housewives*.

The role of Karen McCluskey had already been cast, but the original choice had been incapacitated with health trouble, forcing the show's officials to quickly find someone else.

Joosten auditioned with a scene where McCluskey explains exactly why hitting a child, only once in a while, can keep them in line.

"I loved the fact that (McCluskey) was being used as she is," Joosten said. "I think she was just going to be 'once or twice,' but the response was very good, so they decided to keep the character in the show."

McCluskey's first appearance came in the opening season episode "Love is in the Air," in which she accuses the Scavo kids of stealing from her. A few months later, it got her an Emmy nomination for Outstanding Guest Actress in a Comedy Series.

Up against fellow *Housewives* guest star Lupe Ontiveros, Georgia Engel (*Everybody Loves Raymond*), Blythe Danner (*Will and Grace*), and Oscar-winner Cloris Leachman (*Malcolm in the Middle*), Joosten had some pretty tough competition. But just as she had throughout her career, she looked to her kids for encouragement.

"My sons were there," she recalled. "We were together. They had gone through the whole process with me, from when I was doing community theater and they had been doing their homework on theater seats. It was really important that they be there for that." She won, and her tormenting target Huffman grabbed the Comedy Lead Actress award that year, beating out fellow *Housewives* Marcia Cross and Teri Hatcher.

Three years later, Joosten was back up for the same award – but this time, she was more alone; though Polly Bergen was also up for a quick appearance on *Housewives*, none of the leads made it for 2008. Tina Fey would win the Lead Actress Comedy award for *30 Rock*, and Fey's guest co-stars Edie Falco, Carrie Fisher, and Elaine Stritch were there to face Joosten in the Guest category, along with Sarah Silverman, up for her appearance on *Monk*.

Waiting for the victory announcement, Joosten could feel the heat; several cameras were zooming in on the nominees. On stage, the presenter opened the envelope, and said, "and the Emmy goes to. . ."

Joosten heard her name, but not from the microphone up front. She glanced around; was someone playing a prank on her? Then her moniker was announced, and she headed up for another trophy.

"It was really weird," she remembered. "What I had heard was the earpiece of the cameraman in front of me. They were telling him that I was going to win. The second win was wonderful because it was an affirmation; it showed that the first one wasn't a fluke."

Joosten went back to playing McCluskey, always taking time out for other work – she made small appearances in box-office hits *Wedding Crashers* (2005), *Bedtime Stories* (2008), and *Alvin and the Chipmunks: The Squeakquel* (2009). But in the fall of 2009, she learned that an old opponent had come back; a cancerous spot was found on her left lung during a physical.

"I was devastated because I thought it was a return related to the first cancer," said Joosten, who'd quit smoking and become a lung cancer victim advocate after her first run-in with the disease. "I spent five days crying. I was afraid I would lose my job on *Housewives*."

But the luck that had been with the actress throughout her career came back; not only did she stay employed, but the surgery was less invasive than she'd originally feared, and Joosten didn't lose her hair. By Dec. 2009, she was through with treatment, and back on Wisteria Lane, always happy being the curmudgeon with a warm heart.

"She pretty much says what she thinks," Joosten says of arguably her most well-known character. "I am obviously not the glamour spot on the show; as such, I think a lot of people can identify with someone that does not look perfect. My clothes are from K-Mart or the church basement. She's just real."

She'd stay neighbors with the rest of the *Housewives* for the next few seasons. But as the last go-round rolled through in the early months of 2011, she and the character got a bit closer than anyone ever wanted (along with other real-life cancer patients, Joosten had showed up in Feb. 2011 on *The Bold and the Beautiful*'s 6000th episode, which dealt with the disease).

Ms. McCluskey was diagnosed with cancer, and a large part of the final season was based around the fight. But off screen, the actress' own disease was back once more, and in hindsight, the jokes and one-liners everyone, including her, shot forth about McCluskey's mortality don't seem quite as funny as before.

Viewers saw McCluskey wither away and get ready to pass. They heard her doctors say that there was nothing that could be done. But there were things that they couldn't know about the woman behind the character – this wasn't all an act.

During the last moments of the show finale on May 13, 2012, viewers watched McCluskey breathe her last. Less than three weeks later, Joosten was taken by the same ailment.

"I think when you reach a certain level of celebrity," she said of her advocacy, "you have a responsibility to use your celebrity when you're offered the chance to do so. If or when it comes back, probably other kinds of treatment will be prepared for."

Benjamin Kanes: *Birdman*

All he wanted, all they wanted, all everyone wanted, was to give something new to an audience not really used to or accepting of originality. It was something that no one had expected, and even fewer would have believed could occur, even if they'd known of it firsthand.

It wouldn't be easy. Little in the performance world ever is. It might not even be worth it. Too often, much in the performance world isn't.

With fate tossing one obstacle after another in his way, both from the inside and out, even he started to think it might be easier to just cut and run. Be one of the many too afraid of failure and rejection to really even put out the effort.

That was the story of 2014's *Birdman (or The Unexpected Virtue of Ignorance)* – right up next to *Dr. Strangelove* (1964) with the whole multiple-title practice. It was the tale of Alejandro González Iñárritu behind the camera, Michael Keaton before it, and the rest of a crew struggling through an unthinkably tough task, the difficulty of which might not have been realized or respected once the audience and critics, not always reliably optimistic, got hold of it.

It was the bio of Keaton's protagonist Riggan Thomson, whose acting career had taken him to stardom in superhero mode before, only to leave him dangling when he'd tried to diversify his resume. He was still trying, but, along with optimism, patience isn't a virtue with audiences. To an extent, Keaton himself might have been approaching *Birdman* the same way – he'd been a big star in the 80s and 90s, highlighted with the first two *Batman* films (1989/1992) , but there will never be a shortage of performers hoping to stream into Hollywood's mainstream, and getting lost in the shuffle is all too quick and easy.

The title character of *Birdman* (Benjamin Kanes) confronts and comforts his own alter ego Riggan Thomson (Michael Keaton) in 2014's Best Picture winner.

The feeling was rubbing off on the cast as well, including the fellow playing the impromptu title character. Not Riggan, but the hero he'd pretended to be. Clarification: Benjamin Kanes was pretending to be the character that Riggan, himself a fictional character, had pretended to be.

Just reading about aspects of *Birdman* is enough to wear one out, or at least skip to the next profile. But we're hardly scratching the surface of Kanes' complications.

He'd spend his full part enveloped – except for part of his face – in a heavy costume. He could hardly hear or see. Birdman's wings were about sixty pounds – each! – and he was bolted into them. Filming was in the midst of a New York heatwave.

Under all of that, and he'd have to stay in character for ten, even fifteen minutes at a time – Iñárritu and the rest of the film's scripters innovatively broke the film into less than twenty separate takes. A two-hour-plus film, spread out over so few takes, all of them blending into one another, sometimes requiring the choreography of hundreds of people at a time! One misstep, one wrong look over the face of someone yards in the background, and a day's worth of excruciating work would go the way of the droppings!

"Any one of these things individually would have amounted to one of the trickiest, most challenging things I'd ever played," Kanes recalls. "All of them together made it almost impossible."

Not surprisingly, times came when he thought about walking away before the final called "Cut!"

"There was a full day when we shot an outside scene, and didn't use one take," he recalls. "At the end of the day, I felt that I couldn't do this. I was no good. I was being overly dramatic, reacting to myself."

A crew member came by, and Kanes did a bit of venting, much like he would in character. Then arrived some unexpected sympathy, even inspiration.

"He told me that there wasn't one person on the set who hadn't left one day feeling the way I was feeling," Kanes says. Even co-star Edward Norton, with two Oscar noms down, had had some trouble with *Birdman*, all while doing some self-spoofing by playing the same type of abrasive control freak actor Norton himself is reputed to be.

"That was what I needed to hear," Kanes says. "Everyone working on that movie seemed to know that they were working on something special. This was so hard, but we were doing something wonderful." By the time filming was through, he'd send Riggan a similar message – or, rather, Birdman would.

Kanes almost hadn't become a part of *Birdman* at all. After standing in for Mark Walhberg (and others) a couple of times, he was first *only* asked to do similar work for Riggan, not actually act.

"I told them I wasn't really looking for that job, and I turned it down," Kanes says. "Then I saw casting notices go out, like a regular acting role, someone who was the perfect size and match for Keaton." He called back, and was called in to try out.

"Auditioning, I find to be one of the most tedious, one of the weirdest aspects of the acting world and film world," he says. He headed to Queens to sit down with Iñárritu and others.

"It wasn't just a matter of, 'Can you read these lines?'" Kanes remembers. "It was, 'Do you have claustrophobia? Do you have heat issues?' I put on a mask, and they asked me to talk. I got to improv some stuff, all the things I love as an actor. I love it when it's weird and challenging and unpredictable like that."

They measured everything but his eyelashes to furnish out Birdman's outfit. No Superman-esque tights and capes for this guy.

"This role would only exist in this superhero costume, and superhero costumes are not fun to wear," Kanes explains. "They're extremely restrictive, really tight, really hot. They're not made to make you feel super; they're made to look cool." Even if he's referring to cool in the slangish tone, the weather wouldn't follow suit: New York might get hit hard when blizzard season passes through, but its heat-waves go to the other extreme, and the cameras wouldn't be rolling in the winter.

"The material was so thick that you'd sweat if it was cold out, and here it was in the 80s!" exclaims Kanes, who worked out like crazy to get ready for the shoot. "It was a long process getting the suit on, and if I started to feel anything, there was no quickly getting out of it."

Along with his physicality, just moving around in the getup was part of Kanes' preparation. As production got going, very few people knew how *Birdman* would end up, and he wasn't one of them.

"They told me they were going to send a script, and they just sent a few pages," he says. "I didn't know everything about the character. I was on set for two weeks -- I didn't film immediately – and a lot of times, I would get in the suit and practice being in it, which was really challenging on its own."

As the film seemingly spools through in one continuous take, the story of a man who used to be something more is told. He was once Riggan Thomson, whose Birdman superhero thrilled and inspired audiences of decades before, heroically battling the comic book bad guys in one flick after another, probably making loads of money and winning the libidos of gorgeous actresses.

Now he's just Riggan, barely a blurb on the entertainment pages, seeing a shot at Broadway as his last grab at success. People can't see him as a person, nor any other character but the pseudo-superhero. That happened in real life to former Supermen George Reeves and Christopher Reeve – and probably others – and it's happening here. Is it about putting together a quality product, or is it about having everyone know your name, even if they don't have the first bit of respect for you as a person? As both a person and an actor, Riggan doesn't seem sure himself.

Still, he's not quitting. Enough people have some faith in him that he's got a shot on Broadway, alongside Norton's Mike Shiner, a bigger star than Riggan, not to mention friend (with benefits) of Riggan's daughter.

Birdman really shows audiences who actors truly are when the cameras are turned off and the lights go out, and maybe that's a big reason why it struck such a chord with audiences. Honesty, even the brutal kind, is its own payoff. Not every point needs be made with a jackhammer, and not every homage need be a parody. Keaton's and Norton's characters are probably much like themselves, and Riggan's show is much like the real theater world. When it comes to individuals in entertainment, it's those that do wrong (who probably make up about .000001 of the full profession) that get all the tabloid attention, but the vocation itself is often publicly glorified. Neither side is fair or balanced.

Indeed, there's the eternal mystery of what success truly means. Riggan was popular as Birdman.

Even the play's going pretty well. But a chance meeting with a pessimistic critic reminds him that actor and movie star are two different things, and that being loved and talented can be very far apart. Riggan seems to have mistakenly combined the two in his heyday, and now he's stuck as to what to aim for, or how.

In other words, he's caught in a similar predicament in which Kanes had found himself trapped before. But Kanes had gotten some unexpected, albeit incredibly welcome, assistance, and now he was going to visit it on the fellow who used to play Birdman himself.

Trying to regain his bearings after a decent enough opening night, Riggan can only hope that it's his hangover that's causing his newest, ahem, *distraction*. It's the character he once played, now in full form, in sort-of human form. Plans had started out for Keaton to be both fellows, but now it's Kanes (his mask hiding his non-Riggan form), there to show the man who once personified the superhero he was enacting that things aren't over for him.

"I didn't have the freedom to just create a character," says Kanes, whose scenes were some of the last to be filmed. "I might if the role was just a role, instead of a shared role. It's the younger version of a character who already exists in the film, but also a version of that character that only exists in that character's head, his alter ego. So there was a lot of time where I just had to say, fuck it, let's just make it good."

Much of the script's dialogue has been in monologue form, and now it's Kanes' turn. He's the guy Riggan used to play, and to an extent, the guy he wishes he could be, in some form.

"I spent a day studying Michael, the way he moved and talked, trying to get that into my work," Kanes says. "He has some very distinct physical characteristics. He was playing a character that was very downtrodden, even though he's a high-energy guy. There was a lot of guesswork for me: flipping contrasting pieces of direction and putting it all together to be a character that worked. I had the job of creating the character while at the same time trying to match it to him."

"So you're not a great actor!" Birdman rages at his human form, following the disbelieving Riggan down the sidewalk. "Who cares? You're much more than that! You tower over these other theater douchebags! You're a movie star, man! You're a global force!"

Through the first set of run-throughs, Riggan and Birdman were to be physically similar. Just before rolling, however, a decision made the character much taller than the actor (Riggan or Keaton, it doesn't matter). As if all his other costumed complications weren't enough, Kanes now had to storm around in platforms!

"It was technically impossible," he says. "It was crazy how hard it was, to walk, not to just be not wobbly, but to walk like a superhero and time every one of your moments to every single element of the scene, to sneak behind (Riggan), come up behind his shoulder, slow down behind him."

The scene rolls on. Birdman's starting to heat up even more, and Riggan appears to be responding, perhaps believing what Kanes himself now felt: that the toughest journey is worth taking if there's something special enough at its end.

"There were pages with a lot of movement and a lot of blocking, extras, camera movement, crew members, extras, regular people walking on the street," Kanes says. "Everybody could do their part perfectly, and there could be one background performer who might be a little late, and the entire take would be no good. I was doing things like sneaking up behind the camera, so when it goes back, you're already there. If the camera turns a corner with an actor, you're waiting on the other side to bust through. This was an absolute challenge."

Before filming, Kanes had watched his co-star's work in *Batman*, considered by many to be the best in the series' history, itself rolling from Adam West to Christian Bale. He'd gotten some extra guidance from the old guy behind the Batsuit.

"His suit had been more restrictive than the one I was wearing," Kanes says. "He told me to embrace the role: to focus on being a part of the suit!"

Birdman's about got Riggan back on the team. "You are larger than life, man!" he spews. "You save people from their boring, miserable lives. You make them jump, laugh, shit their pants."

It's like Riggan's already there, even out of costume. He snaps his fingers, and explosions and bullets blast everywhere. The entire film's carried a surreal edge; we're never really sure what's real and what's in his mind. Now we're moving from improbable to impossible, into fantastic levels. And if it was this crazy for us in the outside audience, imagine how Keaton, Kanes, and everyone else felt!

"Moviemaking in general is a huge creative collaboration," Kanes says. "It takes people who are scientists, engineers, builders, people in business, creative people, everyone working together. One of a hundred things can go wrong. That scene had two hundred background actors, fifty stunt people, three pages of dialogue. You're talking about a live street in New York City. You're talking pyrotechnics and tanks, stunt people with weapons. Normally each one of these pieces would be handled individually, but here it's all in one choreographed moment. When you account for the things the special effects people would need in post-production, I'd never seen anything like it."

But the time and place for that sort of worrying and wonder would be later. He still had to hold things together with Birdman's super strength.

"We have to end it on our own terms," Birdman asserts. "Flames. Sacrifice. Icarus. You can do it. You hear me? You are… Birdman." He flies off, and Riggan appears to follow suit, all the way back to the theater.

He might have gotten the inspiration from the most unexpected (psychotic might be more accurate) of places, but who cares? Why does it matter *why* he's doing it? It shouldn't, and it doesn't. What matters is that things get done and done right, and we hope that the appreciation arrives in all kinds of abundance, preferably sooner than later, especially for an actor who hasn't had enough lately. Again, whether we're referring to Riggan or Keaton doesn't matter.

When we give film lovers something that shatters their world like an H-Bomb/A-Bomb tag team, something that ventures into territory that had never been explored, at least not to this extent, it's shooting in the dark. Copying off someone else's success, making a new version of something that's already worked elsewhere, might get an audience to say, "Well, it's nothing new and not as good as what we already saw, but it's OK." OK is enough for some people, probably too many people, but not for those with enough guts to take the tough way out.

It would have been easy to quit, but, even with some outside motivation, Kanes didn't. Neither did anyone else on the *Birdman* crew. And it all ended up being worth it.

"It was clear that people were operating on a higher level," Kanes recalls. "There was definitely this feeling of working on something special. On *Birdman*, you just felt like you were in the presence of a whole new thing, a prevailing energy that people at attention were at a higher level. People had tension, but it was focused, beautiful, creative tension. What we were doing on set was so physical, that never been done before. There was no fallback plan. People were going to film these scenes until they came out the way they wanted, if it took a day or several days."

Did some people dislike *Birdman*? Of course they did. That's unavoidable. That happens with, let's see, *every film that reaches a large enough audience*! But they were the minority. That's why the Academy decided to give it nine shots at awards. Norton got his third nom; Keaton, after three decades in the business, got his first, and you're laid odds he'd have won Best Actor had Eddie Redmayne waited another year to tell *The Theory of Everything* (2014). The screenplay and cinematography got statuettes. Iñárritu's directing was named 2014's best, and so was his Picture.

It all goes to show what happens when we forget the meaning of the word quit. Kanes, and others, had felt it before filming ended.

"There was a point where you felt it, that that was a good take, and some of the relief came," he says. "From my perspective and my experience, so much of what was done had never been done before. Was what we're trying to do even possible? In a normal film with normal coverage, you might have to do several takes, but you know that what you're aiming for is possible: you just haven't quite gotten the pieces yet. That's the apex of the film. For me, inside that suit, what we were doing *was* possible. We could do it. We could make it work. The response to the film shows that it was a landmark film."

John Kapelos: *Breakfast Club*

Did you know that there's a huge inside joke in the opening moments of *The Breakfast Club* (1985)? As we, the audience, are taken on a tour of the flick's setting of Shermer High School, we see a student's photo under a "Man of the Year" honor.

Ready for the shocker? It's actually a picture of Carl, who shows up later as the janitor!

What? What do you mean, you knew that? You've heard it *how* many thousands of times?! OK, FINE! But now let's talk about the backstory and the man who made Carl who he was.

"In the case of Carl, he was a guy who had been a hotshot at the school," says John Kapelos, who replaced Rick Moranis in the role of Carl early in filming. "He'd been really hot shit, and now he's Mr. Clean-Up-The-Shit."

Was Carl's photographic cameo meant to be an inside joke? Was it a self-deprecating remark that legendary late director John Hughes aimed at Shermer? Was it just meant for a quick laugh, something for the quick-eyed to watch for?

Shermer High School maintenance man Carl (John Kapelos) shares some strong street philosophy with the rest of *The Breakfast Club* of 1985.

We'll never know, not the least because the intensely-clandestine Hughes, who directed about half of the comedies in the 1980s and often used Shermer as a backdrop, sadly and suddenly passed in Aug. 2009. But together, Hughes and Kapelos turned a school janitor into, as Carl himself so gleefully put it, "the eyes and ears of this institution!"

"He wasn't some doofus who'd been airlifted in from some other place," Kapelos says. "This guy had a real connection to the high school, and to the kids. He might have even been in a previous incarnation of the Breakfast Club. He was the cock of the walk and the king of the hallways, and he knew that place as a student very well, like those kids knew every nook and cranny of this school."

Yes, Carl might have walked out of the school with stars in his eyes and all the confidence in the world. But along the way, something had gone wrong for the young man. His life had taken all the wrong turns – the same trip that the film's audience is clued in is in store for Judd Nelson's resident delinquent John Bender – and now he was stuck cleaning up other's messes.

Or hell, maybe he'd wanted to be a janitor all along – or just couldn't stay away from his old stomping grounds!

"When I was asked to play the janitor," Kapelos says, "I had no idea it would be a cult classic thirty years later, and even if I did, that wouldn't have helped me at the moment. You look at your script. Look into your heart. Look into the director's eyes and march forward into the future. I used every moment in terms of my presence to move it forward. There's an expression that I've learned in acting; it's that you make yourself serve the art; you don't make the art serve you. I would rather disappear into the guise of a character than make the character serve me, because that's when the work suffers."

To get in custodial character, Kapelos spent much more time secluded in the school's janitor room – Hughes encouraged him not to hang out with the cast to help the spontaneity of the scenes. One scene, that among many others was cut (the original print was allegedly over two hours long), had the janitor morphing into a soothsayer to tell the futures of the club members.

"That was non-scripted stuff that sort of blew it out as to who Carl was," Kapelos says. "There was a whole sequence when I told them where they'd be 15-20 years from now. I looked into the crystal ball, and I said, 'OK, you're going to be a soccer mom, you're a big jackoff cop, you're going to be in jail.'"

Along the way, Carl pops in to torment hapless principal Richard Vernon (the late Paul Gleason), catching the anguished administrator going through confidential records.

"I had an antagonistic relationship with (Gleason) that carried off-screen," Kapelos recalls, laughing. "Paul was a lovely guy: very competitive, and very process-oriented. We used that grit to heighten our on-screen rivalry." When Carl cuts off Vernon with a quick bribe demand in the midst of Vernon's hasty explanation, the surprise the audience sees on Gleason's face is real; his character originally had more lines in the scene.

But all the final decisions came down to one man, and millions mourned at his untimely passing. At the Academy Awards ceremony in March 2010, the *Breakfast Club* cast, as well as Matthew Broderick and Macaulay Culkin, whose careers Hughes helped launch, gathered for a special tribute to the famous filmmaker.

"In death, as in life, (Hughes) was always uber-private," says Kapelos, who also worked with the director in *Sixteen Candles* (1984) and *Weird Science* (1985). "He was very controlling in his work. This is the movie he wanted to be seen. That pride in his work also is what makes him so great and memorable, and what will make his films stand up, as they have. On a human level, I feel horrible. On a creative level, I feel America has lost someone special."

But they'll never forget him; Hughes' films are a constant sight on television, especially *Home Alone* (1990) and *Planes, Trains, and Automobiles* (1987), which show up several dozen times every holiday season.

"We'd do eight, 10, 12, 14 takes," Kapelos recalls, "and then he'd ask me to improvise and let it fly. Like any movie that stands the test of time, like *Rebel Without A Cause* (1955), *Breakfast Club* is about strong characters and characterizations and the effort that the actors put into their work; it's about creating something that's strong and casting it as well as you can cast it. You really had a sense of talking to teenagers in a way they could understand."

For another of his most well-known roles, Kapelos had the unusual task of making a cameo appearance as a real person, forcing him to briefly step into the life of a character, while at the same time blending the actual aspects of the person's persona. For 2002's *Auto Focus*, Kapelos quickly became longtime Canadian TV actor Bruno Gerussi, who hosted the popular cooking series *Celebrity Cooks*.

"I knew (Gerussi) as a TV celebrity when I was a kid," says Kapelos, himself a Canadian. "The important thing in that regard was to capture the essence of a real person. I nailed Bruno as the guy with the curly hair, very jocular."

Still, no one on set could quickly recall the performer, who died in 1995.

"Apparently that was a real schimozzle, as my dad would say," says Kapelos, who hunted down an Internet photo of Gerussi for the makeup department. "Bruno's role was so teeny in *Auto Focus*, but it was important because of the place it falls in the film for Greg Kinnear's character to fall apart."

In the main role of *Hogan's Heroes* (1965) star Bob Crane, Kinnear, his mind warped by sex addiction – and the occasional outside substance – breaks down on the show, filling the air with double entendres and dirty jokes that nearly get him beaten by the women in the audience. The show, which never actually aired (it would be a *YouTube* phenomenon today), was Crane's final public appearance before his 1978 still-unsolved murder.

In the taping, Kapelos says, "Gerussi asks Crane if he's OK. I didn't want to make the guy your run-of-the-mill celebrity host. He knows this is a performer who's having a nervous breakdown."

While Kapelos and the rest of his profession make a living pretending to be other people – real or fictitious – only one person ends up getting the credit (or, once in a great while, the blame) when it comes to acting.

"The real race in acting is not with anyone else," he explains. "It's with yourself. I have to be the best John Kapelos I can be; you have to be the best (fill in your name) that you can be. It's a natural human tendency to look at other people, to say, 'Wow, what an amazing career he has! I wish I had his career!' But you really don't want that, because you have to form your own path."

Just as the best athletes in the world have to practice and work hard every day, before and after they reach the pros, actors have an ethic to develop. All an audience usually sees is the final product, but it's only a small part of one's performing development.

"If you're trying to succeed and you get frustrated," he says to upcoming actors, "don't concentrate on the end result; concentrate on the day-to-day work. Make your audition good; make yourself as refined as possible. You really have to enjoy what you do in a process sort of way – the fame and fortune are auxiliary by-products."

David Kobzantsev: *Bobby*

As I've said earlier, if heading to Hollywood to make your mark in the acting world, it's a good idea to find employment that can be easily left. I hope no one is offended by this, but acting may require a job to be dismissed or resigned from with little or no notice.

That's something that David Kobzantsev learned back in the early part of the last decade. Just after grabbing a role in 2003's low-budget *An Easy Grand*, he was working in a restaurant when someone paid him the most backhanded of compliments.

"The casting director told me that I looked like someone they needed for a re-enactment," he says. "I knew the history for school, but not really the logistics of it."

For a 2004 version of the Discovery Channel's *Unsolved History*, he was called to play Sirhan Sirhan in a dramatization of the RFK assassination.

"What was really cool was that they went into the trajectory of the bullets: how many hit RFK, where the holes were in the wall." Kobzantsev says. "But most of the research was already done by everyone else, and I was just standing there looking pretty."

Just as with his brother John, RFK's death sparked some conspiracy theories. Some said that the shot that killed RFK hit him in the back of the head and was fired from within inches, which would have been impossible from Sirhan, who was standing in front of RFK, several feet away. Others said that over a dozen shots were fired during the assassination, out of the question for a single gun.

A few years after the dramatization, Kobzantsev heard of a drama coming up about the night of the murder – Emilio Estevez's *Bobby* (2006).

"I used that experience (*Unsolved*) as my ammo, no pun intended, to get in for Emilio's movie," says Kobzantsev. "I gave them the tape of *Unsolved History*. I thought it could give me a one-up when it came to auditioning for me." It worked; for the second time in less than three years, he was chosen to play one of the most infamous people in American history.

In one of the most shocking moments in American history, Sirhan Sirhan (David Kobzantsev, with gun) murdered Robert F. Kennedy in June 1968, a story told in 2006's *Bobby*.

"It's funny, because I'm Russian, and (Sirhan is) Jordanian," says the actor, who's actually from Kansas City. "Even in the film, I'm not extremely dark, so it worked. It wasn't an exact historical replica of (Sirhan), but it was close enough that it worked."

With Oscar-winners Anthony Hopkins and Helen Hunt, as well as familiar faces William H. Macy, Estevez's daddy Martin Sheen, Lindsay Lohan, Ellijah Wood, Demi Moore, Estevez himself, and others to contend with, Kobzantsev knew it would be tough for him to stand out, especially in a few-scene role.

"For the audition, I did a lot of research," he says. "I went to the library and found stacks of books on the psyche of serial killers, RFK's last day, and conspiracy theories. I had two weeks to prepare. That research really helped me emotionally connect with the character."

Like the monikers of Oswald, Earl Ray, and Booth, many people will never forget Sirhan's name for all the worst reasons. Kobzantsev, however, delved into the person that he was before the ill-fated gunshots rang out.

"I don't think he was a villain," he says of Sirhan. "I just think he was in the wrong place at the wrong time. He was 23 when he, quote unquote, assassinated RFK."

Sirhan suffered through a fatherless childhood and directionless youth, Kobzantsev learned.

"He constantly was trying to find something to do," he says. "(Sirhan) spent years cleaning horse shit because he wanted to be a jockey. He couldn't find anything worth living for. He was a very oppressed person, a very down-on-his-luck kind of guy."

It's that type of emotion that Kobzantsev shows the second that Sirhan strolls onto the screen in *Bobby*; with less than half an hour left in the flick, Sirhan steps up to the door of the Ambassador Hotel (which, ironically enough, was being demolished as the crew commenced filming) and brushes Estevez's character.

When he walks through the door, Sirhan's like a determined newcomer, like a rookie who's finally getting his turn as a starter – someone who's spent his entire career getting put on the second string, and now finally has a chance to grab his moment in the spotlight. He casts a determined glare at the ceiling, like a freshman trying to intimidate the walls of the menacing high school.

"In my entrance into the lobby, they wanted a close-up," Kobzantsev says. "They asked me to show, through my eyes, what was about to happen. 'You're in the hotel; why did you go in there? Do you know what's going to happen?' I was a guy who was scared out of his mind, but had to keep it together, because it was a huge government event.

"I walked up to the camera, an inch away from my face. On the first take, everybody fell silent. I thought I had done something wrong. I was thinking, 'Oh no, they're going to fire me!' Then an official yelled, 'That was fucking awesome!' I had character shooting out of my eyes, helping understand what was going on at the time."

He's not entirely sure that America will ever get the full story as to what actually went on that fateful night in the hotel.

"Actually, there were more bullet holes in the wall then there are bullets in the gun," Kobzantsev says, awakening the Jim Garrison that lives inside so many of us. "Who else was shooting a gun? Maybe that person, maybe accidentally, shot RFK. Maybe Sirhan was just placed there like a pawn in a chess game, and someone else did the dirty work. He took the fall, and maybe he took the fall because that was the only thing he had going for him: infamy. Now everyone knows who he is. He is branded in history forever. He sits pretty in prison. Maybe that was the exchange. He's going to be infamous forever. I know it's kind of a hard thing to swallow, but I wouldn't doubt it for a second."

That was something that he tried to bring to life in his all-too-short time on the screen ("There was a lot more material in the script with Sirhan than was left in the film, but that happens to everybody," he says).

Originally during the shooting scene, Sirhan was to shoot Kennedy and immediately get knocked down, Kobzantsev recalls. A quick conversation with Estevez, however, allowed him to bring subtlety to the forefront.

"The minute that I shoot, I break down and start crying," Kobzantsev says. "When he shoots, it's a release of emotion and tension and nervousness. Maybe he didn't want to be doing it, and once he pulled the trigger, flood of emotion and exasperation. I tried it and (Estevez) loved it. It showed humility and humanity. It showed that (Sirhan) was a young guy who wasn't sure about doing what he had to do. I wanted to show that battle, that fight that he was having within himself. Maybe there was somebody with his hand on his shoulders saying 'OK, this is what you have to do.' He was kind of forced into it, but it could also be a reason for his breaking down."

To start a biographical film, a three-hour epic, with a tragedy, that was a pretty risky thing to try. Showing its subject taken down by the very violence he had spent his life speaking against was a tough, certainly heartbreaking way to begin.

Audiences knew of the Mahatma's sad, sudden death. Show it, have the audience react, and move on to the story that could finally be told. The epic that would realize the dream that Richard Attenborough had carried for decades, one that millions of Attenborough's British countrymen and those here in America could finally fully appreciate. The story of Mohandas Gandhi, who showed and continues to inspire millions that peace defeats war and love forever triumphs over hate. Those are the messages we still carry from 1982's Best Picture-winning *Gandhi*, which immediately found its place in the classic ranks of filmmaking.

Like Sirhan, the name of Nathuram Vinayak Godse will live forever in darkness for the most infamous reasons; his bullets ended Gandhi's march to independence. Also like Sirhan, the name and the deed are all most will ever care to know. As the film only shows him briefly at the start and end, even it didn't say much about him. By the time his film debut came in Godse's form, Harsh Nayyer knew more than nearly anyone who had ever known the Hindu nationalist whose idolization of the icon turned all the way down to hate.

1982's Best Picture-winning *Gandhi* opened with the icon's assassination at the hands of Nathuram Vinayak Godse (Harsh Nayyer).

"The fact that he was infamous was not a consideration for me," explains Nayyer. "What mattered was that I portray him truthfully." As Kobzantsev would do over two decades later, Nayyer poured himself into the libraries.

"I read every book I could find on Gandhi and Godse," explains Nayyer. "When I arrived in New Delhi for the shooting, I found out where the only living relative of Nathuram lived." He soon got in touch with Godse's young brother Gopal, who'd worked with his brother in the right-wing Hindu nationalist group Rashtriya Swayamsevak Sangh, and arrested as an accomplice, spending over fourteen years in jail.

"I called him on the telephone and asked him a lot of questions," Nayyer remembers. "He was very happy that his brother would be shown in the film. He had his view on what was going on in Indian politics at the time, which I felt was misinformed. They blamed him for things he had not done, and things that he in fact had an opposite view on." Believing that Gandhi had caved in to Pakistan and Muslim pressure, Godse assassinated him just outside the Old Birla House, where Gandhi had been living for a few months before the murder of Jan. 30, 1948, itself just before a prayer meeting.

The house, converted into the Gandhi Smriri public memorial in 1973, became the location of filming the murder.

"It was an experience of recreating history and going back in time, and it was shared by a number of people who were working as extras in the film," Nayyer recalls. "Some of them had been in the same location when the assassination took place, and were telling me about what that experience, years later, was like for them. They said it was like they were reliving the time. That brought a lot of immediacy to my own presence on that location, because it seemed like I was being drawn back into time."

That feeling spread across the set; when many there saw Ben Kingsley, in the midst of an Oscar-winning performance as Gandhi, many touched their foreheads to the ground before him, Nayyer continues.

"It was the Indian style of showing respect," he says. "It was like Gandhi had reappeared, because his likeness was so great."

Immediately arrested and not the slightest bit remorseful, Godse spent a year on trial before being hanged just before Thanksgiving of 1949 (Narayan Apte was also hanged for the killing, and two others got life imprisonment). Gopal, who never denied conspiring nor expressed any regret for it, died in 2005.

"One of the things that came out of (Gopal and my) conversation was the costume I wore in the film," recalls Nayyer. "I talked to the costume designer and my suggestion was accepted." The film's costumes would become one of its eight Oscar victories, along with Best Picture and a directing honor for Attenborough.

"Many people told me that I looked like Nathuram Godse," Nayyer says. "Having seen his photographs, I decided to put on some weight to look more like him. My research had given me a sense of the history of the times. I also watched the shooting of all the scenes that were filmed before mine. That helped put me in the historical moment. I felt I was living in those times."

Heather Litteer: *Requiem for a Dream*

Anyone who has ever battled drug addiction and come out on top has looked back at their past and wondered why. Why they did this sort of thing. How they did what they did for this sort of thing. Who they ever were at all for a time that was too long, no matter how lengthy it was.

Shame. It's a part of the life of every addict who managed to reach the right side of sobriety. Those who even get to ask, though, are the luckiest ones. Many don't, usually because they can't. It's far too late. Too much has been had, too much has been done, too far has been traveled. That might be because of death, and some probably wish it had been. Sometimes the places drugs keep pulling us all the way back to is so much worse.

Issues like this are the ones we typically hit the movies to forget, because they're usually a quick way to step away from these problems, this reality, and step into the happy, upbeat conclusions that usually, often superficially, inspire us just as the last sets of names roll up the screen. However, films that themselves put us in these real worlds and don't have the decency to pull us out at the last second are often called dark, disturbing, sad.

That's unfair. They're just *real*. Far more real than we want to acknowledge.

That's where the gutsiest artists earn their respect. They toss out tradition and go for individualism. They step away from drama and try out actuality. They stand alone in their new world; if people join them, great. If not, well, that's fine too.

Two decades before, Hubert Selby had taken his readers through the darkest neighborhoods of

New York and the darker ones of its drug world, writing the too-common tales of people who lose everything but their lives to drugs, and wish they probably didn't have that either. His story was called *Requiem for a Dream*, but it was more nightmarish than anything that visits us in slumber.

Considering its quality, it seems surprising that it took until 2000 to get the tome to the cinema, but, again, films like this are often considered too risky for those whose names are on the bankroll, or the cast. Investing your green in a movie whose very objective is spellbinding audiences into sad, shocked silence isn't quite an attractive proposition.

It takes a certain amount of trust, a very large amount, to recruit enough funding and performers to put together a film like *Dream*. However, two years before, enough people had believed in Darren Aronofsky to help him fire a debut blast through Hollywood with *Pi*. It was just one film, but it was enough to convince the right people that he could do *Requiem* well.

The producers, of course. And those whose names would rule the billing. In the sad creation that he'd put together, one who'd won an Oscar and two future victors would show up to do things they'd never tried before.

So would the supporting group. WAY back in 1989 (seems like ancient times today, doesn't it?), one of Heather Litteer's pals had brought Selby's first work, *Last Exit to Brooklyn*, to the screen, along with veterans Jennifer Jason Leigh and Burt Young, and newbies like Sam Rockwell. That, next to *Pi*'s success, shoved Litteer towards her *Dream*.

She may look happy, but it's for the fakest and saddest of reasons; Heather Litteer worked her way through a drug-fueled orgy near the end of 2000's *Requiem for a Dream*.

"I loved the darkness of the landscapes (Selby) creates with his characters in his stories," explains the Georgia gal, "and how the characters really take it to another level, as I would as an actress for this particular scene." Her eventual theater career would carry Litteer around the globe, but *Dream* would be her first major time before a camera.

From the start, we probably know the film won't end well. Harry Goldfarb (Jared Leto) and Tyrone Love (Marlon Wayans) are already in the drug trade, and Harry's mom Sara (Ellen Burstyn), widowed and abandoned by her boy, finds her best friend in a TV host.

Then there's Harry's main woman Marion, a role that couldn't possibly have pushed Jennifer Connelly farther from *Labyrinth* (1986), dreaming of one day seeing her name stitched next to Levi and Tommy Hilfiger in the fashion design world. But like the other three, drugs are already in the way of her dreams.

Like it almost always does in the world of drug abuse, nothing stays good for long. Sara gets too into TV, convinced she's going to appear. Harry, Tyrone, and Marion make some serious green, but lose it to people even worse. Desperate to drop some weight, Sara gets on the right pills, but, like a typical addict, goes too far, the last few remaining strings holding on to her mind starting to wither.

Their love just about killed by the drugs, Harry leaves Marion behind on a trip, leaving her to ask, to beg, to screw for drugs a guy she's never seen before.

Those on drugs accept that their new world is a reality they could never have predicted or understood, and it's somewhere they'll never find safety. And if the sheerness of seeing Connelly as a druggie didn't shock us enough, this one may as well be from another solar system.

One advantage that Aronofsky could utilize over Selby is the use not just of vision, but of sound. The term requiem refers to an item created for memory, often involving the sense of hearing. The haunting tone that drums through the film's final moments became its signature tune, but *Dream*'s final reel goes to the other extreme.

Aronofsky's control has removed any such luxury from his performers and viewers, as is everyday for the druggies of the world. The screen starts to rifle like a machine gun, closeups of people's faces throughout. Harry's in the physical hospital, Sara in a mental one, Tyrone in jail. And Marion's going to be the type of actress no one ever hopes to.

Along with another group of desperate ladies, she's putting on a live show, porno in living color, before a bunch of screaming idiots not far from little girls at a boy band show (Aronofsky is one), dousing them with the money they'll probably use for the worst reasons anyway. That's what you do when you'll do anything for drug dough.

Litteer is there as well.

"Playing a heroin junkie and just how far she will go to get her fix and using her body as a last resort," she remembers, "I could relate to the struggles of a young woman with my sometimes tumultuous younger years in the Lower East Side of New York City when I first moved to New York City in 1990."

Addicts do anything, anything whatsoever, to escape what they've made. Not an issue of suffering, only finding a type of pain that's bearable. It's insanity. It's reality. For a drug addict, the difference between the two is difficult to find, the choice impossible to make. It's a world that drugs love to slam their victims right into. It's one that Litteer, along with Connelly and the rest, had to find a cautious way inside.

"Being that the part called for nudity, preparing was more of a mental thing," Litteer explains. "I wasn't really sure what was going to happen. We had had a table meeting to make sure we were all ready to participate. I had to have courage and confidence and I just gave it my all to get the shots we needed as fast as possible, but these scenes took all night. It was one of the most terrifying things I have ever done. I just stayed focused."

That's all but impossible for *Dream* viewers. The music gets faster, louder. The scenes keep jumping around, all four characters in pain both outside and in. They're all going down together, but they can't even be there for each other. There's nobody to pull them up, no one person who sees the problem and tries to fix it, asking to give help or even receive it.

And it just builds and builds and builds until you want to do everything except throw something large and heavy through the screen. You're as caught up in it as they are. You can't help but imagine being in that position, almost wanting to think about what it would be all about. Climactic? Far too subtle a word. Exhausting. Draining. More exhaustion than a marathon runner crossing her first finish line – just from watching a film. No one's ever the same again, assuming they were ever good or right to begin with.

It might be the drugs. For once, that might be the preference. Marion's mind is far from this event, her dazed expression seeing nothing. Even in sex, there's no pleasure, not for her or the other women. The people who are the most aroused, the most enjoying, are the ones that aren't involved at all, the group of rich morons cheering them on nearby, yelling like fools and dropping money like it's trash. Sex should be erotic, relaxing, enjoyable, and this was the opposite. Only a filmmaker and a certain type of crew could take an orgy full of gorgeous unclothed woman and make it sad and depressing.

"It is an iconic sex scene and so is the whole movie," Litteer says. "It is dark."

It's over now. Over for them all. Sara's mind is ruined past repair. Tyrone's in jail (Selby, who died in 2004, plays a guard ready to make his life hell). Harry's arm is gone, as is his love. Marion is alive and at home, but what's there? She's got a new shipment of drugs. She and the women she was with will probably be back where they were soon enough, until (not unless) the drugs become too much.

You see it, you feel it, you understand it. And the last people to do any of these things are the ones that display them at all.

"It is still very hard to watch," Litteer admits, "and this scene has followed me around for the past sixteen years, and maybe not in the way that I had imagined... Being an actor is a life commitment and you can never know too much. Be generous with other actors and listen. It takes so many people to make this artistry, you must work together as a team. It will always come back and show in the work."

Stephen Marcus: *Quills*

The inspiration to entice one to get involved with acting can come from anywhere in existence. The choice to include one in a project we're working uber-hard on can be made for just as many reasons.

It took two rounds for Stephen Marcus to make his way through school — lack of study doomed him the first time.

"I went back to school and worked hard," recalls the oversized Englishman, "and after one year, I left with eight qualifications (I'm very proud of that), one of which was in communications. It involved doing a play and making my own film." Spurred on by a teacher's encouragement, he headed to college to study drama for the next few years.

By that point, however, Marcus already knew where he'd like his career to end up. *Midnight Express* (1978) probably wasn't expected to come across as a feel-good inspirational flick, but, even in a tale of Turkish prison violence, many obtained some.

Marcus was one, and not because (or not *just* because) of main man Brad Davis' work as Billy Hayes, the American who manages to keep things together long enough to escape at the end. No, Marcus saw his own role model in the character of the warden who makes Hayes' life even more hellish.

"I was mesmerized," he remembers. "It confirmed to me that acting was what I wanted to do, and I haven't looked back."

IIn 1996, he learned of a few local unknowns trying to put together a story of some small-town, small-time crooks who decide to rip off a local mob boss.

Marcus went for the role as one of the main men, but ended up with a smaller role of Nick the Greek, a friend of the group trying to fence his way to financial satisfaction. For weeks, Marcus trained his voice to sound like he'd been born and raised in the land of Athens.

"On the first day of rehearsals," he recalls, "(director) Guy Ritchie said he didn't like it and to drop the accent." For quite some time, it appeared that no would else would get to gauge Marcus' vocals either — the film sat on the shelves for three years. But in 1999, *Lock, Stock, and Two Smoking Barrels* smashed through both the British and American cinemas, launching the careers of Marcus, Ritchie, and everyone else involved.

"Shopping for the costume often helps me find the character," Marcus explains. "Once I find the costume, it tells me a lot about the character: if he's smart and crisp, it will have an effect on how I hold myself and present myself and usually means someone who is in control, as opposed to, say, a medieval jailer dressed in rags who clearly doesn't care about himself or his appearance and what others think of him."

In 1996, Geoffrey Rush had brought home an Oscar for playing mentally challenged piano savant David Helfgott in *Shine*. Four years later, just as *Barrels* was blowing the collective mind of action film fans everywhere, he stepped into a role both similar and very different.

Quills would tell the story of the Marquis de Sade, one of history's most (in)famous sexual sadists.

The not too proud owner of a sexual appetite off the charts — including his sister-in-law and enough prostitutes to fill Times Square for a year — and penchants for S&M-type sexual abuse and the use of what today would be considered Quaaludes, the sicko spent serious time behind the walls of prisons and asylums, including two stints at Charenton, an establishment near Paris.

That's the tale that *Quills* would tell. With Rush as de Sade (and spending an uncomfortable amount of the film unclothed!), Kate Winslet would be Madeleine LeClerc, secretly helping him sneak his words outside the walls to publication. For his part, Marcus set out to follow in the footsteps he'd seen back in *Midnight*, looking to play a guard.

News came, good and bad. It was bad that he wouldn't be the guard, but good that he'd have a role, as de Sade's asylum neighbor Bouchon. It was also bad, or at least challenging as all hell, that he'd spend much of the movie silent — and convincing an audition crew that we can pull off something like that isn't just a can of worms; it's a fire barrel's worth.

But just listen to *this* tryout story...

"We decided to do the scene where (Bouchon) is watching Kate Winslet and the others frolicking in the hay," he remembers, "and Bouchon is masturbating. So my audition consisted of me fake masturbating on a chair in front of the casting director."

**Bouchon (Stephen Marcus) was an asylum neighbor to
Geoffrey Rush's Marquis de Sade in *Quills* (2000).**

A tape was sent to director Peter Kaufman, who just had to see this sort of thing for himself.

"When he came to London to begin pre-production," Marcus says, "I met with him and did the scene again. We laughed a lot and he gave me the job." That, however, would be the end of any humor with this character.

As films such as this often do, *Quills* took some liberties with its subject, both making him look better than he probably deserved and surrounding him with people who do much worse. In the film, Madeleine does everything but throw herself at him, not that he says no. She's also clearly a (well, physically) mature adult; in real life, the two got together when she was years underage. Also, in the film, she dies first – more here soon – when it was his passing that ended things in reality.

That, and he's shacked up with a rapist, a pyromaniac, and Joaquin Phoenix's Abbé priest, who's dreaming about schtupping Madeleine's dead body! Yeah, one can take all kinds of cinematic liberties.

In a role probably created for dramatic purposes, Bouchon would be the sex offender. As one of the Marquis' plays hits the stage nearby, Bouchon (the role calls up memories of Lennie from *Of Mice and Men*) gets a bit too affectionate with Madeleine offstage.

"Nearly all of the scenes with Kate Winslet were difficult," Marcus says, "because they were very intimate and I had to be particularly unpleasant in them. The worst for us both was where I grab her from behind and sexually molest her under her skirt. The end result was great, but getting there was traumatic."

In one of the film's most touching (at first!) scenes, Madeleine pleads for one more story from her man, and he's forced to whisper one line at a time through several walls and inmates, creating the game of Telephone decades before Alexander Graham Bell invented the communication device. But this part ends in tragedy as well, as de Sade's words kick Bouchon's emotions and hormones into overdrive, as he breaks out of the cell and murders Madeleine, earning his ass a lifelong trip inside an iron device.

Marcus also acted out the past in *Angela's Ashes* of 1999 and 2001's *Iris*, not to mention getting a little *crazy* in the too-aptly titled *Kinky Boots* film in 2005 that inspired the stage musical!

"If it's meant to be, it will be," he says of acting. "You prepare for auditions, go to the audition, and give it your best shot, then walk away and forget about it until they offer you the job. Don't be afraid to offer them something different."

John Matuszak: *The Goonies*

No matter how old we get, we can still take a quick step back to childhood once in a while. Sometimes films push us in that direction. Sometimes when we're surfing through the bazillions of channels on cable TV, we might hit on a welcome memory, a film that we sat through a few (hundred thousand) times during our early years, and never really left behind.

For me, 1985's *The Goonies* has always been such a flick. I still have it on both VHS and DVD at my house, and I check it out every time it comes on TV. Humor, fun, a little bit of magic and imagination and not too much emphasis on reality – it's all here for the seeing.

The plot is tailor-made for kids: a group of ruffians, depressed about their house being sold – with the adults, typically, too beaten down to do anything about it. The group decides it's up to them, find a treasure map to a weird area (luckily, it's within biking distance!), and end up hunting for sunken treasure that can save their homes. Of course, there's some baddies on the trail as well, so the requisite outwitting occurs throughout, and basically the movies zooms along like a live-action cartoon.

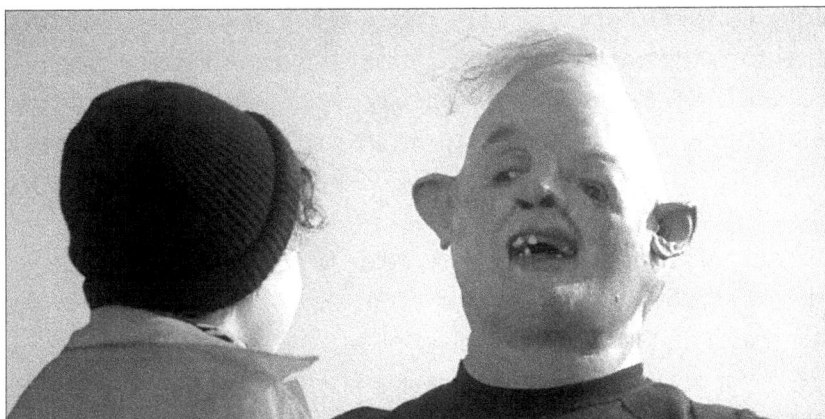

Watching the warm-hearted Sloth in *The Goonies* (1985), you try not to remember that John Matuszak's story didn't have a happy ending.

To be fair, it's also a hell of an inspiration for today's child stars who are nervous about making the jump to grownups: Sean Astin kicked off the career that's been rolling ever since (assuming, of course, that you're familiar with Samwise Gamgee from *Lord of the Rings*) in his turn as impromptu pint-sized leader Mikey, and Mikey's bigger bro Brand is Josh Brolin — yes, the same fellow who should have been Oscar-nominated in 2007 for *No Country for Old Men* and finally was the next year for *Milk*. Martha Plimpton, who plays spunkster Stef, has had a solid career on the big and small screen, including an Emmy-winning turn in 2009 for *The Good Wife* and a starring role as a potheaded young grandma on *Raising Hope* (2010).

Of course, it's more than the plot of the story, as any film that sticks around for so long is. *The Goonies* is about the curiosity and mischief that we all had to let go of when we grew up and developed for the world of conformity. It's about friendship, about sticking together through the toughest times, and the message that the good guys win in the end (and bullies *never* do!), another message that we never truly should allow to escape.

Perhaps just as much as the kids, however, we remember the film's top adult, the kids' main man-child, the one who, like Quasimodo and others, hid a warm heart behind an ugly exterior. In the end, it's Sloth, the (understatement alert!) strange-looking child-in-a-giant body that saves everyone and does it all right just because it's all he knows.

In other words, a switch from the person he was, inside and out. Sometimes that's a good thing, even an expected thing, but in this case, it shatters your heart, and takes some of your childhood innocence along with it.

From (and probably before) the moment he stepped onto an NFL field for the first time, John Matuszak was much larger than life – being over six and a half feet tall and nearly 300 pounds will do that for you. High speed was a factor too; busting through offensive lines to get one quarterback or running back after another necessitates it, and it helped him take home two Super Bowl titles in Oakland.

But, sadly enough, Matuszak's speed and lust for life didn't stop after he stepped off the field, even for the last time. Drinking, drugs, partying, women... eventually that sort of stuff catches up to you, and it did in his case. It's why watching *The Goonies*, and his other films, is a bit less enjoyable than it once was.

Matuszak first stepped onto the screen in the wakeup football drama *North Dallas Forty* in 1979, playing – such a stretch! – a hard-living lineman. In 1981, the same year his football career ended, he played the evil Tonda in Ringo Starr's non-English-speaking slapstick comedy *Caveman*.

"I wanted to be an actor even before I ever touched a football," remembered Matuszak, who fell in love with the profession during a childhood trip to *Rebel Without a Cause* (1955). "I looked at James Dean and I knew he must have had the time of his life getting paid to be so cool."

In late 1984, Matuszak got a phone call from his agent saying that Richard Donner wanted to meet with him. Matuszak strolled through the doors of Warner Brothers, where the director was waiting.

"He took one look at me and started jumping up and down," Matuszak said. "'This is Sloth, this is Sloth,' he kept saying. I didn't know if I should take that personally, but I figured there was something going on that I didn't know." Seconds later, he had the role.

"As Donner explained the part," he said, "I tried to stay calm and collected, but on the inside I was going wild." Not just for working with the man who'd done *Superman* (1978), but with the film's executive producer: Steven Spielberg.

Sloth was the last, tortured child of the evil Fratelli family, and a terrifying sight for the Goonies... until they realize his plight, get him on their side, and get saved from the Fratellis.

"For a job that's supposed to be glamorous, you sure work your ass off," he said of acting. "In that respect, football is similar to acting. In both professions, you have to 'play in pain.' If you're feeling lousy one day when you're shooting a film, you can't call in sick; you have to get up there and perform your part regardless. The moment the camera rolls, just as when the ball is snapped, you'd better be ready to move."

It took two months and a makeup man replacement, but Sloth's artificial look finally came through – which was just the beginning: Matuszak arrived at 5 a.m. every morning, and was in the makeup chair until 10.

Sloth's mask, he said, "was amazing. There were 15 overlapping pieces, including an electronic eye and ears, all of which would move via remote control."

Then he'd be hurrying up and waiting; the minor performers were required to get their work done early in the day, so Sloth couldn't step into the camera until later.

"I would spend six or eight hours doing nothing, lying in a trailer, going nuts," he said. "There were so many glues and adhesives used that my skin was breaking out all over. One of my eyes was even covered with makeup, so I couldn't read. I also couldn't leave the set because a riot would have started if anyone saw me."

But it worked, and it was worth it in the end. Millions of people still remember Sloth's name and turn in the flick (he even got to wear an Oakland Raiders shirt for an inside joke). Perhaps part of it had to do with Matuszak getting so far out of character – when you take a person who made a living tossing linemen around and slamming quarterbacks (on and off the screen) and turn him into a lovable child-like giant, it's talent, and that's not sarcasm.

In June 1989, four months shy of his 39th birthday, John Matuszak died of heart failure – helped along by years of drugs and alcohol abuse. His football and film fans got a strong dose of dark reality; even gentle giants could die young, and from the most unnatural of causes.

Films aren't the real thing, but oftentimes we watch them because we just wish they were – and sometimes we use them to remember people as we'd like to always see them. Matuszak was a depressing story, especially after enjoying the upbeat humor and redemptive nature of his autobiography, as we can't forget that the dark side of real life intervened for him in the end. But sometimes the characters who actors play are easier on us to remember than the people they were, and that's why I – and just about everyone I grew up with – still saw Sloth as something of an overgrown folk hero long after we knew that the man behind him had fallen.

Alice Barrett Mitchell: *Choke*

If you're battling an addiction, there's a few situations you should avoid.

If you're an alcoholic, bartending might not be a wise career choice.

If you're a bit too into gambling, you probably shouldn't move into an apartment above a casino.

And if sex has you in a vice grip, it's a bad idea to get locked inside a small room with a breathtaking brunette who just happens to be in her natural state.

Still, that's the situation in which Victor Mancini (Sam Rockwell) finds himself in the last half of *Choke*, Clark Gregg's 2008 cinematic adaptation of Chuck Palahniuk's novel. After spending much of the film battling sexual addiction – never really sure whether it's a fight he wants to win – Mancini recalls what first voyaged him on the journey: stepping into a plane, into the restroom, and into something that, unfortunately, only happens in the movies: a lovely lady who just wants to enjoy her last remaining jump away from the monotony of her everyday life... by buffing down and seducing the first lucky fellow that opens the door.

Alice Barrett Mitchell (left) played the strong-willed bombshell that unlocked the sexual addiction of Victor Mancini (Sam Rockwell) in *Choke* (2008).

Moments later – obviously, the scene isn't filmed in real time! – the lady puts her professional attire back on, not-so-gently says sayonara, and closes the door in every sense. It's the reality of surrealism, and Mancini, and we the audience, are left to wonder what exactly she did to us.

The actress wasn't a new face in entertainment; millions of daytime show fans probably recognized her right off the bat as *Another World* veteran Frankie Frame, the quirky detective who just happened to be a psychic. But as offbeat as Frankie had gotten during her seven years on the show, audiences had *never* seen her swing this far to the extreme!

Before she can speak the first syllable of her time as the most perfect of surprises, Alice Barrett Mitchell can hardly suppress a school-girl-esque giggle.

"I never in a million years expected to be cast in that role," she admits as her composure comes around. "That was an exercise, a leap of faith by my manager, and it was one of the most unexpected events in my life."

But not the first one; though she'd grown up around *Another World*, Barrett Mitchell never thought she'd one day be seen on its screens.

"My only exposure to soap operas was through my grandmother, who I lived with during the summer months," she recalls (the show kicked off in 1964, when she was in elementary school).

"Her favorite soap opera was *Another World*, so during the summer when I used to do her nails or eyebrows, I would watch the show. She would try to tell me the storylines, and I would say to forget it, because there was no way I could keep up with the show."

Decades later, she'd have an extra incentive to do so; after working sporadically as an actress throughout the 70s and 80s, the role of Frankie came calling in 1989.

"(Getting on the show) was a really happy coincidence," Barrett Mitchell says. "I had been struggling as an actress throughout my 20s, so this really helped me. I was just a lady who desperately needed not to be a bartender anymore."

Notwithstanding Frankie's psychic abilities, Barrett Mitchell tried to find some common ground between the lady and her character.

"Frankie was, in reality, something that evolved from me," she explains. "She always had a lot of spunk. She always was bold, stubborn, and those are the qualities that are in me. The mysticism, the psychic aspect, all of that stuff came in."

Frankie's vegetarianism evolved from Barrett Mitchell's refusal to eat a hot dog during a day of filming. Her ever-present crystal originally belonged to the actress.

After arriving in the show's Midwestern homeland of Bay City on a hunt for the person that killed her uncle, Frankie spent her early time on the show in a schoolyard-fight relationship with Cass Winthrop (Stephen Schnetzer). But just like popular Shakespeare couples Kate and Petruchio and Benedict and Beatrice, the two eventually evolved into the couple that moves from one side to the other in a love-hate relationship.

"The beauty of a soap opera is that it's unlike any other art form," Barrett Mitchell says. "You grow with the character and the character grows with you. You have to do your preparation if there's a major day coming up, like the day your child is hospitalized. You do your preparation under the circumstances. Frankie and I were pretty much a mind-meld."

After the couple faced Cass' genetic heart defect, Frankie suffered a miscarriage. She gave birth to a daughter, but the baby girl was stricken with the same ailment as her father, and the two could only watch helplessly as she lay in the hospital.

"That was intense," remembers Barrett Mitchell, who herself became a mother for the second time just before Frankie got pregnant. "That's when you have to do your emotional preparation. That's when you have to do your as-if work. That's when your training comes in. But I 'lived' Frankie in a lot of ways. It was easy to imagine how stressful that situation would be; as a mother, it's pretty easy to access that." Though her daughter recovered, another miscarriage ended Frankie's mothering abilities.

In 1996, Barrett Mitchell learned that her character was being killed off on the show.

"The problem with having been on a soap for so long is that I have one line on my resume that covers seven years of work," she says. "Many other actors or actresses my age have 40 other jobs, job after job filling up their resume. I had one line, making it look like that was *all* that I did. It looked like I had hardly worked at all. Casting directors, trust me, do not pay attention to soap operas. Leaving *Another World* was just like starting from scratch."

Undaunted, she showed up in several small roles over the next few years, including a short stint as a doctor on *One Life to Live*.

And in the end – again, in every sense – she came back to the lost *World*. After briefly coming back in 1999 as Frankie look-alike Anne (show viewers were betting that she'd steal Cass from his new lady), Barrett Mitchell learned that the series was being cancelled, and her last-ever role would be a reprisal of sorts.

In the finale, which aired in June 1999, Cass and new bride Lila (Lisa Peluso) were set to get married when, in some of daytime TV's most surreal moments, Cass was suddenly abducted by a gorilla. An animal specialist cooled things off, but there was another problem – the priest blew the couple off to head to a poker game. Thankfully, a friend saved the day, and the event, and the show, came to an end.

But for a moment, an old guest arrived. Frankie came to Cass in a dream and gave him permission to fall in love with Lila. She got to spend a moment with the daughter she hadn't gotten to raise.

"Since I had already mourned and moved on when I left the show back in 1996, it was a little different for me," Barrett Mitchell recalls. "It was great seeing the cast and crew again, but because I had already grieved Frankie's end back in 1996, it was a little less burdensome. I was glad to be able to say a final goodbye to the show as Frankie and not Annie, and grateful that Frankie was given a place in the finale because I felt Frankie had been a thread in the fabric of the show and had earned a place at the table."

A few years ago, Barrett Mitchell joined a theater company in Brooklyn. In the early summer of 2008, the group was preparing to put on its annual huge show. As the company director, Mitchell's workload wouldn't fit inside the *Titanic*.

Then her phone rang.

"My manager called me and told me, 'If you decide you don't want to do this, I completely understand. But I need you to know that I would never submit you on something if I didn't think the project was going to be worthwhile.'" Producers bringing Palahniuk's words to action had just lost a member of their cast (she was injured in an accident), and a replacement was on the docket.

First off, they needed Barrett Mitchell to come and audition that very day. Tough, but part of the daily life expectations for an actress.

Then the second provision came with the strength of a lightning bolt; the character was the sultriest of temptresses, one who prowled random locations for indiscriminate sexual encounters with the unsuspecting, one of the last hang-ups left in her repetitious lifestyle. Rockwell's Mancini becomes her latest (and probably not last) piece of willing prey.

"I knew that Chuck Palahniuk's *Fight Club* had been a huge success, and I adore Sam Rockwell," says Barrett Mitchell. "But I thought they would never hire me because I'm old. I'm a middle-aged lady. I had never been naked on the screen, and the time wasn't going to be then."

She hadn't read the book, the script, or even the sides – the individual scenes that performers are given to audition. On the subway to the audition, Barrett Mitchell checked over the material.

"I explained to (the casters) that there would be no callbacks, no scenes, no nothing," she says, "because once I was done, I had to go back and do my theater." She did a quick run-through of the lady, then headed back to work.

Hours later, they called back to confirm – Barrett Mitchell was their 'Woman of the Plane Restroom' (in the book, her name is Tracy). The problem was, they needed her in character the next day.

She and the rest of the company finished out their show and headed out to celebrate. As the sun started to rise the next morning, Barrett Mitchell looked over the script and tried to get to know her new self.

"After they're done, he asks her, 'Why do you do that?'" Barrett Mitchell recalls (the scene is shorter in the finished film, but longer in the book). "She thinks that he's asking, 'Why do you have anonymous sex in bathrooms?' She says, 'Because I've given up cigarettes, and coffee, and chocolate. I've given up everything else, and I'm not going to give up this. Don't think that it had anything to do with you.' That told me everything about her." Much of the dialogue was cut from the final project, sadly enough.

As well as the woman's style of dress, jewelry, and makeup, she continues.

"She dressed in a business shirt and skirt, a wedding ring, with special earrings," she explains. "It gave me so much to work with. It let me know how much was going on with this woman: that she's bored, a trapped person, and this is how she gets her relief. I was able to create an entire life very easily for this woman; this was her naughty little secret."

After learning of the role on a Thursday, Barrett Mitchell was performing it in the wee hours of Saturday morning. That kept in the spirit of the film, which was filmed in three weeks.

"I had this vision that she was working in upper management in an office, though probably not something she was very passionate about. She had children that she loved and a husband that she liked. I think that there's a large segment of the population that misses the end of youth, and she was trapped by what real life is, and I think that that's what these bathroom episodes were about. They made her feel like the 17-year-old doing something that her mommy didn't want her to."

Heading back home, Barrett Mitchell hoped her own children wouldn't pick up on the same message!

"I was thinking, 'Oh my God, how am I going to show my face in front of my kids?'" she says of viewing the scenes. "It's very difficult to watch. I have a lot of pictures of myself at 25 and 30, being thin with tight skin, and none of those things are true anymore. Especially in this culture that values youth above all, it's difficult. But once I get around my physical self, I think it's a great piece of work. The scenes were very respectfully shot so as not to expose too much. I'm proud that I had the nerve to go ahead with it."

It's a feeling that she, and many others in her profession, live to encounter.

"Only come into this business if you absolutely cannot imagine yourself doing anything else," she tells budding performers. "It's exceedingly difficult, but it is a very, very, VERY satisfying life if you're lucky enough to be working. There's nothing more thrilling in the world than being around actors and the other people in the business.

"One of the reasons that I love being in the business is because I love everybody on the set; I love the makeup and hair people and the cinematographers, and the crew. It's a neat, fun group of people.

But 99 percent of an actor's life is not working; 99 percent of an actor's life is looking for work. So you have to have a strong constitution for rejection, you have to have a strong constitution to get up and keep going, and you have to really, really want to do it."

Cindy Morgan: *Caddyshack*

We only wish it were that easy. We only wish it happened more often.

If only we could just walk up to link legends like Jack Nicklaus or Phil Mickelson and say, "Please teach me to hit the links like you!" and have it work. More specifically, we dream of meeting someone who just won a billion-dollar lottery and being able to query, "OK, what was your secret?"

There's no answers, not ones we have the patience for. There are things that you can't teach, you can't learn. Things you just hope for, and only happen to the luckiest of us.

There were plenty of reasons for *Caddyshack* (1980) to *not* work. A first-time director. A leading man new to the cinema world. A supporting cast that hadn't always subscribed to the whole teamwork theory. A storyline that changed by the day.

Cindy Morgan was lucky enough to land in the comedic gold mine that *Caddyshack* became in 1980, the Lacey Underall to Chevy Chase's self-loving golf pro Ty Webb.

And in the midst of it all, a new actress who wasn't sure what the hell she'd just gotten into. Then again, neither were most of the cast and crew.

Decades later, there's really no specific explanation on why the film became iconic in cinematic sports comedy. And she's not sure just how she became such a strong part of it.

It just… did. She just… did.

"We were having a good time," recalls Cindy Morgan. "You can't fake that. There were the best people in the business doing the one thing you can't plan. You can put all the best elements together, but it either happens or it doesn't. That thing they call movie magic? It happened. It just worked."

By the time the golfing flick rolled around in the fall of 1979, Morgan had worked in basically every entertainment field *except* film. Back home in Illinois, she'd called out to listeners and viewers on TV and radio, and even deejayed for a while in the Windy City.

Desire for camera work made her the next in an endless line of stardom searchers wandering west, and Morgan wound up in the City of Angels, commercialing for Irish Spring.

Finally came calling the film world.

Caddyshack was first intended to be all about those with one of the most thankless jobs in sports, right up next to referees, janitors, and groundskeepers: the club-carriers, the ones forced to lug a heavy load around while the golfers they follow try to make the shots and get the glory… and the ladies!

It had been a job that Harold Ramis, Brian Doyle-Murray, Murray's brother Bill, and others had worked through in their youth. Now Ramis, Doyle-Murray, and Doug Kenney had scripted their story to the screen, and, a year after helping script *Animal House* (1978), Ramis was debuting behind the camera.

Chevy Chase, still grabbing for the foothold of success he'd been searching for since *Saturday Night Live* (1975), would be there for a time as local pro Ty Webb, as would Doyle-Murray, Murray, and a fellow named Rodney Dangerfield, trying to adapt the success he'd found in stand-up comedy to the screen. Still, at the outset, everyone expected the film to revolve around the caddies, mainly Michael O'Keefe's Danny Noonan.

And since every hormone-crazed fellow of these films needs a young beauty to lust for, Lacey Underhall arrived, there to spend reluctant time with her curmudgeonly uncle Judge Smails (Ted Knight), himself fending off the loudmouthed blarney of Dangerfield's Al Czervik.

Even in a country club, surrounded several deep by those who, in true cinema fashion, can't wait to look straight down on the peasants of society, Lacey was there to be her true self. The one that flaunted to others what they dreamed of having and holding (some of their dreams came true!), and took the worry of what everyone thought of her straight off the priority list.

"Twelve years of Catholic school left me unprepared for this," Morgan recalls. "I had nothing to lose, and that gave me an edge."

One of the first times we got the visual pleasure of seeing Lacey, however, nearly pushed her straight over the dangerous side.

The caddies take a day off from club-lugging to relax in the pool, and Lacey can't help but snare a few stares as she strolls in; wearing high heels to a pool is a pretty good indication that one really *wants* such attention. But as she prepared to show Lacey off from the high dive, Morgan's nerves were waging their own personal war.

"I'm legally blind," she explains. "All they had were hard contacts back in 1979, and I couldn't wear them. I have a fear of heights, I couldn't dive, and I can barely swim. I had to climb the board blind, walk back and forth on the high board, and then spring, so they could cut to the 'real' diver. There I am in the water, blind, can't swim, don't know where the hell I am."

Fortunately for Morgan (though probably not for us!), her disability kept her from one of the flick's craziest times, where a young girl sees a candy bar floating in a jammed pool and mistakes it for excrement, causing *War of the Worlds*-level hysteria. Some called it a spoof of the legendary *Jaws* (1975) beach scene; others say it was based on a real incident from the screenwriters' past. Maybe, like so much else on *Caddyshack*, everyone just happened to get lucky at the same time.

As filming went on, things started to change, like, say, the storyline – which is kind of important. With Murray, Chase, and others (except one person, who we'll discuss shortly), finding more in their characters than the original script had offered, Ramis started letting them practice the mysterious acting art of improvisation. Murray's legendary speech about hitting the links with the Dalai Lama hadn't been written before, and neither had most of his other lines.

Soon the rest of the cast got in on the action, and Ramis wasn't far behind. On and off the set, the cast started making up all sorts of things as they went along.

"It was 1979, and I think you've got a good idea as to what was going on in that set," Morgan recalls. "With a bunch of young actors, and Harold directing his first film, he was smart enough to follow, and let us improvise. He followed us with a camera, whether we were doing a scene or not."

Lacey's oily rendezvous with Webb was without a script, Morgan says.

"Improv was right up my alley after five years of broadcasting," she remembers. "I had to react with Chevy, not act. He was driving the scene." Knight, known as one of Hollywood's top method performers, was quite irritated and uncomfortable about the film's impromptu manners of filming, she says.

"By then, the script was gone," Morgan says. "The original script was about the caddies, and that storyline went away. We decided to forget the script, get to the set, do hair, makeup, and wardrobe, then get out on the set, and say, 'OK, what are we doing today?' And go with it."

In perhaps Lacey's most risqué scene, she wasn't quite ready to follow her advice, Morgan admits. Gearing up for a mattress romp with O'Keefe, Morgan wasn't prepared to show off more than her acting talents.

She was told to wear her birthday suit to the shoot. She had an issue.

"Back in the ladies' room, I was thinking, what am I doing?" she says. "This isn't me!" Her agent told her to shut up and do it. They wouldn't be working together long. A producer threatened to kick her off the film and blackball the hell out of her name.

Morgan thought back to her past. Not only in the world of disc jockeying, but in sound engineering and other fields. Areas that, even today, women have some trouble breaking into.

"I started out soldering circuit boards for my dad at his auto parts plant in Chicago," Morgan says. "When there's a job to do, there's no BS. Get it done, and get it done on time. When it comes to doing a job and I agree to do it, it's going to get done and done properly." Finally, everyone agreed to do the scene, with just the actors and required filmers there to watch. In hindsight, it was Morgan's final transformation into her character.

"It caused me to go from being very nervous to being very focused," she says. "That was the day Lacey was born."

Right off the cuff came another scene, one that carried a bit more inside meaning than most of the audience had been aware. In the midst of war with a gopher, Murray's groundskeeping Carl Spackler finds his man-cave invaded by an errant white ball one night. Turns out it's Webb's, leading into an impromptu discussion about substance abuse and Carl's career hopes, culminating in Carl's recommendation of violence against Lacey's uncle and a true "buddies for life!" high-five.

It's not a long scene, nor does it have much to do with the main storyline — although such a distinction could apply to much of the film! The scene, written over the course of a single lunch, was created to give Murray and Chase a chance to work together, perhaps heal the troubles they'd had on *Saturday Night Live*.

Did it work? We really can't know. While the scene still comes off at full natural effect, the two haven't worked together since.

Just one more example of the magic that *Caddyshack* became, thrusting it to the upper levels of the best sports films in history, not just comedies. It's tough to even get a golf film off the ground, and, 1996's *Happy Gilmore* and *Tin Cup* notwithstanding, much fewer even try than most other sports (sadly, sports sequels rarely work, 1988's *Caddyshack II* becoming one more example there). But sometimes films like that just happen to work all the way out — just because.

Beata Pozniak: *JFK*

She'd spent months on end trying to learn more and more about her character. Beata Pozniak had researched articles from every printed medium, watched all the documentaries and news clippings, gone over every photograph she could find — without the help of the Internet, which wouldn't envelop the general public for a few more years — but the young actress wasn't satisfied.

Though a familiar face in her native Poland, Pozniak had spent the past few years looking to break through the glass ceiling of American performing, and now was her chance. Yes, the odds were against her — she'd get just a few minutes of screen time in a near three-hour, incredibly diverse film, competing against some of the biggest names in Hollywood.

Still, Pozniak had already passed her first obstacle just by getting the part, and it was time to send chance to the backburner and go for it all. So even with all the time she'd spent, all the books she'd perused, everything she'd done, she knew there was one last well to mine – and in the end, she found the last key to success, a truly invaluable source of preparation information.

"In Poland, I was fascinated with the American way of moviemaking," she recalls, "and so many awesome filmmakers. They were my heroes, and here I am, just dreaming of these people."

After putting a few entries in her acting resume overseas (she also was a calendar model for the Polish national soccer team), Pozniak headed across the ocean in 1985.

"I came (to America) to be in a free country," she says. "I was a very accomplished actor, but I was ready to risk it and start with zero. It was very important to me not to live behind the Iron Curtain. In Poland, there are no agents, no managers, no auditions. It's just like a town where everybody knows everybody and you just wait for a call from the director. It's a totally different system."

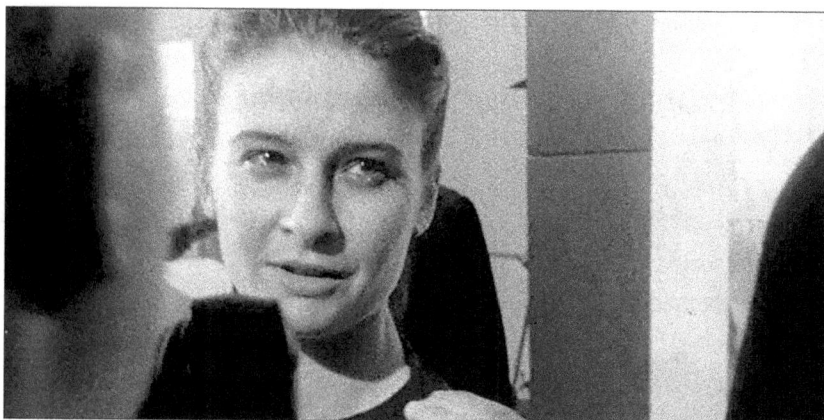

To portray one of the most infamous wives in American history, Beata Pozniak lived with the real Marina Oswald while getting ready to become her in *JFK* (1991).

Pozniak spent the last part of the 80s with small roles in film and television. Then, as the decade came to a close, she learned of an Oscar-winning director looking to put his next mark on the American audiences.

"I heard that Oliver Stone was working on a film called *JFK*," she says of the 1991 film. "It was kind of ironic, because I escaped from politics, and this was a political film. I wanted to work with Oliver Stone; I regarded him as a brilliant filmmaker. The assassination was one of the biggest tragedies in American history, if not world history, so I knew this was going to be a very important film."

Just about everyone who's made it to adulthood in America knows the name of Oswald, as in Lee Harvey Oswald, the only person ever arrested for the assassination of President Kennedy (how guilty he is, if at all, was a question that the film went after, and a matter for another discussion). But not nearly as many know the plight of Oswald's wife and widow Marina, who found herself hurled into the dark spotlight of the public eye after the assassination. Stone needed someone to bring her back to life, nearly three decades later.

"It was a small part, but I thought it was important," Pozniak says. "Coming from Poland, I didn't have a name; I was basically a nobody with name status, and I felt that every small part, every cameo, was important." Combing the newspaper, she learned that household monikers like Jack Lemmon, Walter Matthau, Donald Sutherland, and, in a rare dramatic role, John Candy, were doing short roles in the film.

"I thought about how I could even be considered as part of this project," she says, "but I thought I could at least try and get an audition, meet the producer, just to start the process."

And that's when her marathon in the libraries began. Magazine articles, footage from documentaries, newspaper stories, anything that Pozniak could find that so much as mentioned Marina's name was put to use. One day, she found a photo of the lady.

"I asked a trained photographer to shoot a picture of me as Marina," Pozniak says. "I shot a picture of her from the book, and me looking like her three different ways – when she was in Russia, when she came to America, and when she was more glamorous."

Pozniak sent her photos and resume to the casting directors. A few weeks later, they called back for a meeting.

"They let me know that I'd have to improvise, with no script, no lines," she says. "That is very unusual, for an actor to come in and improvise and make their own lines; what would the character say and do?"

Back in the library, Pozniak tried to imagine how Mariana had felt in her most infamous moments. What would she say under pressure? What would she wear, and how would her hair look? What was she like in a normal, relaxed social setting?

"I knew from the news footage what she would say and how she would dress," Pozniak says. "At the audition, I dressed like I had seen her dress in the articles. I knew that she was fascinated with (longtime French actress and model) Brigitte Bardot, so my hair was like Brigitte Bardot. I had to imagine that I was being interrogated. I'm here with the FBI, how they would put a spotlight on me, put me on camera, on tape, and I had to imagine that I was being interrogated."

The "cops" grilled their pretend suspect, asking her where she was during the shooting. They demanded to know how she and Lee had met, how long they'd been married, everything.

"Thanks to my research, I knew she never called him Lee," Pozniak says. "She always called him 'Alka,' or 'Aleek' (the Russian version of the name). I answered EVERY SINGLE QUESTION as Marina Oswald. I knew every single answer. She was a chain smoker, so at one time, I took out a cigarette. I had tears in my eyes. I *was* Marina, basically."

Shaking with both nervousness and a sense of accomplishment, Pozniak headed home. Another call was waiting for her. This time, she had to do a full scene in Russian.

"I'm at a party, to see if my language was full enough," she says of the scene. "It was like an exam.

I treated it like my first audition. I had to speak Russian. I had to show what Marina would be like if she was elated and happy. They wanted different angles and different scenes. They wanted to see my range."

Pozniak's phone rang once more. This time, the "casters" told her that Stone himself wanted to meet with her.

She'd taken a quick break from her Marina research to look over the filmmaker's background, and checked out all of his previous works (such as 1986's *Platoon* and 1989's *Born on the Fourth of July*, both of which brought Stone Oscars for Best Director).

"I wanted to understand his style of filmmaking," she explains. "I wanted to understand the way he worked with actors. He's a very fast thinker, a very fast decision-maker."

Her words came true quickly in their first meeting. Pozniak headed toward Stone's office, and saw a few people in line. She got comfortable, expecting to be there about an hour.

Two minutes later, everyone else was gone, and she was in.

"Oliver said for me to do the same thing I had done in front of the camera for the casting directors," she says. "He wanted me to do the same thing, just in front of him. He said, 'It's education for me.'"

Like an eager pupil, Stone kept interjecting on his instructor.

"Every time I did anything, he'd say, 'OK, your English is too good!' or 'Can we try that again?' It was interesting to work that way with him, and I think he saw how flexible I was in the scene when he kind of guided me, or broke my thought pattern, or my emotional state. I tried to use a heavier accent, like Marina would do."

Stone asked that she imagine being Marina as an angry housewife, one ticked that her husband was staying out late instead of coming home for the night.

"That was (all he told me)!" she says. "There were no lines; I just had to act it out. I tapped into that emotion. I screamed, I shouted. I was angry. I was in tears. As a mother, I needed him here! (Lee and Marina had two daughters.)"

But Stone still wasn't satisfied.

"He said to me, 'You know, you need to be more angry. I really need to see some anger here. You are so upset that you're really losing it.'" Pozniak went to the extreme, in every sense of the word.

"I took everything I found in his office, and started smashing it against the wall," she says. "He was so surprised, but that was what he needed. The director asked for more, and I gave it to him. I took his books, papers, threw them up and down and everywhere in a huge mess. I was screaming and crying and shouting, I was frustrated. I was speaking half English, half Russian. These little details really helped me in all the interviews I read, because I could use any of them in my improv."

It worked – she got the part. But checking over the script, Pozniak couldn't help feeling that there was something else she needed to do, someone else with whom she needed to meet.

"When you're playing someone who's still alive, it's different than if you're playing Catherine the Great or some other historical figure that is gone, and you just have to imagine what they would say or do," she says. "I thought it was a bigger responsibility, since her family is still alive, and wondered if they would want to be part of this project." Through her research, Pozniak learned that the real Marina still lived in Dallas.

"I called the office and asked if I could really meet her," she remembers. "After all the research I did, I was a little confused, because there were a lot of theories about her. I was very anxious about that, because I just wanted to give her justice."

The filmmakers were concerned that Marina might not want to get involved; she'd since remarried, and just wanted to fade into the background. But Stone gave permission to write to Marina, and Pozniak eventually met with her (she, along with fellow *JFK* stars Kevin Costner, Sissy Spacek, and Gary Oldman, who played Lee himself, headed to Dallas to do advance work for the film, a few months before filming started).

Pozniak met with some locals that knew the Oswalds, as well as some police officers that had been on the job when the murder occurred. Then she finally found her "role model."

"I got to meet Marina, and it was sheer joy because I could hear her point of view," Pozniak says, "and I would write down some things that happened that were not in any book. With that information, I could go back to Oliver with a scene. I could write down the dialogue between her and Lee, what really happened. I could show it to Gary, memorize it, show it to Oliver. She was a beautiful woman with red hair, very stunning." There were scenes of the two meeting at a party, getting acquainted, and falling in love.

The two sat down for some short conversations; Marina had shown up with her daughter and some of her friends, and brought some pictures of her youth in Leningrad.

"You have to build a kind of relationship first," Pozniak says. "But I think she was curious as to who would play her." Then Marina made an offer Pozniak hoped for, but never really expected.

"She asked me, 'You have all these questions for me. Instead of staying in a hotel, why don't you come stay with me?'" Pozniak says. The two would live together for months.

"I had access to a lot of photographs and information that we didn't have before. I saw some footage, where she is dressed in a very glamorous dress, her hair really beautiful. She's thanking the Warren Commission for helping her." Pozniak brought her idea to Stone, and it ended up in the film. All the while, she kept learning about her subject.

"An acting detail that I saw at her home was she would keep her cigarettes in her refrigerator," Pozniak says. "She would go in the fridge, take out a pack, put it back, and while finishing the old one, she already had a new one in her hands. If you were making that up as an actor, who would believe it? I had to use that. These are the kinds of ideas that I got from being in her house and learning from her; her body language, how she sat, how she'd smoke, how she'd look at me. That was great for my character's development."

Pozniak even met film focal point Jim Garrison on several occasions (portrayed by Costner in the film, Garrison played the Supreme Court Chief Justice Earl Warren in his own story. He died in October 1992).

"Jim Garrison told me, 'You did so much research, if I ever need (a new attorney), I'll hire you!'" she says.

Watching over the filming, Pozniak hoped that the film would inspire just as many viewers to check out the facts of the assassination – in other words, to try to decide what truly happened on their own, rather than what was told to them by the media, by the politicians, by others.

"Can we call (Lee) the alleged assassin?" she says. "This film has many questions; it makes people think, read books, articles, questions about what really happened. What was in the truth? Was Lee Oswald a patsy? So many questions. It's an important film for students and future generations to see and think for themselves about what really happened." In real life, Marina wavered on her husband's innocence (though Jack Ruby ended the national matter by shooting Oswald dead a few days later in Dallas; no one else was ever brought to justice in the matter, and Ruby, played by Brian Doyle-Murray in the film, died less than three years after the murder).

Just after the film came out, Pozniak found herself the subject of a new interrogation; had Marina been portrayed by herself or by a performer?

"That was one of the things that many people didn't know until after the film came out, that Oliver had used an actress to portray Marina," she says. "It was interesting, that when you do a lot of research, and you become the character, a lot of people don't know that you played the part, that it was just grouped news clippings. It was funny, but also flattering, in the long run. I think Marina was really happy in the end that the film was made."

Stone got another Best Director nomination, and his film was a Best Picture contender (Jonathan Demme and his *Silence of the Lambs* took the prizes) – and Pozniak kicked her career to the next level.

"It's important to dream and see what you can do. (After) I played a doctor on *Melrose Place* (seven episodes in 1993), I was getting offers as a doctor. Then I was in *Mad About You* (1993), as someone totally different." She played a maid who was in love with Paul Reiser's character. That same year, Pozniak starred in Stone's futuristic sci-fi miniseries *Wild Palms*.

"People don't really know how I look," Pozniak says. "If it's a comedy or something political, I look very different. If you play many villains, people always want to see you as a good villain. For me, if it's a sitcom, if it's a drama, if it's a television series, that's what I'm thriving for. I call my journey an adventure in growth. I like to study my craft and learn more about myself. That's why I became an actress; I like to surprise myself. It's important to take risks and surprise yourselves occationally. We can tap into all those unknown emotions or reactions."

That's why, for her, acting is a building with no ceiling. It's a place where the partakers can never stop learning. It's somewhere where there's always something new to try, a new character to develop, a new persona to take on.

"Find your passion," she says to upcoming actors. "Who is your hero? Who inspired you? Find that, and study that. There's a passion within people that if you work hard, people will want to work with you. They'll give you a break. Everything is possible if you dream."

Emma Ridley: *Return to Oz*

Royalty. Magic. She was experiencing it all.

With the flowing gown of requisite princess garb around her, the young woman smiled down at her welcoming crowd, there to follow her through a harmed land, back to wonder and prosperity. But these types of princesses don't have to do everything themselves; they're lucky enough to inject imagination into reality, and she did so again and again, showing the population that things would be much better very soon.

She'd done this sort of thing for years. So had generations of other girls around the globe that had been enchanted by Disney fairytales, who'd dreamt of stepping into the magic lands of Cinderella, Aurora, and so many other young women of magical monarchy. Ruling worlds with the flick of a wand.

But Emma Ridley went a bit farther than most. She'd walked straight up to the line between reality and fantasy and taken a joyful leap across it. For a few brief months, she didn't just have to just *think* about becoming a princess, or even a queen.

Half a century after American field audiences went to Oz, Emma Ridley welcomed back Fairuza Balk's new Dorothy Gale as Princess Ozma in *Return to Oz* (1985).

The Land of Oz has been a welcome place of escape for over a century. L. Frank Baum had churned out dozens of its stories to the page as the 1900s got going, and youths of today still crowd around the TV to see the same magical tale that audiences of their great-grandparents ushered into pop culture around the globe.

But even after decades of venturing to the land of munchkins, the Yellow Brick Road, and the man behind the curtain, very little of the story had actually been told. Baum's story had stretched for dozens of books, and almost half a century had been long enough to wait to add another chapter to the cinematic tale of Oz.

After arriving on the literary scene in the first months of the millennium with *The Wonderful Wizard of Oz*, Baum had published *The Land of Oz* in 1904, then *Ozma of Oz* three years later. The 1904 story introduced a young boy named Tip, looking to escape from his keeper, the witch Mombi. The scarecrow's now the ruler of Oz — looks like he figured out that triangle equation from the first *Wizard*! — but there's an army ready to take him out. That is, of course, until Tip and his pals run into a lady named Glinda, who lets them know that a few years before, the wizard had handed a baby girl named Ozma off to Mombi to keep the child from rightfully ruling Oz, and that she'd transformed Ozma into Tip.

With Ozma back to normal, Oz becomes hers again. Her title tale begins with Dorothy back in action, a storm stronger than the infamous tornado knocking her off a boat before washing ashore in the Land of Ev, ruled by the Nome King. Ozma and Dorothy meet — the Cowardly Lion is also back in the game — and whomp the King before Dorothy heads back home.

Creating 1985's *Return to Oz* would be tough before Ridley or anyone else got anywhere near it. It's awfully difficult to take two novels and combine them into a film, and still leave it short enough to hold the attention span of the series' typical young viewers. The crew decided to make Dorothy the focal point again, and hand Ozma the bookending side of things.

Once again, Ridley, like so many other young women, had dreamed of becoming a part of her own personal Oz. The role brought things to truthful fruition.

"The role of Ozma was a dream come true for me because I was twelve years old, and I dreamt of being a Disney princess," recalls Ridley, already a ballet veteran at the time, "and then I got to get dressed up every day in beautiful clothes and wave a magic wand, and run around a mirrored ballroom. It was great fun, spending hours on set, running around with Fairuza on set."

First, however, she had to find a side of Oz that not enough were aware of. Ridley roared into Baum's words. She watched the visual adaptations of the story, on stages and small screens. She anaylzed critics' viewpoints of Ozma and her work, and the rest of the queen's counterparts.

But Ozma's not a princess at first — until the last tenth of the film, she's not even named. Dorothy, somehow younger than she was in the first film, can't sleep from her Oz memories, and Aunt Em (now Piper Laurie, and it's tough to imagine a bigger switch from her psycho mother turn in 1976's *Carrie*!) takes her for treatment. Dr. Worley and Nurse Wilson (Jean Marsh, not quite as scary as she'd be in 1988 as the evil queen in *Willow*) are there to champion the whole new electroshock therapy practice, but it's clear that they don't really know what might happen to this little girl.

Fortunately, she's not alone. A mysterious young woman arrives to feverishly let her know that those ominous screams are from those already damaged by the treatment, and, in a storm stronger than the one that sent Dorothy to Oz the first time, the two are off, with Wilson in cold-blooded pursuit.

"I tried to make her very calm, very studious, not crazy and wild like I am now," Ridley says of her character. "I wanted to be humble and befriend Dorothy and wanted her to know that I was on her side, and that we were the only children in this crazy world in the reality and in the movie. I didn't wear any shoes, very country, not a lot of makeup." As the two were in Kansas, Ridley's natural English accent was, shall we say, a bit diluted for the time being.

Toppling down a riverbank, her savior's swept away in the waves, but Dorothy slips into a passing cage to float to... well, no one's sure.

"The river scenes were like a hot Jacuzzi," Ridley says, "all inside, in a sound stage, Fairuza and I splashed away, and the crew was upset, telling us it wasn't safe. It's all make-believe; when you're a little kid, it's pretty easy to play pretend, so that's all we did."

With the Yellow Brick Road all messed up, Emerald City in ruins, and the Tin Man and Cowardly Lion turned to stone, Dorothy and her pet chicken dodge the evil wheelers (who wouldn't be ticked, with wheels for hands and feet?) and evil princess Mombi (Marsh, still lovelier than her green, broom-riding, cackling colleague from the first film). A kindly robot named Tik-Tok, a moose-headed guy named the Gump, and awkward galoot Jack Pumpkinhead (Brian Henson did Jack's voice and some of his puppetry) are along for the trip, which soon has them at the Nome King's castle.

The young girl appears to save all of her friends, but film villains, even the cartoonish sort, don't play fair, and it looks like everyone's done for. But the chicken saves the day, dropping an egg into the King's mouth – and as we all should know, those things are like cyanide when it comes to Nomes!

Back in those familiar red shoes, Dorothy wishes for the City to be back to normal, and atop the lion – who walked on all fours and didn't speak this time! – she leads the group back home, surrounded by tons of thankful Oz-ians. Then, however, she notices someone in a mirror who isn't her.

Indeed, it's the girl who rescued her back at the start. But even we might not recognize her: the hair, the makeup, especially the attire has, shall we say, vastly evolved at high speed.

"I wanted a complete difference between the little girl that didn't have a name and the princess in Oz," Ridley says. "I tried to make it diverse." She's been the young queen all along, trapped in Mombi's mirror until Dorothy vanquished everyone. With the special effects that snared the film an Oscar nomination (*Cocoon* beat it), Dorothy helps her step straight through the glass to freedom.

Several months had actually passed between Ridley's first appearance and filming her second. Once there, she got to live out all of her Ozma fantasies, more than once.

"We got to re-shoot all of the Oz scenes," she recalls, "because the first time they did it, they had me in a gold dress, which they thought didn't stand out enough in the gold ballroom. Much to our delight, we got to re-shoot all the Oz scenes with me wearing a beautiful white/emerald green ball gown. It was actually very itchy and very uncomfortable. They had to squeeze me in, because I was already in adolescence and getting a little bit busty by the time the end of the film came." The time of year's three-digit temperatures probably didn't help much either.

Still, her ruby slippers fit fine, and Ozma used them to send Dorothy back home. Unlike the first one, this whole film doesn't seem to be a dream, as Dorothy awakens aside a river, rather than home in bed, a certain small dog leading a group of searchers to her.

"It was a completely different experience to watch it, as it was to film it," Ridley says.

But after Ozma helped Ridley live out her own dreams over and over again, a few dark aspects of reality crept toward her life. When one steps – or is unintentionally tossed – straight into the nationwide entertainment spotlight at such a young age, it's tough to know where to land. Playing a warm, wholesome model of morality is tough enough on the screen with tons of time to practice and rehearse; doing so in real life, when film cameras are replaced by tabloid ones, often much louder, much ruder, and far too commonplace, it's impossible not to show a bit of fault.

This book is not going to be a fluff piece of tell-all garbage; suffice it to say that Ridley's private life became far too public for a few years in her English homeland, with the drugs, the marriages, the divorces, the young motherhood tales that, as we as Americans know far too well, tabloids just love to beat straight into the ground. But that's over now – just as actresses like Drew Barrymore showed America, Ridley's living proof that one can walk through a few muddy years and come out clean.

And she's not ashamed.

"I'm just one of those people that loved to experience everything firsthand," says the proud mother of three. "I wanted to try everything in life. Everything's a journey and everything's a lesson, and I feel like I'm still learning, and there's no need to ever arrive at the destination, because I'm still enjoying the journey."

That dancing she's been doing since before visiting Oz became Ridley's next career; she now owns a successful dance school in California. But acting isn't so far in her past that it may not someday find a way to the future; with her kids growing up a bit, "I'm starting to get the bug back!" Ridley gleefully admits in May 2014.

"Enjoy the process and stay grateful and say thank you every day, to the universe, to God, to whoever you want to thank every day, for your life and who you are," she says to hopeful performers (Ridley credits becoming born again to her career renaissance). "It's all a self-journey, with self-love, self-empowerment, and self-betterment. If we can learn a few things every day, we're doing great."

Oh, did you happen to notice the other lady that Ridley mentioned a few paragraphs ago? A woman with a very uncommon name who was faced with the task of following in Judy Garland's legendary footsteps as Dorothy without even getting to wear ruby slippers while taking them?

Yes, the Fairuza she spoke of was indeed a debuter named Balk, the same one who'd grow up to be the beauty that entertained and sometimes terrified us in everything from *The Craft* in 1996 to *American History X* two years later.

Not surprisingly, the search for the new Dorothy raged across the globe; this wasn't something anyone wanted to even take the chance of miscasting. As the search roared to the top of North America, Balk first tried out at a cattle call in Vancouver.

As the cuts kept coming and numbers kept dropping, she'd go south for another tryout in Los

Angeles, then across the water to London. Finally, Balk took the Gale gold. Like Ridley, she got started on the *Oz* pages.

"Especially for children, we all want that magical place to disappear to, to be able to go to a world of fantasy," Balk remembers, "and we create that for ourselves as children when we play. It's imagination, and it's an extension of that. For children, as well as for adults, this is that whole world that represents that. As you grow older, if you lose your imagination, you're like a hollow shell. You lose a big part of access to your soul."

Unlike Garland, Balk wasn't just *portraying* a preteen; she actually still was one at the time. As filming stretched into months, Balk started to realize what she'd gone in for with the whole acting thing. She'd carry what she'd learn into more of a successful child-to-adult career switch than many of her colleagues have been able to pull off.

"Every night, I'd go over the scenes for the next day with my mom," she says. "I'd memorize them until I had them down. It was a lot of work, and I think towards the end of the film, I got a little tired, and that's when I began to realize that it was *work*. If you wanted to do it, you had to get up every morning and go and be a professional. As a child, that's kind of a hard concept to grasp, and you have to grasp it like *that*. There's no fooling around."

Sara Rivas: *Manic*

Even in the movies, there's not always a happy ending. The protagonists don't always win, the villains don't always get vanquished, and uplifting music doesn't always rise right up and carry our spirits with it as the credits roll, us walking out of the theater with newfound inspiration we got from fictional characters.

Sometimes we know in advance that that's probably how things are going to go, and films like *Manic* (2001) give us that early impression. Based on a thousand true stories, it's the story of a group of youths victimized even more by the normal perils of the maze-like minefield ominously known as "The Teenage Years."

Pain from within and without. Anger, utter fury at the unjust world that dealt us this hand and wouldn't let us exchange our cards. Even a bit of fear and perhaps remorse, although those can only be displayed in private. Group and psychiatric home residents are fighting the same battle, but those in these places are hardly any kind of team. No partnership here — people in this type of situation are hurting, and it's much easier to spread that around that go heads up against it.

This sort of realism in films doesn't often have the most upbeat of endings, and we expect this. But "un-upbeat" doesn't necessarily mean sad. There's quite a bit of room between happy and heartbreaking. Those two may be the extremes, but there's a huge lot in the middle with plenty of options to fill it up.

One is hope. A reason to believe that the end result of what we see isn't where the residents, the counselors, and everyone else locked in battles with enemies that can never really be defeated hope for… but one that could be soon. Much like the addictions that weld us to booze and drugs – legal or otherwise – mental illness can be held back, but never exterminated. Fighting these things and helping others in the same sort of war, we can only hope that we'll be part of the select few that find a way to rise a bit above them and stay there long enough.

That's what happens in *Manic*. As in most such places – both real and cinematically created – no one gets out unscathed on the inside or out, but some do get out and get a bit better in the bargain. The finale gives us reason to believe that the film's main man will soon become one of these – and someone we met early on, in a sense, already has.

Sara Rivas' Sara (right) became one of many *Manic* youths in the 2001 film.

Sara's an outspoken and all kinds of proud member of the Goth community, one always looked down upon by a society that's always been too intimidated to look them in the eye. The makeup, the dark clothes, the artistic ability – these are things you expect to see. The anger that brought her to this place is more of a stigma of her group that outsiders project on them, but it sometimes comes true. And, as Sara details the family brawls that landed her in the *Manic* land, she becomes a good reason for people to get prejudicial on her colleagues.

"She's the teenager that's angry and has issues with her parents," says Sara Rivas, her real-life moniker a coincidental resemblance to the character. "I know this from personal experiences with my friends, so I can totally relate to everything."

Two years after making her film debut with a similar role in a dissimilar setting, a vampire lass in the rom-com *She's All That*, Rivas stepped into Sara's world, the overwhelming self-esteem she delves from her art not quite strong enough to overcome the rage towards her mom that got far out of control.

"I've had friends that had some issues who stayed in group homes," Rivas says. "I felt like I knew a lot about it, hearing about their issues and problems with their parents. Some of my friends have come to live with (my family) because they were having issues with their parents. It was all kind of similar."

Still trying to make the difficult switch from adorable child star to strapping, intimidating leading man, Joseph Gordon-Levitt got ready to say goodbye to television on *3rd Rock from the Sun* (1996), and the lead in *Manic* was FAR from that or anything else he'd done (*Manic* was filmed in 2001, but not released for two more years). He had flipped on another kid during a baseball game and planted a bat through his cranium, and now Gordon-Levitt's Kyle tried to figure out just what this new world was all about. Surrounded by people much more accustomed to violence than him, and those who'd been its victims, he couldn't know where he was – and, almost always the case at first with residents of any age, he reacted with anger.

There are drug users. Just about everyone's a fisticuff veteran, and most of them were the ones to get it going. Some of them have done it to themselves. One of them may or may not have the dirtiest of issues with kids.

Sara's in the midst of it, not the slightest bit reluctant to dish out the details of her absolute rage towards her mom – almost as much as reminding all of how wonderful her art is. Her own sky-high self-esteem, rare for any group home member, is as intimidating as anything or anyone else there, especially to Tracy (Zooey Deschanel), whose own self-regard is miles under sea level as she tries to hang out with a fellow member of the home's gender minority.

Getting ready for these scenes, Rivas and the rest had visited other similar homes and met others in the situation. They'd sat in on the same group sessions they were now acting out.

"It all relates," she says. "It doesn't matter where you are, how much money your parents have, because a lot of these teenagers still had the same problems. It's true of the world."

Along the way, Rivas found her own role model.

"I met this girl who had *the* look," she remembers. "She had a lot of dark eye makeup."

Much of the dialogue in the group scenes came from these experiences, and the actors themselves, rather than the script, she continues.

"I tried to grab elements from my own life," Rivas says. "Stuff I knew, stuff I'd heard from (the homes), and kind of went from there. It was mostly my own experience. I definitely had personal experiences with teenage angst. I think teenagers just don't know where they belong – too old to act like children, too young to be adults. They get lost in this high school world with other teenagers that can be really cruel and don't realize that it's only temporary."

The residents keep discussing, sometimes in high tones and obscenities. Physical violence breaks out more than once. But we notice that the same pitch-black tones that we saw on Sara's outside and could feel from her inside are starting to lighten up just a bit.

"The idea was that as my character gets better, her mask of eye makeup kind of lessens," Rivas explains. "We used less black."

Still, Sara's art gave her the chance to use all kinds of colors, particularly in her spot-on rendition of a work of Van Gogh. It's her idea of freedom; someone else feels the painter was expressing the same self-created mental prison that pushed the artist to take his own life.

A different kind of artistic expression, however, would tone arguably the film's most important scene. Between sessions, Sara, Lyle, Tracy and everyone else are looking to keep their minds occupied. Someone's gotten hold of a CD player, and one resident's got a great idea.

Music as angry as the people blasts. Lyle and another fellow start the infamous style of dance known as moshing. They start knocking into each other, but it's playful, not malicious. Others start to run around the room.

More and more start to join in.

Pillows fly and trash cans follow. Tables are toppled. Things are thrown.

And it's also one of the first senses of unity we've seen in the film. Just like in a real mosh pit, people knock into each other and laugh. They lift each other up. One person even helps another into a wheelchair and pushes him around. Sara uses the wall for a soccer ball, then takes her own wheelchair ride. As things start to calm down, Lyle and others lay on the floor, laughing in exhaustion and disbelief at what they've done.

It's as if, for a few minutes, they're all free again, free to re-visit a place that many of them probably enjoyed in the most thorough of ways during their time "outside." All the emotion they can't let out through the group discussions is forcing its way outward in the physical sense.

One of the place's head doctors (Don Cheadle, one of Rivas' biggest incentives to step into the cast) seems to realize this. A colleague offers to shut the whole thing down — the doc waves them off.

"We had a blast doing that scene!" Rivas remembers. "We were allowed to go crazy, to get out our aggression. (The crew) was like 'OK, go!' and when they saw something they liked, they said 'OK, do it again! Kick the wall again, now from another angle.' Who doesn't have fun throwing stuff about?"

Eventually, Sara's look and attitude get even brighter, and she's allowed to leave, with Tracy now left without her best friend. But her work, in a sense, will be seen again.

In the closing moments, Lyle's just about convinced that he's as healthy as her, ready to leave, legally or otherwise. Roaring out of the place, he makes his way to a nearby bus terminal. As his ride back to freedom arrives, its side shows a copy of the same painting Van Gogh drew and Sara redid. Remembering the debate of its meaning, Lyle realizes that he's not ready to go back out, and heads back in.

Again, it's not the same finale that movies often show. It's an ending without finality. Not every question gets answered or problem solved. But there's still hope, reason to believe that things for the *Manic* group will be OK. More ready than before to get the help he now sadly admits he needs, Lyle's heading back for it. Maybe the doctor's work will work out. Maybe, just maybe, he'll be OK. And maybe Sara will *stay* OK.

Barbara Rosenblat: *Orange is the New Black*

Heartwarming. Uplifting. Inspirational.

These words are few and far between in the prison system. Rarely do we hear or can we say them about many people involved – the prisoners who find themselves locked in a lonely, violent, angry world (of their own doing), or the administrative staff who are forced to toss their own sense of mortality out the barred and locked doors to keep them in line.

Still, when we're watching these people in the movies – dramatized or documented – we often forget that, despite being locked in something not entirely unlike a human zoo, they're still people. Before they came to prison, they had friends. Families. Jobs. Careers. And as difficult as life in a prison can be, many of them are still up against battles that affect those that never spent any time at all behind bars.

Fighting an enemy that, even after decades of hard warfare with the medical community, still keeps finding thousands of ways every year to take its victims to a sad defeat. One that, once it arrives, never truly leaves. But still, a fight that enough victims have lived through to know that, to every possible extent, it can be won.

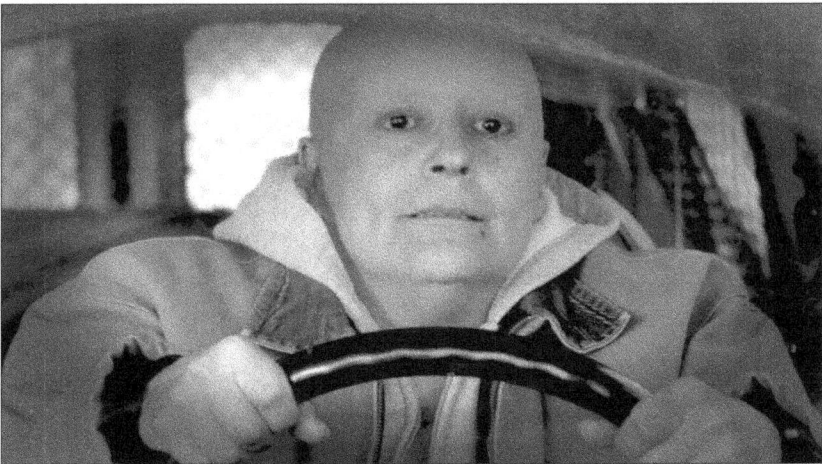

Miss Rosa (Barbara Rosenblat) makes a deserved – well, in some ways – prison escape in the last moments of the second season of *Orange is the New Black* in the summer of 2014.

On both the personal and professional levels, Barbara Rosenblat has been on both sides of the cancer fight; it took the actress's own father. But a character she portrays has put a different human side not just on the disease and its victims, but on a place that society doesn't spend much time even considering, let alone caring about.

"Various people have written to me over the past few years," Rosenblat says of her role as Miss Rosa on *Orange is the New Black* (2013). "It's been very touching. One young man wrote to me, saying my character allowed him to come to terms with his grandmother's journey when she got sick, that he was better able to understand how she dealt with her own illness."

Looking to corner even more of the home entertainment market in 2013, Netflix found the perfect foil in the literary works of Piper Kerman, who did a year in prison for drugs and money laundering. Kerman's 2010 memoir told the tale that would become the company's first original hour-long dramedy.

Early on in the series opener on July 11, 2013, Piper – her last name now Chapman, in the body of Taylor Schilling, makes her way down the hallowed, ominous halls of Litchfield Penitentiary, surrounded by every prison's gaggle of involuntary visitors; the oddballs, the ones who seem to prefer prison to the outside, deniers that just *know* that their sentence will be commuted tomorrow, and those that use the same take-charge assertions that put them to the top of the crime world to get some power here (including one we'll briefly meet in a few paragraphs).

But one doesn't seem to be worrying about any of that. The gal on the bunk below Piper is too old, too tired, and too sick to worry about much except today, and maybe not even all of today.

We don't know why Miss Rosa's at Litchfield, and we're not really worried about it just yet. Her baldness is a sadder sign of a much more current, important issue.

Ovarian cancer, which seems to be already beating her, she sadly confesses.

Still, it keeps her pretty safe in prison. "Nobody fucks with cancer!" Rosa asserts. In a sad way, we only wish she could.

Orange wasn't the first time Rosenblat had ventured into the criminal side of acting, and we're not just talking about her few one-shot deals on *Law and Order: Special Victims Unit* (1999) either. TV wasn't her only medium in the deal. In 2005, video game fans saw her act out local druggie dame Reni Wassulmaier in *Grand Theft Auto: Library City Stories*; a year later, she and Wassulmaier came back for *Vice City*.

"I was a crazed, anti-sexual, coke-sniffing megalomaniac," Rosenblat remembers proudly. "I didn't think I'd ever get such street cred again until I did Rosa."

After just about two days of rehearsal, she stepped in to become a part of one of the video game world's most popular (and, as the two are so often paired, controversial) sagas.

"It was a motion-capture role, where they animate the body and leave the face blank," she explains. "When doing scenes, we acted like we were holding guns, getting off a plane with people on our left. They put all these weird things on your body, and you shoot it. You see your avatar. You move your arms, and she moves. I was looking like the South American Hilary Clinton!"

When she first got involved with *Orange*, Rosenblat went to play another lady with power: she wanted to be Red, the former Russian restaurateur whose power in the prison kitchen extends throughout the facility.

"They didn't know if Red would be Russian or Greek, and Russian is an accent I enjoy doing," says Rosenblat, actually an Anglo-American Polish Jew. "I was nervous as hell when I went in to meet the production people. I did this vitriolic two pages of screaming and snarky language."

A member of the casting crew that would win an Emmy that year for putting together the show's performers reached out and turned off the camera.

"She said, 'How is it that we've never met?'" Rosenblat laughs. "She said, 'I'm going to get you in this prison, one way or another!'"

Two days later, her agent called. Bad news was, she wouldn't be Red; that prize went to Kate Mulgrew, who'd already broken serious sci-fi ground as Janeway, the highest-ranking woman in the *Star Trek* saga. Good news, the crew member had still kept her promise: Rosenblat would be Miss Rosa.

"I asked what has she done, where's she from, does she have a last name?" Rosenblat says. "He said he had no clue. Oh, but she had cancer, and would I shave my head?"

Miss Rosa wasn't around much during the *Orange* freshman year, with Piper and her battles with ex-lover Alex Vause (Laura Prepon, light years from *The 70s Show*) getting quite a bit of time, along with Red's loss to culinary control, not to mention, in her typical scene-stealing fashion, Natasha Lyonne as Nicky Nichols, always there with a spoon ready to stir hell out of every pot.

"I was only in about five episodes," Rosenblat says. "(Miss Rosa) was very faintly outlined. I just knew that she was really, really sick. There was one scene where she said, 'I coulda been a *jefe*!' That's Spanish, so she must be Spanish. Let's give her an accent and see if anyone notices."

It worked – Miss Rosa got a bit more spotlight in season two, and never once had to lose Rosenblat's actual hair to do it.

"If I shaved my head for five episodes, the rest of the year, I'd look pretty silly," she says. Josh Turi, who'd taken home three Emmys for makeup work on *Saturday Night Live*, took three hours to chrome her dome. "The first time he finished, I had this thing on my head, airbrushed to within an inch of my life. It was astonishing, I walked out on the set, and people looked at me and said, 'That poor thing!'

"I did learn something very, very interesting from one of the people on the creative team," Rosenblat continues. "When a character in prison has Miss in front of her name, she has some prison seniority, and people don't mess with her. I learned this, and it helped me form my attitude toward the lines. You do that to become the character you'd already become."

Even the main woman would depart early in the first season, as Piper was whisked away for a trial. Meanwhile, Rosa kept getting a few vacations to the doctor's for last-ditch efforts with chemo – but we also learned a bit more about her.

"In a situation like this, an actor always has to bring her A-game to work," Rosenblat says, "and I had to find an interior life for (Rosa), which I did in my own little mind. You bring the sense of reality of this woman to work, and that freshens her up for the audience. You go in with what's been written for her, and you look at the tempo and the words that are used, the situation she's in, and you start to figure her out. Where does she come from? What does she do? And then we find out what a badass she is! It was fun to find out that I robbed banks!"

Indeed, that was what had forced Rosa to wear the jumpsuit. In flashback mode, Stephanie Andujar played her younger self, part of a trio that made money the most dangerous way. But karma kept sneaking up on the young woman; her first husband was gunned down during a getaway, her second keeled of a coronary during another. Overly impressed with herself, the young gal had stormed into a bank on a whim and on her own. It hadn't worked.

"I met (Andujar) one day while I was shooting my chemo scenes," Rosenblat remembers. "She looked just like my niece." She also ran into Edvin Ortega, who played the only boyfriend of the young woman who stayed alive!

"For some reason, when we looked at each other, there was this odd connection that neither of us really understood," Rosenblat says. "There was some real romance there. I'd never met the guy in my life, but we understood the history that was going on there. It helped me fashion my own opinion of my character. I thought, I can do this!"

Despite the Emmys' classification of *Orange* as a comedy, there was quite a bit of drama, even violence to straddle the line between categories. Still, Rosa's major moment – to that point, as it would soon be passed – came in one of the series' lightest moments.

"Appropriately Sized Pots" showed her at yet another chemo appointment, on a set specially built for the occasion. Enthralled by the deeds of the seemingly kindly old lady with him, a young boy (and fellow patient) dares her to bring her past back.

With nothing to lose, Rosa accepts, helping him filch a few bucks from behind a negligent nurse's desk. The pair gets away, and she doesn't even ask for a cut! Moments later, she learns that his cancer's gone away, for the time being.

"He leaned on me a little bit for guidance," Rosenblat says of the youngster. "His mom was there every day, and we did these fabulous scenes together, him playing an idiot and me sighing at him."

Early on in season two, a lady named Vee (Lorraine Toussaint) shows up. A former foster mom to some of the prisoners and an old prison colleague of Red, she was there to take control, by any means necessary and then some.

It seems to work for a while, with Vee gathering all of her "sisters" and Red losing her friends. But when Vee beats up Red and tries to convince another inmate to take the blame, her control is gone.

As the sophomore season's final episode of "We Have Manners, We're Polite," kicked off on June 6, 2014, we find that she is as well, having escaped. It's about then that Rosa's doctor tells her there's nothing left to try.

"I felt so upset at possibility of ending my life," Rosenblat says. "Dying of cancer in a prison cell, it's terrifying."

Still, even on the coldest day in one of the coldest places in society, she won't have to go that way. Throughout the series, we'd seen Yael Stone's Lorna Morello pull one stunt after another, between driving new prisoners to the holding buildings and Rosa to treatment. We saw her stalk an ex to get thrown into prison, then break into his house while Rosa was at chemo. But a tough chat with the older gal she's grown to care for pushes Lorna to, in a prisoner's own moral way, put someone else above her.

With everyone distracted by a protest outside, Lorna suddenly leaves the prison van un(wo)manned, with Rosa in the back. Calling back to the stunned patient, Lorna gives her one more chance at some kind of freedom, to spend her last moments away from the cell.

The look on her face tells us just how unfamiliar, even frightening, this world is for Rosa. A person who spends a few decades in prison hasn't experienced much in the way of change, perhaps for decades at a time. In our high-speed society, 2015 is a solar system away from 2000, let alone how long Rosa's been away from it. Institutionalized is a tough adjective to assign to anyone, but it seems to have her pretty clenched in its grip.

It takes Rosa a minute, almost too long to take advantage. But then she jumps up front and hauls away. She makes it to the front gate of the prison and smashes right through it – again, what the hell does she have to lose?

If any other inmate in the prison, even Piper, had done this, we'd probably want her caught. We certainly wouldn't be rooting for her this hard. We wouldn't be feeling this type of adrenalin-fueled envy, cheering on someone who takes her last chance to go out on her own terms.

"The escape was the coldest day of my life," Rosenblat says. "It was about four degrees. I must have worn seventy heat pockets on my body that day."

As Rosa busts out into a free world she hasn't seen for several decades, the strands of "Don't Fear the Reaper" make their way out of the radio. Death happens to us all, but that doesn't mean we need to be afraid of it, no matter where we are or how it's happening.

One more coincidence? One more karmic kick? Why not?

Vee just *happens* to be making her way out of the woods a bit up the road. Perhaps hoping to get a ride, she waves to Rosa.

Not happening. All the pain this woman's caused others is going to come right back, in the form of a bumper run-down that gives the ultimate payback.

With Rosa's face starting to alternate between the two actresses who portrayed her, we know this is just about it – not just for the season, but for the character. And while she spent most of her life without freedom, deservedly so, even some prisoners get to go out their own way (she does, driving into a quarry) – especially if they've been fighting a tougher enemy than their colleagues on death row ever will.

Will Sampson: *One Flew Over the Cuckoo's Nest*

Backstage at a Florida theater one late 1970s night, Tim Sampson was hanging out with the man who'd immortalized Chief Bromden, the silent "narrator" of *One Flew Over the Cuckoo's Nest*, which galvanized both the literary and cinematic worlds.

Will Sampson's Chief Bromden says a sad goodbye to the only friend he'd known in decades in the closing minutes of *One Flew Over the Cuckoo's Nest* (1975).

A few years after the film had stormed through the 1975 Academy Awards, taking home Oscars for Best Director, Screenplay, Actor, and Actress (1934's *It Happened One Night* and 1991's *Silence of the Lambs* are the only other two films to do so, as of 2016) the same fellow who'd held millions spellbound with hardly a word had been asked to reprise his role as the chief when the flick made its way to stages.

As showtime inched closer, the performer put the finishing touches on his makeup, then turned toward his younger visitor.

"Live and learn," Will Sampson told his son, "because you're going to be doing this play someday."

The younger Sampson, one of the actor's ten children, maintained a stoic outlook. On the inside, he was grinning in disbelief.

"I thought it was a joke or something," Tim admits. At the time, it may have been. But although Will wouldn't live to see it, his words would one day come true.

Will's journey towards playing Chief Bromden began by going in the other direction. He'd recently retired from a successful career as a rodeo rider, and was settling into a vocation of painting. As he was working as a hunting guide in the mountains that range through the state of Washington (far from his early home in Oklahoma), he learned that some casters were looking for him.

Like all hunters, these people wanted to put their prey on display and be proud of it, to show it off to all their friends. However, they'd hope to do so without the help of a taxidermist.

"He was a bullrider back in the 50s and 60s, and that's how they kind of knew who he was," Tim recalls. "From what he told me, he didn't really want to be in movies. He never had anything to do with acting at all, nothing like that."

Still, the *Cuckoo's Nest* officials finally contacted the senior Sampson.

"They told him about the movie, and he really didn't want to do it," Tim says. "Then he read the book and the script and he decided that it wasn't a bad thing, so he decided to go ahead and do it."

The story, which has been credited with putting a new, more compassionate spin on America's views of its mentally challenged population, tells the story of McMurphy (Jack Nicholson), a wild man-child labeled a sociopath by society, who turns his psychiatric ward into a joyous battle of wills with the evil Nurse Ratchet (Louise Fletcher) and her group of suppressive bully-types who run the ward.

Though the book is told from Bromden's point of view, his role in the film is minor until a gift of gum from McMurphy gets him to say, "Thank you." (In the book, the utterance is accidental, as even the Chief is surprised; in the film, the Chief's words are accompanied by a twinkle in his eye, as if he was the gamesmaster all along, just waiting for someone who deserved to hear his secret.)

For the first time all film, McMurphy's the one that's getting played. For the first time since he showed up, McMurphy has no damn clue what to say or do or how to react. After fooling everyone, including his new friend, into thinking he's deaf and dumb for his full time on the ward, the Chief finally opens up to someone else, his first real human connection in years.

Sadly, as in life, the two are united in death in the film's conclusion, as the Chief smothers a lobotomized McMurphy to save him from a life of tortured catatonia. Just like Morgan Freeman in *Shawshank Redemption* (1994) and *Million Dollar Baby* (2004), Sampson's Bromden is the glue that holds the film together from the background – without a large role in the tale itself, everything starts and ends with him.

While Will the person was a bit more friendly and outgoing than his cinematic character, he had quite a bit in common with Bromden long before putting on the mental facility garb for the first time, Tim says.

"When he did the film, his acting classes were relaxed," he says. "He once told me, 'Every emotion that you're going to portray in film, you've gone through the first seven years of your life. The life that you do is your school.' That's how he took on any role. He didn't have to go to school or class; he just added his own personal touch to it."

In a particularly notable scene a bit past the halfway point in the film, McMurphy angrily discovers that he and the Chief are two of the only residents at the ward by force. Many of the others, including Billy Bibbit (Brad Dourif, who deservedly received an Oscar nomination and a Golden Globe award), are voluntary.

During his upbringing, Sampson had gained a bit of involuntary preparation with his own involuntary confinements; he was unfairly jailed on a few occasions, usually after getting in fights with alcohol-encouraged patrons who wanted to challenge the near seven-footer.

"That was an everyday occurrence in the Native American world," Tim says of the jailings. "Back in them days, a lot of Native American men were thrown in jail for no reason. (But) it didn't bother (Will); it was another lesson learned. If it did bother him, he didn't let it stand in his way as a good man. That was life, and that was what happened. It went on. That was the kind of attitude that he had."

Perhaps Bromden's lack of excitement and emotional connection to the others in the ward wasn't entirely an act either; as Tim points out, his father was never much taken with the actions of others.

"That's how my dad was; he wasn't too impressed with man, and what man had done," he says. "He respected men, and what they had done, but man did not impress him like nature did. In the *New York Times*, he was quoted as saying, 'I'm not awed by man.' My dad had a lot of respect for people like Clint Eastwood, Jack Nicholson, Craig T. Nelson (Sampson's *Poltergeist II* co-star). These men were artists; they perceived their art, and became good at it. He had the highest respect for these guys, what they did."

The cast prepared together both before and during filming; just before the cameras rolled, director Milos Foreman showed them the 1967 documentary *Titicut Follies*, a heartbreaking documentary about conditions for the mentally ill at a Massachusetts prison hospital. During filming, many of the flick's extras were actual mental patients.

Through it all, McMurphy gains inmate after inmate to his impromptu gang; his improvised impersonation of a World Series game, his disruption of ward meetings and refusal to take his medications, his arrangement of a fishing trip (the last scene filmed; the rest of the movie was shot in sequence), and so on. By the end, the men have gained a measure of self-respect and self-confidence, exactly what the nurses and doctors hoped to avoid. In the end, they know that they're not just animals; they're people who deserve better treatment than they'd ever receive at the hospital.

However, in the last reel, McMurphy is lobotomized, and the Chief is all but forced into a mercy killing. And it's the right thing to do – not only would McMurphy have never wanted to live in such a state, the inmates will never see him as such, and the life he breathed into them, the charisma that he put on full volume throughout, will stay with them forever.

But despite Nurse Ratchet's pitch-black intentions throughout, McMurphy still gains a manner of victory in the closing moments; showing more emotion than many of his fellow patients had probably ever seen in him, the Chief hurls a huge water fountain through the window, inciting his "colleagues" to burst out in cheers. In the last scene, we see him escaping, rushing away from captivity and into freedom, taking the steps that McMurphy never got to, going where McMurphy so desperately hoped.

The only scene in the movie that was filmed just once, it's one of the most famous endings in American history. But as memorable as the conclusion proved to audiences across the country and spanning the globe, America's Native Americans, particularly Sampson's Muscogee tribe members in Oklahoma, had even more of a special connection.

"It seemed dream-like," Tim says of the ending. "I was excited and proud of him. It was his first time ever acting in a film, and I said, 'Wow!'

"What he did with that medium, it exposed him to that kind of Native American actor. He became a hero. We were all so proud of him, of what he did and where he came from."

And, as it turned out, where Will would continue to go, and take others with him.

"He found a medium that give him the opportunity to help his people," Tim says. "He told me once,

'Acting is some other job, and what the job does is make you want to help people more.' It helped him do more for his people. That's how he viewed it; he encouraged people to do whatever they wanted to. He took that opportunity to help anybody who needed help, with energy and encouragement, that's what he was all about."

But it wasn't acting that pushed Will forward, or at least it wasn't *only* the performing.

"A lot of people thought he would change," Tim says, "but he never did, as far as tradition, his belief in the Lord and everything. He came from a world where he'd seen a lot of things, and he used it as a tool to enhance people more. He once told me, 'When you get into the high profile acting, you've got to have a reason. His reason was more spiritual: to encourage people, in the spiritual idea, to help us do whatever we wanted to with our lives."

Will kept painting, kept exploring in nature, kept moving forward. And once in a while, he stepped back into the world of scripts and camera. Aside from *Cuckoo's Nest*, his biggest role – at least, on the big screen, notwithstanding his theater work – was as the kindly spirit Taylor in 1986's *Poltergeist II: The Other Side*.

"He accepted it on the condition that he would be the technical advisor on the Native American part," Tim says, referring to the film's Indian ceremonial scene in which his dad assisted, "and (they) agreed to that, so to make it even more authentic and real, he was part of the technical staff."

By that point, Will's family acting predictions were showing signs of realism; Tim did some stunt-doubling for him in *Poltergeist*, as well as on the 1978 television series *Vega$* and 1979 film *Fish Hawk*.

Sadly, soon after *Poltergeist II* came out, Will's health started to deteriorate. In the early summer of 1987, he underwent heart and lung transplant surgery; soon afterward, kidney failure and malnutrition set in. But just as it had throughout his life, Will's spiritualism carried him along on his final journey.

Just before Will's death on June 3, 1987, "He didn't say goodbye," Tim recalls. "That's not our belief. We'd see each other again; that's what we believed as Native Americans. The last time I talked to him, he said, 'I'll see you later.'"

While neither of them knew it then, many would see the Chief again, with the next generation of Sampson behind the portrayal. Just over a decade after his father passed, Tim learned that a new theatrical production of *Cuckoo's Nest* was coming to Broadway.

"When the auditions came around for the play, I thought it was my dad's prophecy coming true," he says, "so I auditioned, and I nailed the part. You can't describe it; there's no words for that feeling, especially when my dad had foretold this. It seemed like a natural thing to do. He was pretty much right when he said things like that."

With a backstory that had been made and re-made for decades, Tim and his colleagues had much more diverse grounds for preparation than Will had enjoyed.

"We did a lot of research, we went to a lot of hospitals, we worked with a lot of patients and nurses and doctors," he says. "We did a lot of research of Ken Kesey, a lot of things to get the whole background of what was going on at mental institutions and those hospitals back in those days. We saw a lot of film and did a lot of research before we ever started rehearsing."

With Gary Sinise as McMurphy, Sampson – despite being dwarfed by his father at *only* 6'3" – tried to regain the muted magic that had turned his dad into a legend.

"Gary Sinise was a quiet, well-spoken man, but when he came into this character, he was a top-notch actor. I thought he was great in the role. I've seen Nicholson do McMurphy, and I've seen Martin Sheen do McMurphy, but Gary Sinise, he was just different; he seemed like he really got into the character. It was like his features changed when he got into the role. His face changed, his walk changed, his voice changed.

"He really helped me out a lot in projecting my voice," Tim says. "He took me under his arms and really guided me through. He helped me out with the role."

In the end, Tim helped the character come full circle. Just as Kasey had used Bromden as the focal point for one of the most highly-renowned literary works ever, and his father and Nicholson had made the role legendary on the screen, he, Sinise, and the rest of the cast brought *Cuckoo's Nest* to the top of one more entertainment expression; in 2001, the play took home a Tony award for Best Revival of a Play.

While Sampson's stoicism and silence were perhaps the most prevelant aspect of his character, someone else went the opposite way – and wound up with an Oscar nomination.

Billy Bibbit (Brad Dourif) stares into his terrifying, and tragically short, future, in the closing moments of 1975's *One Flew Over the Cuckoo's Nest*.

"I did a *lot* of research on people who stuttered," recalls Brad Dourif, who portrayed mentally challenged Billy Bibbit, bullied into man-child mode by Ratchet and the rest of the staff. "I worked with a speech therapist, and worked backwards until I got a stutter that was good."

Stepping out into public to straddle the line between improvisation and reality, Dourif was surprised by what he found, in a positive way.

"You're always very nervous with that sort of thing," he admits. "I would go to Grand Central Station on a really crappy day, and go up to people and ask for help. But lo and behold, the thing I learned is that people are actually really goddamned nice. They would stop, change the way they would concentrate, and focus on me and what I was trying to say until I spat it out. You want to get it in your body. These things kind of eventually make their way into you and make your heart beat a little differently as you respond to the situation."

Amy Sloan: *The Aviator/Gothika/The Day After Tomorrow*

Here's a quick way to recognize a true one-scene wonder.

Watch their scene(s) all the way through a few times. Analyze them. Take them all in.

Then ask yourself: what would the film lose if that scene weren't there?

If the answer is somewhere along the lines of "A whole lot!" you've found yourself a moments-long masterpiece.

A winner of five Oscars (although still not the Best Director/Picture honors that would elude Martin Scorsese until 2006's *The Departed*), 2004's *The Aviator* gave viewers an inside look at Howard Hughes, a millionaire playboy filmmaker and flight pioneer eventually ruined – though this wasn't fully explored in the film – by mental illness, ranging from obsessive-compulsive disorder to agoraphobia to any number of physical ailments, some real, others imagined. In a performance that almost undoubtedly would have won him a Best Actor honor had Jamie Foxx not taken an equally strong step into the world of Ray Charles, Leonardo DiCaprio opened up the dark doors of Hughes' mind and walked straight through, taking millions of viewers with him.

But it's the film's opening scene that truly sets the tone not only for the piece, but for Hughes' entire life. So important to the storyline that Scorsese decided not to run opening credits around him, the audience got a taste of the causes of the man's inner agony.

Of course, to fully understand this, we have to take a step back to even before the film's depictions.

On a 1903 trip through Dallas, Bo Hughes, who'd been expelled from several colleges and lost his money several times over, met and fell in love with Allene Gano, a member of the Texas town's elite. Her family had gotten wealthy off farming and real estate, and it was tough for her family, or anyone else, to understand exactly what the young lady saw in Hughes, who'd recently been through another round of bad financial luck (though he'd founded the Texas Fuel Oil Company, which would eventually morph into Texaco).

Whatever Allene noticed, it was enough; the two were married in May 1904. The next year, Howard, known affectionately to his mother and family as Sonny, was born.

While it's common knowledge today that mental illness, just as with physical ailments like cancer, can be the most unwelcome of inheritances, these things weren't clear a century ago. At the time, few knew that Allene's lifelong obsessive fear of sickness, germs, insects, and small animals (she couldn't stand cats in particular) would transfer to her son.

Amy Sloan played Allene Hughes, the mother who created (or at least aggravated) her son Howard's lifelong germaphobia in the opening moments of 2004's Oscar-winning film *The Aviator*.

Fortunately, in the opening scene of *The Aviator*, Amy Sloan puts it on display, and gives us a glimpse of Hughes' beginnings.

Bathing her elementary-school age son (Jacob Davitch) in a tub of water, Allene quizzes her son's spelling habits. Then she moves on to more important matters.

"You know the cholera?" she asks, in a voice that's both soothing and horrifyingly disturbing.

"Yes, mother," he replies.

"You know the typhus?" Allene inquires. He answers in the affirmative.

"You are not safe," she assures him, looking him straight in the eye like an Oedipal hypnotist.

The scene's less than five minutes long. But for one of the first times, audiences truly got an idea of why Hughes was Hughes.

"What I liked about the role was that, even though it was a small role, it really set the tone for the film's development," explains Sloan, who, like many up-and-comers in acting, jumped at the chance to work with Scorsese. "Some refer to it as the 'Rosebud' scene, a little moment in (Hughes') childhood where things are set in stone." The single word, "Rosebud," set the tone for the legendary *Citizen Kane* (1941), as a journey to discover the meaning of Charles Foster Kane's final word delves into a background study of the (fictional) newspaperman's life.

To become Allene, Sloan immersed herself in readings of the Texan gal and her life.

"I formed a picture in my mind about what this woman would look like," says Sloan (biographers recall Allene as physically striking). "There was a lot of talk about what this woman would look like and why this scene was important in Howard Hughes' life. She was an incredibly overly involved mother, obsessive almost with the detail of Howard's cleanliness, his health, and his well-being. There was almost an oppressive quality to her concern about him. From the reading I did, it appeared that many seeds were sown early in his life."

Helped along, no doubt, by his mother's pleasantly unnerving tone.

"Learning a Texas accent really helped me find the voice for (Allene)," says Sloan. "I thought it was really important to find a voice that was sort of calming, and yet clear and direct. I married my intentions for the scene, my objectives, with the voice that I had found."

Hughes lived a very sheltered childhood, and a theatrical fake sickness at 11 (still a common anti-school tool utilized by children today) enticed a frenzied Allene to hire a team of doctors and nurses while the family stayed at a New York hotel. Later that year, with young Howard away at camp, Allene besieged the officials to keep close watch on her boy's health.

"We didn't want to play (Allene) scary or overwhelmingly domineering," says Sloan (in all fairness, Allene's health fears came true, to an extent; at only 38, she died during surgery for a uteral hemorrhage). "We wanted to play it more subtly, rather than making it one-dimensional. I didn't worry too much about it being a memorable scene in the great scheme of things; I just wanted to make sure I did my job."

The year before, she'd played a not-altogether-different character, albeit in a much more over-the-top manner; as Dr. Miranda Grey (Halle Berry) tries to figure out why she's suddenly locked in a mental ward in 2003's *Gothika*, Sloan plays one of her impromptu roommates, a fire obsessive.

"I did a lot of research about pyromaniacs and the qualities that some of them inhabit in their world view, the way they interact with the world around them," Sloan recalls of her role investigations. "It was a little heavy. A lot of roles like that are hard to take home at the end of the day, just because you have to take on such a mindset, and it can get to be a little overwhelming at times."

In the end, sadly, her role became an underwhelming part of the storyline; deciding that Penelope Cruz's role of Chloe, Grey's former patient and only ally, hadn't received enough development, film officials decided to replace Sloan's character with Cruz's for a few scenes, Sloan says.

"That's one of those tough lessons that you learn in show business," Sloan admits. "As it ended up, I didn't get to do a whole lot, but I continued with the work I had done for the character I had developed."

For another role, star power wouldn't be Sloan's biggest opponent onscreen, or at least not her only one. When the Ice Age – not the cute *Ice Age*! – re-takes over New York City for the first time in dozens of centuries, a group of students is trapped inside a Manhattan library, as a scientist (in true film lore, the only one who could tell what would happen ahead of time) races to save them; after all, his son is one of the endangered.

That's the story of Roland Emmerich's 2004 special effects bonanza *The Day After Tomorrow*. Although, as with fellow Emmerich creations *Independence Day* (1996), *Godzilla* (1998), and *2012* (2009), the graphics are the true stars of the film, Sloan attempted to carve out her own stardom in the midst of a glacier attack, playing Elsa, a friend of Sam Hall (Jake Gyllenhaal) who does what she must to survive in the forced literary wilderness.

"I thought that the movie itself was kind of interesting for a blockbuster film," she explains, "and I thought the role of Elsa was funny, smart, and kind of wry." Elsa's one-liners about why Friedrich Nietzsche was overrated and which books should be burned to stay warm provided the script with some fast-moving humor.

Still, while the acting might not have been the film's main attraction, she and the rest of the cast tried to become the backbone to the physical features that *Tomorrow* showed.

"I did a lot of readings about what those kinds of conditions would be like," Sloan says. "I learned about the conditions in the library, and what a vast ice age what be like, so I would have a greater capacity to portray the physical state changes that happen."

While viewers had the luxury of checking out the finished project with all the artificial insertions already added, the performers weren't so lucky, sometimes having to improvise in every sense of the word, Sloan continues.

"We shot some stuff in the library and we must have been there for four weeks, shooting (only) three or four scenes," she says. "For some of them we had a lot of people in the scene; whenever there are a lot of people in the scene, it exponentially increases the time it takes to shoot it. A lot of footage has to be taken for scenes like that, because there might be a lot of (special effects) later. It was really cool to see how the picture that you develop in your mind and your imagination differs from the end result. Sometimes there's a lot of resemblance to what the finished project ends up being. If you really use your imagination, which is such a vivid thing, if you really let it help you out, it can really mean a lot."

That's advice that Sloan — who, like many in her profession, is oftentimes her own biggest critic — carries with her through every role she goes for, and what she hopes newcomers take with them as well.

"As an actor, it's hard to separate yourself from your work, so I'm always self-critical when I see myself on screen," she confesses. "It's very rare that I'll watch something with clear eyes. I see the flaws in my performance or things that I should have made more interesting. I'll wish I had taken better advantage of things on screen. Tenacity is the name of the (acting) game. You have to keep pushing and be strong; you can't take things personally. If it's what you want to do, you've got to be in it for the long haul."

June Squibb: *About Schmidt/Nebraska*

The words are on the page. The action is on the screen. It's the actor's job to be the medium, the vessel that transports one aspect of performing to the other.

It's how June Squibb approaches her roles. She checks the words. She hears them in her mind —

what and how her character speaks, what others say about the lady she's becoming. For weeks and often longer, she keeps at the script until she can see it in her mind. Then she lets the audience see it through her performance.

"No matter what I'm doing, I just deal over and over with the script," Squibb explains. "That's truly how I work. I find out who (my character) is by delving into the script over and over again. When somebody talks about you, that tells you something about your character."

Indeed, her mind, her talent becomes the bridge and path from paper to screen. And in 2014, for the first time in decades of acting, her route finally led all the way to the Oscars.

But Squibb waited until her 80's for that moment. We can hold out for a few more paragraphs.

"I did a lot of acting and dance in school," recalls the Vandalia, Ill. native. "When I got out of high school, I went to regional theater." After a few years at the Cleveland Playhouse, she headed to New York – and Broadway.

June Squibb scored her first Oscar nomination for becoming Kate Grant, the drill sergeant/matriarch of her wayward-wandering family in 2014's *Nebraska*.

She played a stripper alongside Ethel Merman in *Gypsy* (1962) and sang next to Charles Durning in *Happy Time* (1970) – two tiny parts of her novel-esque theater resume. But entering her seventh decade, Squibb decided to finally jump in front of a camera – and a slightly larger audience than any theater could provide.

And talk about debuts: her first flick just HAPPENED to be a small role in Woody Allen's 1990 dramedy *Alice*, in which title character Mia Farrow explores her relationship through invisibility potions.

"It was a wonderful experience," she recalls. "I adored Woody Allen. He kept calling me back and asking for scenes." As housekeeper Hilda, two days of work stretched into over a month.

Remember the chapter earlier in this tome about networking like crazy? Squibb can testify with an expert opinion about its effectiveness: the casting director on *Alice* remembered her the next year, doing similar work for one of 1992's top films.

Squibb would become Ms. Hunsaker, the secretary that tried to create all sorts of havoc for everyone in *Scent of a Woman*, which ended up bringing Al Pacino an acting Oscar and probably would have snared the 1992 Best Picture honor if *Unforgiven* hadn't been around.

"I loved it," she says of Hunsaker. "She was the snotty secretary, the villain in the piece, caused all the trouble. I thought it was a great little role."

Hunsaker was the right-hand woman of James Rebhorn's Dean Trask, himself all but obsessed with finding out which of his school's students vandalized his office. In roles that ended up shoving both of them towards stardom, Chris O'Donnell is Charlie Simms and Philip Seymour Hoffman is George Willis, whose pals did the damage and threatened Charlie in the bargain.

In front of the whole school, Trask is ready to take them to task. George is all too anxious to rat out his friends to score points, but Charlie's not a snitch. Right or wrong, this guy's not going to stake his future on turning someone else in.

Looks like his whole life's going straight down the tubes. But Pacino's Col. Frank Slade steps in, gives the speech that won Pacino an Oscar, and flips everything and everyone's opinion back around ("Let him continue on his path... because he's gonna make you proud someday!").

"You're always learning something from (Pacino)," Squibb says. "It was a joy to be around him."

As Charlie's schoolmates applaud, Trask's colleagues gather to deliberate. And it's left to Hunsaker to grudgingly read the verdict: George gets nothing, and Charlie's excused.

"She was willing to do anything to help the dean," Squibb recalls. "She wasn't a good woman, per se, but just doing her job. (She) was distressed and upset."

But she's in the minority: the announcement and Slade's "Hoo-hah!" trigger an ovation like a volcano.

A year later, Squibb worked with Martin Scorsese in the Oscar-winning *Age of Innocence*, and soon spent some time on the smaller screens, showing up on *Law and Order*, *ER*, and *The Young and the Restless*. A recurring role as Judge Amy Gray's court reporter on *Judging Amy* showed up, as did some similar work as Jennifer Love Hewitt's grandma on *Ghost Whisperer*.

"The thing about TV is that it's faster (than films)," she explains. "In film, you have the luxury of doing stuff over and over and trying new things. In TV you don't have that. It's a very fast process. If you're a good actor, you know how to work, and you adjust to the different medium."

In 2001, Squibb's agent got a call about Alexander Payne's next directorial expedition. She agreed to do a screen test.

"Alexander told me that the first time he saw the tape," she says, "he wanted me to do it." She'd be playing Helen Schmidt in 2002's *About Schmidt* — alongside a fellow named Nicholson.

"It was a wonderful script on paper," she says, "and working with Jack — if you get a chance to work with people as talented as he is, you leap at it, because you don't always get it. Jack doing it, and working with Alexander, and feeling something with him, that we would understand each other, that was very special."

Helen's the wife of Jack's protagonist Warren, in the midst of a late-life crisis after retiring from his job and not having the first clue what to do with himself. Like Hunsaker before her, Helen's a bit on the mouthy side as well, typical bossy housewife, I-wear-the-pants-while-you-earn-the-money mentality of older couples – but this particular gal has something to hide. We as the audience don't quite know what, but it's obvious that she's a bit ticked at Warren, or perhaps at herself and trying to blame it on him.

Helen won't get to tell; Warren finds her dead on the floor, just before they're about to hop into an RV and head across the country. But it doesn't take long before we see exactly what she tried to keep concealed.

That's because Helen's impact carries on long after her death; Warren learns that she had a forbidden fling with his friend Ray.

"Reading the script," Squibb says, "(I noticed) the few things she says and why she's saying them and building it up. One thing was that she had the affair, and no one knew about it. The other characters say things about your character, and it gives you an insight about what you're playing, what you're dealing with. Her having an affair was momentous in the context of these people."

In early 2013, Squibb got another shot at working with Payne. Per usual, she began with the writing.

"I feel very strongly that the script has all the answers, and that even on stage this is true," she says. "I work the same way from the smallest to the biggest role: I read the script over and over and over again. I go through and deal with the subtext for the person, for the scene, and for the line. The script gives you the opportunity to work by yourself. I take as much time as I can get. I work every day for an hour or two hours. The learning process sticks with you, and it's better than trying to cram it in."

Nebraska told the tale of a family that's found quite a bit more often in reality than in film (none of the shiny, happy Brady Bunch garbage here!). The Grants are a small Montana group with a pair of adult sons still looking for direction, an elderly patriarch whose years of boozing and a new foe in dementia are starting to team up on him, and a razor-tongued mama who stopped caring long ago about what people thought of her and how the hell she sounded. Kate gave Squibb the chance to push a bit farther the characteristics she'd shown as Helen.

"She was unfiltered," recalls Squibb. "Whatever she thought came out of her mouth. I've met people like that, and I have a bit of that myself. I think that was very much a part of who she is. She's fearless. She doesn't care."

Bruce Dern is her husband Woody, determined in his faltering moments of lucidity to head back home to the title state (where the film was shot), to snap up a false lottery victory. His son David (Will Forte) is persuaded to take the wheel, but Kate's not believing a syllable, blasting her family for wasting everyone's time with this mess, even after she follows them to Nebraska.

"I fell in love with the script," Squibb says. "The writing was unbelievable. We did not improvise anything." Including, she continues, a visit to a graveyard, where Kate's venom extends to family members beyond the grave, and punctuates with her skirt-flash to an ex who never knew what he missed!

"Kate was a strong woman with a sense of humor, and she cared very much about her husband and her two sons," Squibb says. "Her role in life was to take care of the three of them."

Woody spreads his tale of false riches throughout the town — it's never really clear if he knows he's lying — but Kate's never fooled, telling off the cousins that fight with him, her sons for believing it, and anyone else taken in by this façade. Still, as the film draws to the last credits, we know that the Grants will probably be OK for now.

"A lot of people told me that at the start of this film, they didn't like Kate," Squibb says, "but by the end of the film, they understood what I had been putting up with and who this husband was, with his problems. We really still were a family together."

Per usual with Payne's films, the Academy took a strong look when it came Oscar time (*Nebraska* marked his fifth consecutive film to win or be nominated for an Oscar). And the flick grabbed more nods than anything he'd done. The script that had stolen Squibb's heart was nominated. Payne was up for top director. His film was there for a shot at the top pic. Dern had scored a nomination.

And so had Squibb, for supporting actress.

"It was great," Squibb says of Oscar night. "The atmosphere was the biggest and the best, and you felt that this was a very important thing that you were a part of." Early on, she was edged for the honor by Lupita Nyong'o's work in *12 Years a Slave*, the eventual Best Picture winner. Payne fell in the directing race to *Gravity*'s Alfonso Cuaron. Matthew McConaughey grabbed the top acting award for *Dallas Buyers Club*. *Nebraska* didn't come through on any of its six nominations.

But for the rest of her career, Squibb's headlines will be extended just a few more very important words.

"From now on," she says, "everything I do, it's going to say 'June Squibb, Academy Award nominee'!"

George "The Animal" Steele: *Ed Wood*

Both of them got started in the wrestling ring as heels (bad guys), equipped with not only the ability to survive between the ropes, but a physical look that opponents and fans wouldn't soon forget. Both of them eventually stepped before cameras and onto screens of slightly larger sizes.

And today, long after their respective careers ended, both still are, and always will be, remembered by fans of film and the mat, though sadly, only one is still around to enjoy it.

In hindsight, it seems the epitome of illogic that *anyone* but George "The Animal" Steele could become Tor Johnson in the underrated *Ed Wood* (1994).

Johnson first stepped into the national spotlight in the 1920s and 30s, and made it into movies shortly thereafter, often playing wrestlers. But it was his ghoulish turn as detective-turned-zombie Daniel Clay in the horrifyingly legendary *Plan 9 From Outer Space* (1959) that pushed him higher than ever before, and has kept him there, four decades after his 1971 passing. He's still seen several times every Oct. 31, and not just on TV; Johnson's huge, bald head was modeled into one of the top-selling Halloween masks of all time.

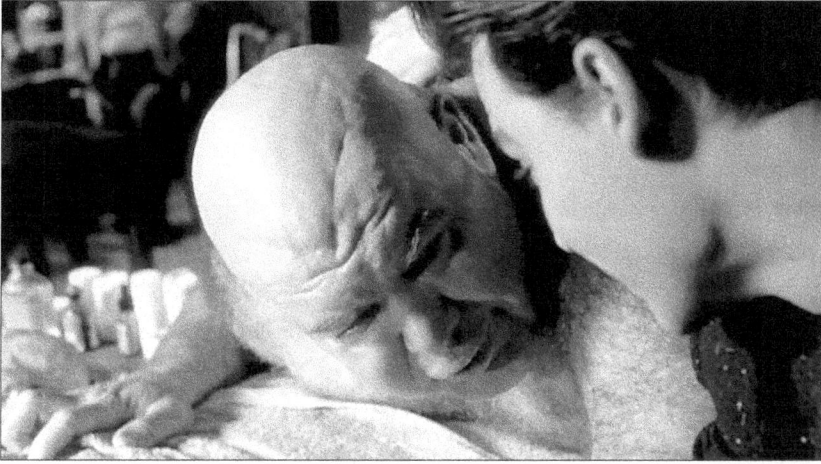

After spending decades as a household name in professional wrestling, George "The Animal" Steele stole 1994's *Ed Wood* by portraying such a performer, becoming Tor Johnson.

Steele first stepped into the squared circle in 1962, under a mask and called The Student. A trip to Pittsburgh for a title match changed his moniker to George Steele (the first name was a promoter's suggestion, the last name for Pittsburgh's top product), and a legend was born.

He'd spend the next few decades tearing it up between the ropes, eventually changing into the lovable teddy bear-ish Animal, who chomped turnbuckles to fans' delight and waved his green tongue, slobbering all over his opponents and speaking in gibberish (he'd been quite the credible interview in early years). After his career ended, Steele was inducted into the World Wrestling Entertainment Hall of Fame, and his personal appearances still pack fans into lines.

Back when his career was winding down, Steele (in real life, he's Jim Myers, who overcame dyslexia to score a Master's Degree and become one of the top high school football coaches in Michigan history, with his school's field being named after him) got a call from the most unlikely of sources.

The man's name was Tim Burton – yes, the same Tim Burton who'd brought Batman back to the big screen, and would eventually become a master of dark humor in films. In the mood to bring the life story of one of his late colleagues to the screen, Burton had a specific role to cast.

He was putting together the story of a man named Wood, long lauded as one of the worst directors in Hollywood history – which, in the minds of film fans, can be just as entertaining as coming up on the other side of quality – a vote spurred on in no small part by *Plan 9*, considered the epitome of horrific filmmaking, the saddest farewell to Bela Lugosi's career.

Burton had his title character down – it was Johnny Depp, with whom he'd form one of film's most formidable tag teams. He had Bela Lugosi: Martin Landau, one of the best ever.

But to cast an uncommon man with a common last name, Burton had to stretch a bit farther. Not a whole lot of 300-400 pound, six-foot-plus performers running around.

"(Burton) wasn't a wrestling fan at all," Steele recalls, "but he was looking for somebody to play the part, and everybody had recommended my name because of the look. Tim called me up and said I looked like a movie star, and I said, 'La, la, that's great!'"

In a very real way, though, Burton was right – Steele might not have had Brad Pitt's countenance, but carrying Johnson's was good enough for this.

"Tor was the first guy to do monster movies without makeup," Steele explains. "It was an opportunity. I think anybody would look for an opportunity to be in a movie. I was born ready."

Sitting in the jammed stands of a match, Wood sees Johnson whomping another opponent. Suddenly in fan mode, he slinks into the dressing room, and asks the main event man if he's ever considered hitting the big screen.

"Not good looking enough!" Johnson responds, in a voice that sounds like an excited loudspeaker. It's a scene that wins the audience's heart in a moment.

"I had a speech coach, and made my voice deeper," Steele recalls. "I watched *Plan 9 From Outer Space*."

Even caught in the midst of a cavalcade of talent – Depp, Landau, Sarah Jessica Parker, Jeffrey Jones, and Bill Murray – Steele still gave Johnson a certain amount of scene snatching, much like the star himself did in the original *Plan 9*. He incorporated Johnson's habit of clumsily and hilariously crashing into doors. He became the victim of a falling fake octopus the group steals through a building. When the full crew is impulsively baptized, it's forced to be outside, as Johnson's too big to fit into the tub in the church.

"It was fun," Steele recalls. "It was a great experience that everybody doesn't get. When you're making a movie, everything is such a slow pace, so you just go along with it. Martin Landau was very helpful. I needed all the help I could get."

But during the filming of the movie, if Steele or anyone else made a mistake, Burton was there to shout "Cut!" and everyone could go back and regroup. In pro wrestling, the sports entertainment business (not quite sports and not quite entertainment, it basically bodyslams the line between the two), people aren't supposed to hurt each other to the point that they can't work the next day, although of course accidents happen.

Life doesn't always work that way. There's not always an easy solution to any problem, and sometimes it can seem like there's no answer at all. Being diagnosed with a disease that can reach out and strike anyone, anywhere, with no set cure or even much treatment is one such situation. In 1988, that's what Steele found himself going through: Crohn's disease, the incurable (or so everyone thought!) and often fatal intestinal disorder, put an end to his career as a full-time mat man.

"I was very sick until 1997," Steele says. "I couldn't leave the house. They carried me out of here to the hospital." The "cures" weren't much improvement; Steele's medications caused diabetes and cataracts, and affected his heartbeat.

Then, slowly, his health came back. His colon had to be removed, but he kept getting better. Eventually, he was back on his feet, back meeting with fans.

And according to Steele, it was due to Someone special.

"If I hadn't gotten Crohn's, I wouldn't have found Jesus Christ as my personal savior," says Steele, who was baptized in 2002 (unlike Johnson, he fit in the tub!). "I got my life back. There's no cure for Crohn's, but I had it, and I don't have it anymore. Crohn's was a blessing leading to the rest of my life. The George 'The Animal' Steele character lives on stronger than ever."

Tami Stronach/Clarissa Burt: *The Neverending Story I/II*

Perhaps the very title and plot of *The Neverending Story* films are indeed a metaphor for something that children desperately need to hold on to, especially in today's electronic world, where books are too quickly becoming obsolete, aside from our trusty Kindle machines.

See, while the cranky old bookseller Mr. Koreander (Thomas Hill, the only performer to appear in the first two films) tried to warn main boy Bastian – twice! – that some books are dangerous, even after making one's way through them, that reading, and the creativity, the originality, the imagination that it all but forces us to have (hopefully, gifts that are instilled in us as soon as we're old enough to recite the alphabet), are our own neverending stories. That the Nothing that nearly destroyed Fantasia lives up to its name by taking away our ability, even our willingness, to dream, to believe, to hope.

It's a message that, many would argue, doesn't ring true enough today, in a world where physical libraries are a foreign land. But reading itself will be around as long as we're willing to take advantage of it, and series like the *Story* (or *Stories*, as it's turned out) can keep reminding us just how magical its worlds can always be.

In 1984, one year after the book made its way to America (it was first published in Germany in 1979), audiences saw the story of a young motherless boy named Bastian (Barrett Oliver), tormented by bullies and estranged from his dad, finding his only solace in the written pages. He reads (and we see) the tale of the story hero and child warrior Atreyu (Noah Hathaway), off to take out the Nothing, slowly destroying his world.

Along the way, he meets a myriad of mythical creatures, takes a ride on film-stealing luck dragon Falcor (did you know that longtime voice actor Alan Oppenheimer is actually the voices of Falcor, the terrifyingly evil wolf-like G'Mork, and the film narrator?), and comes face to face with the lady that the audience has heard so much about, and finally gets to meet.

"I was found in an acting class by the casting scout who was in town auditioning girls," recalls Tami Stronach. "I never intended to get involved with film. It was an accident."

Still, accidents can bring out the best of consequences, and for Stronach, who'd headed across the ocean after being born in Iran, it was a moment in the big screen spotlight; she was named the Childlike Empress in the film.

"After I read the book I was very excited about the story!" says Stronach, who struggled with the rest of the cast through Germany's hottest summer in about a quarter-century during filming.

As the cameras rolled on others, Stronach made her own additions to the script and story that had so enticed her in the first place.

Smarter far beyond her years, Tami Stronach's Childlike Empress tries to keep control as her empire falls to the Nothing near the end of *The Neverending Story* (1984).

"I prepared by... writing down adjectives that seemed to call the character forth — I had a small yellow notebook I took everywhere where I would write ideas down that helped define her for me," she recalls. "I insisted on running lines with my fellow actors during what were supposed to be play dates."

Even in her childlike state, assisted by Stronach actually being eleven at the time, the Empress seems almost maternal. Much like a mother trying to keep a small child calm in a chaotic situation, there's her fear of expressing fear, her forced stoicism, a protective nature over her land and its inhabitants. She knows what's going to happen, and that she can't stop it by herself, but keeps her emotions under control until she's alone, after Atreyu is knocked unconscious as the enemy attacks. That's when the Nothing starts to set in and she finally starts to panic, until Bastian gives her a name, the one that saves her vast empire.

(For over a quarter-century, people have argued about what Bastian actually shouts when he names her, but in the book he calls out, "Moonchild!" so we're going to go with that.)

The first time she saw it, Bastien's shout wasn't the only thing that Stronach and her fellow cast members had trouble understanding.

Clarissa Burt became the gorgeously evil sorceress Xayide
in the second *Neverending Story* flick of 1990.

Watching the final project for the first time "was great!" she says, "but it was at the premier in Germany where the film was dubbed into German – so it was funny seeing myself and fellow American actors deliver lines in fluent German."

By the time the first *Story* came about, Clarissa Burt had already been eyed by about as many as would see it, and on a much larger scale.

"I moved to Manhattan when I was nineteen," recalls the Philadelphia native, "and I had an extremely great modeling career. I was known as one of the top models in Europe in the '80s." Soon moving over to Italy, Burt appeared on hundreds of magazine covers and runways across the world.

Not surprisingly, the film world came calling, and Burt first hit the big screen in *Caruso Pascosky di Padre Polacco*, one of Italy's top-grossing films of 1988. And somewhere in the audiences that stretched around the world sat some members of the crew of the next *Story*.

"They called me, and I went to Munich two or three different times to read for the direction teams," recalls Burt. "I went up one last time, and I had hidden my grandmother's Virgin Mary medal in my right hand the whole time. I wanted that role badly. That film had a really, really strong message for children."

Months later, she finally got the call that she, along with the other 200-plus candidates that had been up for the role, had dreamed of: she would be the evil sorceress Xayide, whose Nothingness threatens to destroy the innocent minds and dreams that the previous Nothing had tried to erase from Fantasia.

That's right – playing the villainess for the 1990 film would be worth helping send the *Story*'s message for Burt.

"Kids get a very, very strong message about the importance of reading," she says, "and that's what it was about: a strong reading epic. The idea of reading because it fortifies your brain and gives great imagery, that was the message."

"I rented the first movie in preparation," recalls Burt, who hadn't seen the first until she snared the role. I read the script a thousand times, and you sit back and imagine yourself in the role and you imagine exactly how you're going to walk through the scene."

Now a bit older, Bastian's world hasn't changed much, apparently not having gotten to take all those wonderful adventures we heard about in the closing moments of the first film (the book actually contains the first two movies). Re-reading the tale that Koreander keeps warning him about, he hears the Empress (now Alexandra Johnes) whispering Xayide's plans to him. Back in Fantasia, he and the new Atreyu (Kenny Morrison) head off to stop her.

The first film, Johnes recalls, "was a very heartfelt, positive story. When you're a kid, and not properly trained as an actress, you just imagine what it would be like to be here, to be this one person with that much authority over a kingdom, a leader over a world." Like Stronach, she underplayed the Empress's emotions.

"I'm not a particularly calm person, but I imagined that she would be calm, so I tried to embody that," remembers Johnes, who'd later go into film production and win an Emmy. "It was a little odd to play someone that had been played before, but I just tried to adjust to the character."

Xayide's already in the know about the earthling, and she's a step ahead; pretending submission and friendship with Bastian (gorgeous women rarely have trouble winning the heart of a teenage boy!), she turns him against his friend, asking that he make one strange wish after another. He doesn't know that her secret machine steals one of his memories after another every time he wishes.

"I wasn't really acting... It's really easy for me to be mean!" Burt jokes. "It was a great role and fun to play the 'mean queen!' It was amusing to be able to scare the heck out of two young boys. Walt Disney said 'I would never make anything my kids couldn't see,' and I would never make anything my nieces and nephews couldn't see."

Still, she and the rest of the crew ran into many of the same problems that Stronach and the first group had found in the German climate.

"I was up in Munich for a very hot and balmy summer, in July and August," she says. I wore two outfits, both extremely heavy, made of sequins with prickly edges on them, digging into my flesh. The huge sound stages were extremely hot. Waking up at 4 a.m. every day and spending two and a half hours a day in the makeup chair was grueling, but I think it helped me get into character. It helped my 'grumpy' performance!"

With Oliver out, Jonathan Brandis took over as Bastian. A decade later, the acting world would be shocked and heartbroken by his suicide in November 2003.

"Jonathan Brandis was the kindest, sweetest, most well-mannered kid on the planet," Burt recalls. "I played off of two really great kids (as Xayide)."

Having already wished away his dead mother, Bastian has one left, and the sorceress hopes he'll use it to go home and leave her to her new controlled land. But his friendship with Atreyu wins out, and Bastian only wishes for Xayide, for the first time in her life, to "have a heart." To care about something besides herself.

A tear spills from her eye, and there's more to her emotion that we'll ever see. A lifetime of feeling that she never felt is coming true and coming out in one. In a blast of light, Xayide is gone. Fantasia is restored, and the Empress helps Bastian get back home.

In 1995, the next chapter of the story arrived, this time with Jason James Richter (of *Free Willy* fame) as Bastian. Hunted down by bullies (Jack Black is one), he and the book slip back to Fantasia. However, the imaginary world finds its way back to his reality, and he and his new stepsister are forced to fight it off.

Back in Italy, Burt went into television production, then radio. In 2014, she launched her own network.

"It's the same thing that made me want to pursue a career in acting," she explains. "Media to me means a camera, a microphone, and what I do for my career. It's a stage. It's just one of those things you know, just one of those things you are, one of the things you're born with and one of the things that's intrinsic in you. I never had an acting class. I never had a singing class, and I had an album when I was in Europe. I never had a modeling class."

Because as much welcome and helpful education as these things can provide, it takes a bit more than them to make it in entertainment, something that can really only come from within, she believes.

"Studying the craft is very important," Burt says, "but I think what is just as important is that it's not just something you want to do, it's something that you really are, and there are some things that no matter how hard you study or how hard you try, it's just not going to be you, not what you were meant to be. A lot of people want to be rich and famous. A lot of people want to be on magazine covers, and in Oscar-winning movies. But it may not have been what they were truly born to do. This is what I was born to do."

Carel Struycken/Ryan Holihan: *The Addams Family*

Typecasting might be a common worry for those who often find their roles defined by their physical stature. Fortunately, Carel Struycken left himself a back door big enough to fit his seven-foot-plus body through.

"I went to film school because I wanted to *make* films," says the fellow who grunted his way through a loveable giant role as butler Lurch in three *Addams Family* films. "The acting was a coincidence."

Struycken's size, brought on by the hormonal disorder acromegaly, often caused others to mistake him for Ted Cassidy, who introduced many television viewers to the hormonal disorder as Lurch in *The*

Addams Family television show (1964), an issue that continued to occur after Cassidy's 1979 passing.

"People would often get upset when I would deny I was Lurch, so it was a bit of a relief when I was asked to play the part (in the movie)," Struycken says. "From then on I would be able to answer in the affirmative. I was living in Hollywood and people kept asking me for low budget movie parts. Because acting was never my primary ambition, I was not overly concerned about being typecast."

Photo52: His height makes it impossible NOT to look down on others, but Carel Struycken made Lurch into the same lovable giant in *The Addams Family* movies (1991, 1993) that Ted Cassidy had on TV.

After playing Fidel in *The Witches of Eastwick* (1987) and a giant on *Twin Peaks* (1990), Struycken finally got to follow in Cassidy's oversized footsteps, as the creepy, kooky, mysterious, and spooky family moved to the big screen in 1991. As if the family butler's size wasn't intimidating enough, his entire dialogue consisted of deep grunts, which Struycken at times managed to vary from frightening to quizzical to even friendly, particularly to the Addams kids of Jimmy Workman's Pugsley and a young Christina Ricci as Wednesday.

"I find it harder to project a presence without dialogue," Strycken explains. "Usually I try to maintain an inner dialogue while doing a scene without lines."

Two years later, he and the rest of the *Family* would return in *Addams Family Values*. In 1998, he'd be one of the few to reprise his role in the TV-only *Addams Family Reunion* (Nicole Fugure and Jerry Messing were the kids this time).

"*Addams Family Values* had the same cast, and a great one at that," Strycken says. "The script also seemed a bit better. So it was great to be a member of the cast again. *Addams Family Reunion* was a pilot for a TV show, with a completely different production team and cast."

Acromegaly has cut short far too many lives, stealing well-known sufferers like Andre the Giant and Richard Kiel of James Bond fame from the entertainment world. The syndrome, which causes unnatural growth in the limbs, hands, feet, facial features, and other parts of the body, can cause diabetes, organ enlargement and failure, and a host of other problems. Fortunately, Struycken had some extra weaponry against it.

"My father was a doctor and always kept close tabs on my health," says the actor, whose growth hormone levels fell after pituitary surgery in 1993. "I have to work a lot harder than before the surgery to stay in shape and follow a low-calorie, very low saturated fat diet, eating mainly vegetables and vegetarian sources of protein. I eat about one egg-yolk per week at most and otherwise egg white only, plus vegetable proteins. I eat a healthy 'Mediterranean-style diet.'"

Still, no healthy diet could prevent him from a quick claw-through-the-carotid assassination from Vincent D'Onofrio's bug during Struycken's small role of Arquillian in 1997 for *Men in Black*!

"In the original script, the two alien ambassadors were more pivotal to the plot," says Stuycken, who played an alien leader trying to keep two planets from going to war. "It was implied in the script that the two ambassadors were old friends, who were both very aware of the critical importance of their mission and the possibility of war between their respective planets. So even though there was not that much screen time, it did not 'feel' like a small part."

At his size, most things probably feel, and look, awfully miniscule.

"Over the years I have become much more appreciative of the art of acting," he asserts. "I am aware of my limitations, but enjoy most parts now more than early on in my career."

Still, it's always important to have a plan B – or C, D, all the way down to Y, he continues.

"A few times I have visited schools for Q+A sessions," he says, "and I am always a bit taken aback by the number of young people who want to be actors or go into professional sports. Such a tiny percentage of people are ever able to make a living that way. So I would not advise anyone to go into acting. It has to be an 'all-consuming' passion – or like in my case, a coincidence."

While Struycken, along with John Franklin, who stepped inside Cousin It's hairy, Morse-code-speaking form for the films, had at least something of a history to learn from for their characters, Ryan Holihan and the fellow he'd become came from nowhere.

The famous Addams clan dance party scene called upon the cast and crew to spread family membership as far as their imaginations could run, and Holihan got a chance to step outside of realism and into the new world he'd been using as a welcome escape for over a decade.

"I was a shy kid with a lot of social anxiety, so getting to play the lead in my school play was really brave for me back then," Holihan says of his acting debut in a middle school play. "When I was younger I found out I could be much more brave on stage than off and it really helped me come out of my shell. This is essentially what keeps me acting to this day. The fact that when you act, you get to be completely free of the consequences of the social norms that restrict everyday life and be someone else. It is always liberating to be an actor because of this reason. It is like taking a 'mini-vacation' from yourself and stepping into someone else's life/body."

Ryan Holihan's Lumpy Addams, the hunchbacked newcomer to the family, hit the dance floor with young Wednesday (Christina Ricci) in the 1991 film.

Like so many other Family members, his was a character that so much of society might frighten away, but found normalcy at home.

"I was still a senior in high school at the time," Holihan recalls of the first film audition of his career. "I was still a completely shy and socially awkward teenager and landing a role as one of the Addams relatives was extraordinary because it made perfect sense to me. I always felt different, and what could be more 'different' than playing a teenage hunchback? That costume, that hair!"

That's right – he'd be putting the next setting in Charles Laughton and Lon Chaney's legendary trends as a brand new, although hardly surprising, Addams addition.

"I always wanted to know more about Lumpy Addams," Holihan says. "He was a completely new character to the Addams Family universe, so that presented endless possibilities. I did my research and there was no hunchback in any of the original cartoons or in the television show, which I watched in re-runs as a child. I was more familiar with the television show, but after I landed the role I looked at the complete canon of Charles Addams cartoons and fell in love with his work. Lumpy Addams was *me* and that is why it was appealing."

Lumpy might have been part him, but others had gone the route of the character called Quasimodo long beforehand, and Holihan looked over some of their work.

"The most famous Hunchback of Notre Dame lived in a bell tower and was a recluse, so I used that as a springboard when I imagined who Lumpy was and why he didn't speak," he remembers. "Using my imagination is always how I prepare for any role. I ask myself 'why.' 'Why' this, and 'why' that, and after I come up with answers, I start to do the physical work."

Lumpy's work there was a bit harder than it looked; as dance music sweeps across the Addams hall (one band member plays a clarinet made from a cobra), Wednesday leads her much larger dance partner through a small routine until Morticia calls her away.

"One of the reasons that I assumed they cast me was because I had musical theater experience and they knew I could move well," explains Holihan, enrolled at a performing arts school at the time of filming. "I had a callback where I worked with Christina Ricci and the choreographer before they offered me the role and there was about a month between that and when we filmed. The costume fittings really informed me about the character as well. They designed this amazing suit for me and that helped me prepare for it. Then they did my hair (it was all my real hair, by the way!) and that helped me figure out just how 'different' Lumpy was."

But as it turned out, he and Lumpy weren't all that far apart at all, as we saw with Morticia's wistfully friendly comment about how long it had been since he'd been around and his hesitant, wide grin.

"The role had no dialogue, even though Morticia spoke to him," Holihan says. "I had no control over that fact, but I did ask myself 'why' and I came up with the reason that the character was shy, like myself."

Tai: *Water for Elephants*

The Johnsons just couldn't figure out the identity of this handsome young fellow.

They knew he was an actor; they were watching him get acquainted with a co-star from his next flick. After rolling through the literary fiction bestseller list, *Water for Elephants* was coming to theaters, and he and director Francis Lawrence had come to meet the title character.

Elephants (2011) would be quite a bit different from his previous works — something about vampires, they understood — and he might have even been looking for advice: the Johnsons' friend had spent *much* more time in front of a camera than he had.

Her name was Tai, and she'd stepped before the cameras of *George of the Jungle* (1997), *Operation Dumbo Drop* (1995), *Jungle Book* (1994), even a Britney Spears video. Now, armed with the training she'd learned at the Johnsons' pachyderm preservation group Have Trunk Will Travel of Perris, California, she was helping him take a new step in his performing career.

Roughly ten times the size of the rest of the cast, it wasn't hard for Tai the elephant to steal the show in 2011's *Water for Elephants*.

They'd learned that Reese Witherspoon would be the film's top female, and the Johnsons had been fine with that – they knew the Oscar winner knew the score in acting. But her male co-star? An unfamiliar face.

"He was super sweet and we really liked him," Kari Johnson recalls of the visitor, "but we had no idea who he was."

The actor and director left, and Kari called her brother to find out the story. He asked the performer's name, and she wasn't quite sure.

"I said it was Robert Patterson," she says. "He said, 'You mean, Pattinson?'" In the background, Kari could hear her nieces screaming.

Indeed, he had been the former – and future, as the last few installments of *Twilight* weren't out yet – Edward Cullen, and Pattinson was moving from adapting Stephanie Meyer's work to the screen to acting out that of Sara Gruen.

But not without Tai's help.

"We've had Tai for 34 years," says Kari, whose company got the elephant from a closing park in Florida. Tai hit age 47 in 2015, about two decades short of the normal life span for her species.

"People think that (elephants are) amazing, but they don't even know how amazing they are. When you live with them, you know everything about them."

Elephants gave film audiences a chance to know a bit more about Tai, and the people who train her.

"We'll get the script and go through it," Johnson explains of Tai's typical preparation process, which lasted a month for *Elephants*. "We take out all the elephant action and decide what she already does and what she needs to learn, and practice whatever it happens to be. (For *Elephants*), they wanted an older elephant, and we knew that the role was very difficult. There was going to be a lot to learn, and she's really quick to pick up on things and really savvy around the set."

With Pattinson as Jacob, a veterinary student who wanders into a passing circus after his parents' tragic passing, and Witherspoon as Marlena, the introverted – in private – wife of the circus master (though we know that they'll end up together from the start) and its top female performer, Tai, became Rosie, the circus' new star attraction (alongside a small Jack Russell terrier named Uggie, who'd soon steal the show of the 2011 Best Picture-winning *The Artist*).

"The best thing is that it takes away from the mundane (parts) of the day," Pattinson says of working with his new four-legged friend. "If you're doing 20 takes of something, and there's a character who's going to be doing something totally different every time, it's always exciting. It's like working with a full-on method actor who's just improvising."

Things may have been fun for Tai, but not for her character; playing the desperate and abusive ringmaster August, Christoph Waltz had to take his anger out on the defenseless, or so he believed, abusing her with a stick in ways that make animal rights activists go straight to protest mode (the film's set several decades in the past, so such groups were much more sparse and liberal back then).

"That was hard," Kari says of the scene. "She never got hit, but we had to get her to react as if she was. He had a little stick with a tennis ball; they added the end with a computer. He wasn't touching her, but it had to look like she was reacting. We had to teach her to move away from him, and to cringe. We don't yell at elephants, but he did, and she reacted to that."

By the way, the scene where Jacob realizes that Rosie reacts better to a foreign language? That was all fiction, Kari continues.

"She's not listening to the actor," she explains. "She's listening to the trainer and doing what the trainer says. The trainer was standing off camera, giving her directions. The actor is just basically a prop in there."

'In there' ends up meaning something new for Pattinson, who gets a trip inside the elephant's mouth.

It was, "the most incredible thing in the world," he says. "You're being lifted up by her gums... She puts just the right amount of pressure on so she isn't hurting you. It's so strange."

Witherspoon, who spent quite a bit of time atop Tai in the flick, also got some elevation from her trunk.

"They had her pick me up, and I just screamed," she says. "She could crush you, but she knows the exact amount of pressure to put on you."

"Reese was absolutely amazing," Kari says. "She did all those mounts herself, and they're hard. They were hard for the stuntgirl to learn. I couldn't believe what she did, and what she was willing to do. There was total trust, and she followed direction."

But Tai still had some new skills to learn, and one of them came in handy during arguably her biggest scene. As his circus descends into anarchy, the workers rebelling and the animals escaping, August finally loses it with Marlena, strangling her into the ground. But Rosie gets revenge, stabbing him dead with a stake.

"One of the main things and the hardest things was getting her to fling the stake to kill August at the end," Kari says. "The director wanted her to swing it in a certain way, like a golf club, which is not normally a movement she would use. If she could have raised it up and brought it down, that would have been easier, but he wanted her to raise it high and follow through, to go in a certain direction."

Of course, by then, the elephant might have been thinking more about the rewards than the work.

"Tai is an elephant that loves to make noise," Kari says. "She's always hitting a stick on another stick or a piece of metal to make noise, so we got a metal trashcan that makes a lot of noise. We started out holding her trunk and letting it go so it hit the trashcan and made noise. She liked that; it was almost like the reward was making the noise. Her treat was to play with the trashcan afterward and bang it around and make a lot of noise. After that, she did (the scene) fast so she could play with the trashcan."

Sadly, after two months of filming in the small southeastern California town of Piru, things had to end, and Tai took it better than her human costars (many snide critics opinioned that they showed better chemistry with her than each other). Pattinson probably couldn't have guessed how much his trip to the Johnsons' would mean.

"(Tai) was the best actor I ever worked with in my life," he says. "I cried when the elephant was wrapped. I never cried when anyone else was wrapped."

Witherspoon felt the same way.

"The day I had to say goodbye to (Tai), I wept all day," she says. "It was one of the most extraordinary filmmaking experiences of my life. You work with actors and directors, but to have this nonverbal complete relationship with an animal that we were all very connected to was very magical... There were a couple of really scary moments on the movie. A couple of zebras broke loose while we were shooting a scene and started bucking and kicking, and we all ran for cover. Camels bit people and spat at them. But the funny thing is that Tai was the most consistent: a calm, just easygoing presence. She was just this incredible spirit."

Harry Waters: *Back to the Future*

When anyone hails Elvis Presley as the king of rock 'n' roll, many people just turn away and snicker to themselves, laughing in disbelief at such a ludicrous label of royalty.

They know the truth. They know who should be sitting on that throne. They think of a fellow who gets *some* credit for the genre – just not nearly enough.

It's a man named Berry. Chuck Berry. And, if a certain film saga told the clear and honest truth (and, really, don't they *always*?), Berry's career got started off of time travel and a family member who happened to witness it.

Temporarily forgetting that he's got to get *Back to the Future* (1985) to avoid a major paradox – you know, one of those things that could destroy the entire universe? – young Marty McFly takes a shot at the musical dreams that have been avoiding him, tearing up and down the stage of Hill Valley High as the graduating class of 1955, including the two people he came back to save, twirls, dips, and dives on the floor beneath him.

Nearby, the band's lead singer sees something special, some seriously "Goode" stuff here.

"Hey, Chuck, it's Marvin," he shouts into a phone. "Your cousin, Marvin Berry! You know that sound you've been looking for? Well, listen to this!" Holding up the phone, he unknowingly unlocks the door to music idolatry.

As is almost always the case in filming, the atmosphere on the set was light years away from what audiences would see. When Harry Waters got Marvin to fire out one of the film's most legendary lines, there was no music, no dancing, little emotion. It was up to him to create it.

The entire dance scene had lasted over two weeks of filming, and now Waters was about to finish things off.

"They did the setup with just me, the crew, and the director," he remembers of the phone call scene. "They said 'Action!' and I did the line. One take and it was done. Now it's clearly part of the American film lexicon." Decades after audiences first went to the past, the future, and back and forth through three films, it's still commonplace for students strolling through Waters' classes at Minnesota's Macalester College (he eventually became the chair of its theater department) and many others, to ask to hear the line in living sound and color.

Before Macalester, before the *Future*, "I was a journeyman actor, always looking for the next job," Waters recalls. "What I found to be important was that I was doing outside theater work. It's what kept my soul alive." In the midst of putting together a new show with some fellow performers, Waters stepped in for a film tryout.

"I had to go in and sing for the casting director," he recalls. "There were eight or ten of us that sang."

Soon, he chatted with a young filmmaker named Robert Zemeckis. "I hadn't even read the script," Waters says. "We sat and talked for about an hour, and I told him how excited I was about a play I was working on." He'd also signed up for a role on a TV series, playing the mayor of a small Midwestern city.

Then, on New Year's Eve of 1984, a phone call came. Zemeckis wanted him to lead the band that helps Marty McFly save his parents' marriage and the entire galaxy. As preparation methods go, he'd have some of the most enjoyable.

Harry Waters reaches out to welcome America to music history as Marvin Berry in *Back to the Future* (1985).

"I had to listen to a lot of old Chuck Berry music," Waters recalls (the TV series he'd lined up was never made). "It was nice to have that kind of homework to do. I had to go back and envelop myself into another genre. I had this group of guys that we created out of our own sensibility of being Marvin Berry and the Starlighters. That made me feel a lot better, being there with those guys."

When it came time to shoot the dance, the crew had rolled through quite a few scenes, then been forced down the same road – Eric Stoltz had originally been cast as Marty, done some work, then left the production (why he did so is irrelevant to this piece). Michael J. Fox had charged straight off the small screens of *Family Ties* (1982) and into one of his first leading roles, and the *Future* group had finally finished with the re-shoots. In the gym of Whittier High School, just below Los Angeles, it was time to go under the sea with newness.

By the time we saw the scene, Marty had already moved back three decades, met his folks, fought off the lustful advances of the lady who'd grow old to be his mom, tried to instill some confidence in his bullied dad, and battled the bullies themselves – all qualities that were still around in his "current" town of 1985, we saw early in the film. However, it was one of the first to go before the cameras.

Gearing up for the shot, Waters and his makeshift band played into character. "There were dancers there, actors, and real musicians," he remembers. "We would jam the entire time between takes. We played 'The Freaks Come out at Night.' The guys would play, and I would sing ballads, standards, R&B songs, and the songs we had to sing."

We'd get a closer look at the fellows soon after. Marty's run outside by a group of bullies, and locked inside a trunk. But it's Marvin's car, and he and the band aren't having that sort of thing, chasing off the bad guys and helping Marty out. However, Marvin's hand is injured in the rescue, and it looks like the show isn't going on.

"Most of those lines I had were ad-libbed, and they kept them in," Waters recalls. "That was when we got to hang out with Michael J. Fox. He had his trailer, and we went in and hung out. We were very happy that he was a nice guy."

Early on, we'd seen Marty try his own hands with his band, only to be cut off by a judge whose ears weren't having it (an inside joke we'll elaborate on in a moment). With Marvin incapacitated, the young McFly steps in to fill out the guitar chords for "Earth Angel," Marvin's voice echoing throughout the gym.

If Marvin's phone call scene was one of the easier shots of the tale, this one was among the toughest. As Marty's dad appears to give in to his cowardly qualities, another fellow steps away with his betrothed. Failure to unite them will knock Marty straight out of existence, and he's about to disappear. As he nearly collapses on the stage, his hand starts to fade out.

"Looking through his hand was one of the most expensive shots," Waters recalls. "It was a $10,000-shot for them to set this all up. Today, you can do it on your laptop, but back then, they were using a computerized camera."

But the happy ending occurs. The father steps forward, shoves away his competitor, and wins the heart of his girl. Marty's back up and whole, and Marvin's grin of relief knocks his voice up a few measures.

As the tune ends, Marty's ready to roll outside and back to 1985. But Marvin convinces him to play just one more melody.

And it almost wasn't the tale of a young guitar prodigy from the evergreens of New Orleans.

"(Berry) was not going to let them do 'Johnny B. Goode,'" Waters says. "The script was saying that this little white boy is going to create a song that was written by Berry." It took a few extra dollars to convince Berry to let Marty impersonate him.

Marvin's advice must have rung true; the same year as *Future* told, Berry started working on the tune. Three years later, he released it, after "Maybellene," "Roll Over, Beethoven," and some other lyrical inventions. Nearly six decades later, the song's still a rock 'n' roll landmark, like Berry himself.

And it brought Waters and his group a new round of stardom: the film's soundtrack reached gold status.

"I have a gold record," Waters marvels, "just because I was in the right place at the right time!"

Oh, that judge we mentioned? It was none other than Huey Lewis — and if Berry truly was the man who made rock 'n' roll, who'd be better to show alongside his words than the fellow who felt its heart still beating? Lewis's "Power of Love" also went gold and rolled all the way to the Oscars, where it was edged for the song statuette by Lionel Richie's creation "Say You, Say Me," for *White Nights*.

Five years later, the saga brought the "To Be Continued" message we saw at the end of part one to cinematic life, pushing Marty to 2015 – as that year actually arrived, we were still waiting on things like flying cars and hoverboards! – to 1985, back to 1955, all over time, including, of course, a new version of the famous dance, bringing back Marvin and his men.

"I had gained some weight, so I had to lose some weight," Waters says of his reprisal. "I had to get back to where I was before." A scene in which Marvin, about to make his call, sees Marty both on stage and crawling in the rafters, was cut, he says.

The third film sent Marty back to the old west of 1885. Clearly, there would be no school concerts at this one.

"How could they find a black band in the old west?" Waters ponders.

You know, in hindsight, *Back to the Future* could have been a bust. Time-travel movies have always been a bit iffy in Hollywood, and this one had many chances to go the wrong way. A teenager goes back in time, meets his wimp of a dad, almost gets forced to make out with his own *mother*, then gets back to the present, only to find that his family's now living the lap of luxury – just because he asked them to go easy on their son, should he light the rug on fire?

Sounds like an uneasy sell. But in this case, it worked through a trilogy.

"It's such a smart movie," Waters says. "It's got enough drama, and the stakes are really high: if my parents don't kiss, I'm going to *die*! It has a great, fun story going back and forth between the 80s and the 50s. There's people that transform and are significant in each plot. It was so smart in bringing them in in such a positive way, a sort of writing on an upscale instead of going for the lowest common denominator. It doesn't pander to anybody. It makes you think, but it also makes you laugh."

Cheryl White: *Well, about everything on TV*

When we're getting started on the small-screen acting gig, chances are that our first few appearances will be of the short variety, a one-shot deal, if you shall. It'll be up to us to get our faces and talent seen for a short period of time, hopefully sparking the match for more, and eventually longer jobs.

That's Cheryl White's *modus operandi*. Despite showing up on over *fifty* TV shows (a number that will undoubtedly have increased by the time you're reading this), she's been there for a single episode on all but a few of them. Everything from *The X-Files* (1993) to *Two and a Half Men* (2003) to *True Blood* (2008), White's appeared – for a short while.

"Television moves very quickly," White explains. "I often do much of my personal preparation for the audition, i.e., working out the character's backstory, clarifying what they want and need. So often I am good to go if I book the job." That's because she sometimes has to go into action the very next day, as cameras roll fast on the small screen.

In 2004, White stuck around for longer than usual on the *Law & Order*-esque *The D.A.*, hanging out for a total of *four* episodes! But showing the importance of networking to an acting career, when the show's crew needed to fill a smaller role on a larger show a few years later, they knew exactly who to call. For one of her toughest roles on a 2008 episode of *The Closer*, White played a woman who helps her husband murder their adopted teenage son, fearing from his violent tendencies and graphic drawings that he'd grow up to be a murderer.

"This was a very difficult character," she recalls. "She does a terrible thing but is not a terrible person: very complex and exciting to portray. This was not a role that I could draw on past experience for. I used my imagination and tried to work as deeply as I could emotionally. I had worked with the actor playing my husband (Jamie McShane) before, which helped tremendously. We had built up a level of trust with each other that made the emotional work safer for us."

By the time she appeared on this episode of *Scrubs* in 2001, it was one of the few shows that Cheryl White hadn't guested upon.

Things weren't safe for the characters of *Nip/Tuck* when White arrived on the plastic surgery drama in 2003, playing a character with over twenty personalities, ranging from the mild-mannered to the UFC-guys-would-run-away-in-fear violent, with names like Justice, Sassy, and Montana.

"I was dying to audition for that role," she says. "I knew it would be extremely challenging. The producers of *Nip/Tuck* actually gave me a video of a documentary about a woman with multiple personality disorder to watch. It helped me tremendously and clarified the tone of the character that the producers were looking for."

Comedies, on the other hand, offer a different, albeit much lighter (not necessarily easier) type of opportunity. *Will and Grace* (1998), *My Name is Earl* (2005), *That 70s Show* (1998); White's been all over the market, including a 2001 episode of *Scrubs*, where she became Maggie, a terminally ill patient who just wants a quick ride on the mattress merry-go-round before she passes.

Demonstrating the above-and-beyond reproach that the show's doctors and nurses always had for their patients, a doctor and nurse go on a quest to find Maggie a one-night man, only to find themselves arrested for solicitation. But before they can give her the bad news, there's a special redemption: hospital lawyer Ted, one of the most tortured characters in small-screen history, someone who couldn't catch a break if someone handed it to him, finally makes Maggie's wish come true.

"That was worth the wait!" she contentedly gasps.

In this line of acting work, White says, "You definitely have to focus on 'finding the funny.' Your timing has to be precise. In the case of *Scrubs*, the writing is so good you can't help but be funny."

Fame might be the final goal of many actors, but it's the manner of getting there that makes the difference. Like in any other line of work, acting won't hand glory to anyone; as White has shown, persistence is one of the biggest keys to making it in the business.

"If you are in search of stardom, you are setting yourself up for failure," she says. "(But) if you are driven to be an actor, a good actor, then you've got a shot."

Matthew Willig: *Concussion*

On a cold Sunday afternoon in September 1992, two teams stepped onto the turf of Pittsburgh's Three Rivers Stadium, the site of so many infamous NFL wars. The stadium had seen its home Steelers drop the legendary Steel Curtain defense on so many hapless offenses during the 1970s, given Franco Harris the room to make his legendary Immaculate Reception catch during the 1972 playoffs, and spurred on the squad to four Super Bowl rings in six years.

Now a recent Univesity of Southern California grad was getting one hell of an NFL initiation; in just the second game of his NFL career, Matt Willig was in the very, *very* big leagues; a new addition to the New York Jets' offensive line, he'd be trying to put the stop on the Steeler defense.

Things didn't go well for the rookie that day; his counterpart Justin Strzelczyk – same position, other team – was a bit more successful, as Pittsburgh won, 27-10.

Over the next few years, the two ran into each other – not literally, both playing offensive tackle – a few more times. Wearing a different outfit for every game – he'd play for six teams during thirteen years in the league – Willig faced Strzelczyk twice more, but the Steel Men came out on top each time. But Willig got his own last laugh, as he'd be a member of St. Louis' Super Bowl champion squad of 1999, one year after Strzelczyk called it quits without a ring.

"I did not know (Strzelczyk) personally," recalls Willig, "(but) in the league's lineman fraternity, you're aware of who else is around, at your position. I remember him being a mountain of a man."

In Sept. 2002, the Steelers lost a local hero, as Hall of Fame center Mike Webster passed away at just age 50. At the time, no one knew how big an aftermath Webster's passing would cause.

Continuing a very sad tradition among NFL retirees, Strzelczyk had trouble finding a new place in society. Bad investments cost him quite a bit of money, and he drank up too much more. He and his wife Keana broke up. He started forgetting things, the resulting frustration driving him to unfocused fury.

As Willig suited up for Carolina for the first few games of the 2004 season (his squad had made it to the previous Super Bowl, falling to New England), western Pittsburgh would soon be rocked again, harder than any defensive line.

On Sept. 30, 2004, Strzelczyk roared down a New York highway, reaching ninety miles an hour. Ignoring cops, other drivers, everything, he moved to the wrong side of the road, smashing right into traffic. Then he hit a truck, and was gone forever at just age thirty-six.

The league, particularly Pittsburgh, was shocked and heartbroken. And it wasn't over; the following June, Terry Long, who'd played guard next to Strzelczyk for two seasons, died after drinking antifreeze, right in the Steel City.

After one more year in St. Louis, Willig hung up his cleats after the 2005 season. By then, he already had an idea for a new career.

Back at USC, he'd already shown up for a small role in 1993's action flick *Full Contact*. Still, it wasn't really Willig's acting debut.

"I was the fifth of sixth boys," he remembers, "and growing up, I was the class clown, so it was sort of natural to have that in me." In his waning days on the Trojan gridirons, a trainer had asked if he'd like to show similar skills before the camera.

Matt Willig and Bitsie Tulloch portray the pain that Justin Strzelczyk and his wife Keana struggled through just before Strzelczyk's tragic death in *Concussion* (2015).

"We were shooting in a small warehouse, and my dressing room was a closet," recalls Willig, who, at 6'8" and three hundred pounds, probably had some extra inconveniences in such a spot! "There was something about it, hundreds of people coming together to create something." Over his career, he'd show up on quite a few TV and radio shows. Just after retirement, he was asked to show up next to former teammate Kurt Warner and some other colleagues for a soup commercial.

"Being an athlete on camera," he remembers, "that feeling came back, even fifteen years later." The acting bug had bitten as hard as football's lure ever did, and he was off and performing for the next few years, including recurring roles on (ready for some serious diversity?) both *The Young and the Restless* and *NCIS* in 2011!

By the time *Concussion* (2015) came around a few years later, too many other athletes had died or suffered all kinds of horrible, incurable injuries from years of getting pounded in the head. In the summer of 2007, Dr. Bennet Omalu had finally given it a name: Chronic Traumatic Encephalopathy, or CTE for short. People (women athletes were certainly afflicted as well) in their thirties and forties were grasped in the evil clutches of dementia, Alzheimer's, and other trouble linked to repeated blows to the head. Over years of football from Pop Warner to the pros, including the thousands of practices along the way, men were taking thousands of huge collisions to the skull. After a while, their brains couldn't recover.

Webster had been the first official case. Strzelczyk and Long had been diagnosed as well (sadly, as of now, the disease can only be found during autopsy). More players in more sports, before and after the film, had been found. By the time this book comes out, it's a safe bet that even more will have been.

In 2013, Strzelczyk's ex Keana McMahon (she's since remarried) sat down to interview for *The United States of Football*, a documentary discussing the potential dangers of America's favorite sport. Learning of *Concussion*, she figured it would be another factual film.

Then McMahon heard starring names like Will Smith and Alec Baldwin. This was a different kind of movie. Eventually, Peter Landesman visited Pittsburgh to see if she'd be a part of the flick he'd written and would eventually direct.

"We had lunch together, and he told me he had written us into the script," McMahon remembers. "He would only put us in if we would sign off on it." Yes, she said "we," because it wasn't just about her – she and Strzelczyk had two children that would see a sad part of their story told.

"It was very important that they approved," McMahon remembers (obviously, while they had lost their dad at far too young an age, her kids had reached adulthood by the time of the film).

They did. Now Landesman and the rest of the crew had to find someone to become Strzelczyk. The film had enough main names from the acting world; Adewale Akinnuoye-Agbaje played Dave Duerson, with Richard Jones as Andre Waters, both of whom took their own lives after losing nearly all to CTE. Getting someone who'd been a part of the game would add just that extra ounce of realism.

"It would have been a shame if had been someone without the experience," Willig says. "It was attractive to me right away. I read the breakdown of the character. I was close to it. I had lived it, to a sense.

I had had a dip in depression: what do you do, post-career? You're meant to be beat up on a daily basis, and now I had that broken-down physical body. I had not had as strong of a depressive trigger that Justin had. Playing a real-life person who had my stature and background was something I wanted to do."

Surrounded by performers with quite a bit more experience, if not necessarily talent, in the profession, Willig wowed the crew at his tryout. "I put on a very emotional audition," he remembers. "They got excited about the idea of getting a player from the NFL that had the acting chops to do this. That was a win as well."

Now it was his turn to meet with McMahon. He met her and the kids.

"I was capable of speaking very openly with Matt, because it had been so long ago," McMahon recalls. "It was easy for me to lay everything out, to talk about every detail of life. I was spilling my guts." She showed stacks of hundreds of writings and drawings that Strzelczyk had used to express the lonely, terrifying place his world was deteriorating into.

"There were random thoughts," Willig says. "Some were unrecognizable, some were beautiful, but when you put it all together, it gave me a nice understanding about who he was and as he evolved into a person who became very scared about where he was going and where his mental state was. It was a treat for me to be able to dive into a character, to be able to pull as much as you can, to find his sense of desperation. As things were going on, he understood less and less about what was happening to him."

There are a few points to make here. Before we learn much of the Omalu protagonist that Smith played, audiences see Webster (David Morse) suffering through his own pain in and out. His body and mind ruined, he's off living in a truck, using a Taser to shock himself into unconsciousness to escape his pain. Strzelczyk comes to visit him, letting him know how worried everyone is – and that Strzelczyk's own mind is starting to go.

The meeting only took place in the storyline, McMahon says, as the two hardly knew each other in real life. A later scene, perhaps the film's toughest part to watch, didn't really happen either.

As one of the NFL's most loyal fanbases cheers on his old squad, Strzelczyk can't handle anything. He smashes up his prized possessions. He storms around the house. He threatens his wife and kids (Bitsie Tulloch played Keana, with Dina Rende and Samara Lee acting out the children).

Then he chokes Keana. That also never occured, says the actual lady. Considering she was already engaged to her now-husband when Strzelczyk died, it seems highly unlikely they'd be in the same house just before his death.

"I told (my kids) about the script," McMahon explains. "I told them, you know the truth, I know the truth, and the truth is important only to you and I. The rest of the world can think what they want, as long as we know the truth. (At the time), there were about eighty players with CTE, and all behave so differently. Peter had to try to cram all these personalities into four or five characters, guys that were abusive, guys, like Justin, that deteriorated."

Strzelczyk storms outside and drives off in his pickup. We don't see him alive again.

But the fans keep cheering. They party, they high five, drink beer, wave Pittsburgh's infamous "Terrible Towels," and worry about the final score, and that's it. It's not that they don't care. They don't know. They don't *want* to know. Once men like Webster, Strzelczyk, Duerson, Junior Seau, and all others who have or will be afflicted with the horror of CTE call it quits, there's always someone else to take their place. And we'd rather hope the new guys win than worry about how the past guys are doing.

As 2015 wound down, McMahon, Willig, and the rest of the *Concussion* crew got to see the action before it fell into the mainstream (Smith's non-Oscar nomination for playing Omalu was one of the year's biggest controversies).

"I didn't know what to expect going into it," McMahon says. "I teared up a little bit at the crash scene. I've had a lot of people walk on eggshells around me, but I've had eleven years, so it's not as hard for me."

She and others had made it just a bit easier, or at least smoother, for Willig.

"You put yourself in the mental state of sitting alone and being by yourself and feeling some things you wouldn't normally do," he says. "Having to cry and having to do other things was just there. It was natural. It wasn't forced. I'll look back on my career, no matter where it goes, and see this role as very satisfying."

As the years pass, more and more athletes will suffer from CTE. With high-contact sports still so high in demand, it's not a question of if, but how many. Omalu's work took the first step in giving it a name. Treatment may be located someday.

Hopefully. Until then, the alumni of such sports can only hope. Hope that they don't wake up one morning and forget where they are, why their spouses and children are hiding, where all their money went. People like Willig.

"There's no question that there are times in the back of your head that you think about that," he admits. "You get depressed. My personal feeling is that players who go through this already have a propensity for it, the makeup of having depression, that type of thing in their DNA. The ups and the downs that, when it comes time for when they do get hit, they're more susceptible to it than others. I'm a pretty positive person. You work the problem and you work the solution. You have to stand up and say, 'I'm going to be a positive guy.'"

Dementia and Alzheimer's are still about as mysterious to the medical community as CTE itself, but doctors have come up with some recommendations that just might keep it away, or at least stave it off for a while. Diet, exercise, and mental stimulation, like learning new languages, doing crossword puzzles, word and number games may just keep the mind stimulated enough to keep it safe from harm. The oft-chaotic, constantly changing world of performing might be a great way to make Willig's mind, his life, diverse enough to stay on the go.

Everyone hopes.

"I feel like keeping my mind active is huge," he remarks. "Being in a business (like acting) where you're constantly staying active, playing new roles, creating new characters, doing improv comedy, having that back and forth when keeping your mind active lends itself to staying away from that sort of depression, the thoughts of where CTE comes in. I've been lucky so far."

Special Spotlight: Ms.'s and Mr.'s of Musicals

The best thing about acting in musicals is that there's no expectation of realism by anyone. It's all-out, no holds barred, no quarter given emotion at high speed. Nothing to lose and everything to gain. Inhibition out the door like 200-mile-an-hour fastballs. It's the place to have a blast and give everyone exactly what they want, what they expect, and what they damned sure hope for. Put the collective pedal to the metal and kick some ass.

Realism? No one expects it – because people don't suddenly break out into tunes and form an impromptu chorus line. Do you think there's people on a bus or at a bar thinking, "Man, I hope someone comes in here and starts singing, because I'll join in right away!"?

Probably not. But that's the wondrous world of musicals. People expect you to grab the screen by the throat and whip it into a frenzy. It's why Anne Hathaway, Catherine Zeta-Jones and Jennifer Hudson – only the most recent – snared Oscars: because they personified a different kind of actress from those who typically take home the statuettes. Ones that we don't expect to be as real as the dramatic, or even the comedic. Just ones who take us into another world (and maybe a better one; who *wouldn't* want to hang out in a place with happy endings and endless rhymes, at least for a while?), a little farther than most movies dare to go.

Going for a musical, give it all you've got, and then don't be afraid to give it just a little bit more. No limits in this place!

T.V. Carpio: *Across the Universe*

At the height of the Beatles' fame, John Lennon got into some trouble for saying that he and his band of British boys were more popular than Jesus.

That quote brought Lennon far more than his fair share of criticism around the world, per usual for the case when the religious right (or totally wrong!) gets involved. Still, even nearly half a century after the group commonly accepted as the music world's first "boy band" cut its ties, the appeal's still here – and perhaps past the healthy levels.

Even before she and the rest of those who'd traveled *Across the Universe* (2007) were through doing their thing on film screens in Rome, T.V. Carpio could feel, see, and especially hear the energy just *wafting* off its audiences.

"Even before the last song, people were standing and clapping for ten minutes!" she recalls. "They loved it there."

When the crew went elsewhere, though, the response was a bit different. The Beatles had been *their* group, and anyone who tried to copy them, skill level and intention irrelevant, it just wasn't happening.

"The British *hated* it," Carpio sadly laments. "Some people couldn't believe we'd touched their Holy Grail." A certain singer named McCartney, however, had enjoyed the *Universe*.

Well, no film pleases everyone. Still, working a plot based on the tunes of one of music's most influential bands into a coherent storyline was quite the challenge. Julie Taymor, who'd help put the script together, was behind the camera, sprinkling songs all over one of America's most turbulent times. The 1960s were the Beatles' years when it came to worldwide appeal: the Fab Four's explosion into America in early 1964 had generated more publicity than just about any other group in history, and they'd toss out four albums in as many years in the late part of the decade.

Dear, dear Prudence (T.V. Carpio) lyrically ponders her future in turbulent
times in the 2007 Beatles tribute *Across the Universe.*

But the rest of the nation was in the grip of fear and terror that only got worse – the Vietnam War was rampant a world away, and racial riots were raging here at home. This *Universe* was a warm, loving place in several ways, but violence and heartbreak were too close as well, and Taymor's tale would work all around it. Jim Sturgess's Jude arrived from Liverpool illegally, and Lucy (Evan Rachel Wood) lost her boyfriend in the fields of Hanoi.

And then there was Prudence (the names weren't exactly an inside joke, as many of the main characters were monikered after Beatles songs). She'd represent another issue that was just starting to come to light in the '60s.

"She was looking for a family, a place to belong, looking for home," Carpio explains. "She was look-ing for a home situation, and she just couldn't find it." The actress had herself spent time on the move; born in Oklahoma City, she'd lived in Hong Kong, Massachusetts, and New York before heading across the country to Los Angeles.

"It wasn't like growing up in the same town with the same friends," she remembers. "Things were always changing." Her character's first appearance would be quite a difference as well.

A high school cheerleader in the midst of an abusive relationship, Prudence can't help but hope and fantasize about another. Someone with whom her relationship is great, if just a little too plutonic for her own tastes.

It's a fellow cheerleader. Yes, a woman. Not an easy subject to so much as speak of back then.

"It was about the discovery of myself," Carpio explains. "We didn't label her as a lesbian cheerleader – she just loved who she loved. It was more about free love, looking for herself, lost. There were so many things about Prudence that I could relate to, and still do." She and the rest of the cast rehearsed for months beforehand, in studios and on the set.

"It was like being in a musical every day," says Carpio. "All I was listening to were Beatles and songs from the '60s, watching videos on the times, on Woodstock. Why would I have run away, ended up in that place, dressed up like that?"

As the football squad holds its own ground attacks and ambushes all around her, Prudence can only wander dreamily across the field, subliminally letting her affection object know just how much she wants to hold her hand. Having a lady do the song was a switch in and of itself; how she did it was another adjustment.

The Beatles originally did the song upbeat and very high speed, like on their legendary appearance on Ed Sullivan's stages in February 1964, a month after "I Wanna Hold Your Hand" had already become America's top song. Friendly, flirtatious, and far from formal could easily describe the Fab Four's tuned tome.

Prudence's version was a bit different. Slow, passionate, full of love, the sort of thing we'd play for someone who we wanted for much than just fun and games.

"At the beginning, we sang it like the original," Carpio says. "Julie said we could slow it down. I sang it once like that, and that's how we ended up doing the song. The whole thing was trying, because I had to sing everything live. But I thrive on challenge." With Prudence rejected and Lucy shattered by her loss, the group ends up in New York, where Sadie (Dana Fuchs) looks to put together a new band. Still, after everyone's personal rendition of "I Want You," Prudence finds that Sadie's sadly heterosexual, sending her into a dark room and a deep depression until her friends bring her to her feet and out of the closet with a new melody.

As any Beatles fan worth their salt could guess, it's "Dear Prudence," a tune Lennon wrote for the group's 1968 album *The Beatles* (known in the inner circles as *The White Album*). It's the story of a lady being implored to "open up your eyes, see the sunny skies," to hear "the birds will sing, that you are part of everything." Lennon called it one of his personal favorites, and his son Sean included it on his own 1991 tribute album, *Happy Birthday, John*.

With the music rising, Prudence is out of the closet (in every sense!) and into the open, soon joining her friends in the chorus and one of the many marches that Americans took against the war not so long ago.

"The way I work, I think about what's happening at a specific time," Carpio explains. "The rest of the time, I allow myself to be surprised by a situation. I don't plan things out too much. I think about the situation and what happened before. But what it comes down to is when they say 'Action!' you don't really think anything, except for that this is really happening, and it's happening for the first time."

They come, they go, they break up, they reconcile as dozens of Beatles tunes play in so many new ways, but things eventually end just like musicals usually do: everyone's back together on a rooftop, more and more people gathering below to take in the magic of the music. It's easy to imagine the Beatles starting out the same way. Decked out in the costumes that snared the film an Oscar nomination, Prudence, Sadie, and others ask the rest to "Don't Let Me Down," as Lucy can't get to see them. But Jude manages to win everyone's heart by reminding everyone that "All You Need is Love," and he and Lucy find each other again.

Then it was across America and around the world, time for the *Universe*-al group to see their creation's impact on the rest of the planet. Some, probably most, enjoyed it. Not everyone did. But, again, that's the case with, oh, every single film that reaches any kind of large audience!

"You can't allow yourself to think about it too much," Carpio explains. "You know how hardcore fans are going to be. That is a test that can happen, and it can impede the work when you try to impress people. The only thing in my power is knowing that what I'm saying or what I'm seeing is coming from my heart. It's a lesson I'm still learning from my heart. So much of what you do is criticized by people, and it's not in your power to control what other people think about your work. If someone doesn't like it, they don't like it."

Joanna Chilcoat: *Camp*

It's not just an act, and it's not just for a show, not part of the production. It's the truth, the autobiography that's been written by enough people to be its own library.

"I'm socially awkward and have trouble making friends, but in theater I always found kinship and acceptance," says almost every drama student, everyone who dared to step onto a stage as the only place to be whom they dreamed of becoming. "Besides the sense of community and of family that I get from performing, for a socially awkward person, there is a great deal of comfort in being able to step outside of my own skin, to walk around in a character's shoes instead of my own and to forget my own troubles for a while."

Maybe not every theater student used those exact words. Perhaps they just came straight from the subject of this piece. But survey any sizable amount of the kids — and probably adults — found in the theatrical companies of America, and you'll probably find quite a few synonymic statements.

We see TV shows like *Glee* and call them unrealistic, but we're only right to an extent. Yes, people don't suddenly break into song and dance routines and learn hardcore choreography in the span of seconds, but clubs like the one we watched for six years on Fox, and the people that join them, are all too real. School drama is a place where the different can find a bit of commonality and stability that the confusing, unpredictable world can never offer.

And yes, two years of drama in high school drama and a college production taught these lessons to a certain guy who took the "socially awkward outcast" label to a new extreme.

Camp's certainly a true story. Not in the typical biographical sense, but in that meaning that the 2003 film tells the saga of every type of student who finds stability in theatrical fiction.

Joanna Chilcoat musically informs us all just where she's *not* going in 2003's *Camp*.

Like the lady we heard from a few short paragraphs ago.

The Baltimore high-schooler was picking up her sister from dance class when the teacher made a quick announcement. An old college friend of hers was trying to make his directing debut, and he'd need a few things. A cast, for example.

Todd Graff's story was from his own past at Stagedoor Manor, one of New York's top performing arts camps. For a quarter-century, thousands of hopeful upcomers have passed through its classrooms and stages – like, say, Natalie Portman, Robert Downey Jr., Zach Braff, and Graff himself. He'd scripted out the story of a similar place in the same state.

He just needed a few people to portray the students he'd once been a part of (Danny DeVito, with whom Graff had worked in the sadly underappreciated *Death to Smoochy* in 2002, was a producer).

"My parents and I went to New York for the cattle call," remembers Joanna Chilcoat, "and after countless rounds of reading and singing, I was called back."

And again. And again.

"Three callbacks later," she wearily remembers, "and the choice for Ellen had been whittled down to me and one other girl." Upon their return to Baltimore, she and her family got the news.

Chilcoat would become Ellen Lucas. She had to start the next day.

"My dad dropped everything and went with me," she says. "What I really liked about Ellen was that she was a real girl, so like myself, with dreams and talent and who was just a little lost. The film emphasized all the things I love about being involved in theater."

Like just about every other theater camp in the history of the world, the place is full of folk with little in common but a dream. An overweight girl, frightened introverts, some gay guys, snobby girls, and a new guy who can't seem to get everyone to believe that he is, in fact, straight.

"Todd's writing and direction meant that everything felt natural on set," Chilcoat says. "I never felt like he was giving me anything I couldn't work with, and he let us have input on dialogue that didn't roll right off the tongue."

After a month in the Big Apple rehearsing for acting camp, it was time to head up to Loch Sheldrake and walk through Stagedoor, transformed to Camp Ovation by Graff's writings. Week after week, the youngsters act out one musical tale after another.

Too innocent to even let her hair down from its pigtails, Ellen, like just about every other gal there, finds herself a bit enthralled with Vlad, the only guy there with the guts to openly admit his heterosexuality. But the stereotypical snobbish girl comes along in the form of Jill (Alana Allen), leading to some typical one-liner action in the midst of lunch.

"I think the hardest scene for me was the canteen scene where I'm 'mean' to Jill," Chilcoat says. "It was the scene that felt furthest from my own reality." Jill's voluntary sidekick – who, like everyone else, turns on her in the end – was a young debuting lady named Anna Kendrick, who'd eventually sing her way to stardom in *Into the Woods* (2014) and the *Picture Perfect* films (2012, 2015), along with yanking down an Oscar nomination in 2009 for *Up in the Air*.

Equipped with a obscenely huge wig, Ellen hilariously charms her way into the heart of one of the camp's youngest performers with her own version of "And I Am Telling You I'm Not Going," the same tune that Jennifer Hudson belted out on her way to an Oscar for *Dreamgirls* (2006).

"Learning that I was going to be singing that song was a crazy, fearful moment," remembers Chilcoat. "Todd showed me a video of Jennifer Holliday singing 'And I Am Telling You,' and watching her perform was overwhelming. It's a powerful song, and when she sings it you feel completely absorbed by it." Holliday won both a Tony and Grammy for renditioning the tune in *Dreamgirls'* Broadway action.

"It was never about me being able to *sing* like Holliday," Chilcoat explains, "moreso about the passion, the energy, and the ridiculousness that a fifteen-year-old white girl would be singing this song in the first place."

Not surprisingly (well, to anyone in theater), the group spends quite a bit of time on the sounds of Stephen Sondheim, *only* about the most well-known theater composer in history, winner of an Oscar

(Best Song of 1990 for "Sooner or Later" in *Dick Tracy*), eight Grammys, and eight more Tonys (i.e., the Oscars for theater). Perhaps an inside tribute from Graff? Maybe.

Up through now, the film hasn't really crossed into true "musical" classification – it's more of a dramedy with the occasional, clearly staged performance. But as their teacher finds himself being grabbed too deeply by depression and booze, the troupe joins up right outside his place and renditions Victoria Williams' creation "Century Plant," rhetorically querying him of, "Hey, do you wanna come out, and play the game? It's never too late!" Soon, he's up, he's out with them, and everyone remembers why they're here. A highlight of the film itself, it ended up as one of Chilcoat's personal favorites.

"In the barn, there was a circle of track with a dolly, which would circle the camera around us as we sang the song two or three times," she explains. "Then they'd take a piece out of the track and make it a smaller circle and we'd do it again. We had recorded everything in a studio in New York City prior to moving up to the camp, so we were singing along with the track at first. But then the musicians started to play, we started to sing louder, and by the end of the day, and it was a long day, it felt so natural, like we weren't on camera, but rather just in our element, jamming with our friends."

Finally, the camp finale arrives.

And who should show? Just Sondheim himself! The performers react like teenage girls to a boy band. At the end of a smash-hit night, Sondheim even gives the campers a way to stay in touch. Maybe he saw some future singers to his tunes.

Still, things aren't going great for everyone. Vlad's starting to spread it around the camp gals, even with a girlfriend back home. But Ellen's satisfied when his comeuppance comes up in the form of a dumping, and it looks like the two might end up together.

And what kind of musical would it be without the full crew joining up for one last song-and-dance extravaganza? In this one, it's "The Want of a Nail," Todd Rundgren's tune.

"The dance numbers are beautiful," Chilcoat says. "The lighting and set design throughout the film are just lovely. Watching it for the first time at the Sundance Film Festival was a surreal experience, I just couldn't believe that I was up on this big screen with all these talented actors and singers. Watching it now, as a director, there are all sorts of tweaks I want to make to my own performance, but I know that my teen awkwardness plays into the vibe of the film."

Did you catch that? That's right: Chilcoat, whose last name eventually moved to Fellows, followed in the footsteps of those who showed her and so many others the welcome world of the performing arts where deviance is normalcy, including teaching drama at her old high school.

"My whole career has been built around creating family through theater," she remarks, "and I'm so grateful for the opportunity that *Camp* afforded me to reach out to thousands of people and create a 'family of freaks,' as I lovingly call my drama kids."

Julie Dawn Cole: *Willy Wonka*

As she watched herself on the screen for the first time of many, there was quite a bit that Julie Dawn Cole couldn't believe.

The youngster found it tough to comprehend just how quickly things had changed for her, how fast the first chapter in her acting career had been written; less than a year before, she'd never read the first words of Roald Dahl's classic children's tome *Willy Wonka and the Chocolate Factory*, and now she and a group of others had brought it straight to the cinema on 1971.

She couldn't believe how villainous she came across; her character Veruca Salt was the epitome of a spoiled little rich girl, light years from Cole herself at any age. As she watched Veruca storm around the screen, blasting everyone she met with words and the occasional shove, Cole hoped everyone recognized that it was all truly an act.

But mostly, she couldn't believe just how huge she looked.

"The strangest thing is seeing yourself so big," Cole recalls. "When you're 13, and you're seeing yourself on a movie screen, you're thinking, 'Oh God, I look enormous!'"

Her journey to acting stardom had begun a few months earlier; in the early summer of 1970, the youngster was making her way through an acting class when a casting director showed up and told everyone about the *Wonka* flick.

"I had to run out and buy a copy (of the book) and read it overnight," Cole says. "We were lined up and judged by experience. It went over several auditions, and it wound down, with a few less each time."

The last audition is her most unforgettable, and for more than one reason.

"I went to read an excerpt from the book," she says. "The script wasn't ready yet." But this practice session was about more than acting — while the final film has a lengthy soundtrack, Veruca's the only one of the contest winners to get her own solo, the immortal, "I Want It Now!"

"They didn't have music yet," Cole says. "I had to sing 'Happy Birthday.'" Director Mel Stuart kept asking her to be meaner and meaner, and it's tough for a preteen to turn down that chance. It wasn't her birthday — although there's going to be a story about that in a minute — but she got a special present: the role.

"That was fantastic," she says. "I didn't know anything about it, except that I'd get to be in Germany for three months. I knew that Gene Wilder was going to play the part (of Wonka himself), but I didn't know who Gene Wilder was. This was in the 1970s, and I was 12!" Despite garnering an Oscar nomination two years before for *The Producers*, Willy Wonka would be just Wilder's fifth film role, though he was already a familiar face on Broadway and television.

Over the next few months, Cole still had to convince the producers that she could do more than act like a snob — singing like one was a different task.

"At that point, it still wasn't decided whether I'd sing or have my voice dubbed," she says. "I was given the song and music. I had to meet with a musical director in London in a room with grand piano."

Julie Dawn Cole was brattiness personified as Veruca Salt in
***Willy Wonka and the Chocolate Factory* (1971).**

With Veruca's arrogance blasting out of her mouth, Cole lyric-ed about wanting "the world, the whole world, I want to lock it all up in my pocket!" and more, and it worked again. While her character in the novel was more of a spoiled little brat who just had more than she'd ever need, Cole made Veruca more evil than most adult baddies before or since ("Make 'em work nights!" she snorts at her dad, who's pleading that their servants are working all day to find her desired golden ticket).

During her first few days in Munich, Cole and the producers worked out her costume designs. They did some recordings. But for the most part, she got to know her new co-stars.

"Three of us were in the same hotel: Denise (Nickerson, who played gum-chewing champ Violet Beauregarde), Peter (Ostrum, story hero Charlie Bucket), and myself. We hung out together, since there was no cable TV in those days. Paris (Themmen, who played Mike Teavee) was a bit younger than us, so we didn't hang around with him that much. Michael (Bollner, the film's Augustus Gloop) didn't speak a word of English, and we didn't speak a word of German, so we didn't really hang out with him."

That's when filming began, and Cole became the sniveling little brat, demanding that the world kowtow to her every whim, looking down upon her fellow winners (in several senses, as she's one of the taller kids), and joyfully pushing around her comically beaten-down father Henry (Roy Kinnear, no relation to current Hollywood star Greg).

"Roy was marvelous and very caring," Cole says. "He became like a real dad to me whilst we were filming, and taught me a few tricks that he had learned over the years, such as how not to squint when the studio lights are glaring at you: close your eyes whilst you look at them, then on action, at the last minute open your eyes, and you should be able to keep them open long enough for the take." Kinnear, who appeared in more than 140 films and television shows during a career that spanned over 40 years, tragically died in 1988 at age 54 after a horseback riding accident while filming *The Return of the Musketeers*.

Eventually, though, the closest thing to the film villain gets hers – but in a different way than the squirrel abduction suffered by the novel's Veruca (special effects at the time just weren't up to snuff).

"I could never see how we could do it with squirrels," Cole says. "There's a difference between a book and a screenplay, so you knew there were going to be changes. Having read the book, I didn't really expect the film to have all the same elements."

Rather, after "requesting" that her dad buy one of Wonka's manservant Oompa-Loompas, it's time for Veruca to tell us what she wants and when.

"The song was very difficult, because it had many sequences in it that I had to get right, and if I didn't, they'd have to re-set everything back up on the set," she says of the "I Want It Now," filming, actually done on her birthday. "There was one sequence where I knock over some boxes, and I must have done it 36 times." Standing atop an egg scale, the impromptu queen looks down – again, literally and figuratively – at her peasants, before the bottom drops out, sending her off-screen and out of the film ("She was a bad egg," Wonka wistfully remarks).

"He was great," she says of Wilder. "I can look back and see that he had the patience of a saint. He had five kids clamoring around him all the time for attention. He was incredibly patient."

After filming wrapped, she and Dahl spoke at a premiere in London, and Cole gifted Princess Margaret with a flower bouquet.

From the moment it wrapped, the film was enclosed in irony; though not a box-office hit, it helped introduce home video to America as one of the first and most highly-rented VCR tapes. Over 30 years later, it's still a cult classic. In 2005, Tim Burton launched the film's remake, *Charlie and the Chocolate Factory*, with Johnny Depp as Wonka and London native Julia Winter as Veruca. Winter's performance gave Veruca a slightly less egotistical edge than Cole, though 21st century special effects allowed her to experience the rodent attack that 1970s technology wasn't ready for.

"She did a good job!" Cole says of Winter.

And even beyond that, the film marked both the beginning and the end for several of its performers. Ostrum never made another film and became a veterinarian; Bollner also stopped acting, returned to Germany, and went into tax law. Nickerson left the entertainment world in the late '70s, and eventually went into medicine, then accounting, while Themmen stuck around for a while before embarking on a casting career and selling real estate. Cole's the only one whose acting career stretched well into adulthood; though she only made a few more films, she showed up on dozens of British television shows for decades, along with tons of voice work.

"It's kind of strange that none of the others carried on, isn't it?" she says. "I was lucky to make the transition from child to adult; not everybody does. I have no idea why some people make it and some don't. I had the right attitude; I was down to earth about it."

About her preparation techniques, she explains, "As an adult, you think about things a bit more. You do a bit more research. As a child, my only obligation was to make sure that I read the lines."

Her reading and research skills took her far beyond the screen; in late 2009, Cole, by then a mother of two, snared a degree in psychotherapy.

"It was time for me to do something that I really wanted to do," she says of her new career.

"(Acting's) a tough business, but you always have to have a quality that's exceptional. It's a huge amount of luck. If you don't get the part, it's no reflection of your talent, and that can be hard, especially for a child. It's not always about being good or talented; it's about having the right breaks."

A few years after the film came out, Wilder was doing a play in London. Afterward, he got a special visitor backstage: a young girl who'd done everything she could to challenge him — in character, of course.

"Maybe," Wilder said thoughtfully, "Veruca wasn't such a bad egg after all."

Sadly, Wilder passed away on Aug. 29, 2016, just days before this book went to press.

Stephanie D'Abruzzo: *Scrubs: The Musical*

I may be a little biased (OK, I'm biased as all hell), but it's always bothered me that *Scrubs* never won a single Emmy or Golden Globe award for acting. Not just for the main characters; the show was a gold-mine for guest stars throughout its run. Dick Van Dyke, Heather Graham, Colin Farrell, Matthew Perry, and other names showed up at Sacred Heart Hospital.

And yet, when it came to acting, or awards in general, *Scrubs* usually got squat. Zach Braff was nominated in 2005 for an Emmy and Golden Globe, and another Globe the next year, but didn't win. The series would be up for the top awards for casting, writing, and overall series a few times over its first few years, but continuously came out statuette-less (it did win an editing award in 2005). Yes, it was superficial comedy for the most part, but this series dared to show a little substance, and sometimes of the dark, dramatic kind that few other such sitcoms dare to try.

But in 2007, that all changed, as *Scrubs* dropped a new tidal wave across the TV landscape. And to think, it would be a virtual unknown — at least, for that sort of entertainment — that would help launch the show into one of the few places it hadn't yet reached. Perhaps following in the footsteps of *Buffy the Vampire Slayer*, which snared an Emmy nomination for a 2001 musical episode, *Scrubs* decided to turn Sacred Heart into Broadway.

The series was always pretty straightforward with its titles, so when the sixth season's sixth show was called "My Musical," viewers got an idea that something new might be at hand. Less than a minute into the episode itself, they found out how right they were.

227

Braff's J.D. and his frequent on-off-perhaps-between companion Elliot (Sarah Chalke) are hanging out in a park when a lady collapses behind them.

They charge over and quiz the semi-conscious woman – but there's a new way of communication today.

"How many fingers do you see?" J.D. asks, his voice suddenly going melodic.

"Call 911, emergency!" Elliot, also in chorus mode, orders onlookers.

"Why are you singing?" the woman asks. Then, realizing her own new pentameter, "Wait, why I am I singing?" The group behind the doctors becomes an impromptu choir, and we're off and running at high melodic speed.

The series newcomer was Stephanie D'Abruzzo, and her character would be Patti Miller – and over the next half hour, she'd make as big or bigger an impact than many others with quite a bit more experience at the acting act. In the end, she'd deserve to be remembered as one of the top one-shot appearances in recent TV memory.

Not that she was all new to the small screen: D'Abruzzo'd long since been hard at work helping some furry friends do their thing on one of TV's most legendary children's shows.

"I was a fan of *Sesame Street* as I had grown up watching the show and listening to the records, and I was also a Muppet fan as well," says the actress, who voiced and "puppetted" several non-human cast members of the show for years. "I chose to go into puppetry at that time because I could play any sort of character I wanted without it mattering what I looked like."

As everyone arrives at the hospital, J.D. and Elliot are back to speaking normally, and it appears that their last performance might have just been a gimmick. But as soon as Patti's back on the screen, the world shifts again.

Hospital head honcho Dr. Kelso and his insubordinate subordinate (and J.D.'s idol/tormentor) Dr. Cox are in full musical mode. J.D.'s friend Turk gets in on the fun, along with the hospital janitor, whose name was never revealed during the entire series (anyone who disagrees didn't watch the finale closely enough). Soon everyone's welcoming their newest patient in tune mood, and she's the center of attention, the newest star in a shining constellation.

"I did not actively pursue this role," D'Abruzzo admits, "because I knew there was no way I could get it. It was not something that my agent would have thought to submit me for, as the show shot in LA and I was not a big enough name to warrant an out-of-town guest spot. I read that they were doing this episode on (the Internet) and instantly got jealous of whoever was going to get the part, because I was a fan of the show and knew that it would be fun to work on."

Back on the show, J.D. and Turk – along with several others in the cast, put on perhaps the most surreal chorus line ever, explaining exactly where the answer to Patti's problem might lie.

Excrement.

Yep- it's "Everything Comes Down to Poo," which, if nothing else, showed that someone could write an entire song about a stool sample.

Patti Miller (Stephanie D'Abruzzo, center) wonders just what's going on with the cast of Sacred Heart Hospital in *Scrubs'* classic 2007 musical episode.

As Turk's wife Carla finally shows up to do her own musical thing, Patti stands back, trying to figure out exactly what's going on here. But as Cox and the Janitor explain in rhyme exactly what it is (or, perhaps, what they are – there's a plethora of reasons) about J.D. that drives them toward rooms with padded walls, D'Abruzzo finally gets to show the skills that snared her a Tony nomination, taking part in the aptly named "Rant Song."

One of the top five musical theater actresses of 2004, she was nominated for a Tony for a musical production of *Avenue Q*, losing out to *Wicked*'s Idina Menzel. But it was her theater skills that brought her and Patti together in the first place — well, that and being on the right stage at the right time, with the right person in the seats. Deb Fordham, an integral part of *Scrubs'* writing squad, had seen D'Abruzzo in another off-Broadway show.

"Somehow she convinced the powers that be to cast me," D'Abruzzo recalls. "That was sheer luck. The role of Patti Miller was appealing to me because it was a job. As a non-puppet, on-camera character. On a major network. On a show I loved. In a well-written, standout episode. At a time when I was unemployed. Even if only one of those things had applied, it would have been a blessing."

She only gets a few lines in this tune, but it's enough to impress Cox into putting the extra effort into finding out what's wrong here. But it's not good news — Patti's musical-soaked perception is being caused by a brain aneurysm just waiting to burst and take her away forever.

Of course, no musical would be complete without allowing Turk and J.D. a few moments to declare their undying love for each other — the two are much closer than just about any couple in TV history — in a manly way, of course.

"We're closer than the average man and wife," Turk explains to Patti.

"That's why our matching bracelets say Turk and J.D.," J.D. blares.

"You know I'll stick by you for the rest of my life," Turk vows.

"You're the only man that's ever been inside of me!" J.D. says.

Before things can come to a crashing halt, Turk explains things.

"I just took out his appendix!" he tells a wondering Patti. Then the two finish out "Guy Love."

"I don't think that anyone who wants to be in musicals should approach performing any differently than someone who wants to be in straight plays," D'Abruzzo says. "Obviously vocal training is important, as is dance training, but I consider those to be wholly separate from the acting elements. I hate to say it, but sometimes the acting in musicals takes a backseat to the singing and dancing, which doesn't help the stereotypes. A good actor with a decent voice should be at home and comfortable with plays and musicals alike, because at the heart of any performance is portraying a compelling character believably and with empathy."

In true musical fashion, everyone gets festive, as relationships are mended and new unions formed, with virtually the entire cast gathering in Patti's room for "Friends Forever." But there's one person who can't share their enthusiasm.

"What's going to happen?" Patti asks in a sad soprano. "What does the future hold? Will I be alive tomorrow? What's going to happen to me?"

"Everything's OK!" the cast assures her as she heads toward surgery. "We're right here, won't let you slip away. Plan for tomorrow, 'cause we swear you're going to be OK."

"We hope," J.D. allows before Cox silences him. But of course, as with most musicals, there's a happy ending, and Patti's just fine.

But it wouldn't be the last "ending" for her, the episode, or, of course, the show. At the next year's Emmys, *Scrubs* finally got some of its just due, as D'Abruzzo's performance, Fordham's writing, and everything else about "My Musical" helped the episode alone garner five nominations, more than any other episode of *any* comedy that season. Fordham, who wrote all or part of every song in the episode, and the rest of the writing staff got a pair of nominations, for "Poo" and "Guy Love." Jan Stevens got a nod for directing the music, as did Will Mackenzie for directing the episode. The show's sound mixing team got a statuette, tying with an episode of *Entourage*.

Once in a while, there comes a TV show episode that actually depresses audiences when it ends. The Christmas/Biker Funeral episode of *Six Feet Under* was one; Beau Bridges' appearance as a handyman on *Desperate Housewives*, the live episode of *E.R.*, the infamous *Seinfeld* "Contest" show, and most of the season finales of *House* might land on the list as well. Because of an actress that few had seen before, this piece became one no one ever forgot.

D'Abruzzo didn't get enough credit for her performance, but she did get a special thanks a few years later. In 2009, as the show went off the air (well, almost – hold on a second here), J.D., about to leave for another position elsewhere, sadly strolled down a Sacred hallway in the last moments of "My Finale."

Turning a corner, he suddenly encountered a huge group of people whose lives he'd touched over the past few years. Patti was one of them.

Note: A great deal of the sentimental impact was removed when someone, or a group of someones, decided to bring the show back for at least one more season in 2010. From a business standpoint, that probably made sense, but for schmaltzy guys like me, this series had a perfect conclusion the first time around. So I'm not acknowledging the relaunch.

"I enjoy singing, though I'm not nearly as good as so many others out there," says D'Abruzzo, displaying a touch of the self-deprecation that *Scrubs* so often showed. "Success as a working actor does not – and cannot – mean stardom. Success, at least to me, means being able to make a living as an actor. That means being able to find work, ANY work, be it in regional theatre or commercials or voiceovers or audiobooks or industrials or all of the other areas outside of feature film, TV, and Broadway. My goal is to become known enough in my community to make it easier to find work, but I fear that the hustle will never end. It does not take much searching to find actors who have done amazing work, or who have won awards, who slowly slip out of the business through no fault of their own. My advice to young people is that if you have an affinity or a desire to do anything else, to do it."

Deidre Goodwin: *Chicago*

Even after years of putting on the same show, finding a way to the newest state (figuratively) of *Chicago* was still a new experience for Deidre Goodwin.

In her college years, Goodwin had carried off the lead role of Roxie Hart, the scorned songstress whose fury-spurred murder of her sleazy gigolo (he'd be a mistress if he'd been a lady; why is there no set term for such a guy?) catapults her into the national spotlight, amid song and dance. Charging to the Big Apple, Goodwin had helped blast out "We Both Reached for the Gun," "Funny Honey," and every other tune that had kept the production rolling across Broadway for decades and thousands of performances.

"My original goal was to be a chorus girl in a million musicals on Broadway," Goodwin recalls. "It wasn't until I was cast in the movie *Chicago* that I started to take acting more seriously and started training for real. I had a long history with the stage production... so I knew it inside and out. The research had already been done: it was just a matter of figuring out the difference between live theater and film."

Yes, the plot, the characters, the lyrics would be about identical for Goodwin. It was the way these things came across that changed a bit. Actually, more than a bit.

June (Deidre Goodwin) did the "Cell Block Tango" in 2002's Best Picture-winning *Chicago*.

After nightclub champ Velma Kelly (Catherine Zeta-Jones, in an Oscar-winning work) kicks off the film with "All That Jazz," things crash apart for her, finding her husband and sister together under the sheets. Hell may have no fury like a woman scorned, but Velma's ready to send them there and find out, slaughtering both. Meanwhile, with Velma in the clink, the new Roxie (now Renee Zellweger), blasts her man away.

With this being the 1920s, a woman doing something so angry, so violent – let alone two, so close together – was foreign to America (assuming we'd recovered from Lizzie Borden!). Not surprisingly, the press eats things up and knocks them out, turning both women into household faces.

Trying to adjust to life on the inside, Roxie finally gets close to Velma, who she'd admired from the nightclub seats for quite some time. Here's where Goodwin got to learn some new lessons about an old tune.

An inadvertent colleague of Velma and Roxie, her June was also in for male murder – and, like them, she had one hell of a good reason. As "Cell Block Tango," kicked off, Velma, June, and the rest of the residents of Murderess Row explain the meanings behind their actions.

"He had it coming," they promise. "He had it coming. He only had himself to blame! If you'd have been there, if you'd have seen it, I betcha you would have done the same."

Goodwin had heard – and sung – it all before. It was the way things were done that gave her a different education.

"Film is different from theater in that you don't start at the beginning and go straight through to the end," she says. "You follow a natural arch in theater, so you have one journey in chronological order, or just the order of the play."

Yes, this would be altered a bit. While theater and film fans heard the ladies' tales in real time, the clock jumped around during filming. We saw one woman proudly crow of poising her cheating boyfriend, another blasting her hubby for going out of his way to tick her off.

And then June elaborates on how her man met his untimely end, drunkenly accusing her of adultery.

"He ran into my knife," she recalls. "He ran into my knife ten times!" By that point, Goodwin had told the tale more than once to the same crew in one take after another.

"'Cell Block Tango' was shot in three or four days and out of order," she says, "so as an actor, you have to be sure to track where you would be emotionally, physically, vocally, etc., in a scene so it all makes sense once it is put together during editing. If you shoot the middle of a scene or the middle of the movie/TV show, first you have to know where you are so when you go back and shoot the beginning and end, things track and make sense on an emotional level while still staying true and in the moment so it, hopefully, ends up as a performance that makes sense."

It certainly did, to all the right people: the flick became the first musical since *Oliver!* from way back in 1969 to take Best Picture, and it nabbed five other statuettes as well. If *Moulin Rouge!* of the year before had kicked off America's newfound re-interest in musicals, *Chicago*'s success blasted it straight into overdrive, with everything from *Sweeney Todd* (2007) to *Mamma Mia! (2008)* and *Les Miserables* (2012) finding their own spots at theaters. Zeta-Jones became part of a star-studded cast that revisited several smashes from yesteryear in 2012's *Rock of Ages*, and Goodwin grabbed a small role to help re-acquaint America with the original British boy band, with 2007's *Across the Universe* leading this nation through the finest works of the Beatles.

"The transition to film was accidental as I never had an intention to do anything other than theater," Goodwin says. "It was only because of being cast in *Chicago* that I discovered I liked it and started working towards that and was able to be seen for and book non-musical roles in film and TV. There is no other way to (make it in musicals) than to just do it. Jump in the water!"

Sarah Lassez: *The Dead Inside*

Zombies. Demonic possession.

These roads get traveled into the ground virtually every year (hell, every month it seems sometimes!) in horror films, and have for years. So why the hell is this profile in a chapter on musicals?

Because in 2011, someone found an undiscovered land in a cluttered world.

A few years before, Travis Betz had written down and directed out 2009's terrifying *Lo*, and Sarah Lassez had been his main object before the camera, another notch on her role of Scream Queen qualifications. Now Betz was up against every writer's tormentor, one that doesn't disappear with Bible, crucifixes, or rifles: writer's block.

It's not a question of if or even when that eternal enemy hits authors, screenwriters, journalists, poets, cartoonists, anyone who hopes to prosper from adding pen and paper. It's how often. So Betz looked outside and in, and found *The Dead Inside* (2011).

He dumped his mental obstacle on the main character of his next tale, a lady who'd done well writing a string of zombie novels, but couldn't figure out the next sentence, let alone chapter. And he added a recent memory of seeing Lassez do her thing on one dark karaoke-jammed night.

"(Betz) called me one night and asked if I wanted to make a movie," Lassez remembers. "I said yes. He said 'It's a musical.' I said that was even better."

Now it was a question of meeting quite a few challenges. Her Fi (yes, that's her name) is the author with the virus that had forced Betz into creativity. Her boyfriend Wes (Dustin Fasching, who also produced the film) would be about the only other person we'd see – albeit in more than one form – for the majority of the film.

Fi had hit the same issue that so often turns into a plot hole with fiction – how do the characters get through a locked door? We see her creatures, the undead, pondering the problem. Knocking didn't work. Smashing it didn't work. The whole "When in doubt, have two guys come through the door with guns," failsafe trick philosophy probably couldn't come into play here either.

What else? The two are forced to straddle the line between cheerful and wistful, pouring a glass of wine into their souls to the tunes of "Fucking Heart." Betz lets us know early just what we're in for.

It's eating away at Fi, and authors' common alcoholic ally isn't doing enough. This thing is pushing her mind far away. Self-harm. A new personality, this an entity named Emily who – typical demoness – hides a sex bomb inside an innocent act. She claims to be from the past, using Fi to resurrect the motherly love she once held.

But hey, what's a better stress reliever than a sudden outbreak of song and dance? And when those tunes happen to carry labels like "Doomsday," and "Zombie Apocalypse," we're clearly in a holds without bars state.

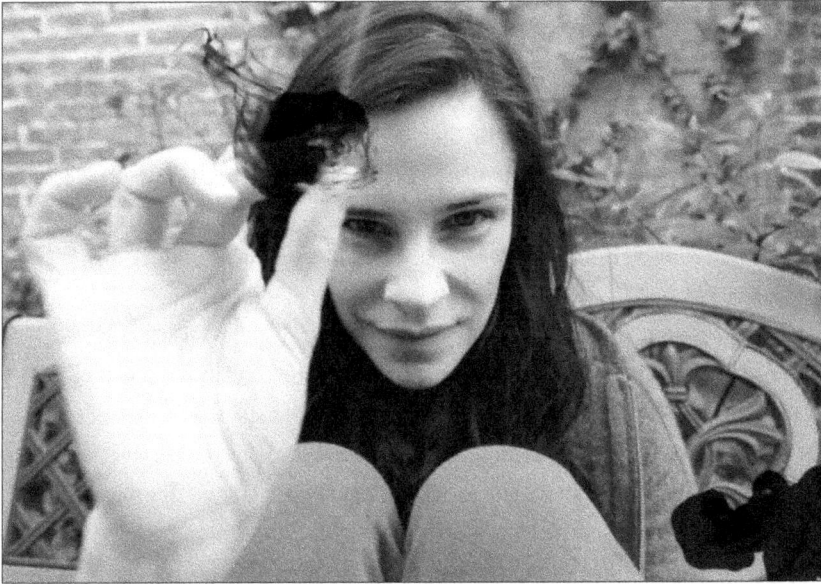

Showing that even in musicals, there might just be a place for horror, Fi (Sarah Lassez) casts an evil smile of the entity slowly stealing her soul in 2011's *The Dead Inside.*

"I did some research on possession," says Lassez. "We worked a lot on the music, recording all the songs ahead of filming. It was a really challenging role and I felt that if that was the last film I ever did I would be satisfied. It's hard to top that role for me. I strangely enough had a harder time with the role of Fi than as Emily. But my favorite part was playing Harper the zombie." Yes, yes – Lassez and Fasching also played the zombies that Fi attempted to biograph (wouldn't it be a great racket if actors got paid equally for each role they played within a film?).

Things get scary. They occasionally get bloody. But where Fi once showed an amazing ability to break into sudden song alongside Wes, now Emily does as well, even while in frightening mode. We hear the musical stories of how she lost her son, how she died, how she returned, and how she made it inside Fi.

Emily keeps showing up, and not even the local priests are willing to fight this fight. Fi's still look-ing for the inspiration to get her Harper through the door. It's really tough to tell just who the film's leading lady truly is. Everyone's got a problem to solve, and it seems like just one key will open all the doors, but no one seems to know where the lock lays.

And they never will. *Dead Inside* doesn't reach the typical happy ending we usually find in musicals. Then again, when *Night of the Living Dead* basically set the zombie trend back in 1968, that didn't leave us upbeat either.

Maybe while finding a new way across an old landscape, Betz decided to pay a special inside tribute after all.

Kelley Parker: *Moonwalker*

It's certainly not a field for everyone, but the entertainment business is just right for those who get a special appreciation right out of it. Singing, dancing, and acting can give just the right people a rush, an adrenalized trip to Utopia that may never truly end.

Many people don't even take the time to try, but those that do, well, they may never leave it behind, and that's by choice.

"I was actually an incredibly shy and soft-spoken child, and dance, later acting as well, was a way for me to be confident and it became my way of communicating," remembers Kelley Parker, whose ballet career kicked off before kindergarten. "My love for dance is still strong after all of these years, and the lessons I learned there helped me greatly in my acting. Acting is just as much about what you are saying with your body, as it is the words that you speak, perhaps more so. The thing that kept me in both for so long was that natural high that you get from performing. I loved both equally, and when I had the chance to combine the two worlds, I always jumped at it."

Still, for others, the high she mentions might have been just a bit *too* pleasurable...

Long before his sudden passing, the question was being pondered: who *was* Michael Jackson, in all reality? For someone who couldn't so much as cough without tabloids blaring it like a loudspeaker from hell for his entire life, the man, the performer, the father... the number of people who truly knew who this fellow was wouldn't require both hands to count. The line between the person on the stage and off it was never really clear, if it existed at all.

Many felt that Jackson was never comfortable in society, that the character on the stage and screen was too big a part of him to leave behind. That he didn't step out of character because he simply couldn't, and even when the physical and emotional demands he tried so hard to meet proved too far away, he never left the entertainment life behind. Jackson proclaimed that the tour he would embark on would be his last, but we'll never know if he would or could have followed it up.

Seriously, what would he have done had he not been famous? Can anyone possibly imagine this fellow trying to work at a regular job, interacting with others? It's tough to even consider.

Reality? It was a relative term for the guy, mainly because he had the power — mostly financially — to manipulate it. To create his own special world where he could be alone, or at least in control. And while it certainly wasn't the popular or even common viewpoint, there were some who felt that the excessive – to say the absolute minimum! – time he spent with the much younger crowd was a way of experiencing the childhood he lost on stages and before cameras.

That's a debate that will probably never end. But for now, let's look back at a time in Michael's life when it didn't look too suspicious.

Years after "Thriller" and "Beat It" had kicked the holy hell out of the music world, both in sales and video usage, Michael went *Bad* – and the whole world did indeed decide to answer right now, as the album and the tour that accompanied it rocked the world. But as the *Bad* man's stage romps came to an end early in 1989, it was time for him to shock the entertainment world in a new way – from the big screen. Just like anything else he ever did, it was very different than what many of us had ever seen.

Named after just one of the dance steps that made him a legend in the department, *Moonwalker* (1989) fired "linear-eality" straight out the nearest window, and if anyone but a household name like Michael Jackson had tried it, the film probably wouldn't have even been funded (the singer raised much of the bankroll himself). Still, it was one of the first glances of Michael the person that we managed – whether we liked what we saw is another story.

The flick – which, unlike Michael's fans in South America and Europe, Americans never got to see in the theaters, as it went right to homes in Jan. 1989 – starts out straightforward enough, as Michael belts out "Man in the Mirror" to Wembley Stadium, a montage of African kids and historical figures rushing by (John Lennon's face is shown, and that has more than one meaning a bit later on). The next part's truly a "Retrospective," as we hear bits and pieces of everything from "Don't Stop 'Til You Get Enough" to "Billie Jean" (can you imagine how many women that song made life hell for? Even today, ladies with either of those names probably get beaten over the head with it) to "We Are the World."

After that, however, things get a little... iffy. First off, there's a parody of "Bad" with kids, with Michael's nephew Jermaine Jr. out there, and Brandon Quintin Adams playing Michael's role. But that's not even close to how crazy things get in "Speed Demon" (both the title of the short and the song it's named for).

Now back into adulthood, Michael's outside the video and the character, when suddenly a group of fans (in claymation mode!), led by the infamous Noid of Domino's Pizza villainy, start chasing him around the set. On a motorcycle and attired in a rabbit suit – oh yeah, that's *so* inconspicuous! – Michael speeds away, clayfully morphing into Tina Turner and Pee Wee Herman (!) along the way.

Soon enough, though, it's time for a rough time in "Smooth Criminal," and the first people we meet are three of Michael's young pals. There's Adams, now playing Zeke, leading his fellow homeless pals through a tough night out. His friend Sean is Sean Lennon, John and Yoko's boy.

And then there's Katie. By the time she stepped into a new persona before the camera, Parker and her friends had been in the *Moonwalker* world for quite some time. But it's not quite time for that.

While many fans of just about any age would have loved to work alongside Michael throughout his career, Parker didn't take things too seriously just yet.

Michael Jackson as a musical action hero? With the help of Kelley Parker's Katie, it happened in 1989's *Moonwalker*.

"I was called to audition for the role of Katie, for what was originally just going to be an extended music video," she remembers. "I was not really a huge fan of Michael at the time. *Thriller* had come out when I was five, and my parents were not popular music fans, so while I knew who Michael was, I didn't really get how massive a star and talent he was. I think this may have actually been instrumental in my getting the role because when I met him I was rather unfazed by it. I was working with a lot of big actors at the time, and to me he was just another actor!" Her acting debut had been four years before in an episode of *Highway to Heaven*, not to mention a host of commercials.

Still, before and while other parts of the film were coming together, she had a new person to become. While the young lady had originally been intended as more of a feminine model, Parker made things a bit more realistic, knowing that the homeless don't have the means for "proper" female living.

At the tryout, Parker recalls, "the other girls were mostly dressed in fashionable dresses, with their hair perfectly placed, and lip gloss on. I, on the other hand, came in dressed in old jeans and overalls, with messy unkempt braids and a face full of freckles! To me, it made more sense that Katie was a tomboy."

It worked, but she and the guys would spend a month on set before their first call to "Action!"

"Michael was funding it, and kept expanding it, so we just kept showing up for work!" Parker says. "They were rehearsing and filming the 'Smooth Criminal' video, and they had us there 'just in case' they needed us."

But even without an assignment, the trio still worked to get ready. Watching Michael and his dancing partners do their thing, hanging out with Adams and Lennon, Parker could feel Katie stepping (high-stepping and otherwise!) through her mind.

"It allowed me to be submerged in the world of 'Smooth Criminal' for weeks before having to appear as Katie. It was an incredible opportunity, because Michael and the dancers were so committed to what they were doing, and to embodying the characters at all times, I got to truly live in the 'world' of *Moonwalker*."

But while Neverland – neither Michael's nor Peter Pan's – wasn't always a happy place, neither was her new world. As Michael and Katie search the woods for the kids' dog, they happen upon the dark house of Frankie Lideo, and Hansel and Gretel didn't have it this hard.

It's Joe Pesci as the self-proclaimed Mr. Big – we know he's a bad guy because he lets spiders crawl around his place – is looking to get the world addicted to his drugs. Still, Michael's got a way out, suddenly turning into a sports car and running down some of Big's men.

The kids escape, and end up next to a nightclub, which Michael magically turns into a performance of "Smooth Criminal" itself. But Big's not done, nor does he personify the song title, blasting hell out of the club and rushing Katie back to his place, having Michael beaten down in the process. But just as Big's about to make the girl his first needled victim (remember, it was almost two more years before Pesci got outsmarted by another youngster in *Home Alone*!), Michael... morphs into a robot, blasts the Big boys back where they came from, then switches into a spaceship and flies off.

Big's not done, commandeering a giant cannon to fire at the kids. But the Michael-ship comes back and wastes him one last time, then skitters skyward.

"There is a scene where Joe Pesci is throwing me around a bit, and that was a tough scene for me because it was so physical and emotional," Parker says. "The take that made it into the film, I was actually injured while doing it. Joe was to push me to the ground, and I tripped falling backwards and was not able to catch myself, so I landed on a mic battery pack that was right at the base of my spine. In those days the packs were these giant metal boxes that they would strap to you!"

The kids sadly make their way back to the closest thing they have to a home, only to see Michael appear from a fog. Now back to the club, it's suddenly become a raging concert hall, huge audience included, along with their missing dog.

As Michael and his group launch into their own version of "Come Together," one of the many tunes that Sean's dad helped elevate to legend (Jackson's cover would appear on his 1995 putout *HIStory*), the kids make the song title true one last time.

"After I got the role and the 'extended video' turned into a film," Parker says, "the writer was basically writing as we went along, so there was a great collaboration that happened between the writer, director, and actors in discovering who these characters were. We did have a lot of green screen shoots, which are always interesting. You really have to use your imagination as to what it is that you're reacting to. It was quite fun to see it with all the animations for the first time."

Look, while the enjoyment of performing arts, hell, his absolute *need* for it, that Jackson showed for his entire life is the most extreme of scarcity, among rarities that make lightning-striking look commonplace, it's important to remember, and define, the line between realism and fantasy that he never seemed to comprehend. For her part, Parker moved behind the camera, helping to choreograph everything from tours for Madonna and Britney Spears to episodes of *Dancing With the Stars* and even on to 2013's *Frozen* (yes, even animated song and dance teams are sent through rehearsal!), along with writing a few ballets of her own.

"Make sure you have hobbies and friends that are not performers/performance related," she tells the up and comers. "I say this because as an actor you HAVE to experience life, and the bubble of performance life is removed a bit from reality. Plus it will keep you grounded!"

Of course, nearly a decade later, things had changed for Jackson.

Mainly, they'd gotten real. The mythical creature we saw on stage, his aura was starting to fade. The person that Jackson was, who we really hadn't cared to know and who he hadn't much cared to share with us, we were getting a new picture, and not always a nice one. We heard stories. Tales of his frolics with kids at Neverland. A child sex charge that many thought would get Jackson in the worst kind of legal trouble (it turned out we'd have to wait until 2005 for that, and even that ended in an acquittal). We really didn't *mind* not knowing much about Michael Jackson the person, as long as he entertained us to the high extreme on the stage and screen.

Now things were changing, and Jackson changed along with them, willingly or otherwise. It was time for him to show a new side. Someone who didn't always have to live inside the character.

He'd certainly shown some self-mockery in *Moonwalker*, and would do so again in 2002 in a hilarious *Men in Black II* cameo. 1996's *Ghosts*, though, was a bit different.

Repeat – a bit, not *that* much! There were definitely some remnants of *Thriller* here. Again, he'd be dancing with the undead. As John Landis had helped Jackson a decade before, he'd have some legendary help here too – Stephen King wrote the screenplay, and Stan Winston directed and showed the special effects skills that won him four Oscars.

There would be some contrasts as well; a group of locals were creeped out by a hilltop mansion infringing on their ability to name their town Normal Valley, and the Maestro that lived there. The kids insisted that he was a decent guy – which might not have been such a smart twist after Jackson's legal issues – but there was an overweight, thickly bespectacled, incredibly self-worshipping city mayor who wasn't having this fellow in his Valley.

But once they arrive, the Maestro himself appears. Yes, it's Jackson, not even changing himself for character's sake. And just as with *Thriller*, he had some friends around to add super to natural in all the right ways.

For the Maestro's paranormal backup, the film crew looked right at home. Kelly Konno had danced in the background of three of Janet Jackson's world tours, and Shawnette Heard had been with her on the Janet. (period intentional!) World Tour that traveled the globe before ending in London the previous May.

A decade after *Thriller*, Michael Jackson again danced with the undead for *Ghosts* (1996), and Kelly Konno was one such reincarnation.

Neither had known Janet's older bro too well, but working with Michael Jackson? Would *anyone* have said no?

"It's the chance of a lifetime," Konno recalls. "As a dancer, you don't get those calls very much. I would have done it for free." (She didn't have to!)

"It was a no-brainer," echoes Hearn. "It's Michael Jackson! He's one of the ones that made me want to become a professional dancer." They and over twenty others would become the Maestro's macabre musical mob, tearing it up and down to "2 Bad."

"It allowed me to explore my danceability in a new way," Konno recalls. "Dancing for Janet, we're girls, we're human. Now we're ghouls, and it gave us the freedom to act a little crazy, to make it look scary and as ghoul-like as possible." Filming went on for over a week, with the troupe taking up serious residence in the local makeup chairs. There, there was plenty of time to think.

"It wasn't hard to get into character once you had that professionally done makeup, that mold on your face," Heard says. "You'd look in the mirror and it would be easy to translate that character into the scene. Michael was very clear on what the story was about. The makeup helped with that, along with the choreography and the set design."

Along the way, she felt herself slipping into the Maestro's surrealism, and back to her past at the same time.

"I grew up watching *Thriller*, and now I was in this world with Michael Jackson, in this fantasy world with monsters," she explains. "Stan Winston would yell 'Cut!' and we'd all be really dazed. Everybody would look at each other and say 'Did we just do that?'"

Meanwhile, Konno felt a new direction leading her towards the future. She'd danced through a small role in the 1992 underrated John Ritter comedy *Stay Tuned*, but hadn't really thought of acting as her career.

Yet.

"I didn't consider myself an actor back then," she says, "but when you get into all that ghost makeup and ghoul makeup, you really start to embody the character. That was unexpected for me, pretending I'm a ghoul and a ghost and doing things I never thought I'd do. I just allowed it to fully overtake my body. When Michael Jackson's right in front of you, you give it your all."

By the end of the impromptu concert, everyone seems to want the Maestro to stay before them forever. But that jerkweed mayor insists he's out, and the Maestro collapses into dust.

Come on, you didn't really think that was it, did you? The mayor parades out, only to come to face blimp-sized countenance with the Maestro, just outside. Turning back, everyone sees Michael's man standing there, and realizes there's goodness in his magic, albeit not always of the visually appealing sort.

By the way, that mayor, who's been full of himself to the forehead all along? That was Jackson too.

The film, which found its way into the *Guinness Book of World Records* as the world's longest music video, helped kick off Jackson's *HIStory* World Tour that September (it would be Jackson's final global tour), and kicked his albums *HIStory: Past, Present, and Future, Book I* and *Blood on the Dance Floor* into the public eye. Heard was right along with him, dancing into *HIStory*.

"I remember rehearsing in this huge hanger," she says. "I was amazed, being around these talents from every area, from choreography to the director to Michael Jackson the artist. I remember the feeling in my stomach when I heard Michael, and saw those seas of people. It was one of the best experiences of my career."

The acting bug had taken a bite of both women; Heard and Konno each got musical with Jackson's longtime friend Eddie Murphy in *The Nutty Professor 2* (2000), and Konno's peppered her resume with all kinds of TV shows since. Still, she, like, well, about *everyone else* who ever worked with Jackson, will never forget it.

"I was so honored," she remembers. "It's something I'll treasure for the rest of my life."

Jerry Sroka: *Godspell*

The next time you're perusing upcoming theater productions in the local newspaper or web site, check to see if *Godspell* is coming to town. Chances are, if it hasn't yet, it'll be there shortly.

On the stages of high schools, community theaters, Broadway, and everything else, the story of a group of people musically acting out the 'greatest stories ever told' has been a staple of theater productions for decades.

As I looked over the auditorium of Hampton, Virginia's Kecoughtan High School in the spring of 1997, I felt a bit of the *Godspell* magic myself. Along with the rest of our drama club (though we were modern enough to label it our personal "Theatrical Agency"), I'd been spending the past few months putting the story together, and it was ready to go.

Along the way, the group had learned a bit about Christianity, but even more about performing. Between the telling of parables, we'd found our own ways to make the story our own – interacting with audience members in mid-production, firing out one-liners that evoked howls from the viewers, and adding our own personalities to the people we'd become.

Decked out in huge overalls and mismatched sneakers, I became Herb, who tells the story of the Prodigal Son, and becomes the pitying slavemaster in the tale of a man who learns the value of forgiving those who trespassed against him. With my horribly non-musical singing voice fortunately lost in chorus, we belted out "Day By Day," "We Beseech Thee," "Light of the World," and the show's other tunes.

And as we carried the crucified savior through the audience on the last night of my high school theatrical career, I couldn't help but notice that several of the audience had joined us in spellbound tears, after spending much of the evening in hysterics. The show had had just as strong an effect on its viewers as its performers, a mark of success for any production. We had been allowed to turn ourselves into our characters, to make the play ours, to take advantage of its non-linear, laid-back nature and turn out a superb production.

Perhaps that's the magic of the play, one of the main reasons it's been done by so many for so long. Part of it deals with simplicity; like *Our Town*, *Godspell* is performed so often not only because of the beauty of its storyline, but also because it doesn't often require large, expensive sets and props that take forever to find and construct. It's a simple story that everyone gets a chance to tell, and, in their own way, recreate. Performers often develop their own costumes, think up their own quirks to the play, and incorporate their own improvisation and physical comedy. Emmy-winning Jane Lynch of *Glee* fame credits a high school production of *Godspell* as one of the kick-starts that pushed her into an acting career. Future Oscar winner Jessica Lange was in a cast once, as were eventual comedy household names Eugene Levy, Gilda Radner, and so, so many others.

Now let's meet someone who helped take the show from theatrical to cinematic national prominence in the early 1970s...

Just as with most young actors, Jerry Sroka got his start in local theater. But also like many young actors, he didn't know when the right person, the giver of big breaks, would be watching.

A veteran of summer stock and a stand-up comic since his high school years, Sroka, who'd just convinced the military not to send him to Vietnam, heard of an upcoming show called *New Talent*. In the vein of *Star Search*, the program gave the less experienced a chance to show their stuff.

"I had sent out about 150 notices that I was going to be on," he recalls. "Every agent, every casting director, everyone I could think of."

He headed out, blazed his audience with comedy and drama, and wowed the producers, who told him he'd done a great job.

Problem was, Sroka couldn't find anyone else who'd happened to catch him.

"The producer said he didn't understand (why I hadn't gotten more attention)," he says. "He wished me luck."

Back on the career-starting trail, Sroka spent the next six months handing out more resumes and headshots, working night jobs to roam about during the day. One day, he stepped into an office to make a personal delivery.

Suddenly, a gentleman came up to him.

"Were you just on a show?" he asked. Sroka said that he had been, and the fellow invited him into his office.

Lynne Thigpen and Jerry Sroka sing out the oldest stories in the Book in 1973's *Godspell*.

"He turned out to be an agent," Sroka says. "He said that he had enjoyed my act, and that there was this show having an audition. I had no idea what it was, what it was about, or even that it was a musical. It was about simply getting a foot in the door, getting a job."

As it turned out, *Godspell* was already running at a nearby theater, and some producers wanted to make their own show and take it around the country.

At the audition, Sroka was asked if he knew the story of the Prodigal Son, the tome of a young man who convinces his father to give him a third of his estate, only to waste it away before returning home to his understanding parent.

"I said I was Jewish, and didn't know anything in the New Testament," Sroka says. "They explained it to me, and I got up and did it. I did a different voice for each character."

The casters said he'd get a call. Three days later, he was at New York's Promenade Theater, telling the Son story again.

Then he was asked to sing. Sroka was experienced, but unprepared. An official told him to fire off "Happy Birthday."

"I did it," Sroka says, "but in a lounge lizard version." No matter; it won him a role as Herb.

To get ready for his role, Sroka headed to the theater to watch another group cast the *Spell*.

"I couldn't get out of my seat," he recalls. "I was laughing, crying. It was, it still is, one of the great nights in the theater."

Like the others who'd become those of the Bible, Sroka and the rest of his troupe brought their own creations to the characters.

"We were just inventing through the day," he says. "We would bring things to the stage manager, try it out, and hope it worked. By the time you got home, you were exhausted, both mentally and physically. When we got to intermission at our first run-through, people were laying down from exhaustion."

Godspell hit the stages in New York, Los Angeles, everywhere. One night after a show in Boston, Sroka was hanging out at a cast party.

"I was sitting on the floor, half-wasted," he recalls, "and there was a Bible."

He picked it up, and flipped through the Testament. Sroka turned to a cast member.

"I said, 'Oh my god, the whole show is in here, and some of the lyrics!'" he says. "'Did you know it was right out of the Bible?' Everybody thought that was really funny, that I'd been doing the show for three months and had no idea where parables were coming from."

Shortly thereafter, the cast members started hearing whispers that Hollywood was going to turn their production to the screen. They heard that Columbia Pictures, which had bought the film rights to the play, was going to send random representatives to shows.

One day after a show in Toronto, Sroka learned that a Pictures person had shown up — a week before. Then he got the same call that had reached him nine months before: someone new wanted him to be Herb.

Back in New York, Sroka remembered what had got him there to begin with.

"I knew that show after doing it eight times a week for months," he says. "I knew it inside and out; I'd never missed a show, much to the dismay of my understudy. There wasn't any preparation to be done, except to be put together with people from other companies. But like me, all the members of the cast from other companies knew the show in and out."

That helped them develop even more new improvs and comradeship techniques, he recalls.

"It was just reading a script and saying, 'What can I do with this?' Most of it was on the set, on the day of shooting. Basically we just fooled around and played; everybody had an improv background." Unlike most films, *Godspell* was shot nearly in sequence, all over New York, including a routine atop a then-unfinished tower of the World Trade Center, which Sroka says is still tough for him to watch today.

Theater veteran Victor Garber used his film debut as Jesus to kick off a career that made him one of the film world's most well-known character actors, snaring small roles in 1997's Best Picture of *Titanic* and 2008's *Milk*, which brought Sean Penn his second Best Actor award. Tragically, cast members Jeffrey Mylett and Merrell Jackson died before age 40, and David Haskell, who played Judas, departed at 52. Lynne Thigpen, who'd become known to millions of children as the chief on the game show *Where in the World is Carmen Sandiego?*, passed in March 2003, one month before the premiere of her final film, the Adam Sandler box-office hit *Anger Management*.

"That was tough," Sroka says. "We shared this bond. Friends come and go in your life, and whether you lose contact really depends on you, and it's a real blow. You shared something that only the people in the company knew about. It was a wonderful thread, and when you lose that, it really hurts right to your core."

The film finally hit the screen in 1973, and kept the theatrical fires burning, as *Godspell* continued to Broadway for years afterward and still rolls today.

Over the next few years, more and more audiences would continue to see and hear Sroka in all sorts of contexts; he voiced characters in the box-office hit *Antz* and on a 2000 episode of *Family Guy*. He showed up on *Murphy Brown* (1995), *Seinfeld* (1993), *Ally McBeal* (1998) and other shows.

A few years ago, a friend called and asked him to help out her daughter's school production of *Godspell*. He'd end up the reluctant director.

"There were between thirty and forty-five kids on the stage at a grammar school production," he says. "I said, 'This can't work; there's not enough time.'"

A few weeks later, the kids were wowing their own crowds. In the back of his mind, Sroka knew why.

"It's a combination of a story that everyone knows, the music, and the approach to it," he says. "All of the elements come together and make magic, and that's what happened here. Someone's always doing *Godspell* somewhere."

Chapter Four:
Character Performers

*H*ave you ever had this sort of conversation while watching a movie?

You: "Hey, who is that guy? I know I've seen him before, but I don't know his name."

Friend: "Me neither, but he was (character X) in (movie X)."

You: "Oh yeah! And (character Y) in (movie Y)!"

Friend: "Yeah, now we've got him!"

That's the type of talk that usually revolves around character actors. They're the epitome of supporting role-players in the acting world. They usually don't see their names at the top of posters or in tabloid headers (not that that isn't a good thing!), but they're the backups that make the storylines complete. If the stars are the faces of acting, the characters are the spine, and maybe even the heart.

"I try to make each of the characters different," says late character actor Paul Benedict, who had a longtime recurring role as Harry Bentley on *The Jeffersons* (1975) before snaring short roles in *The Addams Family* (1991) and *Waiting for Guffman* (1996), among other films. "I think the trick is to cement in the reality, to make it logical and real to yourself. Once there's a reality, I think you can make it as crazy as you want it to be."

Let's meet some of our more well-known character actors and actresses – this way, the next time we have the above conversation, we'll be able to fill in the blanks!

Here's why it's so important for newcoming and upcoming performers to learn about this part of the craft: this is how and why actors get work. Stardom might seem nice before you have it – and many who have it will probably attest it isn't all it's cracked up to be – but character acting is oftentimes much steadier. The paychecks aren't as great as for the A-listers, but they're usually quite a bit more common. These are the people that recive and certainly take full advantage of the chance to diversify their skills at the craft, to play one character one day, a totally different one next week, and someone light years from those a very short time later. This is what film casting crews look for when they're trying to find someone to give some work; someone who can do anything at a moment's notice, then switch to something else and do it even better.

"The character actor is there to make the lead look good," explains George Segal, himself a long-time character star. "The lead is the one that falls in love with the girl, and the character actor is the one who sees the absurdity of everything that's happening."

Character actors are the ones that often show up for small roles in movies and one-episode jaunts on television, so their acting checklist gets all of its marks filled in at high speed. But that's the sort of thing that helps a name get out and a reputation spread – these are the people who know how to network, who know how to put a positive spin on their characters and get as many directors and producers saying, "Sure, that person was a delight to work with."

Erick Avari

The films could not, at the outset, appear to be farther apart in the shared spectrum of qualities. Neither then, could the characters between them, even if two were indeed the same person.

One was an action flick, blazing with gunshots and special effects, roaring straight out of the starting gates of reality and smashing through supernaturalism all the way. The other, lighter than the weight of air itself, a typical romp in the land of comedy where people act like the kids they wish they once were and those in the audience can't help but crack up, in reaction and memory.

Indeed – *The Mummy* (1999) and *Mr. Deeds* (2002). Who could possibly tie those films together with a common thread?

One man could – because in both, he'd found the basis to pick exactly the sort of characters that have been filling up his resume for decades.

"I was actually passionate about being a stage actor," Erick Avari says of his performance beginnings. "I studied the classics and that was my specialty. While on a two-week vacation in L.A. from New York City between shows, I dropped in to see my agents in their L.A. offices. They started sending me on auditions and I booked the first two I went out on. That was over twenty years ago and I'm still in Los Angeles!"

But the journey's been rolling for even longer than a pair of decades.

"I loved airports, especially the international terminals," he recalls, "and as a teen I often went with my parents to pick someone up or see someone off. I'd be too excited to get any sleep the night before as I was drawn to every aspect of air travel. From a deep inner desire to fly like Superman to a fascination with the multi-cultural world all gathered together under one roof was more stimuli than perhaps what was good for me. But looking back at it I guess I was always attracted to 'characters.' Unique, distinctive, each with a personal story that gives them a different perspective on life and relationships. As a character actor, one gets to fill in the holes with back stories that have always come readily for me and I relish the opportunity to disappear into one of those many passengers I saw as a child."

Erick Avari's acting career has taken him through time and space and around the globe – but his turn in *Mr. Deeds* (2002) showed that Avari never forgot how to have fun.

The first time we meet the tortured Cairo museum curator, Dr. Terrence Bey is truly in comedic pain himself. Hardly able to shake off his disgust at the flubbish nature of employee Evelyn Carnahan (Rachel Weisz), who just turned his library into a disastrous domino set, Bey checks over an artifact she brings, a puzzle box and map that just might lead to the City of Dead, which just might hold treasures beyond belief – but so many have died trying to find it.

To her face, he calls it fake; however, he's got a hidden motive himself. Bey later meets with his fellow Medjai warriors, deciding Evelyn's too dangerous to live. However, when Evelyn returns, Bey lets her know that the Medjai's only there to prevent *The Mummy*'s (1999) title character from completing his multi-millennium mission to plaque the Earth full of death and destruction.

In Cairo, the mummy Imhotep makes it back to existence, stealing Evelyn and ordering his followers to take out her friends. But Bey helps everyone else down a manhole cover to escape, sacrificing himself to save the group.

"I loved the 'red-herring' treatment and the arc of the character," Avari recalls, "his noble efforts to preserve the integrity of his 'cult' and the script was a hoot to boot. Add to that a trip to Morocco and I was sold!"

On the other hand, 2002 brought us the latest entry in Adam Sandler's resume, the story of a young man named Longfellow (man, wouldn't it have been something if this film had inspired new parents across America to gift their arrivals with *that* moniker?) who suddenly finds out he's a billionaire, via an uncle named Blake he never knew who'd built an entertainment company worth Bill Gates type of green, before he was suddenly frozen to death on Mt. Everest.

Avari's Cecil Anderson and fellow Blake businessman Chuck Cedar team up to bring young Deeds back to the Big Apple, and Cedar's already casting a big dark eye towards the fortune he's secretly manipulating to make his. This guy Deeds is a perfect patsy for such a skilled sleazebag, and his impromptu rendition of "Space Oddity," the tragic story of Major Tom, who bypasses the outer limits too far to return, doesn't help much in the way of credibility.

But Cecil might just be an OK guy, not totally blinded by seriousness and folding green. One duet of "For here… am I sitting in a tin can!" later, we know exactly who the hero of this partnership will become.

"My eagerness to do *Mr. Deeds* can be summed up in two words: Adam Sandler," Avari says. "I had heard great things about him from colleagues who had worked for him and that was enough reason to jump at the role."

Individually, there was clearly enough in each role to at least take a shot at them, blasts that rang true for the character performer. But, "Cecil was, like Dr. Bey in *The Mummy*, a character that made a journey. It's always more fun to play a part where the character evolves in some way, or if not, has an arc and has a change of 'heart.'" And not just his own — Deeds' new friend manages not only to save his job, but finds Lothario love with a local lady.

The character acting category is especially known for its avoidance of typecasting, and Avari's resume bounces around with the mobility of the attacking aliens he helped battle in a small role in *Independence Day*. Bey wouldn't be his only self-sacrifice: as Tival, the servant of Helena Bonham Carter's Ari in *Planet of the Apes* (obviously the 2001 remake!), he saved his friend Daena (Estella Warren) before ape champ Attar took him out. Ironically, Michael Clarke Duncan, who played Attar, would get over on Avari again two years later in *Daredevil*; as Avari's Nikolas Natchios tried to protect his daughter Elektra (Jennifer Garner), Duncan's aptly named Kingpin sent Colin Farrell in Bullseye form to whack Nathchios.

Still, Avari would step FAR from his usual work and into a much more welcome and common example of animal service in 2009's *Hachi: A Dog's Tale*, the true story of the title Akita and the role he played in the lives of a college professor and his wife. After his master suddenly passes, the dog maintains vigil at the train station where they first met for the next ten years, helped along by the culinary offerings of nearby hot dog culinarian Jasjeet.

"I played Jasjeet the hot dog vendor, and a departure from the suit and tie roles I generally find myself, when I'm not in robes, that is," Avari says. "I'm a huge dog lover and enjoyed working with the human and animal cast on the film very much."

Along with those, just a few of the thirty-plus times film fans have seen Avari, there's also been dozens of TV shows, from aside Will Smith on *Fresh Prince of Bel-Air* (1990) to the sci-fi worlds of *Babylon 5* (1994) and a couple of *Star Trek* series to the action of *NCIS* and *NYPD Blue* (1993).

"Finding a character is always tricky as a guest star, so the best bet is keeping it close to yourself," Avari says of the multitude of small-screen work. "You try to find ways to build layers into the character, (as) you don't have the the luxury of time that you sometimes have with films. On television, the dialogue is denser than in most films. There is more exposition to get through and one is always aware of the remote sitting in the hands of the viewer, if you get my drift."

Of course, we shouldn't forget *Zork Grand Inquisitor* and *The Librarian: Return to King Solomon's Mines*. Video games, they were.

And the diversity Avari has shown doesn't just come from the role side of things: the India native (he's the great-grandson of Jameshedji Framji Madan, one of the first household names in Indian film culture) has shifted between characters of dozens of ethnicities. In 1988's *The Beast of War* (it's also known as simply *The Beast*), one of his personal favorites, Avari plays Samad, an Afghan crewman there to help a group of Russian soldiers in their early 80s war against the mujahideen fighters in Afghanistan. Suspected of secretly helping out his countrymen, Samad's set up and slaughtered by George Dzundza's blackheart Cmdr. Daskal, who himself gets comeuppance from a group of stone-wielding women.

"It got caught up in studio politics and was given a very limited release," Avari recalls. The film didn't do much when it first came out, but, perhaps assisted by public interest in America's wars in Afghanistan in the 1990s and 2000s, turned into a cult classic when it came out on DVD in 2003. "I'm often stopped on the streets with words like, 'That's one of my all time favorite war films.'"

Several years after going to battle at home (in the planetary sense!), Avari found himself about to become part of a slightly more foreign form of combat. Led by James Spader's Egyptologist linguist Daniel Jackson and Kurt Russell's Col. Jack O'Neil, a team of researchers find their way to another galaxy, passing through the *Stargate* (1994).

Eventually, they run into a group of locals whose language isn't far from the Ancient Egyptian that Jackson knows so well. Avari, however, wasn't familiar with it – until a crash course got him ready to become Kasuf, the chief of the Abydonians.

"I was initially reluctant to read for the part," Avari remembers, "because, as written, he was 80 years old and I was 42, so it seemed like a long shot. There also was very little on paper for the character in terms of dialogue."

Then his agent uttered the 'I' word that actors love so much.

"I've always loved to improvise and thought it would be fun at the very least," he says. "It was! The language was particularly challenging and I relished every minute of it. I worked with Dr. Stewart Smith, an Egyptologist at the University of California, Santa Barbara, to learn an approximation of the language. I spent hours playing with the rhythms and even the pronunciation of the words that Dr. Smith had laboriously reconstructed. He was also on set with us to continue the work and eventually I felt comfortable enough to be able to improvise lines in our version of Ancient Egyptian."

He also turned toward more recent versions of the writings and art that millions of *Stargate* fans would see, in a more dramatized form.

"I studied hieroglyphs and Egyptian paintings to familiarize myself with the way they help their bodies and the gestures that would have influenced the Ancient Egyptians, just like people today are influenced by the images they see on television and in films," Avari says.

After spending so many decades believing that the Egyptian god Ra was truly the one to follow, Kasuf and his forces are shown that Ra was a false deity all along, helping the crew escape back to their home planet.

But it wouldn't be Avari's last trip through the gate; he'd reprise Kasuf on a few episodes of the TV series *Stargate SG-1* (1997).

"People above all have intrigued me," Avari says. "I often think, 'What must it be like to walk a mile in that person's shoes?' And from there, I love to let my imagination fly. That's what I love about character work."

Brenda Bakke

From the moment one steps onto the audition stage to the final cut, Brenda Bakke hopes that performers in every area, every venue, every era keep one word in their mind – the thing that everyone's asking for, just a little bit.

Respect.

"Do not ever leave your clothes on the floor when you have wardrobe," the longtime character actress says to upcoming performers. "Respect your wardrobe people as much as you would a producer. Respect every aspect of every person in the show, from the driver to the producer. Acting is a whole community, a whole team effort. The universe only works if you turn it. Everybody on the set is as important as you are. The most important person is everybody: every driver, every gaffer, every best boy, everybody is important."

It's a message she's been sending to fellow film alumni for over two decades – from Oscar-winning flicks like *L.A. Confidential* (1997) to underrated TV series like *American Gothic* (1995), which spent a year on CBS before being revived by the Science Fiction channel.

"That was my best character ever," Bakke says of Selena Coombs, the schoolteacher in the *Gothic* series about a small South Carolina town called Trinity, in which horror, drama, sci-fi, and comedy clashed, oftentimes in the same episode. "Selena was closest to me as far as characters I've played, as far as her humour and her pain. I think it's a gift when an actor is able to play something close to them."

Selena was the seductive, albeit vulnerable, schoolteacher of Caleb (Lucas Black), jealous of his estranged father, monikered Lucas Black in nothing but irony (Gary Cole) and the relationship Buck shared with Caleb's cousin Gail (Paige Turco). Along the way, Caleb's sister Merlyn (Sarah Paulson) showed up to defend him, which wouldn't be too unusual – except that she'd long since passed away.

Brenda Bakke portrayed sultriness in reality as Lana Turner in *L.A. Confidential* (1997) and in spoof mode in *Hot Shots: Part Deux* (1993).

Character development begins on the written page, but that's only a small part of who the character will become. How they evolve and where they end it is up to the person portraying them, Bakke continues.

"Almost every role has something that you can pull out of your personal life, even from the smallest observance. And if you don't understand it, you need to find a way inside yourself to create it," she says. "That's what real actors do. I got the part because I had her spirit and her sense of humor. Laughing when there was a tragedy, I can do that. It's easy for me. It was about understanding the pain of being somebody that feels like they are misunderstood."

She'd gone to the larger screen scale of horror in 1995, helping the infamous Cryptkeeper kick off his directing career, taking his *Tales from the Crypt* to the cinema in *Demon Knight* (OK, Ernest Dickerson actually was in the director's chair!).

William Sadler's drifter Brayker and Billy Zane's evil Collector arrive in a lousy part of a lousy town in New Mexico, chasing each other over a key that could unleash the Collector's demonic pals upon the world. Hiding out in a church, Brayker runs into the locals, like a lovely lady of the night (not in a good way) named Cordelia, and Charles Fleisher's postman Wally, who keeps sending unrequited love her way.

"Most of the character of Cordelia came from the written page and from my imagination," Bakke recalls, "but I also related to her having to prostitute herself, a weak person having to do whatever was necessary to get by. Her oblivion to Charles Fleisher's character's feelings for her was a subtext of not wanting to be attached to anyone, something that at that time was of utmost importance to me personally."

Looking for Cordelia's spirit within (which would become the Collector's property, as he possesses her early on to kill Wally before being taking out by Brayker), Bakke sat down to utilize the verses, looking for Cordelia in Bakke's creation "Dirty Sheets":

I's the cat
sits by the windows
I's the cat
sits waitin'
I's the cat
paces my amusements with wantin' death
Oh, pet me
and I's lick my's self
Hatin' you's for havin' fingers
to opens windows
Gimme yours dirty nailed moneys
an' clomps a'ways down stairs
I's curl up
on my bed
a' stained sheets

For her most-seen role, Bakke had to take quite another tack for her portrayal of Lana Turner in 1997's *L.A. Confidential*, the epic of police corruption that probably would have taken home Best Picture had a certain film about a giant sinking ocean liner not been around.

"My manager at the time knew the casting director quite well, and she said, 'Brenda Bakke's face looks right for that character!'" Bakke says. "When I went to meet (director) Curtis Hanson, he held a picture of Lana next to me, and said 'OK, go learn her voice.' The interesting thing about that project, is that they wouldn't let the smaller cast read the entire script. It was all very hush hush."

That kicked off two months of intense Turner training for Bakke.

"I worked on her voice for weeks, listening to the soundtrack from many of her films, mostly Peyton Place, just trying to mimic her voice," Bakke says. "I was learning her characteristics, her timing. I had to BE her. I was the only person in the film that was a real person. It was a little scary." Paolo Seganti played Turner's boyfriend Johnny Stompanato, whose relationship with Turner would resemble something from a Hollywood screenplay in 1958, when Turner's fourteen-year-old daughter Cheryl Crane stabbed Stompanato to death when he beat her mother (the death would be ruled a justifiable homicide).

All of it for a scene that lasts but two minutes, yet still gives the film one of its few forays into comedy; Turner douses a police officer (Guy Pierce) who mistakes her for a prostitute impersonating the actress.

Of course, one of Bakke's other roles was a just a bit more light and easygoing; in 1993, she played Charlie "Topper Harley" Sheen's love interest Michelle Rodham Huddleston (one guess where the middle name comes from) in *Hot Shots: Part Deux*. She and Sheen spoofed *Basic Instinct* (1992), *Rambo* (1985), and many other films – that is, before Harley finds out that Huddleston's actually the bad guy.

"*Hot Shots* was total fun," Bakke recalls. "There was no approach. There was no character. It was all voice, body, and jokes. That was the easiest job I ever had. It wasn't really acting; it was all timing and voice."

Still, even the most slapstick of flicks requires its own amount of time and effort to get in character, she continues.

"Comedy requires a certain kind of preparation," Bakke explains. "You have to know your character. What they want, what they desire, what they're thinking every moment. A character you play is much more important than playing real people. You have to know their emotions; you have to know what they're feeling."

Susan Blommaert

Of all the interviews I did for this book, Susan Blommaert was one of the toughest.

Not because of procrastination – she got back to me faster than about ninety percent of the people I heard from.

Not because of rudeness; she was very polite and well-spoken (or well-written in this case, as this was done by e-mail).

Just because, like many of her colleagues, Blommaert prefers to let her screen work speak, yell, laugh, and cry for itself.

"Acting in front of a camera was never a conscious decision on my part," she recalls. "I'd been working in the theatre and just started getting auditions for film and TV through my agent. As it's really difficult to make a living in theatre alone, the opportunity to work more was certainly welcome. I came to acting rather late in life – mid-twenties, actually. I discovered I liked being involved in creating something that might make people laugh or cry or think."

For *United 93* (2006), she represented Jane Folger, a six-time mother and grandmother who, alongside her sister-in-law Patricia Cushing and others on the fated plane, thwarted the terrorists attempting to crash it into the Capitol Building or White House. They forced it to crash into a Pennsylvania field, killing dozens while saving thousands. The filming of the movie kept in time with the atmosphere of the tragedy; without much scripted action, the performers had to imagine and improvise what the victims went through on that horrific day.

Susan Blommaert (right) as Jane Folger comforts Rebecca Schull's Patricia Cushing in *United 93* (2006). Sisters-in-law from New Jersey who had a combined eleven children, Folger and Schull were on their way to a vacation in San Francisco on Sept. 11.

One of her first main roles came in 1989, playing Missy, a terminally ill woman in *Pet Sematary*, the adaptation of Stephen King's horror novel (King intentionally misspelled the title in the way a child would probably spell it, perhaps referring to the importance of children to the storyline) of pets that come back to life – only with some psychiatric issues.

"The chance to work on a Stephen King project was exciting and challenging," she recalls. "Missy was a housekeeper from Maine who was dying of cancer and decided to take her life. I began preparing for the role by speaking to as many local residents as possible, working on a Maine accent and consulting with a psychiatrist about what state a person may be in during the last few moments before taking their life. Then you just try to live that life and take that life in front of a camera."

She was there with Johnny Depp and Winona Ryder in *Edward Scissorhands* (1990), next to Meryl Streep and Philip Seymour Hoffman in *Doubt* (2008), and Liam Neeson in *Kinsey* (2004). She's showed up as a judge in *Ally McBeal* (1997), *The Practice* (1997), and three versions of *Law and Order*.

"I never think in terms of making my mark in a film... just to be true to the world and the character," she says. "Character actors are lucky in that we often get parts with unusual and exciting traits to portray. The character needs to be solidly and clearly portrayed, as there is often little time for an audience to get to know you."

As with anything else in acting, performers get to step into unchartered territory, if for only a few small minutes, and become other people, all in the smoothest of manners. It's a form of transformation.

"I feel my job is to bring a character to life in a full and natural way and then work with the director to honor the script," she says. "My preparation for a role is the same for theatre, film and television. I personally begin by spending lots of time living in the words. I feel my job is to try to bring the character to life in a full and natural way and then work with the director to honor the script. "

Wendy Crewson

Being recognized in public. Being congratulated, cheered, occasionally high-fived once in a while; hey, it's all part of the perks of fame.

Heading to her kids' school to grab them up, Wendy Crewson experienced this sort of thing several times all the way over. Millions had recently seen her become the ex-wife of Tim Allen's Scott Calvin in the smash hit *The Santa Clause* (1994), and now some young locals were lucky enough to meet the lady they'd only known before as Laura Miller.

"I was the darling of the recess group at school," recalls Crewson, who'd reprise the role in a pair of *Clause* sequels. "They would say to my kids, 'Oh my gosh, your mom's in *The Santa Clause*!'"

Of course, had the kids recognized Crewson from a role she'd done just the year before – in a film that, admittedly, people of such an age shouldn't be watching to begin with! – their impressions might have been just a *bit* different.

"I always wanted to be an actress from long, long ago," recalls Crewson, "from my stellar appearances as the Virgin Mary in a Christmas show when I was five. You want a little longevity in your career, and you sure can't have that if you just want to be the pretty leading lady, because of course, that all goes. I like the idea of being a character actor, someone who can put themselves into the idea of a character and become that: not a personality, per se, but somebody who can walk in their shoes."

If there was a film in recent memory that came farther out of nowhere than 1993's *The Good Son*, particularly in the days before up-to-the-second news and social media, it would be tough to find. Millions had so recently seen Macaulay Culkin hilariously torment a pair of bumbling burglars in *Home Alone 2* (1992), and now here he'd gone to the other end of the spectrum and even farther, in full *Bad*

Seed mode as a murderous young boy, complete with brutal in-family killings and F-bombs! Nostradamus himself would have been like, "Wow, none of my predictions even *touched* this one!"

She played a comedic mom in *The Santa Clause* films (1994, 2002, 2006), a terrified
one in *The Good Son* (1993), a scared one in *Air Force One* (1997), and a sad one
here in *Better Than Chocolate* (1999), and it's diversity like that that turned
Wendy Crewson into one of America's top supporting actresses.

Elijah Wood, embarking alongside Culkin on the journey from child star to grown-up one, was Mark, staying with Culkin's Henry and the rest of his cousin's family, Mark's mom sadly passed and his dad away on business. The Evans family has had its own brush with tragedy, as infant Richard drowned shortly before the story begins.

Crewson was Henry's mom Susan, in the worst situation a parent can be forced through. A new mom at the time herself, she stepped into a situation impossible to even imagine.

"Having children prepares you for a lot of things," she says. "It's the best thing in the world. It opens your heart in so many ways. Once I was a parent, there were avenues that were open to me that had never been available before, and the area of how do you survive after you've lost a child? The fact that people don't see that in their children and want to be the last to recognize that in their children, was so fascinating to me at that point, a real chance to use all these big emotions that I suddenly had on screen."

As is almost always the case in films (and, as she stated and society keeps showing, far too common in reality), Mark's the only one smart, or at least gutsy, enough to realize how dark Henry's inside truly shines. He shoots a dog with a nail gun. He causes his sister to fall through some ice and nearly drown. He plays all the gullible adults like instruments.

All without the first hint of emotion. Clearly, he, like most evil cinematic kids, has no concept of good or evil, only doing something that he can't see why anyone would disagree with.

But Susan can't be fooled forever. As one sad coincidence builds on the other, she comes to realize that her son is everything any mother worth her salt raises a child not to be.

"The content was a little disturbing, but I thought it was very interesting," she says. "I love that final moment on the cliff. Sometimes you do a movie just for one scene, and I thought that was going to be a fascinating moment." It was that and so much more.

Henry's cover is blown, and now his only choice left is to take out the only two who see it: Mark and Susan. A nearby cliff has long been Susan's place of Zen, but now it might be her final bow, as Henry shoves her off, leaving her dangling on the side.

Mark grabs Henry, and Susan manages to make her way back up as the two beat the hell out of each other. But just as they roll off the cliff, she manages to grab one in each arm.

What can she do? What could anyone do? How could anyone have the first damned idea? She could go over too, and they'd all be done. If both died, she'd never forgive herself. If one did, she'd always ask the ultimate "if" questions. But she can't save both, and her rationale doesn't have the time to apply here.

"We shot on an actual cliff," says Crewson (obviously, she and the boys weren't *literally* inches from death!). "I was wired down, and the two children were wired to the cliff. It was so cold, with the wind coming off and biting through to the bone with a little skeleton (filming) crew huddled around me."

Even the hysterical strength that we might find in such situations is starting to go for her, and we can see it in her frantically tortured face, and Mark's; Henry's the same stone cold he always has been, just knowing that Mommy will save only him.

But although we can't see Susan's mind, it might just be flashing back to Richard. The daughter she almost lost. Her own life, which will never be safe (as won't be so many others) if Henry lives.

In a flick as shocking to the public as *Son* was from the moment it was released, it's only fitting that it should have just as astonishing an ending; Susan yanks her hand out of Henry's, sending him plummeting down to the river below, his body quickly washed away. She yanks Mark back up, and he clings to her like letting go will kill him.

"There were so many other things whirling around," Crewson remembers. "Sometimes, in the moment, feeling the adrenalin, hanging there, looking at the waves crashing below, it all becomes quite real. It's a horrifying moment, and you can let the actual situation guide you and do your best at just trying to survive, and it comes across."

The next year, Crewson lightened up with her first go as Laura. In 1997, she became the first lady to Harrison Ford's president in the action smash *Air Force One* ("Get off my plane!").

"I got to work with Harrison Ford!" Crewson remembers. "For that alone, I would have read the phone book. Playing the first lady was a thrilling experience. I had done a lot of little things, and then there I was in a great big blockbuster. I didn't understand the scope of the movie until I went to the premiere, and it was so much bigger than what I'd ever imagined." She'd hit blockbuster action hard again in 2000, going to the mat with Arnold Schwarzenegger in *The 6th Day*.

Playing the title role in *At the End of the Day: The Sue Rodriguez Story* (1998), however, gave Crewson a new career challenge: to become a real person who'd lived and tragically passed away, rather than sticking fully to fiction.

A Canada native like Crewson herself, Rodriguez was victimized by Lou Gehrig's Disease in her early 40's. A few years after people like Jack Kevorkian brought the issue to public view in the United States, Rodriguez fought her country's laws against assisted suicide.

She didn't live to see her goal; in September 1993, the nation's Supreme Court narrowly voted 5-4 against her. Five months later, however, Rodriguez defied them by medically taking her own life. Not until 2015 did the Court reverse itself on doctor-assisted suicide.

As her subject wouldn't be around for a conversation, Crewson launched into waist-deep amounts of research, a future cornerstone of her acting career.

"I look for as much footage as I can find on the person," she explains of the flick. "I look for radio interviews, books that have been written about them, people that have known them. I love playing a real person because it's just a treasure trove of fabulous information you can gather and use as an actor. I really enjoy the process of transforming into someone I can actually see and hear, and the idea of getting far away from myself in the character, taking all those little pieces of them that I can relate to and walking through those doors to explore their character. You want to do justice to them, and if they're not around, to their story. Then everybody else gets to see a little piece of them too." She'd later help tell the life tales of Nelson Mandela's wife Winnie, and of Matthew Shepard, whose brutal murder helped turn America's tide against anti-gay bigotry.

1999's *Better Than Chocolate*, however, gave Crewson the chance to show a side of her own autobio. On her own for the first time, Karyn Dwyer's Maggie has a great loft to live in and someone special to share things with. Then, as many have in the iffy economy, she's forced to accommodate, as her mom Lila's depressingly forced to move in.

So upset is Crewson's Lila that she doesn't realize that Maggie and her close friend are, well, more than galpals. Hijinks ensue as Maggie tries to keep it secret.

Crewson actually had a bit more in common with Maggie than Lila; after over two decades of marriage and a pair of rounds of motherhood, the actress herself publicly came out as a lesbian.

"I used a little bit of my own mother (as Lila)," Crewson recalls. "I loved her naiveté, and I loved the change she goes through. She sort of comes to terms. As a mother, I loved the thing about being blind to your child, and suddenly realizing what was happening, and I loved her transformation."

Mary Crosby

The question became more famous than the answer.

After spending the summer of 1980 waiting to see the puzzle's final piece be added, the show's fans had to wait even longer – a writers' strike knocked the show's premiere past September, through Halloween, and even almost to Thanksgiving.

For three seasons, millions had stewed all over the misdeeds of a scheming Texas oilman and those that we couldn't wait to see get all kinds of revenge. At the end of the past year, someone had.

But who? As more people than had ever sat down for a sitcom in American history couldn't wait to know, the query finally reached an answer.

Just who shot J.R.?

And as *Dallas*'s legendary "Who Done It?" episode tale started to be told on Nov. 21, 1980, even the person who'd done it wasn't sure.

Of course, Mary Crosby had carried out the act. Her Kristin Shepard had spent over a season trying to sex her way to the Ewing oil fortune, having an affair with Larry Hagman's legendary protagonist himself – and if that's not sleazy enough by itself, J.R. was married to Kirstin's own sister! But, per usual for the character, he'd backstabbed, lied to, and otherwise generally pissed the hell out of her – just one more in a list of many, and well from the end.

So finding out that Kristin had held the gun that nearly ended his reign forever wasn't *that* surprising. Still, Crosby was ready to be shocked herself. It sounds crazy in a time where the Internet has made secrecy a foreign term, but the *Dallas* crew of way back when had gone to the ends of the universe to hide the facts.

"The producers were incredibly smart," Crosby recalls. "*Everybody* got to shoot Larry. The makeup artists, the script supervisors, the producers, we all shot Larry. Larry even got to shoot himself!" If any readers are having eerie flashback feelings right now, these are the same techniques *The Simpsons* creators used in the (almost as legendary) saga spoof of "Who Shot Mr. Burns?" in 1995, which ended the cartoon's sixth season and started the seventh.

"It was set up in such a way that nobody actually knew," Crosby recalls. "I had an idea, but there was no absolute certainty as to who shot J.R. It was flexible, so if word got out, it could have easily been somebody else."

Crosby's small-screen debut had come in a role that couldn't be farther from Kristin had it been in a different galaxy. Her dad's Christmas TV specials entertained American families throughout the 60s and 70s, and she'd been alongside Peter Pan before finishing kindergarten.

"I was Wendy's little girl," she recalls, "and Peter comes in at the end, and we go flying off together. You're pretty much ruined for any other career if that's how you get to start."

Colleen Camp had actually started off Kristin's work in *Dallas*'s second season; when she didn't return for the third, producers needed a new Jezebel. Crosby could hear the strikes already called against her.

After becoming the one who shot J.R. Ewing on *Dallas*, Mary Crosby carried
on her family tradition of entertaining audiences for decades.

Not just because they might worry that a former cute little child star could play gorgeous evil. Crosby's family issues could have been brought to play as well.

"They were very hesitant that the public would not accept Bing Crosby's daughter, Bing Crosby of *White Christmas* (1954), and Minute Maid commercials, doing all these nasty, dastardly things with J.R.," she recalls, "but they took a chance on me, and I'm very glad of that."

That's right; her dad was Bing Crosby, and if you need that name explained, you're probably not the type to read a book like this anyway — though Chevy Chase's hysterical solemn vow near the end of *Christmas Vacation* (1989) has probably caused many tough holiday seasons for Crosby and her family!

"For me, it has always been easier to play somebody who's quite different than who I am," Crosby explains (her mom is Kathryn Grant, Crosby's second wife). "I'm an old-fashioned girl, a tomboy. It's easier for me to do that than to play a nice, All-American girl, because it's more likely to be incredibly boring. Kristin was anything but boring. Larry Hagman was one of my greatest teachers. He taught me to hit my mark and find my light, how to have so much fun being a bad guy."

After she's revealed as J.R.'s trigger (wo)man, the main man of Ewing, fearful that his crimes will come out at trial, buys her off and sends her away. Kristin returned briefly in the fourth season, only to overdose on drugs and drown. But Crosby and Hagman stayed close for the rest of his life; he walked her down the aisle for her second wedding and was godfather to her children until his Nov. 2012 passing.

So yes, one role and one special last name were all Mary Crosby would ever need to have her moniker entered in the household ranks. But it's certainly not all we *should* know about her.

Let's talk about it. Let's discuss an acting career that's stretched out over a few decades. And, even more individually than one with such a length, an attitude towards a tough profession that should never be the slightest bit tough to locate.

"As an actress, every single thing that I've done has been wonderful in one way or another," she remembers. "I have learned to develop interesting relationships, and I have had adventures and life experiences that I wouldn't trade for anything. I feel that it's really important as an actor not to take yourself too seriously. That's not to say you don't take the work seriously. I take the work that I do and the kind of jobs that I do very seriously. But I have to be aware that some of the stuff I've done is not in any way good, except for providing a little entertainment to people."

You see, the final project is always the end goal, but not the only one. There are more reasons to get into the acting business and stay there than just getting a good review from the critics and/or hoping against hope that your film breaks the bank. You need a skin thicker than concrete to be a public figure in this sort of work, and worrying *too* much about ticket sales and critic reviews will sink us like a stone.

That is, if it's all we worry about — and it's going to do a hell of a number on our self-confidence if it does. Anyone in the business for any extended time (and this is really hard for performers who have this happen early on) will hit a project that people just don't like, or even see, or one that might even make the actress say, "Shouldn't have given the OK to that!"

But it doesn't have to be that way, and we don't have to let it. Even the misfires that we usually don't realize until hindsight can't bother us too much. It's about looking back at any job, any work that we put some serious effort into, and finding something that the work taught us. Whether it was what to do or what to avoid, there's something there to learn, and if we find it, we can even be proud of something that didn't go the full way we'd hoped.

"It's a life in which about ninety-two percent of actors are out of work," Crosby says. "You can be the flavor-of-the-minute, like I was on *Dallas*, and still be out of work for most of the time. And yet, the experiences that I've had and the people that I've met are priceless. I'm incredibly grateful to be an actress."

After remaking Doris Day's renowned work in 1981's *Midnight Lace* (she'd put together an updated version of *Stagecoach* a few years later), Crosby traveled to the future for 1984's *Ice Pirates*. She was Karina, the bratty ruler of a land where water's become rare enough to reach gold values (*Waterworld* in reverse!). She's kidnapped by Robert Urich's handsome pirate Jason, who ends up helping her look for her pappy, himself lost searching for a new and much wetter world.

"The idea of playing a swashbuckling princess was just great," Crosby recalls. "Everybody, growing up, likes to play make-believe, and doing that kind of a movie is just playtime. Bring the princess was easy; roles that are a little more challenging are the old housewife or girl next door, because it's very hard to do those and make them have depth." Unless, of course, said wifey gets an up close and quite impersonal view of a different kind; Crosby did so as the wife to Pedro Armendariz's Governor Riley in 2005's *The Legend of Zorro*, Antonio Banderas' masked Lothario slicing and dicing his way to heroism!

Right around her Karina time, Crosby started learning a few of her own trademarks in the annals of character acting. Some she'd picked up from her father, others she formed on her own.

"Dad never watched anything he did more than once," she remembers. "He'd watch it at the premiere, and then he was done. We wanted to see one of his movies, and he'd be off watching basketball. That's fairly true for me. I'm really not interested in watching what I've done, but when I'm on the job, I love to watch the dailies, because then I could see what I was doing and where I was going." She'd play a schizophrenic murderer in *Dead Innocents* of 1989 and a wronged wife the next year in *Body Chemistry* (critics called it a watered-down *Fatal Attraction*, and Crosby doesn't really disagree).

"On certain roles, if I found a hat or an article of clothing that told me something about the character, that would help," Crosby explains on her personal prep choices. "There would be a moment in my life when I could think of some vulnerability in my character. What was the softness? What was the wound? What created the action? With each character, it's about finding the opposite of what the action is. What is the reason for it? It's about combining little bits of the outside that can help me from the inside."

It was tough to determine what was more twisted about 1997's *Cupid*. Was it a) that it was a horror film with a romantically comedic title, b) that Zach Gilligan, who'd played the warm, caring Billy Peltzer in the two *Gremlins* films, was now a killer, c) that his Eric was having an affair with his sister Dana (Crosby), or d) that the two were massacring those who had rejected the other? (or rather, ?!!!). Who in hell could even decide?

"Doing things that are further away from who I am gives me the freedom to do what I want, to explore, and to play," says Crosby, who starred beside *Hellraiser* (1987) heroine Ashley Laurence in *Cupid*. "I've been around some fairly crazy people, and it's not hard to go there, or at least it wasn't for me. The advantage of doing movies that are not, quote unquote, art, is that sometimes, as an actor, you can play. You can take chances and you can do things that you might not want to do otherwise."

It's like she says, what she's said for years, and what she's been learning and showing throughout a career that's been all kinds of successful. Perhaps not in the self-important eyes of critics or box-office numbers, but in hers, and in those of everyone else with the right kind of viewpoint towards a profession that's tougher than the world we saw in *Ice Pirates*.

"It's a grand adventure, as they all are on one level or another, even if it's a terrible movie," Crosby says. "Every job that I've ever had, and some of them were *really* terrible movies, the people that you get to meet and the places that you get to go, it's always an interesting adventure. You can develop friendships for life, and that's such a gift."

Ami Dolenz

Acting is an art that has been around since humanity itself wandered down the interstate. But to get in character, Ami Dolenz uses a different artistic analogy.

"Think of it like a canvas, and you have different color paints," the third-generation character actress tells performers in training. "The paints help you create different emotions, and the script helps it. You start reading it; does your character act like *this* when *this* happens. I even take characteristics from my friends. When I'm with somebody, I recognize something about somebody, and I kind of steal it."

Being *around* acting was a lifelong thing for Dolenz; she's the granddaughter of George Dolenz, who appeared in dozens of films in the 40s and 50s, and her dad is Micky Dolenz, he of the Monkees. Getting into it herself, however, was another matter.

Being the child of a teen idol, she said, "got my foot in the door, but I still had to prove myself. This is such a hard business to get into."

An early victory in the acting category of *Star Search* (1983) got her rolling, and led to several one-shot appearances on television, including a recurring role in the late 1980s on *General Hospital*.

"(*GH*) was like going to college for acting," Dolenz remembers. "I learned a lot, not just about building a character, but for basics: finding your light, finding your mark on the floor, just working with professional actors who have been in business for such a long time."

Then the movies came calling — and, as perhaps more with the 80s than any other decade, the clichés were along for the ride.

a. "Incredibly Gorgeous, Popular Character Somehow Ends Up In Love With Loser." Following in the footsteps of *The Breakfast Club* (1985), Dolenz took her turn here with a small role in *Can't Buy Me Love* (1987), alongside a Patrick Dempsey that no one dreamed would even become McDreamy.

b. "High-Speed Makeover Suddenly Turns Introverted Nerd Into Campus Lordship." Dolenz's star-making role would set things in motion for *Clueless* (1995), *She's All That* (1999), and other such films.

1989's *She's Out of Control* launched Ami Dolenz into the upper ranks of the performing world.

At the beginning of 1989's *She's Out of Control*, Dolenz is Katie Simpson, complete with glasses, braces, and a weakness for high-speed dance routines in her room. Her dad Doug (Tony Danza, who'd ironically hosted Dolenz's *Star Search* victory), is heading off for a business trip, and Katie's about to get the end-all, be-all of 15th birthday presents.

Contact lenses. Mouth metal moved out. A trip to the tanning salon. Even some new clothes.

When Doug gets home, the phone's ringing off the hook for Katie, and he's not sure why. Then her date for the evening arrives, and Doug's question gets answered.

Strolling down the stairs is the woman that Katie always dreamed of becoming — physically, at least. Makeover might be too weak a word for her change; transformation would be more appropriate. This is a type of gorgeousness that rarely happens, even in the movies. It's part *Pygmalion*, part *Taming of the Shrew* (translated for 90s audiences into *She's All That* and *10 Things I Hate About You*), and an all-new woman.

Her date's the luckiest guy alive, and he won't be the last one to knock on the Simpson door (*Diff'rent Strokes* [1978] star Todd Bridges even cameos as an extroverted water deliveryman). Soon, Katie's out, everywhere, with everyone, and Doug, without a wife to help out (at least, when the movie starts), isn't sure what to do.

"The part that I found intriguing was that it was like playing two different characters," Dolenz says. "She was very homely in the beginning, and then she got to change, and become so self-sufficient. Her personality changed. Everything changed for her, and freaked her father out. When you shoot a movie, you don't shoot in sequence, so I had to jump back and forth during production."

During preparation, she used her own background, and what she'd learned back in high school, a lot of which was not from teachers (remember, Dolenz was 19, but playing 15).

"I considered myself kind of young for my age," Dolenz says. "I didn't grow up very fast, and I wasn't a big partier. I really had to go back and think about how I was back when I was 15. I went over my yearbook, and started trying to get back the feeling of being 15."

She remembered the days of cliques, school socialism (in a good way!), and the battles with self-esteem that bother us all in those seven long teenage years.

"I used my own personal background," she says. "For lots of girls, it's about finding yourself. I used personal growth: dealing with adolescence, dealing with friends, and school, and cliques, I brought a lot of myself into the character. When she changed, I wanted to make sure she was still likable." That's fair; unlike many in her position (at least, in films), Katie never gets too big of an ego or develops a full-blown diva attitude – maybe she wasn't quite as *Out of Control* as the title made it seem.

Near the end, it's prom night, and Katie and her date Timothy rock the floor in a routine choreographed by Paula Abdul. But at a party afterward, Timothy tries to venture into forbidden territory, and Doug shows up to make things right.

By the way, that Timothy kid? A decade later, he'd be a household name as Chandler Bing.

"I was very happy when Matthew (Perry) got *Friends*," Dolenz says. "It was really fun working with him."

After starring alongside Jennifer Aniston, another future *Friend*, in 1990's ill-fated-but-very-underrated *Ferris Bueller* TV show (she played Sloan; Charlie Schlatter was the title character), Dolenz went back to on-screen beauty, playing a genie named Jeannie in 1992's *Miracle Beach*, the story of a guy with luck only slightly better than Aladdin who discovers she who makes the wishes real.

"It was so weird, because I had a lot of leeway to do what I wanted," Dolenz says of the character. "It wasn't really based on anything. I thought, 'Do what you want, she's a genie!' It was a lot of fun to create her and do what I wanted with her."

Horror came next, as roles in *Witchboard II* (1993), *Pumpkinhead II* (1993), and *Stepmonster* (1993) pushed Dolenz into the "Scream Queen" ranks next to Heather Langenkamp and Jamie Lee Curtis.

In horror, Dolenz explains, "A lot more screaming and physical stuff is involved, but I just try and go with each character. Go by the character; if it's horror or comedy, it's about the story and the character."

Richard Dreyfuss

Throughout his acting life, Richard Dreyfuss has done a great deal of encountering.

At the age of nine, he encountered his mother in the home kitchen and announced his plans to take the acting world by storm.

Glancing away from the dishes, his mom became a teacher.

"Don't just talk about it," she said.

Taking her advice to heart, Dreyfuss headed down to the local Jewish Community Center and encountered one audience after another, as he became a fixture in its dramatic programs.

"I never stopped auditioning until I was 27," he says. "I never stopped, ever. I mean, my ambition, my acceptance of my designation as an actor, my self-definition, my ambition to achieve it totally and completely, were all born in that instant – like the Big Bang Theory." (obviously, long before the TV show of an identical moniker!)

Two decades after making box-office history with *Jaws* (1975) and snaring an Oscar in 1979 for *The Goodbye Girl*, Richard Dreyfuss nearly grabbed another statuette for *Mr. Holland's Opus* (1995).

Though much of the Hollywood public didn't realize it until later, its first encounter with the then-youngster came with a whiz-bang cameo in *The Graduate* (1967), when he showed up just long enough to blurt, "I'll call the cops!" Not until his black-white portrayal of Baby Face Nelson in 1973's *Dillinger* and a sensitive upcoming underclassman in *American Graffiti* that same year did the American film world truly notice the $100 bill in an ocean bottle.

Speaking of oceans, Dreyfuss had his most terrifying encounter there in 1975 with *Jaws*, considered the film world's first-ever "blockbuster." Two years later, back with Steven Spielberg, Dreyfuss showed that he meant something, and was, in fact, important, (echoing the film's screenplay) in 1977's

Close Encounters of the Third Kind, which started off the "friendly alien" trend that Spielberg moved Earth with a few years later in the form of *E.T.* (1982).

Dreyfuss believed, "that this particular project had a noble agenda... It wasn't just a sci-fi movie; it wasn't just about monsters from the id. It was that we are not only not alone, but that we have relatively little to fear. That really was a huge statement and I... wanted to participate in that." In 1979, he said hello to a Best Actor Oscar for *The Goodbye Girl*, then the youngest-ever award winner.

"I had a love affair with acting as real, as certain as having a nuclear pellet embedded in my chest," Dreyfuss remembers. "Acting is more fun than a barrel full of monkeys. Acting is glorious. Acting is spiritual. When you make people laugh, when you make people concentrate on you, you are giving a gift."

The actor, he continues, "knows that he is the mechanism, the Rube Goldberg device – the thing that is the connective tissue between understanding and appreciation and that genius."

If Dreyfuss wasn't endowing film fans from the screen, a different group of viewers might be watching him perform; his well-known patriotism might have pushed him to a history teaching career had the acting bug not gone chomping.

"Many think that going to school is a big drag and boring," he says. "But then you get out of school, and you find that when you learn something, whether it's two plus two, how to kiss a girl, or where Ghana is, you can feel a sense of pleasure right here." He taps his chest.

"That pleasure is built into the system. It's built into evolution. It's built into community. When you say something clearly, when you think a thought, when you come up with a good idea, you can feel it physically with your body. That's evolution's way of saying to you, 'Pay attention, because there are rewards here.'"

Then in 1995, Dreyfuss was himself encountered in a new way, by an audience too young to remember *Close Encounters* and who may have allowed his Matt Hooper role to be overshadowed by Chief Brody, a giant shark, and *Jaws*' legendary soundtrack. But they indeed paid attention, and the rewards arrived. He'd get to send the message – in character at least.

It was the story of a man with so much time for everyone – except those who needed it most. An American character/period piece in which three decades of the country's most famous era (in the bright or dark sense) set the tones for turning points in a life that finally came around to where it belonged. Idealism was his mindset at the start, with realism arriving at the end. And reality wasn't all that bad, not all the time.

Mr. Holland's Opus was the 1995 story of a music teacher who believed that notes on a page were a treasure map to fame and fortune, only to discover that the map's directions were the students that he inspired, and the son, born deaf, who he finally learned to exchange gifts (not the type given at Christmas) with, every day.

First came the musical aspect; Dreyfuss had been hearing and belting it out – mostly in private – for years, but playing it would be something else entirely.

"The most difficult aspect was the piano," he says of Holland's self-composing scenes early in the flick. "The hands have to be just right." Attending a music appreciation class helped him there, and he worked with a deafness consultant to get down some sign language basics.

Then came the conducting that Holland did while leading the school band through a parade, in generations of classes, and in front of packed school auditoriums – including one at the end that so many in the profession deserve and so few ever get anywhere near. That came from Michael Kamen, who'd jammed with Pink Floyd and worked on the sounds of *Die Hard* (1988) and other films. Dreyfuss studied Kamen's baton work between takes.

And Holland's ploys helped him see a little closer just how thin the line between the two men's careers was.

"Teaching is very much like performing," Dreyfuss remarked. "A teacher is an actor, in a way. It takes a great deal to get, and hold, a class."

The talent to age 30 years in every sense over a period of two and a half hours (a mark shattered in reverse by Brad Pitt in 2008's *Curious Case of Benjamin Button*) was business as usual – almost.

"No one had ever asked me to play 'a life' before. I get to age through 30 years. The idea really challenged me… What was really disconcerting was they used all these wigs and stuff to get me to look younger, but in order for me to play 60, all they did was show me."

It was a side of him that many had never seen, and that no one had seen for all too long. His work in the title role gave him Golden Globe and Academy Award nominations and some of the warmest reviews of his career.

"I succeeded at an unlikely goal and discovered that I was much more comfortable in the pursuit than in the attainment," Dreyfuss says of his acting prowess and unintentionally of Holland's teaching career, "that achieving the assumption that I was an actor was not half as much fun as proving I was.

"I just… do it," he says. "There's one question I've never been able to answer, and that's about my process as an actor. Glen Holland was my favorite teacher. He was my fantasy of becoming an adult.

"I find, without sounding too stupid," he continues, "that within everyone, in all of us, there's Hitler and Jesus. What you have to do is find the appropriate Hitler and the appropriate Jesus and bring them out and show them."

When getting the chances to do so, he's been a bit more fortunate than many in the business.

From almost the moment he first took that Center stage, Dreyfuss says, "there was really no month that was not devoted to acting. I had a nuclear pellet. It never wavered and it never ended and it never weakened. And it was a pulsing, driving, absolute part of my life that created all of my momentum and absolute certainty about my future. So that I went through all the years of teenage struggling and looking for work, and TV and agents and all that, thrilled. Thrilled because I absolutely knew that at the end, I would make it.

"Absolutely without question."

Bill Erwin

Once in a while, you get a person who personifies a certain type of acting, and elevates it to a masterpiece. Certain actors have something about them that every other performer, experienced or otherwise, can look at and say, "Wow, I need a bit more of that in my repertoire!"

Indeed, there are some performers who truly characterize their characterization. And the next participant here in *Before the Camera Rolled* has shown generations of audiences and actors exactly what it means to be a character actor.

"To me there wasn't any other world other than the imaginary world," remembered Bill Erwin, a consistent presence in the acting world since his first role in 1941's *In the Army Now*, "and I wanted somehow anyway to become part of that world. I did – and I'm as enthusiastic today as I was when I started seventy years ago!"

Bill Erwin (left) did it all and did it all again over nearly seventy years in the acting world.

For many profiles in this book, I tried to choose a small few that especially helped performers stand out, that really allowed them to show their stuff. But with a resume that alone would fill a few chapters of this book, it was better to take the overview route with one of Hollywood's little-known legends. Erwin showed up, usually in the background, of over 200 films and television shows (weird fact: despite appearing on over 100 shows, his longest stay on any one in particular was an eight-episode recurring gig on *Growing Pains* in the late 80s and 90s!).

He was the man in the airport that Catherine McAllister convinces to sell her his tickets to get home to see her son Kevin in the 1990 box-office smash *Home Alone*. He hung out with Steve Martin and John Candy on a plane in *Planes, Trains, and Automobiles* (1997), with Leslie Nielsen in *Naked Gun 33 1/3* (1994), with Christopher Reeve in *Somewhere in Time* (1980), and with Walter Matthau in 1993's *Dennis the Menace* (Erwin's natural gift for clean, lighthearted comedy was simply off the charts).

"Walter Matthau was the most warm, caring person I worked with," Erwin said. "I'll always remember him as the symbol of the project."

A former Yankees veteran in *Mad About You* (1998). A doctor on *Star Trek: Next Generation* (1990). A joyful tormentor of hapless George Costanza in 1993 on *Seinfeld* ("Can you change my diaper?"), which snared Erwin an Emmy nomination – criminally, the only one of his career. His farewell appearance as a ping-pong champ on *My Name is Earl* (2006). He did it all a few times over.

"There are no small parts, only small actors!" he quipped. "My fellow colleagues and I were never afraid to take a 'small' role. Before shooting I would know my scene inside and out, and prepare well. I've never felt, when I've agreed to do something for a producer, that I wouldn't give him what he wants."

That's because, like so many others we'll met in this book, Erwin always believed that some are just made and meant to perform.

"I have never considered NOT being an actor!" he gleefully admitted. "Any role that you get is more likely to be your own being than you think. It won't be difficult at all if it's right for you."

And, like so many others, he advises that the play's truly the thing to begin.

"Eat, live, breathe, live theater, and learn as much as you can," he told acting's newcomers. "I would advise anyone to do as much live theater as they can. It is the base of all the roles you will be likely to be called for."

And how to join him on the ranks of wonderful "character" acting? Well, that's not too difficult either, he continued.

"Every actor is a character actor!" he said. "I don't really think it is important to distinguish 'character,' as we are all acting. It was about the people, and the people were important. There are just so many wonderful things that happened to me. I look back on it, and sometimes it seems like it's only yesterday."

Editor's note: Bill Erwin passed away on Dec. 29, 2010, less than a month after his 96th birthday. We thank him and his family for their help on this book – he was truly a pleasure to interview.

Leo Fitzpatrick

Throughout the mid-1990s, millions of people met the cast of *Kids*, the 1995 all-too-realistic story of a day in the life of a group of youngsters (who, like so many of us once were, are at the age where they know absolutely everything), a day filled with sex, drugs, booze, violence, a desire for more of all four, and not a single thought about tomorrow – or even an hour from now.

In the center of it all, there's Telly, an (unfortunately) ordinary kid in a sadly ordinary world. In the first scene, we see him making out with a girl whose main worry should be passing seventh-grade pre-algebra. Eventually, he sweet-talks her into handing over her virginity – and two scenes later, bad-mouths her and forgets she ever existed.

But he's more than just a predator; early on, we meet Jennie (Chloe Sevigny, at the start of a career that's made it all the way to Oscar nominations and Golden Globe wins) one of Telly's earlier conquests, who, on a whim, goes to get an STD test with her promiscuous friend Ruby (Rosario Dawson, another bright star just starting to shine).

Despite openly sleeping around and around, Ruby's clean. But Jennie, a virgin but for Telly, comes back positive for HIV.

The heartbroken young woman spends the rest of the film searching for Telly, who never even acknowledged her after his innocence theft, but it's too late – just as she finds him, he's in the midst of deflowering – and probably infecting – another middle-school-age girl.

After the film came out, Telly found himself a target. On the New York subway, on the streets, in the skateboard shop he worked at, he noticed people giving him dirty looks. Some would even call and threaten him.

Leo Fitzpatrick's Telly and Justin Pierce's Casper exchange typical hormone-crazed pleasantries in the 1995 coming-of-teenage drama *Kids*.

The problem was, he wasn't actually Telly at all. Once the cameras went off and the crew went home, he was Leo Fitzpatrick, a skateboarding freak from New Jersey who'd happened to stumble into the movie business.

"The weird thing for me was how many other people thought that I was truly that character, because I was almost the opposite of that character," recalls Fitzpatrick. "I was shy and awkward, not tough or whatever. I was really scared; I'm as average as you can get. But a lot of people truly thought that I was a jerk, and that was kind of weird for me."

Practicing his skateboarding trade in the streets of New York as a youngster, Fitzpatrick ran into a fellow named Larry Clark.

"(Clark) liked skateboarders, and the lifestyle they represented," says Fitzpatrick. "He'd be up on a skateboard with a camera, which was weird, because he was like fifty years old. He really became a part of the kids' lives."

One day, Clark told Fitzpatrick and his friends that he was making a film, and that he wanted them all to audition.

"It seemed sort of bullshit at the time," Fitzpatrick admits. "I was just a skateboarding kid. I'd never thought about acting. It wasn't something I aspired to. That was so foreign to us, somebody putting us in a movie. But I decided to try out. I thought we would go and see what happened."

Perhaps it was his inexperience, natural talent, or a little of both, but Fitzpatrick turned his own dark side into Telly at the audition.

"I didn't really try to act," he explains. "I tried to be myself, with (Telly's) words in my mouth. I didn't really know what I was doing, but the reason that it worked is because it wasn't subconscious; I wasn't trying to act and be over the top. I felt kind of overwhelmed. The more I overanalyze it, the worse an actor I become."

Then the parts were handed out, and Fitzpatrick, Justin Pierce, who played Telly's friend Casper, and the rest of the cast hung out, mainly between skateboarding extravaganzas.

"We already had the bond of skateboarding, so we would hang out all night anyway," Fitzpatrick says. "It was like *Lord of the Flies*; there were no parents. We could hang out, drink, smoke weed. It was our life, so we already had this bond. But this wasn't between us; it was between every skateboarder in New York City."

Still, as filming began, the two main men hadn't exactly forged a strong bond.

"Me and Justin were so young, and our egos were crazy," Fitzpatrick says. "We weren't good friends during filming; we were arguing between takes, cussing at each other. Larry said to us, 'You guys can't be arguing. You have to be best friends.'"

A nervous film official pulled the two aside and told them to memorize the entire script, roughly 100 pages.

"We had to recite the whole movie," Fitzpatrick says. "But (scriptwriter) Harmony (Korine) was such a great writer. We were never really searching; we just knew the next line, so everybody could feed off each other. People think that there's a lot of improv in that movie, but there's not. Harmony knew the way we talked, and he knew how to write it."

Fitzpatrick notes that he was one of the few actual minors in the film (despite the age of their characters, Pierce and Sevigny were both of adult age by the time filming began).

"My mom had to sign off on (me participating)," Fitzpatrick says. "She didn't agree with a lot of the things that were said, but she knew that it was real. Larry was a father too; she knew that he wasn't trying to exploit anybody. A lot of people thought that Larry took advantage of us, but it was the opposite; he showed us all a ton of respect."

Filming was originally slated to begin with a long scene of Telly and Casper strolling around the city, plotting out their plans for the day (involving, not for the first or 22nd time, sex, drugs, and the bong arts). However, rain knocked the cameras inside, and Fitzpatrick's acting career began with the film's first scene, a seemingly endless kiss between him and the first girl.

"That was kind of awkward for a 16-year-old kid, for that to be his first scene in acting," says Fitzpatrick. "But that was about it. After that, nothing else seemed really strange."

And for a large segment of the film's audience, it didn't seem strange at all. It was new — no happy ending, not a lot of exceptionally likable characters, not one's typical Hollywood putout, but something that told the story of America's youths in a way that few films had before, or since.

"It was about the honesty," Fitzpatrick says of the film's appeal. "A lot of kids tell me that *Kids* was the first movie that turned them on to movies. It made them think, 'Wow! This is about me and my good friends!' It's not a movie about skateboarding or New York; it's a movie about trying to find your place in the world. Kids at that age aren't really interested in bonding with their parents; it's them and their friends against the world."

After filming, Fitzpatrick dropped out of the acting world's sight, making only one more film over the next five years.

"I don't think I was old enough to deal with auditioning and agents and people kissing my ass and me having to kiss other people's ass," says the actor, who spent a year in London during his time away from the cameras. "I wasn't into that. I still wanted to be a kid. I wanted a better understanding of how I wanted to (act), and I wasn't going to let anybody bully or pressure me into doing it another way. Having people tell me what to do was very awkward." He came back at full force in 2000, knocking out three films and a one-shot appearance on TV on *The Practice*.

In August of that same year, after appearing in the 2000 Ice Cube sequel *Next Friday* and a few episodes of *Malcolm in the Middle*, Pierce hanged himself in a Las Vegas hotel.

"It's strange," Fitzpatrick says of the suicide. "It was a mistake. The life I grew up in and the world I live in, this kind of thing happens, and it just sucks. But you deal with it the best you can."

2001 brought quite the diversity for Fitzpatrick; he helped Clark put together the true crime tale of *Bully*, the story of a group of Florida friends who trap and kill a tormentor. Fitzpatrick spent time with some sufferers of cerebral palsy to play Marcus, the similarly afflicted boyfriend of Selma Blair's Vi in the anthological *Storytelling* (Marcus and Telly each got laid within moments of their films' opening credits, which has to give Fitzpatrick some kind of record!).

Turning back to television acting, he had a recurring role on the HBO series *The Wire*, and later come back to HBO for *Carnivale*. Fitzpatrick also appeared on a few 2007 episodes of *My Name is Earl*, including the show's pilot, alongside boyhood hero Jason Lee.

"I don't think people understand how important to skateboarding Jason Lee was," claims Fitzpatrick (the actor was a common sight on the professional skateboarding circuit before turning to acting). "I don't think he really knows that. He was as cool as he could be."

To an extent, that's how Fitzpatrick seems to feel about his own career – the coolness comes not only from his feelings in front of the camera, but from exactly how the end result of his work matters – to him, at least.

"I have different reasons for working, and none of it's for seeing myself," he says. "I like to try different things to see if I can do them. I wanted to do a sitcom comedy, and I don't know if I did it well, but I tried at least. I don't really watch or care about the end product; I just enjoy acting. I just do it one day at a time; there's really no right or wrong way to go about acting. The only thing I would say is to be true to yourself; if it doesn't feel right, then it's not right. There's no reason to rush things."

Because in the end, as important as it is to impress the casting directors that choose you and the people that pay to see you, the only person a performer needs to prove anything to is the one in the mirror.

"To me, it's not about awards; it's about respect, and having a career you can be proud of," Fitzpatrick says. "It took me a long time to get to that place, but that's how I feel about it. I wanted to have a decent career, and know that I did it my way."

Kurt Fuller

It's tough to portray an actual person onscreen, as opposed to a fictional character. There's less leeway when it comes to creating a character – an actor needs to learn to give their own version of their model's voice, persona, characteristics, even physical stature. Chances are, there might be someone watching who is familiar with the person being portrayed, and they have an extra manner to judge the strength of one's work.

Indeed, one must go the extra mile to act like an actual person, which is why the accolades are generous when it comes to real-person portrayal: performers from Robert De Niro to Julia Roberts have taken home Academy Awards for becoming real people.

Still, when Kurt Fuller walked into his role for the 2002 Bob Crane biopic *Auto Focus*, he had one extra hurdle to cover.

Fuller was becoming Werner Klemperer, Crane's longtime friend and co-star on *Hogan's Heroes*. Not only would he have to become Klemperer, who enjoyed a four-decade acting career before his death in 2000, but he'd have to also do double duty as Klemperer's *Heroes* character, the bumbling, lovable Colonel Klink.

Basically, Fuller was an actor playing an actor... playing an actor!

"I remember being a big fan of that show," Fuller says of *Heroes*, which ran from 1965 to 1971. "At the time, I wasn't politically aware, I wasn't worried about who the Nazis were and who the Germans were and what happened in World War II." Crane's Hogan (Greg Kinnear in the film) was the leader of a group of POWs in a Germany camp, comically sabotaging their Nazi guards with a myriad of hidden tunnels and tricks.

Before he took on the role, Klemperer (who as a child fled the city of Cologne with his family to escape the Nazis, winding up in New York City) said that he'd only become Klink if the character never succeeded, and that the Nazis were portrayed as buffoons.

Playing both Werner Klemperer and Col. Klink in 2002's *Auto Focus* was just a new challenge for Kurt Fuller, doing his acting thing for nearly three decades.

"He was worried about the political correctness of it," Fuller says. "That's a show that probably never would get done today, the way it was done."

Fuller headed to New York City's Museum of Television and Radio.

"You don't see much of Werner other than that iconic role," says Fuller (Klemperer's portrayal of Klink won him a pair of Emmys). "I asked for all the clips of interview shows that he did, of which there were very little. He was on the *Mike Douglas* show, and he narrated *Peter and the Wolf* and *A Christmas Carol* and things like that. I watched them all over and over and over and over again, and I watched every *Hogan's Heroes* that I could find."

Fuller used Klemperer's background in the music world for an extra springboard to his character; a concert pianist and violinist, Klemperer sang on Broadway stages for years, even spoofing his own talents with Klink's ear-breaking violin sounds.

"I sort of got hooked into him when I realized that he basically sang the role," says Fuller (sharp-eared viewers will notice that Klemperer's lines were often delivered with an aura of soprano-ship near the end). "When I hooked into that, that's when I had it. The central thing about him was that he was very, very musical."

That's why, while Fuller only a got a few scenes in *Auto Focus* (including one where Crane's sex addiction leads him into a hallucination where everyone, including Klink, temporarily goes into psycho-nymphomaniac mode), he straddled the thick line between the actor and the character.

"When we were working, we were doing actual scenes from *Hogan's Heroes*," says Fuller, obviously discounting the dream scene. "Greg Kinnear and I would go into a room and watch it, watch it, watch it, and then go do it. We'd rehearse it."

When becoming an actual person, Fuller says, "You don't want to imitate; you want to recreate, and there's a fine difference. I'm not a guy doing a Vegas act of Warner, so I had to go back be Warner Klemperer and do Clink, but not try to copy him, just to embody him. It's subtle and hard to define, but it's a real difference."

And for the character actors of the world, who often don't get much screen time to do their thing, it's business as usual, he continues.

"As character actors, the things that you do for love and the things that you do for money are often two different things," Fuller asserts. "I've done plenty of really lousy movies (1991's *Bingo*, 1989's *No Holds Barred*, and 2009's *Van Wilder: Freshman Year* come to mind), and every single one of them was for money, because I have two kids and I'm a character actor, so I'm kind of a volume guy. I don't make the big bucks. I don't get blamed for anything, and I don't get the credit for anything; it's my job to just keep working. But for every three mediocre movies you make, you have to make one really good one. If you don't come up with a really good one, it hurts your career." Fortunately, he managed to show up in not just *Pursuit of Happyness* (2006), *Midnight in Paris* (2011), and *Ray* (2004), but box office hits *Wayne's World* (1992), *Scary Movie* (2000), and *Anger Management* (2003).

"The best advice that was given to me came from Michael Apted (director of 1988's *Gorillas in the Mist*)," says Fuller, who's also been on the small screen in *Psych* (2009) and other TV tales. "He said, 'When I was a director, I said I would direct any place, any time I could.'

"That's what I'd say to actors. You're an actor, go act. If you're in class, act with people who are a lot better than you. Everybody gets a break, everybody gets an opportunity to shine, but most people don't know it, and don't take advantage of that. You just have to keep getting better and better."

M.C. Gainey

If his name wasn't household, M.C. Gainey's acting career certainly was.

Like many in the character acting field, he often traded screen quality for quantity early on, commonly showing up as a member of the justice system on both sides of the law in *The A-Team* (1983), *Knight Rider* (1982), and *Simon and Simon* (1983), among other action TV work throughout the 80s. He played a buffoonish convict in *Designing Women* (1988), and showed up on dozens of shows for the rest of the 90s, though his biggest small-screen work would come later. On the silver screen, Gainey got the chance to show a bit more variety, jumping into everything from comedy (1986's *Soul Man*) to the family (1992's *Mighty Ducks*) to action (1997's *Breakdown*). Still, in the span of about five minutes, Gainey's career backflipped, spun around, and shot off like an agitated meteorite.

One day, on the front porch of Gainey's Laurel Canyon home, the phone rang. His old pal Alexander Payne's voice came over the line.

"(Payne's) a great guy," says Gainey, who'd appeared in the director's earlier work *Citizen Ruth* (1996). Payne said he had a potential role for Gainey in his next film.

The plot? The character? The cast? None of it was too important at that point.

"I said, great, I'd do it, just because I love him and would jump at any opportunity to work with him. He said, 'Well, you may need to think about this. You need to talk about this part with your people.'

"I said, 'No, I don't need to think about it. I'm doing this part, pal.'"

However, there was one slight provision: he'd be naked for about the entire appearance – from the back, the side, and even the front.

During one shot, Payne told him, "It'll be your naked ass next to a TV with George Bush's face on the screen."

With that, things went into overdrive.

"I said, 'I'm in, baby!'" Gainey crows. "'That should have been the first thing you said! My ass and George Bush's face?! Get me the setup!'"

So started his emergence in Payne's 2004 winery-centered comedy *Sideways*, the story of two men off to find themselves during a wine-tasting trip through California's vineyards. Paul Giamati (who MANY felt should have been Oscar-nominated for the role) was Miles, an English teacher looking to give his pal Jack (Thomas Haden Church) a social sendoff before marriage, while Jack, a has-been actor, can't keep his Lothario-esque libido down pat during time on his own.

In the end, Jack's hormones nearly get both men severely beaten. But they gave Gainey a chance to steal the show.

Jack's managed to seduce a lovely young waitress, whose husband comes home and finds them in *flagrante delicto*. Now Jack, revealing the scared child he always was, is on the floor before Miles, crying that his wallet, with his wedding ring, was left at the house, and it might be the only chance he has to hold on to his real love.

Like any good friend (well, some of them, maybe) would do, Miles heads back to the home. His amateur burglary skills showing, he makes his way through the home, and to the bedroom. Apparently quick to forgive, the husband (Gainey) is back in action with his wife, and the dirty talk is flowing.

With Bush on the TV, joining him in some inadvertent voyeurism, Miles can't help but stare, suddenly looking as though he's rubber-necking his way past a truck pileup. But just as Miles grinds up enough courage to snare and steal the wallet, the husband spots him, wearing a hat and that's it, and the race is on.

Neglecting his in-the-altogether state, the fellow hauls after Miles, barreling out of the house, across the lawn, and down the street (fortunately, jogging doesn't seem to be a popular pastime in this neck of the woods at this time). By the time it's over, audiences are either jaw-dropped spellbound, or howling in laughter – or maybe switching back and forth between the two.

"The really weird part was running down the street of Lompoc, California, naked, with the cops blocking traffic on both sides of the street," Gainey recalls, "and all the people who lived on that street hiding in their houses looking out the windows. I could hear them laughing! It was a very liberating experience. We shot it early in the morning, and it was very cold!"

Ever since, the minutes-long cameo has become a newfound milestone in his career.

"Every room I go into, every meeting I take, every audition I go into, everybody has seen me naked!" he says. "It's just a given. Everybody in the business saw (*Sideways*), so they've all seen my junk. They say, 'This time, you get to keep your clothes on.' Once you've done that, you've got nothing left to hide." It's working; Gainey's become an even bigger mainstay in films, with small roles in hit films like *Are We There Yet?* (2005), *Dukes of Hazzard* (2005), and the smash *Wild Hogs* (2007).

But, hey, it's all part of a character acting career – as Gainey can't wait to tell you.

"A character actor is someone who's really acting," he explains. "He's not just posing and looking good; he's doing something. He's created a personality. There's something going on there that's interesting."

Gainey calls early character stars Ward Bond (veteran of over 250 roles), Thomas Mitchell (Oscar winner, 1939's *Stagecoach*) and Victory McLaglen (Oscar winner, 1935's *The Informer*) three of his all-time favorites.

"Whenever they were in something, man, I was all over it," he remembers. "Back in the old studio days, character guys worked all the time perfecting their characters. Not so much anymore; now you have to do it on your own, because there's no studio to hire you 52 weeks out of the year."

As the 1980s grew near, Mike Conner Gainey (he's named after Mike Conner, the first Irish governor in Gainey's home state of Mississippi) headed off to drop into character. Before his first role, however, drama came calling. When Gainey went to the Screen Actors Guild, he couldn't use his real full name; Mike Connors (1967's *Mannix*) was still going strong in Hollywood, and similarity was a dirty word. Sadly, Connors died in late January 2017, just weeks before this book was done.

"This was back in 1977, and you couldn't get an audition in this town if you weren't in SAG," says Gainey. "I had to do something on the spot." As a tribute to screen legend W.C. Fields, he went by his initials.

After working alongside Kurt Russell and fellow character performer J.T. Walsh in *Breakdown* (1997), Gainey heard that a new action flick was in the works. Jerry Bruckheimer, with whom he'd always wanted to work, was putting together an explosion-dominated, action-jammed story of a group of criminals who hijack a plane. He'd gotten Nicolas Cage, Ving Rhames, John Malkovich, and others for the film – and he was calling it, simply enough, *Con Air* (1997).

He certainly seemed at home while piloting *Con Air* (1997), but action's just one of the many genres that M.C. Gainey has tackled in his career.

Arriving on the set, Gainey recalls, "I walked in and saw all these guys that I'm always competing with for jobs, and here we all were, all in the same movie. That doesn't happen very often. These guys were all really badasses. There were cannibals, mass murderers, really badasses." Note: he's of course referring to the *characters*, not the actors playing them!

Gainey was Swamp Thing – fortunately, bearing little resemblance to his sci-fi film/TV namesake! – and the Thing's backstory appeared from nowhere.

"I was on a buyout," he says. "That's when they pay you a lump sum to do a movie, and you don't get any overtime. In preproduction, they took us all into a trailer, and all of my buddies were getting these giant tattoos.

"I'm thinking to myself, I don't want that, I don't want to spend an hour in makeup everyday when I'm not getting any overtime. So I just got a marijuana leaf on the back of my hand, and that led me in my thinking about my character."

Unlike many of his fellow passengers, and despite his intimidating appearance, Swamp Thing wasn't a killer, or even especially violent, Gainey says.

"He was a guy who could fly planes," he explained. "I created a backstory that he had flown in the military, flown in the oil fields. Then he started flying some pot, and started flying some coke, then he crashed a plane loaded with coke. They'd put him in the federal (prison), and he had escaped a couple of times." He also called the performance a tribute to Donald Sutherland's aptly-named tank commander Sgt. Oddjob in the 1970 Clint Eastwood action flick *Kelly's Heroes*, the saga of a group of American soliders trying to steal treasure from the Nazis.

Character actors are great at showing flashes of personality with simple words and gestures, and Gainey did so from Swamp Thing's first appearance.

"When my first shot came up, I looked at the plane, and I started smiling," he says. "The director (Simon West) asked me why I was smiling. I ran it by him, and he said I was absolutely right."

After his criminal colleagues take over the plane, it's left to the Thing to step behind the controls and lead them through the air, to a non-extradition land.

"From then on, whenever there was a gunfight, whenever there was violence, Swamp Thing would be on the plane, looking down at all his friends, shooting each other and blowing shit up," Gainey says. "Swamp Thing's the happiest character in that entire world. He was somebody who wasn't gritting their teeth and looking through blood-filled eyes."

For his role as Rosco P. Coltrane in the movie adaptation of *Dukes of Hazzard*, Gainey took a different tact from the former sheriff.

"No way was I going to try to be Rosco P. Coltrane the way the great James Best played him on TV," says Gainey. Playing Coltrane for six years on the show and in some subsequent TV movies, Best made him into a "coo-coo"-spouting, light man-child, the perfect foil for Luke, Bo, and Daisy to fool one week after another.

"James Best was a great Mississippi actor," says Gainey, who appeared on a 1982 episode of the *Dukes*, portraying (shockingly!) a hostage-taking thug. "I didn't want to do an impression of him, so what I did was to be the meanest cop you could ever imagine, the kind of cop that would ticket an ambulance or a hearse, the kind of cop that nobody liked. I made him a hyper, pseudo-macho guy with the spurs on his boots and longest handgun in the world, just trying to make him an asshole."

He showed a different side of law enforcement in a turn as a police detective trying to get a confession from a legend in a different area during one of the most notorious crime investigations in American history.

In the summer of 1981, a group of people robbed the home of drug dealer Eddie Nash in Laurel Canyon, a suburb of Los Angeles. An infuriated Nash found porn icon and longtime customer John Holmes, who'd allegedly helped plan the robbery, and got him to give up the names of those who'd committed the act. Days later, a mob (how many people were there is unknown) attacked a house where some of the robbers were staying, beating four people to death and putting another in a coma. Holmes' fingerprints were found at the scene, but it will never be known just how much he actually participated, if at all. No one was ever convicted of the murders, though Holmes was tried and acquitted, and did time for contempt of court.

The event was dramatized in 1997's *Boogie Nights* (loosely based on Holmes' life). Six years later, Gainey became Billy Ward, a police detective and friend of Holmes in *Wonderland* (Val Kilmer plays Holmes himself).

"I used to live on the Wonderland street, a few blocks over," remembers Gainey. "I remember walking down there and seeing the aftermath (of the murders). When the homicide cops couldn't break this guy's story, they call in this other guy who can break his story because he's Holmes' friend.

"What drew me to this were the scenes I shared with Val Kilmer," he continues. "A recurring theme in a lot of my decisions is working with people that I want to work with, even if the part sucks; on *Terminator 3* (2003), I had a five-line part because I wanted to work with Schwarzenegger." He played a bar bouncer in the film.

To become Ward, he continues, "I see vice cops as being incredibly jaded, incredibly cynical and world-weary, so I just added that part of myself to get in touch with those feelings. That's how they live their lives, because they see the worst of people, day in and day out for years. I looked to that part of my psyche."

For one of his more famous TV roles of the past few years, Gainey had to check out a different side, one that, even after decades on the screens, he still hadn't really touched upon. For the first few seasons of *Lost* (2004), he became Tom Friendly, a member of the menacing group of Others that threatened and even imprisoned some of the crew of Flight 815 on that ominous island.

During a particular episode, Tom's assigned the extremely enviable position of looking after Kate (Evangeline Lilly) before her meeting with fellow Other Ben (Michael Emerson). Kate declares that she's not showering in front of him, and Tom makes the shocking statement that she's just not his type.

"I decided that if she's not your type, then you're gay!" Gainey says. "She's just that perfect a woman. I decided right there, if she's not your type, then Sawyer is." From then on, during scenes with Sawyer (Josh Holloway), who'd eventually kill Tom, or Jack Shephard (Matthew Fox), Gainey used a particular sense to show his preferences.

"I started thinking gay thoughts," he says. "I never manifested anything, but whenever I was with Matthew Fox, I would *gaze* at him. In scenes with Sawyer, I would ogle him. I thought of what a horny gay man would think if he was on an island with these guys."

During a scene where Tom and Shephard are tossing around a pigskin, Gainey says, "I threw it as if I had never thrown a football before in my life, because (Tom) had never thrown a football around. He had no interest in football, but if Jack wanted to throw a football around, he'd do it."

It's all part of everyday life for a character actor, something that Gainey hopes to continue for much, much longer.

"Character actors, many times, go through a progression," he explains. "I started out as Goon #3, worked my way up to Goon #2, the murderer, and now I've moved into the 'He looks sort of like a goon, but he's probably a lovable old grandpa!'

"I don't know if you've heard 'The five stages of an actor's career.' Step one is 'Who is M.C. Gainey?' Step two is 'Get me M.C. Gainey.' Stage three is 'Get me an M.C. Gainey type.' Stage four is 'Get me a young M.C. Gainey'

"And stage five is 'Who is M.C. Gainey?' That's been true as long as films have been made. Those five stages apply to all character actors. I'm somewhere in stages three or four, and trying to put off the fifth stage as long as I can."

James Gammon

Don't try to name all of James Gammon's acting roles — you'll be up all week. Trying to rattle off what he *didn't* get done, however, might, *might* fill up a page.

"I don't know that I've done everything," Gammon said. "My first work was at a play in Hollywood in 1964 or 1965. I belonged to a theater group. I kind of kept going."

In 1966, he showed up in *Gunsmoke*, *Bonanza*, *Batman*, and some other TV shows before hitting the big screen for the first time the next year with an uncredited part in the Paul Newman classic *Cool Hand Luke* (1967).

Indeed, there isn't much in the acting world that Gammon hasn't seen or performed in himself. But for one of his more well-known roles, he looked to someone with a ton of experience in another area.

In the late 1980s, Gammon's extensive network opened up a bright new connection. Back in 1982, he'd played the sheriff in a television version of *The Ballad of Gregorio Cortez*, the story of a Mexican American wrongfully convicted of murder.

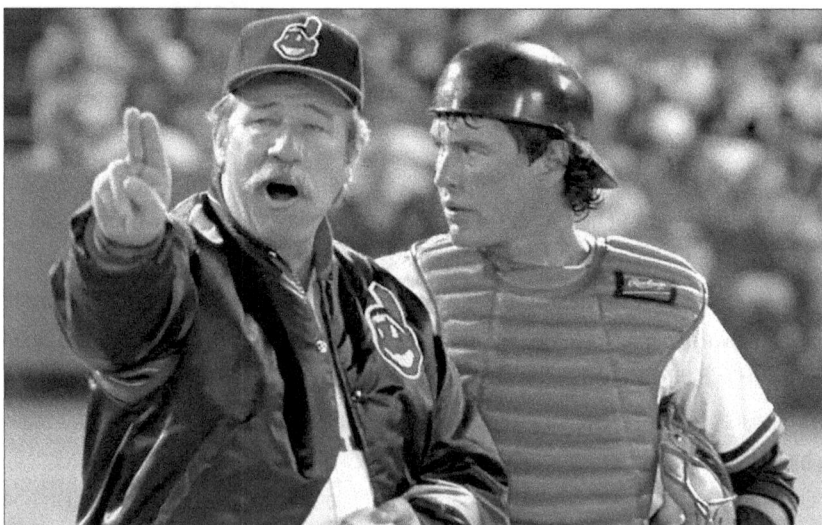

James Gammon's career spanned decades, but he'll never be forgotten for becoming Lou Brown in the two *Major League* films of 1989 and 1994.

As the decade came to a close, director David Ward was putting together a film about America's top sport, and Ward's then-wife Rosanna DeSoto, who'd worked with Gammon in *Cortez*, suggested her former co-star.

"The studio was thinking about using an English actor," Gammon said. "She told them to think about me."

Then he had a new role to think about.

"If you're in Los Angeles, you're a fan of the Dodgers," he said. "They came to town about the same time that I came here." After getting started in Brooklyn in 1883, the team moved across the country in 1958.

"It was a major league film," Gammon said of 1989's *Major League*. "It had many fine young actors just starting out." The film was a springboard to relative newcomers Wesley Snipes and Rene Russo, and Dennis Haysbert was in his most memorable as voodoo slugger Pedro Cerrano until the TV show *24* came out nearly two decades later (on the other hand, Charlie Sheen's background as a high school pitcher gave Rick "Wild Thing" Vaughn one of the most realistic fastballs in movie history, firing off at 85 miles an hour).

Working toward the character of manager Lou Brown — who, as could probably only happen in Hollywood, goes from working at Tire World to the top of the American League in a single year — Gammon observed Bobby Cox, the legendary Atlanta Braves skipper who, as of the opening of the 2017 season, was one of only four managers in pro baseball history with more than 2,300 wins.

"I used (Cox) primarily to give me the guidelines for what a manager looks like, and how he basically acts," Gammon said. "I learned from the way he moved, his manners. He was the one we came to when we said, 'That's a baseball manager.' I used him as a guideline, and it was a good thing I did. Bobby Cox is all for every player he's had."

Scenes were actually filmed at Milwaukee's County Stadium, near to which Gammon's wife coincidentally grew up.

Like just about every baseball manager at some point, Brown had to deal with owners who didn't want to spend enough green to make a winning squad, and butted heads with new owner Rachel Phelps (Margaret Whitton, who sadly died of cancer in Dec. 2016).. His shortstop Roger Dorn (Corbin Bernsen) could always hit the ball, but couldn't field it — until a pep talk/castration threat from catcher Jake Taylor (Tom Berenger) straightened him out. New pitcher Rick Vaughn (Sheen, like anyone could ever forget him in this!) was a flamethrower in the high 90's, but couldn't find the plate with an atlas.

Or maybe it was just his vision — one pair of horn-rimmed glasses later, Vaughn was going like Nolan Ryan himself.

"The scenes that I liked the most were the quieter moments, the ones when I was trying to help a member of the team," said Gammon, who called the scene where Vaughn first meets his eyewear one of his personal top shots.

While another newbie rubbed Brown wrong at the start, working off-screen was a blast, he continued.

Snipes was Willie Mays Hayes, who hit like (baseball legend Willie) Mays and ran like (1908 Olympics marathon champ Johnny) Hayes. But after seeing Hayes foul ball after ball into the top of the batting cage, Brown decided to lay down the law.

"You may run like Hayes," he deadtones to the rookie, "but you hit like shit."

Egged on by a "twenty pushups for every pop-up" drill, Hayes makes the team — and makes his first-ever putout with a Mays-esque basket fly ball catch. Heading back to the dugout, Hayes is all smiles, and Brown reached out for a high-five.

"Nice catch, Hayes," Brown says, his face expressionless as a blank chalkboard. "Don't ever fuckin' do it again."

But, hey, it was all an act.

"Wesley Snipes is one of the finest actors I have ever seen," Gammon said. "He's all the way in, all the time he acts. It's hard to take your eyes off him; he's so funny. I loved watching him and his work. Even if he wasn't with me, I enjoyed watching his work."

Audiences felt the same way about the *Major League* bunch — the film spawned two sequels (Gammon only reprised his role in the first one, in 1994).

"Lou Brown is a very popular character in society," Gammon said. "A lot of people related to him. I think he had a sense of humor. He truly loved his ballplayers. He was one of those guys that you just like. He was a good man. He was all about his players, all the time."

Author's note: On July 16, 2010, Gammon passed away. I thank him for his contributions to this publication, and send my condolences to his family, about whom he spoke very highly during our conversation.

Lee Garlington

For almost two decades, Lee Garlington has been explaining to her field's newcomers exactly who's who and what's what when it comes to the acting business.

A few times a year, the longtime character actress stands up with the Screen Actors Guild/American Federation of Television and Radio Artists signups and gives them an orientation (that's the nice way of saying it — some would probably go with "boot camp") about the business end of the acting business.

"I have a lot of sayings and philosophies about acting," she says. "There's no better teacher of humility than the entertainment business. My philosophy on Hollywood is that if you're willing to do it for free, eventually, they'll pay you to do it."

Still, as with any such work, the first step — and the overwhelming majority thereafter — have to come from the performers themselves.

"If you come up (to Hollywood), and hustle, or do standup, or if you do improv, you do theater, write your own screenplay," Garlington continues, "you do whatever you can to get yourself out there. It really is a town of 'Last Man Standing.' This is not the land of probability; this is the land of possibility."

But just as with any chance-taking extravaganza, there's always the shot at victory, at success, especially for those that never stop playing and always find new shots to take.

"You're here because anything's possible," she tells her makeshift classes. "If you aim for the sky, you may never reach the roof. If you aim for the roof, you may never get off the ground. Dream big! Aim big!"

It's coming from someone who knows. Garlington's been a consistent presence around the Golden World for decades, from showing up for a few scenes in blockbuster films to coming THIS close to being the main woman on one of television's landmark shows.

Getting to get close to Robert Redford, if only for a scene, would be enough to take a role for most actresses; Lee Garlington got to do so and more in 1992's *Sneakers*.

"It's an interesting phenomenon, being called a character actor," she says. "The difference between television and movies is that when you go on movies, you're going to shoot a page or a page and a half a day, where in television shows, you're going to shoot six or 10 pages a day. The difference is the luxury of time and the luxury of lighting. With film, you have much time and many takes; it's different in television. In TV, you have to do it fast and hit it hard: different styles, different takes."

Her first credited role came as a grouchy waitress (not the last time she'd take on such a part) who discovers that her newest co-worker has, well... quite a past.

His name is Norman.

Bates, that is.

Garlington was Myrna, a small role in *Psycho II* (1983), the story of a boy, his mother, and everything that happened decades later.

"At first, I thought Anthony Perkins (whose performance in the original will forever be imitated) was the strangest person I'd ever met," she says. "But then I thought he was so charming, so funny. He and I argued all the time — politics, movies, music, over everything. I amused the shit out of him. He knew that we could have a solid argument." Four years later, she'd reprise the role in *Psycho III*, which Perkins himself would direct.

"Myrna was the mean waitress, not a happy person," Garlington says. "Tony would slide up next to me and say, 'OK, you have a date with a guy you wanted to go out with for five years, and you're afraid that if you don't get home and get ready, he'll leave.' That was how he would mold his actors."

After steady work, mostly on television, for the next few years, Garlington nearly got into a school meeting fistfight with Amy Madigan during a rough scene in the 1989 Best Picture nominee *Field of Dreams*. As Beulah Gasnick, Garlington rallies her colleagues to ban the works of author Terrence Mann (James Earl Jones), labeling them everything from pornography on up. But Madigan's Annie Kinsella – armed with her husband Ray (Kevin Costner) at her side – has had just about enough of this anal-retentive self-posturing, and suddenly sermons into a monologue about the meaning of freedom and the importance of love and peace.

As the women toss back and forth diplomatic isms like "Nazi cow" and "horse's ass," and nearly come to blows, the audience quickly switches to Annie's support, and Beulah's motion is overruled.

"In my close-up at the end of that scene, I turned red," Garlington says. "Every part of my body was furious. I was near tears, I was so hurt."

That same year, a new show hit the small screen, and no one could have ever predicted what an impact it would make.

It was the story of a New York comedian and his off-beat friends. But more specifically, it was the show about nothing.

When *Seinfeld* kicked off in 1989, it was called *The Seinfeld Chronicles*. Kramer was still named Kessler. And the name Elaine Benes wasn't even in anyone's vocabulary yet.

At the show's start, the female focal point was Claire the waitress, dispensing sage advice to Jerry and George as they dropped by the restaurant that would become a trademark setting throughout the show. Viewers of syndication can catch her ridiculing George in early episodes ("Claire, you're a woman, right?" "What gave it away, George?").

Playing Claire might have been an even bigger step to superstardom for Garlington. But after the pilot, the producers decided to trade Claire in, and Julia Louis-Dreyfus got the call to show heroine glory.

Being switched out, Garlington says, was "one of the most painful experiences of my life. You can't get much prouder than being able to say that you were a regular on *Seinfeld*."

Remember the last *Seinfeld* episode, when the gang went on trial and all the recurring characters came back to testify against them? It didn't go over well with critics, but it was probably the right thing to do; anything else would have had people saying, "Oh, like we didn't see *that* coming!" Anyhoo, it would have been hysterical to see Garlington come back as Claire and tearfully blurt something like, "Yes... they got me fired – and to top it off, I was even blackballed from the whole area!" That would have been self-mockery at its finest ever.

Heading toward realism, Garlington showed up in the 1990 TV film *Killing in a Small Town*, playing Peggy Blankenship, whose husband has an affair with Barbara Hershey's Candy Morrison. The two women collide, and Blankenship is killed with an ax, a crime that paralyzes the tiny Texas city.

"(Hershey and I) spent three days in a room with an axe, our hands covered with fake blood," Garlington recalls. "Playing these southern Texas characters, you had to work to get the energy going, and then you had to cover, because they didn't reveal their emotions. It was draining and emotional to play this character. It really resonated with people, because it was so true. I want to do things that are interesting, challenging, real, poignant."

In 1992's *Sneakers*, however, she got to go the other route, playing a doctor with a full-blown wild side. As Martin Bishop (Robert Redford) and his team of superspies ply their trade on Gunter Janek (Donal Logue, in one of his first film roles), a mathematician with a few secrets that could change the electronic world, one of his colleagues shows up for a late-night conference.

But it's quickly clear that the relationship Janek shares with Elena Rhyzkov is a bit more than professional, as the two quickly start relieving their past passions.

"Let's do what we did in Mexico City," a breathless Rhyzkov gasps as things start to get hot and heavy.

"Hmmm," wonders an admiring Bishop, in one of the film's slapstick-esque one-liners. "I didn't know you could do *that* in Mexico City!"

"That was a fun role!" says Garlington. "A makeup man that I had worked with, he and his wife were from Romania. I went over to their house, and I had them say all my lines on tape for me. One of the things I've learned is that as long as you're consistent, nobody cares. You have to sell the energy of it."

Later, Bryce poses as a private investigator to sneak into Janek's office, only to be surprised by Rhyzkov. But with some fast talk about Janek having a secret marriage and how only Rhyzkov can save him, he quickly turns the doctor to his side.

"The scene with Robert Redford was one of the best scenes I've ever done," Garlington says. "She was fun, kind of an uptight woman who thought she was being betrayed, but under the exterior, she's a very passionate woman."

Variety is the spice of life for any character performers, and reliability is another — it's something that Garlington's been putting on display for her entire career. There are ways to do one's job without reaching out for the spotlight, and it's the sort of work that many newcomers and character actors employ for a large part of their careers.

"My roles are usually there to service the story," she says. "It's not about me; it's about giving information to move the plot along. I'm a firm believer that films are the director's medium. For me, if I'm given a role, that I can, in any way, feel like I can sink my teeth into, I evaluate how good the piece is. If it's a decent role or a decent shot, I'm not too worried about whether I like it or not; I'm going to show up and do the best job I can. If I get the job, great, and if I don't, it was meant for somebody else."

That's a message that she's sent to generations of upcoming performers, from both the screens and the head of the SAG/UFTA classrooms.

"I have three definitions of success in Hollywood," Garlington explains. "One is that you get back on the horse one more time than you're knocked down. Two is that success happens when opportunity meets preparedness. The third definition is happiness is wanting what you have, not having what you want. I have so many friends who are far more successful than I am, who are miserable because they aren't where they wanted to be. I have complete gratitude for what I have."

Irma Hall

There's going to be an extreme theme running straight through this profile. You'll hear the same word, the same *name*, quite often. Because it's the same source that's kept Irma Hall going.

Going through one of the most unpredictable careers a person can take on, even one that she started much later than others, and on a huge whim, no less! And, in some special way, going through just about every one of the roles that have landed her square on the list of "Top Character Actresses" in the film world.

Mother Joe (Irma Hall) spreads her word along with His in 1997's *Soul Food*.

You'll figure it out long before the end of this profile. Let's focus on Hall for now.

Like many in this chapter, she didn't really consider acting a remote possibility until it took its own surprising step into her world; Hall led generations of Texas through their grade school years from the podiums of language (foreign and otherwise) until one fateful day in 1972.

A freelance reporter in the very spare time that teachers enjoy, Hall was assigned a conversation with a young filmmaker named Raymond St. Jacques, in town to spread the word about his film *Book of Numbers* (1973). So wowed was he by her journalistic work that St. Jacques asked her to become an impromptu publicist for the flick.

But that wasn't all – a chance hearing of Hall reciting poetry at a local writing club showed the director that there might be even more to his welcome discovery.

"I was not even thinking about acting – it just happened," Hall recalls. "He said I had a lot of natural talents that should be developed. They were all excited; I had no idea what they were talking about." But that wouldn't last – soon after, she was playing Georgia Brown (not necessarily the "Sweet" version!) alongside St. Jacques himself.

"I learned it all by doing it," Hall says of her first few roles. "When God gives you a challenge, you're obligated to develop it. It had something to do with teaching, which was what I was doing. For the next twelve years, I continued to teach, while I was learning the craft. Everything I learned about acting, I learned on the job. More and more roles kept coming. I guess it was what God was giving me to do." Health problems for both Hall and several of her family members ended her teaching career in 1984.

"I tried to sub in Chicago," she says, "but I would never be able to sub because every time they would call me, I'd have to be out of town or on stage, so it was all God's plan. (Theater) is the cornerstone for me in learning the craft. Stage work is the mother." After nearly two decades on stages and screens of every size, Hall finally got the role to slam her straight on the acting map. She didn't expect to become a centerpiece of the 1996 drama *A Family Thing*; it just sort of happened.

Or maybe, not just once again. "It was God's work," she says. "I had auditioned for the role of the midwife, and gotten that part. Then I went to Rochester for a play and met a young lady who'd been born blind."

Fascinated, she watched the lady help in getting the local handicapped community to see Hall and the rest of the cast show their trade. The two spent time together, more and more throughout the public. Hall got an unexpected education in the life of those who can't see.

"She didn't use a cane, and she knew where everything in her house was," Hall remembers. "She liked all kinds of music." Heading back to Chicago to do her *Thing*, another surprise awaited.

"My manager said they'd gotten a call for me to be Aunt T," she says. "I hadn't even considered that." But she taped an audition and sent it down to Memphis, where headliner Robert Duvall was waiting.

Soon enough, she headed to Tennessee to meet him. Hall worked out one of the Aunt's several speeches, then did a scene with Duvall.

It worked: she snared the largest role of her career. But what was even more ironic – or perhaps divine! – was that Aunt T herself was blind.

"I said, 'Oh my goodness, they want me to play a blind woman!' How wonderful does God work?" Hall says. "I thanked God I'd spent all that time with this girl (in New York) and remembered how she had behaved, except for the part when I had to use a cane. I thought people used the cane so that other people would know they were blind. I didn't want to look funny."

One day, she stepped outside to grab a newspaper. A blind man just *happened* to walk by with such an instrument.

"I just followed him around for almost an hour," Hall says. "I noticed that he used the cane like an antennae, knowing if something was there in front of him. I just recalled all that I had observed."

Duvall plays Earl, whose mother posthumously reveals that she wasn't his biological mom – that would be a maid who Earl's dad raped, and who died having him. Earl has a secret family in Chicago, and she'd like for him to go find out. Once there, he meets a fellow named Ray who he engaged in mutual tormenting as youths.

Earl couldn't know that Ray, played by James Earl Jones himself, was actually his half-brother. But Ray's (well, now both of theirs) aunt, Aunt T certainly did. She'd always known that Earl existed, and now Ray and his family would welcome their uncle and brother.

"Since I have not been trained in school, I go back to my childhood days," Hall says of her self-training for Aunt T. "That's something that's never gotten out of me. I went to that particular state of mind and became blind. I was counting steps all the time. I practiced sitting at the table, handling my silverware, using my cup. It's not the real world, but that's how I prepared for this role. People thought I was blind for real."

A final monologue from the aunt reveals that her sister always wanted Earl raised by his believed mom, who helped save his life in the delivery. It might have been that that convinced the Chicago Film Critics to gift Hall with their Best Supporting Actress honor (Billy Bob Thornton, who helped write the screenplay, would win an Oscar the next year for transcribing *Sling Blade*).

"Acting is a metaphor for teaching," Hall says. "I always said I was a teacher who acted until I got the Chicago Film Critics award. "After *A Family Thing*, my status changed from a day player to an actress."

Right around the time she hilariously slapped around both Martin Lawrence and Tim Robbins as a sharp-tongued mama in *Nothing to Lose* (1997), starred with Rene Russo and a monkey in *Buddy* (1997), and helped Shaquille O'Neal try out his action style in *Steel* (1997) – few performers can boast of such diversity so close together! – Hall grabbed a role even more matriarchal than Aunt T.

After all, the lady's *name* was Mother Joe, trying to hold her battling family together in the surprise smash *Soul Food* (1997).

"The first thought that caught my eye was Mama Joe's name," Hall remembers. "My mother's name was Josephine, and my children called her Mama Joe. My mother used to have dinners every Sunday at her home in Chicago." For many cultures, many families, food and meals often have little to do with nutrition, or even hunger. It's about the togetherness that family dinners represent. Even if we do so by obligation, even force, it's a way to hang on to a sense of connection and the bonds of family that can slip away in the midst of careers and, well, life itself. Family is something that we should always be able to rely on, and all too often people don't realize this until the bonds between us are broken, perhaps beyond repair.

For too long, the dinners were all Mother Joe had left. With daughters who knew how to hammer each other's buttons and a brother who might not have left his room if the house were ablaze, the dinners were just about the only time the family could be bothered to care just a little bit – and the only other one who realized this was Mama's grandson, and film narrator Ahmad.

"I have a boy and a girl," Hall says, "so the reality of her having three girls was different. I had known many people like that, so I recognized her right off the bat. She was the kind of mother who was there for her children."

Sadly, not for long, as Mama's diabetes gets too strong for her, stealing her leg and eventually her life.

"My grandmother was an amputee, and she had died from diabetes," Hall remembers. "I had an uncle who had a speech impediment. We called him Uncle Pete, and there was this uncle in the story named Pete. I said, 'Wow, this was so close!' I did a *lot* of praying, and God told me to do it." As is all too often the case, it takes the sympathy of a loved one's loss and the wisdom of a child to get the family back together, with even John Watson's Pete stepping back into the family.

Three years later, the film moved to the small screens of Showtime, with Hall the only performer to follow it there. Over the next four years – longer than any other primetime drama with a black cast – she and Mama showed up in spiritual form to lead her family through even more tumults.

"I was dead already, and I was coming back in their thoughts," Hall says. "It was an interesting thing." Early in her career, Hall visited with residents of a nursing home to become a character that, like Mama, was a bit older than Hall herself.

"I spent time with old people so that I wouldn't be a caricature of the old," she recalls. "I wanted to tell their stories so no one would ever forget them."

Herself a nurse, she got to boss Robin Williams around in his title role of *Patch Adams* (1998). "I went up to Robin and told him that *Mrs. Doubtfire* (1993) was one of my kids' favorite movies," says Hall, who also played a nurse in the 1991 action film *Backdraft*. "He joked that *no one* had ever told him that before! It was an honor to work with him and to learn more about my craft from him. I just observed him as an actor on screen and as a human being." Also in 1998, the former English teacher stood alongside another American icon to visually create a literary legend, a small part of *Beloved*, starring a lady named Oprah Winfrey.

"My way of preparing is to read the script a lot, and to find out a lot of the clues that the other of the script has given me," Hall says. "That gives me a background. I would advise anyone who wants to be an actor to go to school for it. I read the book several times and prepared for it by knowing as much about the time as I could. I learned about the people and what they were like, dressed like, talked like, what was going on in that era."

She formed the form of Ella, a former slave trying to save others, such as Oprah's Sethe and Thandie Newton's title character, the mother and daughter whose supernaturally dark tale is beyond any kind of human comprehension for Ella and her friends.

"Ella was a slave, and had escaped herself," Hall says, "and was on a mission to help out as many slaves as possible, and help them adjust to a new way of living. She knew that role pretty well as soon as she came into contact with the main people, helping them adjust to freedom."

In some ways, Hall's last role to chat about her had more in common with the performer than any she'd played in the past; in others, it couldn't have been more different. The same could be said for the men behind the camera for *The Ladykillers* (2004).

Like Hall, main lady Marva Munson lived for her church and the word it preaches. Unlike her, Munson became the target of a group of con men that couldn't steal a bag of air without breaking six bones.

"I knew her right off the bat," Hall says. "I knew that it was cut and paste getting into her, but I knew her."

While *The Ladykillers* was jammed with the same dark comedic tastes that Joel and Ethan Cohen had thrilled us with in *Intolerable Cruelty* (2003) and *The Big Lebowski* (1998), it wasn't their original creation; Alexander Mackendrick, with Katie Johnson in the leading role, had shoved the story across England half a century before. Unlike Marva, Johnson's Louisa Alexandra Wilberforce wasn't the religious type, preferring to inadvertently entertain others with her eccentries.

That's one reason why Hall, for all of her preparation, didn't watch the original as she got ready to be Marva.

"I didn't want to be swayed by it," she says of the first film. "I was doing a reading for the audition, and they stopped me in the middle of the first paragraph. I was very, very surprised."

Led by Tom Hanks, playing a bad guy for one of the only times thus far for him, a group of thieves holes up in Marva's basement. Under the guise of a band, they're about to dig out a tunnel from the basement to a nearby casino and take all the winnings they're not entitled to.

But, again, these guys would get lost going through an open door; not only do they foul up one attempt after another, but Marva finds them out, and there's only one thing left for them to do to shut her up.

Hey, why would we be surprised about what happens next? If these guys couldn't do robbery, how could they even think they'd get away with murder? Indeed, through one mishap after another, they manage to bump themselves and each other off, culminating in the death of Hanks's masterminding Goldthwaite Higginson Dorr, Ph. D., knocked out by a falling statue and hanged from a bridge. Perhaps, in one more way, something stronger was at work on these clowns' karma.

And that sounds just like the perfect way to bring this to a full-circled close. Script reading, character backstories, the same tools that so many of her colleagues utilize have brought Hall all kinds of success.

But she'd never have made it without the One that guides her through it all, acting and otherwise.

"Acting was never my plan," she asserts. "It was all God's plan. I've always looked to His direction. I was lucky, although I prefer the word blessed. I'm still learning this craft. Once I made a decision, I'm living with it through Him."

Randee Heller

The Karate Kid (1984) may not be considered the mother of all sports films – although many have it ranked reasonably high on the list – but one of its stars has her own distinction there. She'll forever be known as Lucille LaRusso, the scared but tough gal who stayed by her son Danny as the two stepped into a strange, even dangerous new world and made it all the way through to triumph, a surprise hit that spawned an Oscar nomination (albeit not for her), three sequels, and a remake (not to mention, of course, an overload of folding green!).

Even today, decades afterward, "I've got Lucille in my back pocket," recalls Randee Heller. "She's there, in my toolbox, ready to rear her head, very close to my heart."

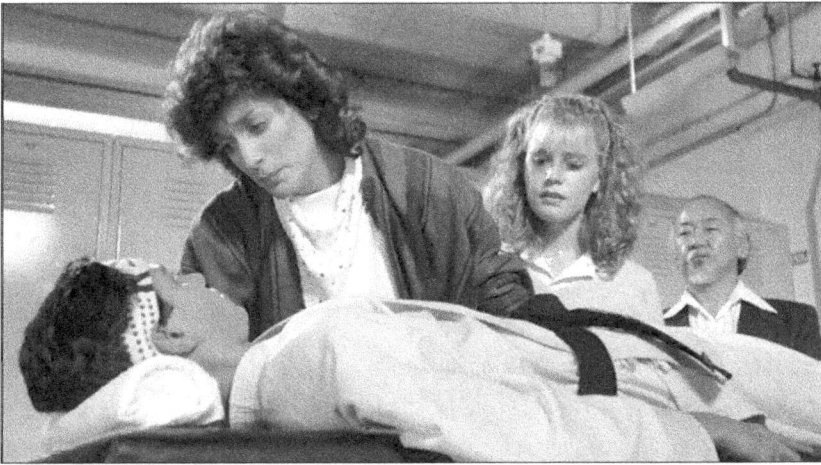

Being Daniel LaRusso's mom Lucille in a few *Karate Kid* films turned Randee Heller into Hollywood's idealized sports mother.

Like many looking to take their first step through the door of the acting world, Heller got rolling on the stages of musical and summer stock back in her New York homeland. Also like many newcomers to the profession, she grabbed hold of a special springboard to see things more clearly and follow them more deeply, day by day and production by production of *Godspell* just off of Broadway, then decided that *Grease* was the one that she wanted. They wouldn't be the last times she'd make music on stage.

"I got into musicals, and that combined with acting," she remembers. "That's when the bug got to me. It got to me, rather than me having a dying passion for it."

Not long after, Heller learned of a new show that a lady named Joan Rivers had helped put together. It took a year between knocking out the pilot and the actual start of the show, but 1978's *Husbands, Wives, & Lovers*, one of the first hour-long sitcoms, took Heller all the way to Los Angeles and kept her there for a very long time.

But she didn't have to wait a great while for her big-screen debut, ironically in the same type of flick that became her career landmark. In the waning days of playing the title role of *Welcome Back, Kotter* (1975), Gabe Kaplan was taking his own first steps into movies. In true Hollywood fashion, *Fast Break* (1979) was the tale of basketball nut David Greene, whose coaching career didn't even reach high school. But out of nowhere, he gets a shot to lead a backwater college team with a last gasp at stardom.

As they're so often forced to in real life and otherwise, his wife was made to follow and suffer as her husband searched for fame and glory. Heller would be Jan, that very wife.

"I thought this was my Hollywood break!" Heller says. "I'd been going on every audition I could get, and if I got a role, it was attractive to me. This was a nice role for someone in their first movie shot."

The same year, *Soap* was gaining a foothold in the always-uncertain world of prime-time soap operas. Near the end of 1979, the producers decided to introduce a new gal named Alice. Groundbreaking for the time like a quake ranked 10 on the Richter Scale, the lady was... a *lesbian*!

OK, maybe it wouldn't be the first time homosexuality had been in the public eye on the small screen – not even the first time on that show, as we'll discuss in a moment – but Alice would factor more into her show's happenings than many lady-loving-ladies had before.

"I had just had a very expensive perm in my hair," Heller recalls. "It was long, very full. When I got to the job, they were very worried that Alice was too wild looking; they couldn't have a lesbian character with something so fashionable and forward. There went my $100 perm. They wanted to make her look very straight." Whatever the hell that meant.

Even in rehearsal, Alice couldn't act on her sexual urges, the crew not even allowing Heller and her girlfriend to kiss while practicing. Ironically, she'd end up falling for closet case Jodie (his name spelling gives something away there, doesn't it?), played by a fellow named Billy Crystal, before the show became a victim of the religious crackdowns of the "smut" in the entertainment world at the time.

"The rest of the country was not ready for that," Heller says. "The networks were scared. It didn't even occur to me that it was something out of the ordinary. That's why the show ended. I'm laughing at it now, but it was too bad."

TV roles have peppered her resume since, but arguably none as much as a relatively short showup on AMC in 2010. For the first four years of *Mad Men*, Bert Cooper had occasionally chatted about his secretary Ida Blankenship at the ad agency, but she'd never actually been seen. Then Cooper's coworker Don Draper drove his own secretary away with a one-night stand, and Blankenship came in to lead *his* office. Heller was Blankenship.

"She was classically the comic relief," Heller says. "They needed that character. She was sort of poignant in that way. They gave her great lines. It wasn't hard to just deliver the lines and hit your marks."

Unlike many who'd worked with and under (tsk, tsk!) Don, Blankenship treated him like the normal, flawed folk he was, letting him know what he'd done right and when he'd screwed up.

"They wanted a really, *really* strong New York accent," Heller says of her prep work for Blankenship. "I learned it from my grandparents, my parents, the whole *meshuga*, as we say."

Through six episodes, Blankenship waxed Don into line, then took time off for cataract surgery.

"You had no idea what was going to happen next," Heller says. "You can't build on anything or any backstory, so it was totally being in the moment of doing this character and having her in this moment. It was moment to moment, like life."

Tragically, her and Blankenship's time on *Men* would slam to a halt, the lady suddenly dying of a heart attack at her desk.

"They had some stuntmen to teach me to do it," Heller says. "Falling forward, slumping, it hurts your arms and your head. They padded me up and put this foam sponge thing on the desk that I aimed for. It looked great." Blankenship brought her an Emmy nomination for Outstanding Guest Actress in a Drama Series; Loretta Devine would take the award for showing up on *Grey's Anatomy*.

Many thought that this might be it for one of the icons of American entertainment. Many figured that Barbra Streisand might just call it all quits after proving just how *Timeless* she was in the 2000 concert tour that gave audiences around the world at least one more look at her talent.

As it turned out, they were all wrong, although many certainly didn't mind that. Still, as Streisand's story flashed back to her own musical beginnings, Heller played the mother that watched her daughter take the first steps toward entertainment.

At long last, let's go to the role with whom Heller (along with her co-stars Ralph Macchio and Pat Morita) will forever be associated. Not far from *Fast Break*, she got another shot at sports cinema, this time in more of a dramatic sense. Nearly a decade after inspiring the nation behind the cameras of 1975's *Rocky* (Internet rumors will falsely tell you that Heller had a cameo in that), John Avildsen was putting more of a family twist on the sports world.

"I will never forget reading the script," she says. "I read it, closed it, and said it was a gem."

With little more than a teenage son and a few possessions, Lucille LaRusso picked it all up and moved to a new part of America, far from her former home and the passing of her husband.

"I loved the fact that it was a single mother, something that was not present often at the time," Heller says of the flick. "Now, it's a prevalent kind of character, but then, it was kind of an iconic role. You didn't see a lot of single mothers get in the car and go cross country with their children. I loved that she was courageous, a survivor making a good life for her son."

Stuck in a dead-end job and a dingy apartment, Lucille tries to piece something together for her boy, himself getting a seriously tough time from neighborhood bullies. Until, of course, the complex maintenance man shows him the glory of the martial arts.

"I prepared the way I prepare for everything," Heller says. "I thought about the character and how somebody in that situation would be challenged. What were the obstacles, and how would I overcome them? How I could make a better life for me and my child? I got into the life, the being of the character and her circumstances, because she had nothing but a car and some boxes, and she was trying to make a new life for herself. I didn't have a role model, I didn't know anybody, so I had to pull it out of my own self and my own heart."

As Daniel and Mr. Myagi begin their secret adventure together, Lucille stands back, just hoping that her son will find himself and his own success in this new activity. With nothing but a few people believing in him, Daniel makes it all the way to the local karate tourney finals, finally blasting down his arch enemy as Lucille leads the cheers for one of the film world's top underdogs.

"It had a huge heart, and it still holds up," Heller says. "It's about survival, being heroic and following your dreams. There's so many elements of being a success in the face of a lot of obstacles, and yet it's very sweet and kind and has a lot to it, and I think it really touches everyone on some level. Whether you're a single parent, whether you're married, whether you're a kid who has to endure all the teasing and the crap in high school, it's about a little guy who makes it and triumphs. It's about being a winner in the face of so many obstacles."

Pregnancy kept Heller from reprising Lucille in the sequel two years later as Daniel and Miyagi went to Japan, but she came back for part three in 1989 to cheer on Daniel as he battled a new round of local opponents.

Morita, who'd scored a Supporting Actor Oscar nomination for the first film, became Miyagi one last time to train Hilary Swank as *The Next Karate Kid* in 1994, and Jackie Chan took over the role with Jaden Smith as his new student in the original's 2010 remake.

Still, even decades after Lucille came about, few film sports moms can get anywhere near Heller's mark for the sort of role.

"I love being a character actress," she says. "I am a character. I never played the leading lady, and I always loved being the character actress. Just for the opportunity to perform, to entertain, to make people laugh, to sing, it's been very good."

Lindsay Hollister

For male actors, being on the hefty side isn't usually a big problem. John Goodman became one of the most famous husbands in TV history during his run as lovable Dan Connor on *Roseanne* (1988). Kevin James was one of television's top stars on *King of Queens* (1998), and continued his roll on the big screen with *Hitch* (2005) and *Paul Blart: Mall Cop* (2009). Kevin Smith's name — and girth — became iconic in the independent comedy film scene throughout the late 1990s, both as a director and street philosophy-firing Silent Bob. John Candy, who hovered above the 300-pound mark throughout his career, was one of Hollywood's top men of comedy throughout the 70s and 80s, though his weight undoubtedly played a role in his tragic, far premature death.

In fact, getting fat (if only for a film) can elevate some fellows to stardom. Vincent D'Onofrio's poundage jump to play the tortured Pvt. Pyle in *Full Metal Jacket* (1987) launched a career as one of the acting world's top character performers, and Robert De Niro won an Oscar by grotesquely transforming himself into an obese, troubled Jake LaMotta for *Raging Bull* (1980).

But the same doesn't really hold true for ladies with a few extra pounds. All too often, these women are used as sight gags, the social outcasts that everyone mocks, and other such mishmash.

Lindsay Hollister hit the dance floor hard with Steve Carell in 2008's film version of *Get Smart*.

It's a road that Lindsay Hollister has been forced down more than once in her life, and long before she stepped in front of a camera. Like too many other hefty women of this age (and, for that matter, about any era), she's been a victim of the plus-sized prejudice.

The downward looks? The behind-the-back snide comments? She's been there, and heard that.

Ironically enough, however, it was those very experiences that helped Hollister build a common ground with her first role.

As has happened about every time he puts out a new show, audiences flocked to David Kelley's TV high school drama *Boston Public* after its 1999 premiere, and a young woman, a new Los Angeles addition looking to get her foot in the door of the acting world, was no exception.

"Of course I was thrilled to go in for a guest star role on a major network as it was one of my biggest auditions to date," says Hollister. "I didn't think in a million years I would get it, though, so when my agent called me as I was driving back from the producers' session, I almost had to pull over to the side of the road."

On the show's tenth episode (easily titled "Chapter 10," as *Boston Public* really went the extra mile to help its fans keep track of the small-screen happenings), rumors ran through Winslow High about the mysterious beatings of three male students. Eventually, suspicion went all the way back to the most unlikely (or likely, if hindsight really does have perfect vision) of suspects: Christine Banks, who'd decided that she wasn't going to get called "The Blob" one more goddamned time.

"Christine was a dream character to play," Hollister recalls. "A girl who was mocked by her fellow students, but fought back. That had been me in high school. I think kids who get made fun of on a daily basis either become introverts or sassy mouths. I had been the latter. I knew her and understood the frustration she had. She just wanted to be a normal kid, but her size would never allow that."

Deciding to turn her aggression into a positive, the faculty shoved Christine straight onto the wrestling team, making her into a local sensation. But just as she wins the big match, tragedy strikes the young woman.

Before her time on the show was set to expire, Hollister sat down with Kelley for the first time. Faced between graduating Christine and killing her (what a pair of extremes!), the two decided on tragedy, and the heartfelt sentiment that it often brings on TV. Just after her triumph, Christine is suddenly struck down by a heart attack.

"I was sad," Hollister says, "but as an actor, I would rather have gone out the dramatic way. More people remembered my character because of that final episode. The funeral scene had flashbacks of my character's journey. My friends and family were a mess! Many said they felt like they were watching my funeral, it was so sad."

The next year, she helped launch another of TV's top shows, scaring the righteous hell out of a couple of plastic surgeons on the third episode of *Nip/Tuck* (2003). Playing the title character in "Nannette Babcock," Hollister was a woman pushed over the edge when the surgeons wouldn't do a liposuction on her.

"When reading a character on the page, I start to get a feel for how it feels inside that person's skin," she explains. "With Nanette Babcock, I just felt a heaviness on my chest. That feeling you have when you're really depressed? I knew how it felt, to feel worthless because you don't look like an image in a magazine." One of the doctors tries to set her up with a shrink, but it's too late for Nanette, who ends up ending it all with a gun.

"I purposely did not practice or prepare for her suicide," Hollister says. "I sat on the floor after they brought me onto set and waited as they did final touches around me. There was a ton of pressure to get it in one take because of the blood effect. I thought about all the women who have beat themselves up over image. Over weight. Over beauty. By the time the camera was at the point where I was supposed to put the gun in my mouth, I was there with Nanette. I was dead on the inside from all of the pain."

Once again, she played the tortured target of bullies on a 2004 episode of *Law and Order: SVU*, then got the tables turned on her the next year on *Scrubs*, playing a wiseass gastric-bypass patient challenged to lose the weight herself. Self-mockery was the key to becoming Xena (no, not the warrior princess!), the nerdy cashier who throws herself at Jason Lee on *My Name is Earl* in 2006.

"I loved that character from the moment I got the audition," she says of Xena. "I think the roles actors end up getting are the ones that they just *know* from the start. The ones that you sit inside of, instead of on top of; basically, *being* the character, not playing a stereotype of one. Regardless of the screen time, I try to live inside of that character and play them with everything I have. I think good character actors through the years have stolen entire shows by doing that. The one key to acting for film and TV is the same: think it and the camera will pick up on it."

Hollister stepped away from comedy for the next few years, attempting to steal shows from the stars of *The Shield* (2007), *Cold Case* (2005), *Desperate Housewives* (2006), *CSI: New York* (2008). Then her biggest big-screen role came, as she and Steve Carell put on a routine that rivaled *anything* on *Dancing With the Stars* in the 2008 box-office smash *Get Smart*.

"The audition came up to be in a Steve Carell movie and I was geeked!" Hollister exclaims. "I loved him and it was a huge studio movie. I would have stood in the corner and scooped ice cream if they had wanted me to."

After a quick, action-less audition, she and about 10 other girls headed to a four-hour dance workshop to get the routine down.

"That was pressure," she says. "I'm not a great dancer! Somehow I pulled through and did it twice by myself with the dance instructor on tape for the producers. I still didn't think I would get it."

A week later, she got a call to come in for one more tryout. Expecting to be up against her competitors once again, Hollister got ready for action.

Then she arrived, and director Peter Segal was the only one there. He asked if her schedule was open that summer.

"Of course I was free!" says Hollister, who'd spend a good part of the next June hanging from wires during the scene, including a part where Carell casually lifts her into the air.

"It was an amazing experience," she says of the film. "If I could do one film like that every year, I'd be a happy camper!"

Will she get her wish? It's tough to say, and not just because of the unpredictable nature of the film world itself.

"I am typecast because of my size — that's just a fact," she says. "Do I wish there were more roles available to me? Of course. It's extremely limiting out there because character actors get half the chances leading actors do anyway, let alone if you are overweight. This industry simply doesn't embrace a fat woman. It's difficult to become a name as a big girl. Hey, I should know, because I'm still trying!"

But while her characters don't often follow suit, her career also signifies a victory. It's a message of inspiration.

Her career is a triumph. Not so much over typecasting, which isn't necessarily a negative thing, as we've seen throughout this book. But it's helped to lower the superficial dangers that Hollywood, like much of society itself, practices all too often.

Before she went into the performing profession, when people looked at Lindsay Hollister, they saw a large girl.

Once she made her mark in the game, they glanced over and saw a large actress.

Because of people like her, one day, people may take the time to look her and many others over, and take away the adjective in that phrase.

Mark Holton

It might not appear too difficult to play an evil character in film; after all, how hard can it be to pretend to be a jerk and get everyone angry at us?

But it's actually tough to portray an evil character in film; there's a fine, fine line between someone who's evil for no purpose other than to give the flick an villain (which almost always results in a subpar film and/or performance), and someone whose evil is based in some sort of reason, no matter how disjointed or irrational the reason may be.

Mark Holton, however, went a step further: to undertake one of the darkest personas in American history, he had to step into the gray area between horrifying fiction and far-too-real-realism.

Quite a switch for someone known for about two decades for hanging out in the background of family flicks.

One of Holton's first major roles came as Scott Howard's (Michael J. Fox) caging teammate Chubbs in the 1985 film *Teen Wolf*.

"There was nothing about the script or role that appealed to me," admits the actor. "I was just starting out and needed credits." Still, he managed to turn Chubbs into a likeable shlub, a guy who uses a jerk façade to hide his lack of self-confidence, an all-too-common sight among high schoolers.

"The last thing I wanted was a formula Hollywood delivery system for fat jokes," Holton recalls. "I decided Chubbs was a football player, just filling a gap in the basketball team and wasn't too enthused about it. I tried to give him a bit of an edge and attitude."

Indeed, Chubbs seems a bit underwhelmed with the on-court happenings in the film's opening minutes, particularly since his squad loses its first game 71-12. However, after a secret family curse turns Scott into a slam-dunking werewolf and local hero, the team barrels toward the top of the standings.

Even so, Chubbs still seems like a spectator who happened to stumble out of the bleachers and land in a uniform; he never really seems to be giving it his all, even snacking on an apple at mid-court during one contest.

For the final game, against the same squad that whomped them just after the first credits, Scott decides that if he can't do it without supercharged animal assistance, he and his squad shouldn't be champions at all.

That's when we truly find out just how important Chubbs' role is.

Remember Holton's comment about not wanting the cheap obesity joke used at his expense?

Despite his nickname, his physical stature never really becomes a script issue — until the end, when one short smartass comment turns his character all the way around. Trapped near the top of the key, Chubbs, always a reluctant shooter, searches for an open man. But he's trapped in front of a taunting defender and a desperate crowd, nearly pleading with him to put one up.

Nearly two decades after becoming comedic villainy in *Pee Wee's Big Adventure* (1985), Mark Holton went to the realistic side as John Wayne Gacy in 2003.

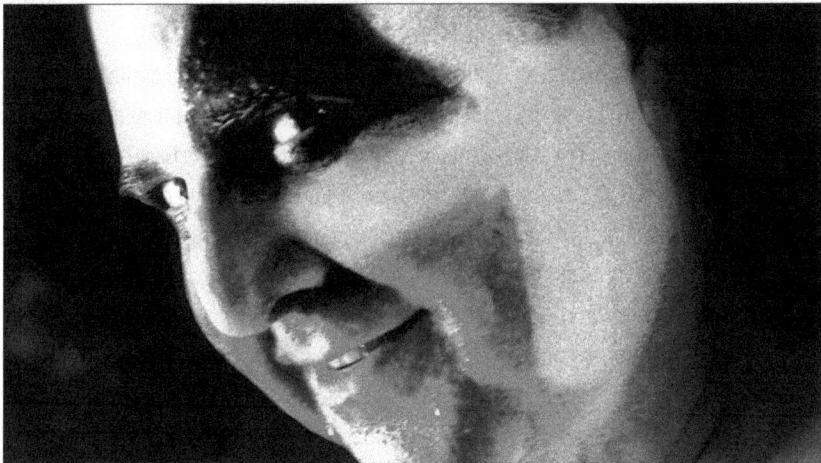

"Shoot it, *fat boy*!" blares a villainous opponent. Chubbs' visage goes from stoic to building fury in about six milliseconds, and he swishes a jumper.

A hilarious look of surprise rolls across Chubbs's face as the crowd cheers, and it's at that moment that he truly becomes a team player – not just on the court, but as a member of the school. The team rushes back – with Scott, all 5'5" of him, swooping and driving past several foot-higher defenders throughout – and takes home the championship. As an added bonus, he and Chubbs get carried off the court in the final moments.

Scott didn't do it alone, and Chubbs wasn't his only helper. But it's important to show that, despite Scott being the hero of the game and the film, basketball is still truly a team sport.

Note: Holton was one of the few original cast members to return for the less-successful 1987 sequel Teen Wolf Too *(Jason Bateman replaced Fox), which revolved around a college boxing squad.*

Aside from *Teen Wolf*, Holton's most visual role of the 1980s came the same year when he played Pee-Wee Herman's nemesis neighbor Francis in the Tim Burton madcap flick *Pee-Wee's Big Adventure* (1985).

"Francis is the only other child played by an adult," says Holton, "and I was free to be as broad as Paul Ruebens was with Pee Wee. I wanted the role because it was a well-written second male lead and would give me a chance to paint with a broad brush."

After appearing on screen with the classic, "I-know-you-are-but-what-am-I?" exchange with Ruebens, Holton takes a hilarious solo turn as a makeshift sea monster in his huge bathtub, only to get ambushed by Ruebens, who's sending his man-child Herman on a furious, frantic search for his stolen bicycle (in the end, Francis gets his, blasted off Herman's launching bicycle seat like a human rocket).

For the next few years, Holton showed up for a scene or two (or maybe even five or six) in flicks like *A League of Their Own* (1992) and the Michael Keaton heartwrencher *My Life* (1993), or on the small screen in *Seinfeld* (1994) and *Deep Space Nine* (1996).

Then in 2003, for one of his first top billings, Holton went to the other end of the acting spectrum, light-years away from some of his early work. He decided to become one whose name will live forever in the annals of infamy. He took the title role in *Gacy*, the story of John Wayne Gacy, the respected community leader, birthday clown, construction business owner, husband, father of two... sexual predator and serial killer, who solicited thousands of innocent young men and murdered (at least) 33 of them. Holton had to channel Gacy's mysterious sexual allure, his horrifically violent nature, and even a bit of remorse, which Gacy shows near the end of the biopic.

"You use whatever information is available to you when playing a real person with a known history," the actor says of his preparation habits. Researching his character, Holton headed to a Hollywood library and found a new publication on the man who buried dozens of victims in the crawlspace of his home, and dumped other bodies in a nearby river.

"The book hadn't been on the shelf long and had only been checked out by a few readers," Holton says. "Inside was a hand drawing in pencil of a naked Gacy with a smaller boyish figure. In black ink someone had added a rope around the boy's neck. In another color of ink was added the word DREAMS above the drawing by another reader."

As if the bare facts of Gacy's case weren't enough to bring his obscene nature to the forefront, his drawings, in hindsight, opened up a whole new dark door, as his artwork portrayed several violent, disturbing acts (it can be seen in the film, and was a common sight on television in the days leading up to his 1994 execution). In his portrayal, Holton balanced Gacy's effective business style with his closed-doors torturous, predatory nature, making him a Norman Bates-esque mama's boy with a barren wife and a lust for violence.

Holton found himself trapped inside a world of fear and anger – not only because of the mindset he adapted to play Gacy, he says, but because of the atmosphere on the set; he recalls a film official dropping lit matches from a ladder to keep everyone off balance during filming.

"I left the set every day wishing I could scrub my brain out with a toilet brush," he admits.

Ernie Hudson

Today, it might not seem so long ago. To the man who'd become a household name and face around the globe in acting, or the fans that can't wait to remind him of *this* role, or *that* one. With hundreds of entries up and down his resume (even if we don't count his decades on the stages), there's far too many to pick from.

Maybe that's why it's so easy to remember when performing, for a good paycheck, was just a hope. A possibility. A chance that so many might have, and so few see reach reality, for reasons within and without.

"When I came into acting, it was a dream I had," he remembers. "I didn't know any actors. I believed, I was taught that when there's a dream, something that stays with you, even if it seems far away or something that you've never seen anyone do, if it stays on your heart, then it's coming from the universe. It's coming from a source. It's coming from that greater place, and it's for you, but you have to somehow believe in it. I believe that it comes from a source."

Wherever it came from for Ernie Hudson, it worked. And it's still working hard, decades after his career began in southern Michigan. Odds are well against anyone hoping to make a living in acting, but Hudson had some strikes there as well; his mother died when he was a few months old, and he never knew his father. As the civil rights movement stretched, far too slowly for the tastes of many, across America in the 1960s, crime was rampant too. Riots raged across his Benton Harbor hometown throughout the 60s, and many who lived long enough to reach adulthood would spend it looking out from behind bars.

"Growing up in the projects, not in prison or dead, like so many of my friends," he remembers, "it's who I believe I am and who I know I am. In spirit, we are all connected; all one. The good news is, nobody's better than you. The bad news is, you're not better than anybody else."

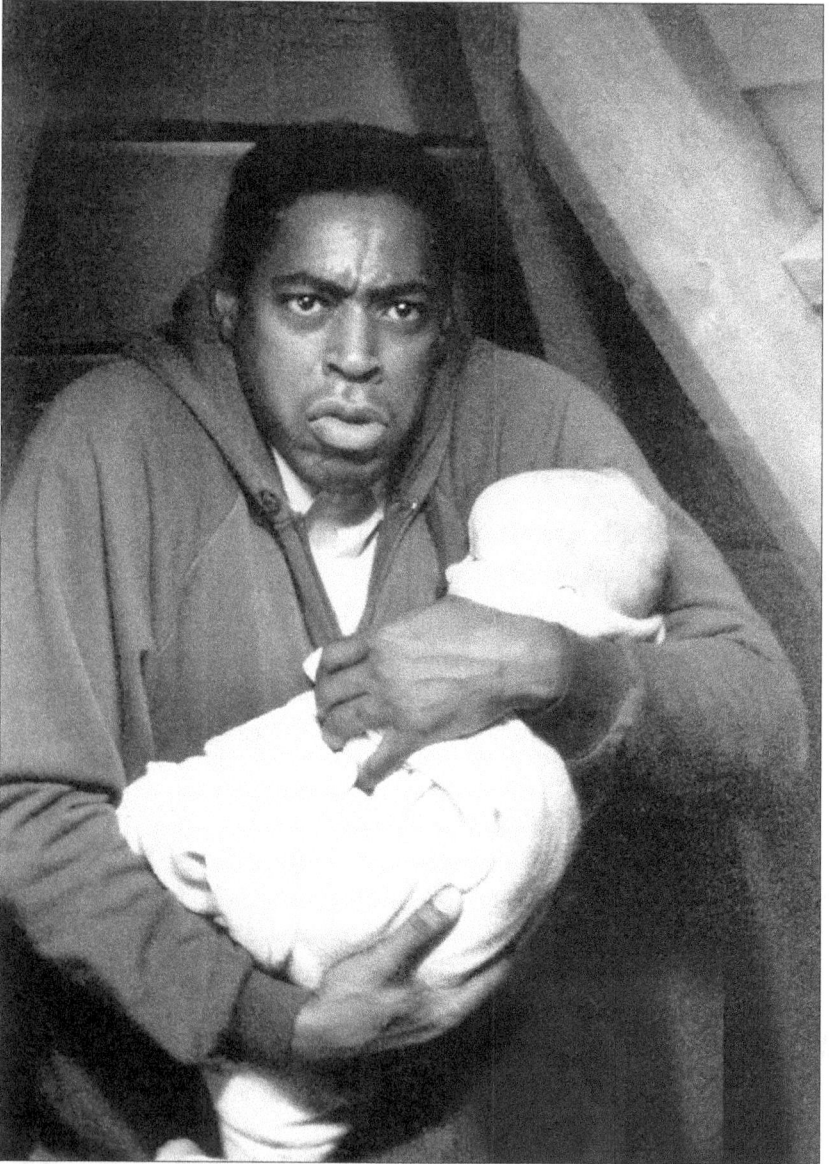

Just as he has for much of his four decades on screens large and small, Ernie Hudson traveled the heroic route in 1992's *The Hand That Rocks the Cradle*.

Yes, yes — many of our memories of Hudson go quickly to his role as Winston Zeddemore in 1984's *Ghostbusters*, as well as its sequel five years later (and more recently, his brief cameo in the all-lady *Ghostbusters* reboot in the summer of 2016).

But while that's the first place most minds go with him, hopefully they don't stay there, as there's so much more to chat about, as is often the case for those in the character acting genre.

When he first got started, Hudson remembers, "My kids had to call me by my character's name. I would study a lot. If a character lived an experience that I didn't know anything about, I would try to go right along with the policeman or be in that world, to get a sense of it. It's nice to be able to play me, but if it's a really interesting role, the work you do makes it worth it. As an actor, acting is believing. You want to create the world and make it believable that you would be someone to fit into that world."

He's been in many, and some were far from welcoming, not just in the script. *The Crow* (1994) will never be forgotten, and we all wish it was only because of the film's greatness. Hudson was Albrecht, a warm-hearted cop trying to help a rough city in the midst of a crime wave, especially some locals who lost a good friend the year before.

The friend was Eric Draven, murdered along with his wife by a group of gang members. Draven was Brandon Lee. Everyone knows where this profile is going.

One March 1993 night, Hudson and Lee, who'd worked together a few years before on the show *Broken Badges*, sat down for dinner.

"I was complaining," Hudson recalls. "I hadn't been able to break through. There were guys that seemed like they were doing things, and I wasn't invited. Brandon was very encouraging. He told me he had signed a three-picture deal, was getting married soon, buying a house… to hang in there, because it was going to be OK."

The next day, Lee was dead.

"None of us ever know what's coming next," Hudson says sadly. "Whatever your situation is, focus on the good stuff, because who knows what tomorrow's going to bring?"

Two years before, he'd shown something different, though just as admirable as Albrecht. His Solomon wouldn't get much screen time in *The Hand That Rocks the Cradle*, but he'd make a hell of a difference.

As is often the case with the mentally handicapped, people like Solomon tend to always do right, as well as they can. It's the sort of thing that makes you hopeful that some people are just born right. As the Bartel family welcomes their second addition, a baby boy, Solomon becomes their new friend, an impromptu handyman and babysitter.

But they're slowly being victimized by Peyton Flanders (Rebecca De Mornay, who I think should have been Oscar nominated here), who just *happened* to volunteer as the family nanny. They don't know — although we do — that Peyton's just lost her husband and newborn, and that she's going to get her form of revenge on them.

By any means necessary. Peyton's lies get Solomon kicked out. But just as she gains the upper hand on the family, he shows back up to save everyone.

"That role was very special to me," Hudson remembers. "I did a lot of research and went to homes, spending time with mentally disabled patients to be able to portray the character in a way that wasn't a caricature."

And while playing the hero would become a hallmark trademark of Hudson's career, his turn in *The Substitute* (1996) put a spin on his work that few expected, even partway through the flick. The principal of a school overrun with rebels with a deadly cause, his Claude Rolle's found to be their secret partner, dealing in loads of cocaine and cash to back it up.

"I was a bad guy, but you didn't really know that," Hudson remembers. "It's nice to play a character that you haven't played before. It was fun, and it kind of freaked some *Ghostbusters* fans out." For six years on HBO, he'd be just a bit more moral as Leo Glynn, the warden of the title location of *Oz* (1997).

While he (fortunately!) had no personal experience to act out incarceration, Hudson had seen some a decade before, portraying a San Quentin inmate alongside Nick Nolte in *Weeds* (1987).

"We shot at a lot of prisons," he remembers of *Weeds*. "I met so many young people who had done stupid stuff, and were in there for a long time. It was just heartbreaking. When *Oz* came along, it was important to do. When I see actors do what they do well, it's great." The network's first original hour-long drama, *Oz* laid the groundwork for future cultural icons like *The Wire*, *Six Feet Under*, *Game of Thrones*, and *The Sopranos*.

"If (a role) is funny, I can be funny," Hudson remarks. "If it's serious, I'll cry for you. Your kids make you more than what you are. A lot of guys sort of avoid that responsibility, but it's the best thing that can happen to you, because you step up." He has four sons (Ernie Hudson Jr. played inmate Hamid Khan on *Oz*), and some grandchildren that love to watch *Ghostbusters*.

"There are so many things outside of us that are warning us to be afraid of each other and protect ourselves," Hudson explains, "but if you can just let go of that fear a little bit, this is a great place to be and a great time to be here. When I became an actor, I stepped out on that faith, and I believed that that source would direct me, guide me to where I needed to go, and it didn't fail me. All of us are tapped into this creative force."

Chapelle Jaffe

"Acting means finding a way inside of another person, or another persona," explains Chapelle Jaffe, "understanding the world from that person's perspective; finding out what makes that individual unique and what motivates that person to commit to her actions. It means finding something about the character that makes them worth knowing and remembering, whether you personally admire and respect that character or even if you do not, you must find the human elements — the contradictory aspects of a person — the fragile heart of a good woman making damaging choices, for example."

Jaffe's fellow Canadian countrymen (and women) got their first strong look at her in a Genie-winning (equivalent to an Oscar) performance in Allan King's 1978 screen-adapted stage drama *One Night Stand*, playing Daisy, who allows a young man to charm himself into her apartment. But the things that seem too good to be true tragically are, and it turns out that he's a killer, forcing her into a fight for her life.

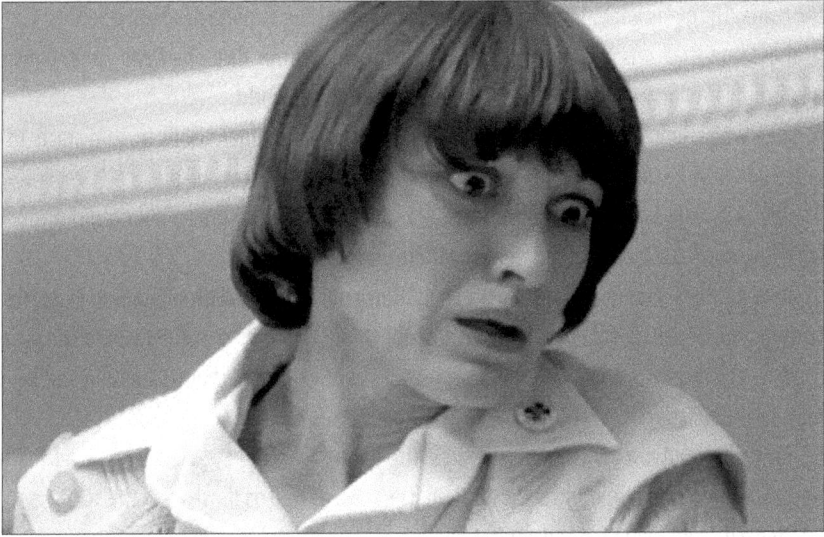

After her own terrifying presence was seen in *The Dead Zone* (1983), Chapelle Jaffe played a fortune-telling soothsayer in 2004's *The Butterfly Effect.*

In 1983, she got a shot to play a small but important part in a flick directed by another of Canada's biggest film names (Jaffe is from Toronto) — and one of the planet's biggest in literature.

Johnny Smith is a schoolteacher with a loving family and a lovely lady just waiting to be his wife, and everything seems fine. Driving home one night, he's in a horrible accident. Years later, he wakes up from the coma. His girl is gone, his career is kaput. But something strange has happened.

In the scene that sets the tone for David Cronenberg's horror flick *The Dead Zone*, Christopher Walken's Smith is laying in a hospital bed, far away from the real world.

A nurse who's seen this sort of thing before (at least, at the time) strolls in, and starts to clean Smith up. Suddenly, he grabs her arm – and his new power goes on scary display.

Staring at a wall, Smith sees another place, at the same time. There's a young girl trapped in a burning room, and it's the daughter of the lady there with him.

"Your daughter's screaming!" he blurts to her. "Hurry up! There's still time!" At first, he seems to be just sputtering gibberish. But then he starts to describe things that only an insider would know, and the nurse realizes she must act upon what he is saying, and because of this chance meeting and her belief in Johnny, her child is saved.

Up until she tried out for the nurse's part, Jaffe hadn't read the Stephen King novel the film is based on. Afterward, she flipped straight through its pages, as well as those from the script.

"With each script, you read the entire script very carefully, and see where your character fits into the story as a whole," Jaffe explains, "and in terms of the nurse, it was clearly necessary to elicit a specific response of belief in Johnny's unearthly power; to believe that he is recognizing something no one else can see. Within the story, this is the first instance of his power; he knows what is going to happen."

In another of her smaller roles, the youth in question wouldn't be so lucky.

In 2004's *The Butterfly Effect*, she played Madame Helga, a fortune teller who sees a dark future for young Evan Treborn (played, at various ages in the film, by Logan Lerman, John Amedori, and, for the most part, a fellow named Ashton Kutcher).

"That was really interesting," she recalls. "It intrigued me because it was such an odd little role, and the idea of the film, in terms of its central idea, was quite fascinating, an examination of cause and effect; the idea that you can look at the past and change the past, but the result is not necessarily for the better."

As Evan and his mom Andrea arrive to have their fortunes informed, Helga herself can't believe what she sees: the youth is wrong for the world. He's not a bad person himself, but the world would somehow be better off without him.

It's unimaginable to even think this, let alone say it to someone, but Helga manages to do so. She looks for all the world like the villain of the piece, but as it turns out, she's right.

"It's quite a turning point for him and for his mother, because Madame Helga says, in essence, that he was never meant to have been born, because he's not right for this world," Jaffe says. "She's important because of what she says to him: the scene demanded an impression with a mysterious overall effect on the character being addressed."

Jaffe would have a much darker effect on both her co-stars and audience in one of her biggest roles – but this one requires a bit of background.

Around the mid-1860s, Indian Residential Schools began to open up around Canada, designed to teach Native Canadians of the area to act more "white." Often sprinted thousands of miles from their homes and families, roughly 150,000 children were taught to speak English, learned other non-Native Canadian cultures: basically, everything they had ever known was wrong, and that white, Christian culture was simply the way to be, that Indian life would never lead them to success.

But even beyond that, the children were subjected to all sorts of horrors. Sexual and physical abuse was rampant at the schools – many children died of the abuse they suffered (many more committed suicide), and girls who became pregnant as a result of the abuse were forced to have abortions. This went on for almost a century, as the final schools in Canada stayed open until the 1990s.

This is a story that, like much of the plight of Native Americans, needs to get quite a bit more publicity in America, and maybe this book and its readers can help spread this word a bit more. In 1989, the TV flick *Where the Spirit Lives* told the story of young Ashtecome (Michelle St. John), a young Native Canadian abducted off to a school where, in remembrance of the Alex Haley novel and film *Roots*, has her name changed to Amelia. Forced through assault and abuse for the entire time, she, in the spirit that lives somewhere inside us all, somehow manages to escape with her mind, her life, and her identity intact.

At the time the film came out, the reality of the residential school horrors was only starting to stretch across Canada, Jaffe remembers.

"It was just being made known to the general public how extensive the damage of the residential schools was," she says. "That horrendous information had burst upon the scene, and so began the rush to have something done for the people who had been so grievously injured."

When the film first came about, Jaffe was cast for the role of Miss Appleby, a teacher who falls in love with one of the young students, but takes full control of her, abusing the student in all senses of the word.

"In terms of going about playing a character with whom you have a violent disagreement," she explains, "you must come to understand the world from the perspective of that character, and suspend your own personal judgment on that character. To see the inside of her, the preparation was understanding that history, and separating myself and my own feelings from that particular woman. She was a very young woman, a teacher working at a residential school who fell in love with this young girl and took the young girl as her lover. That is wrong, but I had to put myself aside, to understand her and her motivations, and realize that in her actions, she was very kind to that girl, and very watchful to the well-being of that young girl, but at the same time, she took advantage of her."

Playing a character that the audience fears is one thing; playing someone they out and out despise is another story. That's the situation that Jaffe found herself in when she got ready to be Miss Appleby.

"In terms of being a person who looks at the film, and the artistic process in which I'm going to be involved, and playing the character," she says, "I had to make a separation between the character and myself. If I stand back from that, and look at (Appleby), I am completely opposed to her, and what she did. And yet in order to be able to play that character, just as with any character, you have to understand the way they look at the world and their place in it, from inside that character. And within that film, the wrongs that were committed had to be indicated."

For her, the role wasn't just about her prowess as an actress; it was being part of an ensemble that helped illustrate to the audience a terrible but true story that had been visited upon thousands of families across their land for over a century beforehand. *Where the Spirit Lives* was about telling thousands, even millions, a story that many had tried to hide but still needed to be told.

"This was a terrible tragedy in the history of our nation," Jaffe says. "It was very important to be a part of this film, so that the general public could see this story and understand how completely wrong this was and how necessary it was to make reparation to all these people and try to make the lives of all the people affected by this tragedy better, even so many years later."

Over the next few years after the film's release, the Canadian government started working to put together a compensation plan for the victims of the program, and in 2007, Canada's federal government announced a compensation package of $1.9 billion for the schools. As of April 2010, about $1.5 billion had been paid out to over 75,000 cases. In April 2009, Pope Benedict XVI apologized to the victims; many of the schools had been run by the Catholic Church.

"I think we need to understand what happened and have an opinion about things that are wrong in the world, and do something about that," Jaffe says. "I was playing a character that people were going to loathe and I knew that, and I am not personally in disagreement with that." All in all, it's part of the job for any character performer, any actor in general – not only to do their best in the role given, but make the role significant. Making a film is a team effort; the whole is more important than each specific individual part.

"The process is one of understanding the script, of understanding the character, of doing the research that is necessary," Jaffe says, "to understand the context of the film, or the television show and the presentation of what the character is trying to do, I must know what the director wants and how the director is looking to present a particular topic. In terms of understanding how the story is being told I must clearly see what choices the writer has already made in telling this particular story. An actor's role is to be at one with all that, and to be in front of that. The role of the actor at all times is to be absolutely true to the character you are playing."

Susan Lynch

The legendarily hypnotic ones of a vampire.

The cold-blooded ones of a killer.

The naturally sad-looking, darkly lovely ones of an immortally beloved sea resident.

While millions of eyes have watched her on the screen for decades, Susan Lynch has seen more than her own share of pairs, sometimes all too close.

"I like the lack of repetition," she explains. "I like the feeling of total concentration of all departments before a take. What I enjoy about filming is the absoluteness of being in the moment. I love the sensuality of creating different people, how they look/speak/behave."

Susan Lynch (right) played one of the final victims of arguably history's most infamous serial killer in 2001's *From Hell*.

One of her first major roles, though, involved putting together something a bit different. *The Secret of Roan Inish* (1994) told the tale of a young girl, looking for semblances of normalcy after the death of her mother, who learns the local Irish folktale of a selkie, a mythical half seal/gorgeous woman who just might be a relative of hers. With mermaids already a common sight on the big screen, Lynch had to get ready to become a different sort of sea lass.

It was a chore she couldn't wait to take on.

"I spent a lot of time with seals," she remembers. "To me, they look like they are constantly teary eyed. It helped with the sadness of the selkie character. (Director John Sayles) told me to slow everything down like I was underwater. That was really interesting."

Later in 1994, the character that gave larger American audiences a look at the Irish lass was part of a group known for their dark sensuality, with a good helping of murder right along with it: she had a small role as one of the title characters in *Interview with the Vampire* (1994).

"It was an experience being on a Hollywood set," recalls Lynch, who snared the role after impressing the crew during a 1993 appearance on the British TV series *Cracker*, "but, acting-wise, it wasn't particularly stretching. I let my costume and vampire fangs do the work. I loved playing poker with the other vampires in the downtime."

Four years later, it was back to Ireland – at least, that's where the film was set – for her first shot at comedy, as she played Maggie in *Waking Ned Devine*, the hilarious 1998 tale of a small Irish countryside, frantically scrambling to even out the winnings of a man who died of shock from a winning lottery ticket. With the winnings of the man (Ned himself) in her hands – she has a son whose father just might have been him – Maggie decides that sharing it amongst the village is just the right thing to do, ending things in a mini-Woodstock on a hill, celebrating the new economical boost atop a huge hill.

"It just was a funny film," she remembers. I wanted to be part of it. The humor was all on the page. I love to do comedy and don't get much of an opportunity, so I love this film because of that."

Up with Johnny Depp, Heather Graham, and the Hughes Brothers in 2001, Lynch became Liz Stride, the witty extroverted impromptu leader of a group of prostitutes (Graham's Mary Kelly was one of her followers), looking to eke out a living on the back streets and alleys of the 18th-century London of *From Hell* (2001). That is, until the amateur surgeon known as Jack the Ripper – in legend, as his real name was never fully revealed, despite the library's worth of books each declaring indisputable proof as to who the Ripper truly was – began terrorizing the jolly streets. Stride becomes one of his victims.

To get ready for her role, Lynch went to London itself, taking part in the Jack the Ripper Walk, in which visitors stroll through city streets, seeing the sections where the Ripper's victims were found – there's many more buildings and other landmarks there now, but the same pavement upon which they fell and pubs in which they drank are still around.

"I also did lots of improvisation with my fellow prostitutes," she says. "Even before 'action' we improvised. I felt very free with the Hughes brothers and the other actresses. It's a good thing to feel that. It makes you braver. Liz Stride was a pretty brave character."

Lynch grabbed a far different side of historical reality in 2007 in *Elizabeth: The Golden Age*. While Cate Blanchett was earning her second Oscar nomination for playing the English queen (she'd nearly won a statuette for 1998's *Elizabeth*), Lynch was Annette, understudying for the Queen's cousin Mary, Queen of Scots, herself put on by two-time Oscar nominee Samantha Morton, an old colleague of Lynch.

"I worked with Sam Morton at the Royal Court years before," Lynch says. "We were so close, like sisters almost. Then for a period of time we lost touch. Through *Elizabeth* . . . we reconnected. I just used our relationship for Annette, our bond."

But it's all part of daily life for a character actress, where the only thing consistent is that nothing's even remotely the same. The sets, the directors, the castmates, and certainly the roles . . . everything's changing faster than cable channels manipulated by a hyperactive remote controller.

But diversity is the long name of the acting game for those in that particular spot in the business. Different is the most common adjective. One day, they're the heroine; the next, the bad guy's sidekick. In one film, they're in the past, the next, the future. At some point, they might (*might*) step into the present. Perhaps more so than any other category in the performing arts, character actresses get to go all-out, everywhere, all the time.

"To me, being different people is key," Lynch explains. "Our industry isn't always enamored by actors morphing into different characters. The character is the key. I don't want to look/sound like ME unless that is undeniably emphasizing the character, and, don't get me wrong, sometimes it does, but not all the time."

Marguerite Moreau

As she skated onto the ice for her role in the first *Mighty Ducks* flick, Marguerite Moreau had quite a bit to think about.

As she came off a television role in *The Wonder Years* the year before, the 1992 Disney youth hockey flick was Moreau's first big-screen venture, and she had a shot – a slap shot, that is! – to prove herself in a new area. Perhaps the Hernet, Calif. native could show the poise and presence needed to convince Hollywood that she was at the start of a long career, one that could make her the next star to shine over the star-spangled land for decades.

Well, she did. But back then, no one could have prophesized how much her areas of concentration would change, though the location wouldn't.

"I don't know how conscious I was of being specifically interested in that part at that age," Moreau remembers of her turn as Connie, "any more than any other part that I got the opportunity to audition for. It was a character that I could know and like." Whereas previous youth sports films had made gender integration the entire focal point of their films – the 1976 Walter Matthau/Tatum O'Neal flick *Bad News Bears*, for just one example – the *Ducks* flicks downplayed it, helping film audiences accept it as a normal part of youth sports competition.

Oh, and by the way, Connie and Marguerite having the same last name? Not a coincidence.

"That was nice," she says. "They let me pick my last name, and I had my real name, which was nice, because you could see my name (on my jersey) and know that it was me. My grandfather appreciated that."

Between skating lessons at the camp that she and other members of the cast attended for a month before filming, Moreau kept her eyes on the screenplay and her mind on Connie's supporting, but important role.

"Getting ready to play Connie at that age meant reading the script a bunch of times and learning our lines," she says. "I didn't really have any formal training at that time. I was just doing my best." She, star coach Emilio Estevez, and the rest of the group did as well; the flick brought in about $50 million in America alone. It set the stage for a sequel two years later – and that's when things went the wrong way for Moreau's concentration. The role of Connie was important to her, but it had quite a bit of competition.

"For part two, I tried not to be distracted by the boys," says Moreau, who doesn't care to name names of who specifically drew her attention. "That's why I went into the second saying, 'Do your job! Stop flirting with the boys!' At that age, we were all at the age when that was distracting." Rather than taking on the local group of opponents, she and her merry band of Ducks battled the world, met all-time great Wayne Gretzky, and brought home a set of Junior Goodwill Games gold medals, slipping past Iceland in the final process.

**Her three-time membership in *The Mighty Ducks* laid Marguerite Moreau's
path to becoming one of the acting world's top stars.**

Still, nothing distracted Moreau from her acting career; after reprising Connie in the second, and then (as of this writing!) the last *Ducks* sequel in 1996, she appeared in *Wag the Dog* (1997), *Mighty Joe Young* (1998), and other big-time films.

"I felt that I had had some success, which gave me a lot of confidence," she says. "It started to teach me about myself and about the world, and I was craving learning about how to communicate with others and putting myself in other people's shoes. I had the tools to know that, and acting gave me that."

Those were just some of the tools that helped her major – and eventually take home a degree – in political science (between school on-stage acting roles, of course!) at Vassar, which her early on-screen earnings paid for, she says.

"I had some really great parents that instilled some really great values in me. I wasn't allowed to go and spend my money. I was always expected to empty the dishwasher. I was a young girl, self-conscious and wanting attention, the wrong reasons to go into the business. I grew myself and learned, and I wasn't given anything too quickly."

Including the Vassar degree, which took years before she could stroll across the stage, mortar-board atop head, and grab the degree, she says.

"I went to college and graduated to make sure that I didn't want to go any other avenues," Moreau explains. "I could tell that when I was running from play rehearsal to class with gum in my hair and hoop-skirts. I do a lot of volunteering in the political world, but I think I've really found a lot in life with (acting)."

Even if that wasn't always her main career path, she continues.

"I come from a very political family who were always talking about current events at the dinner table," says Moreau. "I had a romantic fantasy of being the first female president until I found out what they actually did, and I was like, 'Whoa! That's a hard job, really out of my reach!' It just wasn't for me."

But, fortunately for audiences around the world, acting indeed was – and her modes of preparation have changed since the days of Connie, says Moreau.

"I didn't really have any technique, now, having been in classes and learning as much as I can," she says. "I prepare by reading the scripts and breaking them down, understanding the story (and) what my role is within the story. What's the objective of that character? What drives her in life? I further break it down, understanding her emotional condition and how she changes throughout the story."

To get ready, and stay so, for one of her biggest TV roles, Moreau had to carry her own words for several weeks. Different from her earlier short show-ups on *The O.C.* and *Lost*, both in 2005, she visited Grey Sloan Memorial Hospital to become a special part of *Grey's Anatomy* in 2013 as Dr. Emma Marling. A maternal-fetal surgeon, Emma turned down a full-time shot at Grey Sloan so as not to get re-involved with her long-ago ex Owen Hunt (Kevin McKidd).

"As a performer, we never stop changing," Moreau says of acting teachings. "We never stop performing. We never stop evolving. We never stop growing. Those are the lessons that every budding actor should ascertain.

"Never be afraid to learn, because the classroom is like the gym. It's a place to keep all the acting muscles warm and strong. It's a great place to build confidence and to grow yourself. It's important to stay clear to your job, whether it's television or movie acting. It's a hard thing to feel truly satisfied, because there's always something to be reaching for. You just buckle down, do the work, and tell the story – and you'll have a great life."

Marnette Patterson

Even when you're pretending to be so many other people, sometimes you just have to be yourself. Be your own person.

Not the one that gets caught up in so many of the dark stereotypes of American entertainment culture. Not pay too much attention to what people who have never even sniffed your profession, let alone been in the same area code as you, are saying and writing about you and your colleagues, just waiting, hoping for someone to screw up in the professional or personal sense.

It's about being you, the performer that shows up to do what needs doing, at the top of your game. Not about worrying what those who live to find flaws are telling themselves and each other.

That's not always easy for those who stay in the profession for years, even decades. Some say it might even be harder for those who try the jump from child to grown-up star. We, as the public outsiders, are hardly even surprised anymore when we check out a tabloid, electronic or print, and read about someone who hit it big in acting decades ago, now reduced to sadly staring back at us from a mugshot.

Ignoring that mess doesn't make you ignorant, hardly so. It just means that you, like every other performer, have more important things to worry about – like, you know, the next job!

That's how performers like Marnette Patterson have managed to break right through the negative stereotype of child stars (which, when you consider how many have done so, appears to be the rule rather than the exception anyway). Still, after spending decades in the business before even finishing up her 30s on screens of all sizes and performances of just about any type – this will be all kinds of clear shortly – even Patterson was ready to kick back for the time being.

"I almost stopped acting," Patterson admits. "Two seconds from saying maybe I'll take a break..." Then one of Hollywood's most legendary names and one of 2014's most well-known films came calling. Patterson's role wouldn't be huge, but its meaning would be.

Just as she was about to walk away from acting, Marnette Patterson stormed out of the first moments of 2014's *American Sniper* – and, fortunately for Hollywood, back into the business.

"My family has a history in the entertainment industry," recalls Patterson. "I think it's in my blood. It was a hobby to start with. I absolutely loved it. It was my 'soccer.'" Her aunt Dana Dillaway was herself a child star, playing Rock Hudson and Liz Taylor's daughter in *Giant* (1956); forty years later, Patterson had a small role in a TV biopic of Taylor.

Her first movie role, however, had been on the other side of the acting gamut. Using the whole "demonic kids" angle was a staple throughout much of the *Nightmare on Elm Street* series, and as the characters of 1989's *Dream Child* looked for a way to fight off dream master Freddy Krueger, viewers kept seeing the same group of evilly angelic young girls we'd first met in the first *Elm Street* of 1984. Somehow ignoring the blood and gore surrounding them, the group stoically jumped rope to the simple, yet terrifying reminder to the victims that, "One, two, Freddy's coming for you..."

Patterson was one.

"I was so young but so excited to read for and get my first movie role," she remembers. "They had to cut a large portion of my part because we went really late and, because of the child labor laws, I was forced to stop working after 2 a.m. I was so disappointed at the time. I'm like 'I got this! I don't need to leave!' They still had to send me home."

She certainly didn't want to leave *Camp Nowhere* five years later. Surrounded by colleagues who'd step through to grown-up star right next to her (Joshua Jackson and a debuting Jessica Alba were two), Patterson was Trish, who'd help her friends form their own camp into the best summer experience anyone would have — as we know, kids are *always* smarter and more resourceful than adults in this type of flick!

"I auditioned and just fell in love with the character because she had aspects of myself," Patterson recalls, "and yet was so much more dramatic."

She grew as a person and actress in front of TV audiences over the next decade, playing the daughter of a famous actor for a year on *Movie Stars* (1999) and a telekinetic/pyrokinetic witch in 2006 on *Charmed* (have to mention this — Patterson also voiced resident comic strip brat Lucy Van Pelt on a pair of *Peanuts* TV specials!).

"There were transition years for sure," the actress remembers. "It was actually much harder to transition from comedy and sitcom to drama. Now that I do a lot of drama, it seems like I have to convince and show people I can do comedy. Go figure!" The next role, however, would be far from humor. It would be far from anything else she'd ever tried. In 2000, Patterson stepped into a sort of horror much scarier than the supernatural stuff she'd seen back on Elm Street.

Until 1991, Lancaster, Pa., was best known for being the unofficial home of America's Amish folk. The city residents can only wish that was still the case.

Right around that time, teenager Laurie Show moved to town with her newly single mother. Over the next few months, the high schooler met Michelle Lambert and her boyfriend Butch Yunkin. Butch started flirting with Laurie.

Then he allegedly raped her. Michelle, herself already carrying his child, went haywire. Ludicrously blaming the victim, she ran a campaign of verbal and physical abuse against Laurie and her family. Helped along by Butch and another friend, she cornered Laurie alone at her house just before Christmas of 1991. Bound and stabbed repeatedly, Laurie managed to tell her mom what had happened before she died.

The next summer, all three were convicted in the murder. As of this writing, Lambert, who gave birth to Butch's child, and her friend were still incarcerated; Butch, who only drove the girls to commit the murder, got less time.

In 2000, the case, which brought new anti-stalking laws to fruition in the area, turned to the screen in *The Stalking of Laurie Show*. For one of the biggest roles of her career, Patterson played evil as Lambert, with Jennifer Finnigan as her victim.

Patterson read interviews that Lambert, whose own version of the story has changed several times, gave from her time behind bars.

"It was a fascinating story to me," she recalls. "A sociopath at seventeen? What that girl had in her brain to stab a girl to death was fascinating to figure out. I would have to get in a zone and be so awful and cruel to Jennifer Finnegan, and then after they called 'Cut!' we would both burst into tears and hug each other. It was pretty intense now that I look back."

A decade after the first group of *Starship Troopers* battled crazed arachnids across the galaxy, the war moved to a new planet, one in which the two-legged were hopelessly outnumbered, for the film's first sequel in 2004. When part three, *Marauder*, came about in 2008, the story jumped ahead a decade as Casper Van Dien brought original hero John Rico back to battle. Under a bug attack, war vet Omar Anoke and Captain Lola Beck (Jolene Blalock) abandoned ship and took an escape pod to the distant planet OM-1 (anyone else having *Empire Strikes Back* [1980] flashbacks here?), and Rico's sent to bring them home.

Alongside her colleagues, Anoke's assistant Holly Little looked to her faith to save her, even as the critters killed her boyfriend.

"I loved Holly Little because she was so... sort of fanatical about her faith," says Patterson, who hadn't seen the first two *Trooper* flicks before becoming Little. "She was such a sweet, innocent girl, yet deep down she was probably the strongest of all of the characters."

Filming down in South Africa, she and Blalock were hit hard with illness during rainy, cold nights of filming. But Rico arrives to save and bring them home (Anoke is killed beforehand). He's elevated to general and Holly to chaplain. As we see war protestors using religion for protest and propaganda reasons, some being hanged for their actions, however, it's clear that the war isn't over, though, as of 2017, a fourth chapter hadn't emerged.

After all of that, and many others we don't have time to cover here, Patterson was ready for a deserved breather from her career. Consistency and reliability had long been demonstrated across her resume – she could take some time off and have enough reasons to be given a way back into the game when her sabbatical ended.

"You need to know when you really do need a break," she explains. "It's a tough business, but so rewarding."

In 2014, a fellow named Eastwood embarked on the next stage of the directing career that had won him a pair of Oscars. Over the past few years, America had come to know the name of Chris Kyle, many personifying his name right along with the wars in Iraq and Afghanistan.

Kyle had discussed his accomplishments in his autobiography *American Sniper*, and now Eastwood, armed with a new and much sadder ending than the book, got ready to show the story. Most placed Kyle straight at his killing of more enemies than any other Navy SEAL sniper the nation would ever know. They and others were probably just as aware of his own tragic murder at the hands of a fellow former solider in 2013.

But there was much more to his story – like why Kyle had stepped into service to begin with. Before he'd even considered it, the young Texan was content to ply his trades in the never-stable professions of farming and rodeo riding.

Unfortunately, someone else wasn't happy with those lifestyles. Making a triumphant return home from a rodeo rocking, Bradley Cooper's title character runs right into his girlfriend Sarah...and the fellow she's doing extra overtime with between the sheets.

Patterson was Sarah. *That close* to stepping all the way away from the profession, she'd suddenly hit one of the biggest roles of her career.

"The experience was amazing," she recalls. "It was a lot of improv, and Clint Eastwood said to me 'Just make sure you say the last line.' So I had to give my character a reason for why she cheated on Chris, which wasn't scripted."

She'd worked hard to come up with an explanation, as so many hypocritically have while caught up in such a moment.

"What'd you expect?" started Patterson's created impromptu monologue. "You drag me out here, then run off with your damn brother every weekend! You think you're a cowboy, 'cause you rodeo? You're no cowboy. You're just a lousy ranch hand and a shitty fuckin' lay!"

"I believe girls are not just 'slutty' and people are not just 'mean,'" Patterson explains. "There's catalysts, things that provoke that behavior. That's what I had to find for Sarah, and everything I came up with stayed in the film."

With his career on the rocks and his relationship gone, Kyle had crashed into a life roadblock. Then, even before the Sept. 11 attacks or the new Iraq invasion years later, his countrymen were attacked overseas, sending both he and his brother into a new vocation, one that brought Kyle to the national public eye — whether for the right or wrong reasons depends on who is asked.

Not surprisingly, Cooper and Eastwood both brought home Oscar noms, though the film's only victory would be for sound editing.

"Even though the role was small, it was an unforgettable experience," Patterson recalls. "I was sort of questioning myself, and then had Bradley Cooper say 'You are completely in the zone,' and Clint Eastwood, who doesn't give a lot of feedback, giving me a thumbs up after each take, and the producer saying 'Wow. She has real acting chops,' was all wonderful feedback to hear. As actors, we can't see ourselves, so it's important to know we are doing exactly what we intended to convey."

Before I finish with this piece, there's a point I need to make here. I'd originally planned to write a chapter on people like Patterson who made the jump from child to grown-up star, but didn't get enough feedback. That's fine — we can all think of others that can join her in the successful group, from Drew Barrymore to Sean Astin to Kurt Russell to whoever else we can name.

Look, acting can be a great profession to pursue, at nearly any age. But on the flip side, there are just as many reasons not to stay in it, and many of them can be found on the lips and minds of those who might have torn up the screen in their early years, but looked for a new line of work right around the time of adulthood. We're not going to list monikers here, but many of us could probably name a few performers that looked so natural in front of the camera in youth-hood, only to disappear from the screens before getting to ply their trades at more grown-up work.

As alluring as stardom can seem to those on the outside looking in, this might fall under the category of something that appears so wonderful until we actually have it. Constantly being bombarded by fans for autographs, interviewers (and authors!) that ask the same inquiries over and over, or those that ask personal, dirt-digging questions that are no one's business, certainly isn't for everyone. They may find that, while acting itself is fun, film acting isn't the thing for them — theater might be a more attractive option, for example. And some may not even like acting at all — there's millions of other professions out there, and performing isn't for everyone. We may look at people who didn't have long careers and wonder why, but we rarely consider that maybe they just didn't *want* one.

In hindsight, that may be one of the safer ways out: we can all recall the tragic stories of child stars who have battled mental illness, gotten into legal trouble, and, as has been too often the case, wound up in places worse than jail.

"The experience of stardom when one is not old enough to deal with it," explains John Lindon, a psychiatrist who has taught at UCLA and treated many performers in his practice, "causes a severe distortion not just of reality but of inner reality... You would think that child actors would have an excessive, inflated idea of their own worth. In actuality, it is just the opposite. They feel they have no inner resources and suffer from a terrible lack of self-esteem. To grow up *normal*, we need the stability that comes from having a fairly well-known set of people to deal with who react in fairly predictable ways." Fans of movies, music, and virtually every form of entertainment have notoriously short memories, and as loving and loyal as they may seem when we're at the top of the world, many will leave at hyperspeed when the next performer has a big hit, and finding out just how small many people are can knock out our self-worth like a right cross.

Still, we can always find people like Patterson, and so many others, who decided to keep playing the game far into adulthood, and keep winning at it. But leaving the acting profession is a choice, and for many, it's the right choice. People like her made the decision to stick with it as their generation switched. That alone doesn't make them admirable, but the talent they showed in both sections of the performing game certainly does.

Raynor Scheine

We sit in the audiences at films, theaters, even in our living rooms staring at the small screen. We watch performers do their thing for us, transforming into this person, at this place, in this time. A week later, we might watch them again — the same performer, yes, but someone else, somewhere else, sometime else.

What we don't always consider or realize, though, is that we might have been their models at some fast point. They might have learned something from us. Just by taking a walk down the street, grabbing a bite in our favorite restaurant, standing up and cheering at a ballgame, perhaps starting a "who can bust the screaming sound barrier" contest...

Doing all of that and so much more, all that action that we do all the time and take so far for granted, we might see ourselves on the screen or stage someday, in some form. The words we spoke, the movements we made, the way we conducted ourselves — we might have just inspired someone right into the next great mark in an acting career. Sometimes we just have to *be* to become role models.

"They key is observation — simple observation," explains Raynor Scheine, "observing humans here and there, interactions, culture. I spend hours just sitting outside, just observing life. Watching people, just being a keen observer of humanity." That's probably a more common technique that we the public ever realize. As Scheine and his colleagues have shown, it can be effective if one just *happens* to be performing such experiments at just the right time.

Scheine (it's not his given last name — say his names together to get the pun there!) started out deep into Virginia (not too far from where this piece was transcribed!), and never ventured too far north, at least not mentally or for very long. He ventured over to Richmond's Virginia Commonwealth University and made off with a drama degree, then put it to use on stages in North Carolina — and, yes, in New York and Los Angeles, which appears to be something of an initiation ritual for performance as a whole art!

Now let's talk about the flicks. Let's talk about how Scheine's shown so many different times and ways what an actor can learn just by making the world his personal observatory, and the ease that sort of experience affords such a performer.

We saw it in *Fried Green Tomatoes* back in 1991, when Sheriff Curtis Smoote arrived from his Georgia patrol-land, in Birmingham's Whistle Stop to find out just what happened to this Frank fellow whose truck's on the local lake floor.

"That was a wonderful story," Scheine remembers. "(Smoote) has this wonderful monologue. I did it for the audition, the same way in I did it in the performance. It was exactly what they wanted." He does find Frank, although he doesn't actually *realize* it, in a plot twist that it took a hell of a set of guts for Fannie Flagg to try when she wrote the book four years before. If you haven't seen it, check it out; it'll mean a hell of a lot more if you see it, rather than read it here.

Back to the point, though, Smoote was the type of fellow that Scheine had seen hard at work for decades.

"I'm from the south, and I knew many people like him," he explains. "I've been around southern culture all my life. I know those people."

That's not to say that his form of sociology has always been a positive, however. Three years after directing *Tomatoes*, Jon Avnet went to Mississippi to start *The War*, the story of the Simmons family, struggling in tough times while their dad Stephen (Kevin Costner) looks for freedom from the demons that followed him home from 'Nam.

Sheriff Curtis Smoote (Raynor Scheine) can't guess the spectacular succulent secret of the Whistle Stop Café barbecue in *Fried Green Tomatoes* (1991).

Typical of the south of the time, we're talking large families. We're talking racism. And we're talking about the family down the street that's all too anxious to stigmatize their Lipnicki surname with bullying, brawls, and booze.

Perhaps personified in the proud papa himself, his first title just Mr. It was Scheine. Unfortunately, the performer was a bit accustomed to this social setting as well.

"I'm familiar with many types like Mr. Lipnicki," he says wistfully. "He was not very smart. He was probably an alcoholic. I was acting mean and drunk, and I'd seen a lot of that in my life."

He got some unpleasantries out of character as well, injured when Costner slams him to the ground. It got worse the next year in *The Quick and the Dead*, his Ratsy blasted by backstabbing boss Herod (Gene Hackman) while fleeing town.

"I was supposed to fall at the gunshot," Scheine says. "I did, and I fell right onto a cactus. I was pulling those prickly spine things out of my skin for days."

Ah, but for the days of sitting on a witness stand, being led through Joe Pesci's photo-collage cross examination in *My Cousin Vinny* (1992), or Woodstock (complete with two pairs of glasses), walking, not leading his pal Ace Ventura (1994) down the information superhighway, before hacking was particularly cool ("C'mon, Ace, I thought you had a challenge for me!")!

"You come up with a way to do it, and it has to be spot-on," he claims. "It's the correct thing for that character at that time. You time the words in the line. There's nothing special. You just be in the moment and be with who you're acting opposite. It's just a matter of learning the words so well, you can do them three or four different ways. They will do many takes, and the editor chooses the one that's the best."

In two years, Scheine got two extreme views of an American tragedy; a year after playing a Congressman alongside Daniel Day-Lewis' Academy Award-winning title work in 2012's *Lincoln*, he played Dr. Samuel Mudd on TV in *Killing Lincoln*.

"I read about the characters," he remembers, "what they were like and what they did, and I looked at pictures of them. You try to look the part, and look to the costume and makeup to help you."

History tends to make Mudd's reputation as dirty as his last name; he's mostly known as the doctor who set the leg that John Wilkes Booth broke while jumping to the Ford Theater stage after firing the shot that changed American history. Mudd went to jail for conspiracy (what he knew ahead of time will probably never be known), and that's about all most of us know about him.

But that's not enough. Scheine got a chance to tell it all.

He showed us the yellow fever outbreak that engulfed Florida's Fort Jefferson, the one that Mudd battled in the fall of 1867, unsuspectingly returning to practice until the disease disappeared. It's why President Johnson pardoned him in February 1869, allowing him to go back home to Maryland, back to work in medicine and the family farm, where he died in 1875.

"I thought he got a bad rap," Scheine expresses. "In prison, he helped save a lot of people. They let him out, and back to Maryland. He became a hero in the end."

More roles have come for him since, and many more will. All along the way, he and so many others in the profession continue to watch and learn from the very people they'll soon be entertaining.

"You see people's behavior, and you pick the best one that you can use in a role," he says. "Outside in a park, at a Bingo parlor, you're just observing life. You hold the mirror up to nature."

Rusty Schwimmer

Most audiences saw the stars, the names that had enticed them to check out the films to begin with. Rusty Schwimmer looked a little deeper.

She could see it in them. She could hear it from them. And she might, just might one lucky day, be able to pass it on to those viewing her.

"When I was younger, I saw a lot of plays or movies," recalls the Chicago native, whose name comes from being nicknamed by her grandpa, seeing his redhead granddaughter sleeping away her first hours. "I would see that the person having the most fun was the character actor. As a kid, you think about what is the most fun. As I got older, I still was working for the fun, but also looking into the subtleties of being a character actress: where they were from, what experiences they had. I could almost see their experiences being worn on them, rather than the person who was the lead."

Long before she became one of the acting world's top character actresses, Rusty Schwimmer dreamt of being one in her first years in Chicago.

For a show revolving around death, *Six Feet Under* breathed some serious life into HBO from its premier in June of 2001. For five seasons, the stories of the Fisher family, their friends, and the funeral home they ran became and stayed one of HBO's highest-rated series, taking home nine Emmys, three Golden Globes, and a ton of other honors.

Like the millions of others lucky enough to experience *SFU* (like one author who subscribed to HBO just to watch it!), Schwimmer'd been wowed by the Fisher clan and its experiences with death within and without. While most of said viewers would be lucky enough to stay on the outside and watch within, she'd go inside the world, a burden and opportunity fighting it out.

"I was really afraid I was going to screw it up," Schwimmer admits of her break on the show. "I loved that series so much."

As the series so often did, "It's the Most Wonderful Time of the Year," began with dark humor mixed with tragedy. It's the holidays (though the episode aired in April 2002), and Marilyn Johnson's husband Jesse Ray heads off to be a department store Santa — it's obvious that the collective girth in this marriage comes from both being jammed with life as much as anything else. But just as he passes a group of kids, a car comes out of nowhere, and they can only sit and watch as Santa dies violently before them.

It might seem rough, and it was, but anyone who'd watched the show up to then wasn't so much as blinking.

They might not look so as a group, but biker communities are known for being there for each other and their area, as anyone willing to spend any time with them attests. Charity runs, biker drives, even tragedy, these people are their own community, and it's all but heavenly to them. Not just for the

Christmas party that Jesse's funeral becomes, complete with countless kegs and Lynyrd Skynyrd, but Marilyn's final farewell.

Without so much as a moment's hesitation, she hands her personal photo (for inside the coffin) to Peter Krause's Nate Fisher.

Years before, it had been in *Hustler*.

"I love playing women who show their sexuality," Schwimmer explains, "because a lot of times, they take that away from character actors. I went in there thinking she was a hot chick, always on the back of some guy's motorcycle. I'd been living in Los Angeles for a while, and I saw a lot of the motorcycle people come through. I'd see the women there. They were hard looking, but had a certain freedom about them. When this character came up, I thought about a lot of these ladies. What are they like, ten years later? What would be going on there?

Hopefully, none would ever be in Marilyn's oversized shoes (some undoubtedly had been). But if they were, they'd hopefully be lucky enough to have so many around to help. As her friends and family celebrate Jesse's life, rather than mourn his death, she takes a brief moment with Nate, unable to resist the urge to discuss a bit of her bedroom past and flirtatious future with him.

"I felt that Marilyn wasn't necessary from Los Angeles, but somewhere out west," Schwimmer says. "I made her a little more casual and less educated than I was. I found that she didn't cry a lot, and she laughed a little bit more. She had a tendency to be very dreamy talking about her husband. She was grieving, but she thought of him in a much more joyous light. I played with dialect, like I do with a lot of my characters."

Let's talk about that, as she has in just about every speech pattern possible over the past few decades. Like many at every level of her profession, Schwimmer starts with the script. As she did as a young viewer, she looks past the words, and then adds some of her own.

"I was taught that the author is God, so what the author says goes!" she explains. "If there isn't information on something you need to know, you have to fill in the blanks. If it's good writing, you can connect the dots really easily. I break it down by writing everything the author says about the character: how she sighs, how she laughs. Then I write everything that other characters say about her. Then I write everything that I say about myself. Usually, when you write all of that down, you're not only getting familiar with the character, but you're finding a pattern."

Her hometown Chicago speech came in handy early on, as Schwimmer's lovely face was bashed in in 1993's *Jason Goes to Hell: The Final Friday* (misleading, as he came back a few more times).

"I had to learn how to swear for that one!" she recalls jokingly. "I used a Chicago accent, where A's are hard and really nasally." The year before, she'd been a cop in *Candyman*; the next year, she showed up for a *Tales from the Crypt* go-round.

Schwimmer went a bit farther south in 1996, playing the mom to young Jo Harding (Alexa Vega, who'd become Helen Hunt in grown-up form) in the terrifying opening to *Twister*.

"We had to take a course in what to do if a tornado came," she remembers. "If you couldn't be in a cellar or ditch, you just laid down in a fetal position with your butt up and head down." Making it to a cellar wouldn't save her husband, sucked up and out by a twister, somehow causing an unnatural obsession with the disaster in his little girl.

"While we were running from the house to the cellar, getting hit by wind machines and jet engines, I could barely keep myself up," she remembers. "There was lots of screaming."

Spending time in the past, recent and *way* back, would become a fixture of her career. A bigger audience would end up seeing her in a small role as the caring wife of a prison warden in *Amistad* (1997), but jumping over to New York and back nearly a century handed Schwimmer a tougher job in 1995's *A Little Princess*.

With her dad off fighting for the Brits in World War One, Sara Crewe (Liesel Matthews) shows up at a boarding school in the Big Apple. Per usual for this kind of story, it's run by a lady hiding a pitch-black heart behind a caring smile, with Eleanor Bron's Miss Minchin in the Nurse Ratchet-esque role (actually, the Trunchbull from *Matilda* the year before might be a better comparison).

"For a period piece, you have to breathe a certain way, stand a certain way," Schwimmer says. "Your posture is changed. You're not even allowed to slouch." She was Amelia, Minchin's sister, whose unexpected friendship with Sara gives her a boost of confidence Amelia never knew existed, pushing her on to something else.

"I was scared of my sister, and I showed it with my hands," Schwimmer says. "My hands were never below my waist, because I was afraid my sister would haul off and hit me." Reading up on older times, she learned just how tough women had things back then — it wasn't a question of if, but of how much.

"I read about how people stood, how their hair was, how they were in partnering up," she remembers. "A lot of times, a woman would never go into the drawing room, because that was where men were discussing war and money. I've heard it said, to be a really good actor, you have to be a psychologist, a sociologist, and a historian. You can't just know your lines: you have to know the human condition and the history, if you're doing period pieces. You have to know how these women stood, or didn't stand, or walked." Or in Amelia's case, ran — as in, escaping with her secret crush as her sister's world implodes.

She'd be the one pursued in *The Perfect Storm* (2000). Watching his fellow crewman on the *Andrea Gail* look for love and occasionally find it, Michael "Bugsy" Moran (John Hawkes) can only chat up local bar babe Irene Johnson, monikered Big Red — it's tough to say who had a more insensitive nickname.

Here would bring Schwimmer some old and new manners to get ready.

"Once we got to Gloucester (Massachusetts, for filming), we had a week," she remembers. "John and I were the only non-famous people there, so we acted like we were from a few towns over." With her alongside Diane Lane and Mary Elizabeth Mastrantonio and Hawkes cast with Mark Wahlberg, John C. Reilly, and, oh yeah, *George Clooney* (who, to be fair, hadn't had his star rise too high just yet), their names wouldn't be too near the cast list top.

"That let us practice our accents," Schwimmer says. "The Gloucester accent is a bitch! We said 'convasation' instead of conversation!" But they also got to spend some time playing softball and doing some bar-hopping around the town, hanging out with folk who'd lost their friends that sad week back in October and November of 1991, when the real *Gail* was caught between a pair of weather fronts and a hurricane, something that no crew in American history (that we know of) had ever faced.

"When we first see Irene, she's nursing two brown drinks," Schwimmer recalls. "If I drink, it's usually wine. Brown drink, that's bourbon and scotch. I had a friend who was a connoisseur in scotch and all things brown, and he knew what that was like. I felt that Irene would drink Jack (Daniels!) and Coke, so I drank a few, and I found myself a little more belligerent than usual." As Irene would be, with no one knowing that the *Gail* would find a tragic place in American history (ironically in the worst of ways, 2011's Hurricane Irene would become one of the deadliest storms the east coast had ever suffered through, killing over sixty and causing nearly $17 billion in damages).

"The only way I could talk to him was to be belligerent," she continues. "It really informed the character. If I haven't had the experience, I go to the person who has had it." For the only real-person role of Schwimmer's career (Irene had been a dramatic creation), however, this would be in the severe negatives.

It's sad that this sort of thing was rampant so recently, but it wasn't until 1988 that the first class-action (i.e., group) sexual harassment lawsuit took the first step against such an epidemic. For over a decade, Lois Jenson and other female mine workers in Eveleth, Minnesota were abused (if not physically, than every other way possible) with sexual harassment and other hostility from their male colleagues, of the gender majority of the time and career. After almost a decade of putting up with this garbage, Jenson and other women finally made legal history with the suit.

And as long as it had taken for the lawsuit to be filed, the liability trial didn't start until 1992 (the next year, the company was ordered to lesson its workers on the concept), the civil trial until 1996, and the settlement unreached until Christmas of 1998! Although, by this point, sexual harassment had become a common public topic in America, and many steps had long since been taken to fight it.

In 2005, the film version came out in *North Country*, with Charlize Theron in Jenson's role, renamed Josey Aimes. Oscar-winners Frances McDormand and Sissy Spacek were there beside her. And so was Schwimmer, their friend Big Betty.

"We were given the absolute privilege of hanging out with the women we were portraying," Schwimmer remembers. "That's iffy because you must respect these women, even though you're taking them apart and learning how they tick so you can portray them correctly. When you're meeting these people, you watch them go through their lives, and you stay as objective as possible. You're talking to them, and they lived through this. You have to be incredibly compassionate without being too subjective."

Helped along by some serious research from director Niki Caro in her own Hollywood debut, Schwimmer and her co-stars learned the *Country* background. They spent time together, drank together, established some friendships. They also learned just how dark some of the ladies' pasts had been.

"There was one woman, about fifty years old, a petite blonde woman," Schwimmer says. "You'd never think she was working in mines, driving big trucks. She said to me, 'I get a little crazy when guys treat me like crap. But it gets really old when you're a grandmother, and someone calls you a cunt.'" She'll never forget the look on her face, the sound of her voice, the pain of the memory.

"Seeing how tired she was made me think about how her resting face should be," Schwimmer says. "It was not a pretty picture, but it informed us of what kind of treatment these women had."

But Caro also wanted some realism in the pseudo-workplace (whatever she wanted, it worked, as Theron and McDormand were both Oscar-nominated!).

"We had to get certified to work in the mines," Schwimmer remembers. She learned to go rock hunting as much as Big Betty herself would have.

"I was the one crushing rocks to make the iron," she says. "I was in this huge pitch, trying to see. It was like the arcade game where you try to pick up stuffed animals with a claw. But instead, you had to crush it, on a grander, much more dangerous scale." She and the rest of the lady miners were kept separate from the other crew during filming: different lives, different backgrounds, different portrayals.

Country showed us some of the worst that sexual harassment can be, but some felt it didn't show enough, and they'd earned the right to feel that way. One scene has a woman inside a porta-john, only to have some morons tip it over. Might seem funny as a frat-boy practice joke, but the victims weren't laughing – some of them had had to worry about such an occurrence every time they needed to use the facility.

"Afterward, the women were bit disappointed because it was worse for them than what we saw," Schwimmer admits. "But for the most part, I think they were really glad the story was told."

Michelle St. John

If we need to lose weight for a role, we go on a diet and start working out more. If we want to gain weight for one, we don't do much other than eat donuts and cheeseburgers (ah, heaven!).

We can grow our hair or shave it. We can get a tattoo, or have one erased.

But no matter how much training we undergo, how many classes we take, we can't make ourselves learn how to be younger.

We can learn to act younger. It may not take much time in the makeup chair to look younger. But we can't step into a time machine and subtract a few years for the want of a role.

That nearly derailed one of the biggest parts of Michelle St. John's career.

When she was 18, she and screenwriter Keith Leckie, among others, had been talking about putting together *Where the Spirit Lives* (1989), which would tell the horrifying stories of the borderline-concentration camp upbringing forced upon thousands of Native American and Canadian children for over a century. It would be the story of Astohkomi, a young woman separated (stolen might be a better word) from her family and forced into a school that educated them not on reading, writing, and arithmetic, but on how to leave their "Indian" lifestyles behind and how to be more white and Christian... in other words, in the eyes of too many from the past, how to be better (for more information on this, and the film, see Chapelle Jaffe's profile in this chapter).

Michelle St. John (above, right, in 1998's *Smoke Signals*) has spent much of her career acting out the tales of Native American heritage, from the sad to the uplifting to the animated musical type, as she voiced a character in 1995's *Pocahontas*.

St. John and Leckie improvised their way through the storylines, putting themselves in the position of the unimaginable. St. John started reading up on how the schools were created, and why they lasted from just past the Civil War to the 1990s. She even met with many who had suffered through the horrors of these places (many were abused and/or killed during the process).

Soon, she was beyond ready to be Komi. Unfortunately, the film took another three years to be made. By that point, St. John was 21, and many felt that the gap between teen life and adulthood would be too wide for her to jump back over.

Fortunately, she wasn't one of them. As the shooting schedule finally fell into place, St. John snared some tapes of the Blackfoot dialect to work on Komi's tongue.

"I spent hours and hours listening and practicing, trying to find the rhythm of the language and feel comfortable speaking it as effortlessly as I could," she recalls. "I also spent a great deal of time trying to build an accent for (Komi), as she speaks more and more English during the film — an accent that was appropriate to a new English speaker and that was tricky."

With a new culture, a new *life*, jammed into her psyche, Komi's shoved from teacher to teacher, witness to physical and emotional abuse, and eventually taken and all but enslaved by one instructor (Jaffe).

"I thought that creating a physicality for Astohkomi that reflected her response to her surroundings would take me out of my 21-year-old sensibilities and help me to appear younger on screen," St. John explains. "The physicality I created is quite subtle, but in some scenes you can see her being a bit awkward and fidgety; uncomfortable in a scratchy wool dress, etc."

For many actors, even those who have been working "steadily" (i.e., two or three jobs a year) for years at a time, comfort is nothing to get used to. That's why working needs to be part compassion and part consistency, knowing what to do for the experience, what to do for the diversity, and what to do for a quick few bucks.

"There is something equally terrifying and exhilarating about acting," St. John explains. "While you have the opportunity to explore aspects of human experience and emotion, you also have to allow yourself to be vulnerable amongst your fellow actors, director, and audience. I think most actors fear they will fail miserably and often second-guess themselves, and finding a way to rise above that fear and find fulfillment in the work and the dynamics among the performers you're working with can be very satisfying."

She helped explore another travesty of Native American culture a few years later.

Like St. John, Helen Betty Osbourne was a member of the Cree tribe, living in Manitoba, a former residential school student. Just before Thanksgiving of 1971, the teenager was kidnapped, sexually assaulted, and beaten and stabbed to death.

With lost evidence, no witnesses, and little public regard for the local Native female population, the case lay dormant for 16 years. But in 1987, a man was finally convicted of her killing.

However, the local Aboriginal community got another shock less than four months later, when a Winnipeg police officer gunned down J.J. Harper, the executive director of the Island Lake Tribal Council. This led to an even bigger outcry concerning the treatment of Natives of the land.

As the trials came to an end, St. John found herself glued to the local TV screens, learning all she could about a justice that took far too long to be done. In 1991, her interest would pay off in the TV flick *Conspiracy of Silence*: she'd be Osbourne.

She utilized some of the same preparation techniques that worked so well for *Spirit*, sitting down with Lisa Priest, who'd written the book on which the film was based. St. John also interviewed several people from Osbourne's area about the case, racism in the area, and the woman herself.

"Betty's mother Justine testified," she says, "and it was enormously painful to watch, but I was so moved by Justine's strength and grace and her grief, talking about her girl." In keeping with her daughter's dream of becoming a teacher, Justine saw a scholarship fund launched in Helen's honor and a school named after her.

Things lightened up a few years later, as St. John joined fellow Native performers Irene Bedard, Russell Means, and others in Disney's animated *Pocahontas* (1995). She'd be the speaker for the title character's best friend.

"Over the years, I have had the good fortune of doing a number of cartoons," St. John says, "as well as lots of 'looping' and voiceovers as well. Like most actors, I really enjoy voice work; it's a lot of fun and you don't have to get all dolled up to go to work. There wasn't much to prepare for Nakoma, and the process with Disney was a new way of working for me. I never saw a full script. I would only see the pages of the scenes I was recording on the day I recorded so I never really knew what the big picture was. That made it very challenging in some ways, but they know how to make it all work in the end."

Four years after she and Evan Adams made things happen in the 1998 dramedy *Smoke Signals*, they went back to work in *The Business of Fancydancing*, a character study of a young gay Spokane man (Adams) who returns to the nearby reservation at which he grew up for the funeral of his friend, meeting his ex-lover Agnes (St. John) along the way.

"Evan Adams and I are very old and very close friends," she says, "and working together is always a fantastic experience."

For one of the first times in her career, the only true preparation St. John needed came from herself – herself as a Native who longed to teach, a lady who experienced the culture, kept far too separate from the civilizing mainstream.

"A big part of an actor's training is getting to know and understand yourself and human experience," she says. "We need to be open to constantly learning about ourselves and how we make choices in life, what motivates our decisions and how they impact the people in our world. This personal growth can not only help make us better actors but it can also make us more aware of our inter-personal relationships as well."

Fancydancing has long since been another asset in that department for generations of Natives, and those that wish to learn more about it. The step was created by Native Americans of the 1920s and 30s, inspired by war dances from the past. Popularity of the style has gone up and down over the past few decades, but it's still a staple at festivals across the world.

"Even though the script was really strong," St. John says, "(Director Sherman Alexie, who wrote the book the film is based on) was very interested in improvising, giving the power to the performers to truly own what we said and how we said it. In most cases we started with what was written and then we would talk through it and then improvise when the camera was rolling. We were very fortunate to have such faith and trust between us and likewise that was true for all of the other actors in the film. It was a labor of love."

That's always a great attitude to have about acting in general; love for acting alone can sometimes get a person into the business, and keep them there, at least for a while.

"It's important to develop a healthy sense of self-esteem too," she says. "This business can be very challenging and as actors we are rarely in control of when we work, the kind of work we do and the quality of it."

Mike Starr

Mike Starr couldn't wait to get to the *Goodfellas* set in 1990. He'd come THIS CLOSE to snaring a role in *The Last Temptation of Christ* two years before, and now he was finally grabbing the much sought-after chance to work with a directing legend named Scorsese and a fellow named De Niro.

"It was one of the few roles I've ever campaigned for," Starr says of his role as Frenchy in the 1990 flick. "Frenchy was real a fun-loving, funny type of guy. He wasn't the clichéd mobster; he was a cargo supervisor who was a thief. I felt I was at the right age and had the look. I thought I could play this."

He's not always a good guy in the films, and sometimes not even there for long, but Mike Starr almost always comes across like the type of guy you'd like to sit down with for a few beers.

After making his way through the Nicholas Pileggi book *Wiseguy*, on which the film is based, Starr transcribed a letter to casting director Ellen Lewis.

"I don't think I've ever done that before (writing a letter)," he says. "I said, 'You probably get a lot of these, but I really think I could play this character really well!'"

It worked, and he was off to work. But less than a week into filming, Frenchy was dead.

Not because the character had been deemed unimportant enough to cut, the fate of all too many performers at some point. Simply because the director decided to make one of the film's most well-known montages the first to go before the cameras.

As a sad but somehow soothing tone plays in the background about three-fourths of the way through the film, viewers are treated to a musical horror show, as "whacked" henchmen show the pain of knowing too much after a robbery coverup starts to go awry.

One henchman is found in a meat-chilling truck, frozen solid as a side of beef. A man named Johnny Roastbeef and his wife, gruesomely slaughtered in their new car, are stumbled upon by a group of children. And Frenchy and another fellow are literally tossed out in the trash, as garbagemen find them in a dumpster, fresh bullets in the brain.

"Martin Scorsese did all of the deaths in the first week," Starr recalls. "Johnny Roastbeef's death scene took seven hours, but, *man*, did it pay off in the film!

"When we got in the dumpster, there was carved up, shredded lettuce, and some old treasury money," he says. "The freaky part was that I got dumped into a hopper, and the guy showed me that the blades were off. My legs were sticking out, and the huge dumpster was going up, iron to iron. It was good acting exercise because I had to totally relax; the first couple of times, my eyes were blinking. When you see the shot, you think, 'Wow, that's cool.' Now the rest of the time, you just get to show up, hang out, and ad-lib."

Hanging out was Frenchy's M.O. for most of the film; he hung out at a bar with Ray Liotta's Henry Hill and Robert De Niro's Jimmy Conway, discussing plans to heist an airport in Queens (Starr's birth-place). Working security at the joint, he hung out with his back turned while Henry, Tommy DeVito (Os-car-winning Joe Pesci), and the rest of the gang robbed the place. He even hung out at Henry's wedding to Karen Hill (Lorraine Bracco, still not quite as lovely as she was a few years later in 1999's *The Sopranos*), where a scene when Frenchy trades insults with another character was cut from the final product.

"Frenchy was from Long Island, out near Hempstead, where I went to school," says Starr, a Hosftra University graduate. "When I was growing up, I didn't hang out with those types of guys, but at the neighborhood bars, guys like them came by. I didn't find it a tremendous stretch for someone to say, 'Wow, I wonder if he can play this.'" His brother Beau showed up early in the film as Henry's no-nonsense father.

"We all wanted to work with Scorsese, and I thought this was going to be an interesting film," Starr says. "I knew people similar to that. *Goodfellas* isn't about the mob; these guys were a crew, but it's almost the opposite of *The Godfather* (1972), almost a contra-positive of *The Godfather*. It's a different life. It's about guys making scores."

Despite fellows like De Niro and Frank Sivero (future human popsicle Carbone) crossing over from the *Godfather* series, Scorsese took mob-like pains to create a difference between the two, even forbidding ad-libbers to speak Sicilian in certain scenes, Starr recalls.

"It was so simple," he says, "not simplistic, but simple the way Scorsese got rid of the debris. He set up an atmosphere that was so clean, made it so easy to work on the scene. It was so clean that you couldn't be distracted. If he trusted you, he let you do anything."

Just before it was time for the soon-legendary henchmen roll-call introduction scene, Scorsese asked Starr to discuss things with De Niro.

"I was like 'What?'" he says. "But all (De Niro) did was ask questions. He gave me so much respect and made you feel so comfortable. He had a way of helping you relax. He just talked about our characters' relationship. 'What do you think of this? How well do we know each other?'"

"I liked the fact that Frenchy was an 'Up' guy, because a lot of times in the genre of mob films, a lot of people are talking like this," Starr says, dropping his voice to a deep monotone. "Frenchy was an 'Up' character who just loved stealing and was a lot of fun. There was this big adventure to him."

With Frenchy, it was easy to get the impression that thievery wasn't done for the money, and he didn't like the potentiality of getting hurt or hurting others; at least, those weren't his main priorities. With this character, it was just about seeing if he could do it, the challenge of someone thinking or saying that it couldn't be done, and proving them wrong. Any personal gain, for Frenchy's wallet at least, was secondary.

"When I got to the set, there was a detective there, and we hit it off right away," Starr says. "He said, 'You must be playing Frenchy.' I said yes. He said, 'You're perfect.' He started telling me about the real guy (on whom Frenchy was based), and later on showed me pictures of the guy with his family, and then the guy dead."

During a night of filming at the airport, Silvero made similar queries, he continues.

"He asked me how I was going to play the role. When people say that to you, sometimes you don't know what to say, but he was making a very good point. I asked what he meant, and he said, 'Just the way you are with me, that's the way (Frenchy) is.' We became friends."

Remember, likeable, in the cinematic sense, doesn't necessarily mean just wanting to see someone and hoping that they win the fight; many horror fans go to the movies to cheer for the monsters, but not many of them would want to invite Jason Vorhees out for a beer afterward. Mobsters may not be quite as bad, but when killing and cussing at the volume they do in such movies, it's quite a task to make them likeable as people, to honestly care about the characters you're watching.

But with his sense of humor and egregious grin, Frenchy, along with several other characters in the film, managed to get the job done. Sure, we knew he was helping steal from innocent people and hurting others, one way or another, but we couldn't help but think he'd be a great guy to invite over for the game on Sunday anyway.

"I wanted to do it like I was shot out of a cannon," recalls Starr, who utilized the improv techniques he'd picked up in his first major big-screen role alongside Robert Redford in 1984's *The Natural*. "I wanted to be this guy that had this tremendous joy, and I was thrilled by it. Frenchy wasn't the guy who shot people; he was a thief, and he loved doing it."

A year later, he'd ironically do it again, reprising Frenchy's role for the TV movie *The 10 Million Dollar Getaway*, which depicted many of the same events as *Goodfellas*, albeit in a more politically correct fashion!

Still, television's nothing new for Starr, who's been appearing on the small screen since a 1978 *Hawaii Five-0* episode, ironically entitled "Small Potatoes." *Home Improvement* (1997), *House* (2005), *Scrubs* (2004), *CSI* (2012), a long role on *The Young and Restless* (2011), he's done just about them all. But his dark comedy still shines at times, from his unrecognizable turn as a drunken clown in 1989's *Uncle Buck* (don't believe that's him, do you? Go back and check it out — it's worth it!) to a stalker kidnapper who inadvertently commits suicide in 1994's *Dumb and Dumber*!

"With character actors, people count on you to perform," says Starr. "It's like you're a relief pitcher or good offensive lineman. You're not the quarterback, but people count on you to make that block. It's about having people that believe you can do it." He'd get to work with De Niro again in 1993's *Mad Dog and Glory*.

"I take 'character actor' as a compliment," he says. "To me, it's saying that you can play various characters. I don't even know where the term comes from. Maybe it's something that comes from the studio system, like, 'Oh, bring in the character actors!'

He recently found an article on a place called "He's That Guy," encompassing 10 actors whose names weren't known, but film roles were. Starr was one of the 10 'That Guys.'

"I was very lucky and very fortunate to be put in such company. I think (a character actor) is someone who plays all types of characters. But if someone said to me, 'Ah, you always play yourself,' I would say that that's strange — I'm not *this* guy, I'm not *that* guy."

Hannah Taylor Gordon

If there were a list of books that should be legally required to peruse, Anne Frank's story would be at the top. It's the world through the eyes of a young woman with the same dreams as many of the time, who never knew that, just a month after making the first few entries in the book she'd received as a thirteenth birthday present, she and her family would be thrust into a world of almost indescribable evil.

Or that her words would be read more than any other biography in Earth's history. That her writings would tell one of the saddest stories of all time, and somehow manage to send a message of hope.

But, even after her musings have been interpreted and studied by generations, moving to plays and screens over and over, there was still more to Anne's life than her words could tell.

"I cannot emphasize enough what a wonderful woman she was to play," remembers Hannah Taylor Gordon, one of many to lift the burden of becoming Anne. "She was immensely dramatic, immensely emotional, incredibly inquisitive, fiercely passionate, everything I was at that age."

Not all of us are aware of what Anne Frank did, what she wanted, long after that heartbreaking day in August 1944 when her family was betrayed, then hoarded off with treatment worse than cattle to one concentration camp after another.

We know she didn't live through the Holocaust. But how she suffered, as so many did in that sad time and place, in the infamous Auschwitz and eventually in Bergen-Belsen, how she was victimized by fellow prisoners, how her sister died right next to her. . . maybe not everyone is aware. And how she died — of typhus, like the goddamned Nazis weren't enough — just weeks before the British arrived, it just breaks your heart. And wondering what she might have done, or what would have happened if her diary hadn't been discovered after the war, you just don't want to even imagine it.

We wish that Anne could have been there to find her own diary, and tell us the rest of the life that she deserved to live.

Hannah Taylor Gordon shows the glance up into hopelessness that so many innocent Holocaust victims were forced to finally take in 2001's *Anne Frank: The Whole Story*.

That was Taylor Gordon's challenge. *Anne Frank: The Whole Story* (2001) showed us more of Anne's life than her diary could tell. Rather than the title character's work, it's based on Melissa Müller's 1998 work *Anne Frank: The Biography*.

Just two years before, Taylor Gordon had helped send a different message of inspiration through the saddest of times in *Jakob the Liar*, as Robin Williams' title character stretched the truth into an uplifting message to so many others stranded in the hopelessness of a concentration camp.

Including Lina, the young gal he'd hidden away in the hopes she might escape.

"Robin was portraying something very serious, warm, and earnest," recalls the woman who was Lina. "It was different from his usual stuff. It had light moments, as much as you can have in a Holocaust movie, but it was so far removed from anything else that he'd done." That, along with *Jakob* arriving around the same time as *Life is Beautiful*, an Oscar winner with a similar theme, kept the film from getting the credit it should have.

"I cannot tell you enough about how amazing it was to be in a movie with Robin Williams," Taylor Gordon explains. "I look back and know that I learned so much from him, having to do a scene with such a genius with his words. He never stuck to the script, and for a ten-year-old to come to the set having prepared my lines, and for them to go out the window, it was a little bit nerve wracking, but it made me learn. It made the movie fifty times better."

She and Williams would stay close until the world (far past the acting land) was shocked and heartbroken by his tragic passing in August 2014.

"Robin created a kind of magic in every single movie," she remembers. "He really was a force of that crazy genius. There was nobody like him. To spend time with him, to sit with him, to talk with him,

I learned everything about acting. I'm a very instinctive actress. I go by what my feelings are on how an actor, how a character would feel – if I were in that situation, what would I feel like. He was so much the same, and it rubbed off on me big time."

To become Lina, she also studied up on the Holocaust, not expecting it to come back in so handy when rumors began to spread about the newest cinematic chapter of the Frank family. Steven Spielberg was in talks for the film, but a deal wasn't reached.

The casting crew, Taylor Gordon remembers, "was looking all over the world. I probably auditioned four or five times. They chose me because I had an uncanny resemblance to her at that stage." Her acting ability was quite the asset as well. Knowing the film wasn't based around Anne's original words, Taylor Gordon only checked it over once.

"I was mostly going off the script, and what I felt a thirteen-year-old girl would be like," she remembers. "I had a lot of people advising me: the director, the producers, my family explaining World War 2 to me." She'd spend several months filming in the Czech Republic, and visited Auschwitz and other places that the Nazis had acted out their horror.

Anne's final diary entry fell on Aug. 1, 1944, just days before her family was sent to the Westerbork camp in the north Netherlands. That's where Taylor Gordon's portrayal took audiences in directions past the book.

The young lady becomes an impromptu role model to other young captives, telling stories at the camp school (as much of a "school" as could be established in such a place), including one tale she herself had written as a student.

But then she's sent to Auschwitz, probably the most infamous camp of all. It became the setting for some of the toughest scenes to film, Taylor Gordon says.

"We were on the trains going to the camps, filming at 4 a.m., filled with extras," she remembers. "It was snowing, dogs barking, people crying, all for filming. We went in to get our hair shaved, and it felt so intense. It really provoked us and made us feel a lot. Everybody was crying, because they were so moved." She and the rest of Anne's family actually had their heads sheared for the scene.

"We had our hair shaved, and we had makeup put on our body to look like scabies," Taylor Gordon says. "It was an intense experience: very real, but not frightening. The cast and crew didn't want to make it terrifying."

A scabies infection sends Anne and other family members to Bergen-Belsen in northern Germany (her dad Otto, played by Ben Kingsley, stayed behind, and was the only family member to survive). Her mother Edith (Brenda Blethyn) passes early in 1945, and Anne and her sister Margot are left alone with desperate hopes and memories.

But that's not enough to sustain them. Wracked by starvation, typhus, and we'll never fully know what else, Margot passes away, and Anne sadly follows, gone at age fifteen. It's believed that they died in March 1945, just weeks before the camp was liberated.

The Emmys named *The Whole Story* as 2001's top miniseries, and it also scored a win for art direction. Taylor Gordon was up for the lead acting award (Kingsley and Blethyn were also nominated), but was edged by Judy Davis's title work in *Life With Judy Garland*.

The Anne Frank Foundation maintains the family's original home back in Amsterdam, one of the world's top tourist attractions. It also battles the same bigotry that planted the Holocaust's seeds back in the 1930s. Taylor Gordon became a part of the organization after her portrayal.

"I've given speeches, been at conferences," she says. "I have so many letters from schoolchildren who have watched the miniseries, telling me my work is the only thing they have to hang on to. Anne Frank is an icon."

Putting a new spin on legendary tales would become a hallmark of Taylor Gordon's career; in 2006, she'd appear in the latest version of *The Ten Commandments*, with Dougray Scott as Moses. Hollywood remakes and/or modernizes Bill Shakespeare's work every few years, and 2012 gave Taylor Gordon and some others their chance to tell a new tragic tale.

It's the story of a young man who goes mad with power, a feeling spurred by his wife, who seems to feel that she should be running the show. He kills the king of Scotland and takes the throne, but it's never enough, and never would have been. Convinced that someone's out to get him (probably right) and that his authority can't cease enforcement, he kills again and again before losing his mind and his life (his wife does as well) to the war that didn't have to happen.

Yes, it's *Macbeth*. Yes, the wife in question is Lady Macbeth, whom many consider to be Shakespeare's most darkly intelligent character, right down next to Iago, Brutus, and others. Everyone from Vivien Leigh to Judi Dench to Angela Bassett has grabbed the role.

Now it was Taylor Gordon's turn.

"There is no better character in the theater for a female than Lady Macbeth," she claims. "A lot of actresses are old when they play her, because what people take from the play is that she is this crazed, damned woman who's deeply twisted inside. How could you have that much in you if you were young? But I think what Shakespeare intended was that she *was* young. It's just my opinion, but I think what he intended was that she and her husband were young kids completely caught up in a whirlwind, dramatic situation they didn't know how to repair." Fresh off a small role in *Captain America* (2011), Marek Oravec became the title man.

By then, Taylor Gordon had shown Shakespeare's work all over Europe's theaters, including the Lady herself.

"I love literature, and I love Shakespeare," she explains. "To play her, I roamed around, completely freaking out, filled with anger and volatility, dramatic and wild and deeply dark. It helped that I had dark eyes – dark, flushing angry eyes."

Early in her career, Taylor Gordon had briefly played the young version of Elizabeth Lavenza in *Mary Shelley's Frankenstein* (1994), acting out the lady who steals the young doctor's heart before he starts nabbing body parts (Rory Jenkins played the young doctor, with Kenneth Branagh and Helena Bonham Carter in the adult modes).

Back on television two decades later, she became Shelley herself in the 2014 docudrama *Frankenstein and the Vampyre: A Dark and Stormy Night*.

"I am *very* interested in (Shelley), her work, *Frankenstein* itself," she asserts. "When they approached me to play her, I dive-bombed straight into it. You can't get a more daring, different kind of woman for her time than her. The only thing you can ask for as an actress is to play interesting characters, and it makes a major difference when the woman is a strong, different character, rather than average." She poured over the literature by and about Shelley, who wrote out one of horror's most legendary tales in her early 20's.

"I thought she was bold, pursuing very strange darkness in her mind through her writing," explains Taylor Gordon. "You can't get better than that. She was weird, very strange, and there's definitely an aspect of that that I have. She was inquisitive, dark, kind of morbid, and I have certain aspects of that in my own personality. I delved as far as I could go. The fantastic art and literature from that period, I fell straight into them." That same year, she'd get involved in a different type of recreation, showing up in *Jack Ryan: Shadow Recruit*; Chris Pine became the fourth fellow to play the Ryan man we first met in Tom Clancy's legendary words.

"I've played some awesome women and girls, who are very special for an actress to portray," Taylor Gordon remarks. "I don't know what the next twenty years of my acting career will bring, but having played Anne Frank, Lady Macbeth, and Mary Shelley, it's already been very exciting."

Richard Thomas

If you've been checking out screens of any size over the past few decades, you've probably seen Richard Thomas.

He showed up between grade school classes as Oliver Twist in an episode of *DuPont Show of the Month* in 1959, and spent most of his adolescent and teenage years popping up on one-shot appearances in one TV show after another.

In 1971, Thomas landed his biggest role to date, showing up on over 100 episodes of *The Waltons* as John-Boy Walton, whose journaled entries told the story of his father Jon (Ralph Waite) attempting to lead his western Virginia family through the Great Depression and World War II, work that scored him an Emmy in 1973.

Fans of the much more recent *Gilmore Girls* got a special look at the Waltons' home, as the Dragonfly Inn that Lorelei Gilmore helps buy and renovate was actually the family's former residence.

Three years after getting John-Boy started, Thomas brought the big screen to the small screen in his role as Henry Fleming in *The Red Badge of Courage*. It set the stage for one of the biggest roles of his career.

In 1979, the same year that Thomas left *The Waltons* (Robert Wightman reprised John-Boy for the series' last three seasons), he became a member of the German army.

After spending years of his childhood in front of TV audiences as a member of the Walton family, Richard Thomas made the switch to grown-up star in films like 1990's *It*.

But only in character; his performance as Paul Baumer, the young, carefree optimist who devolves into a hardened war veteran in the World War I drama *All Quiet on the Western Front* has been used as a tool for years of school history teachers. A remake of 1930's Best Picture, it's the story of a young man who believes the life of a solider to be exciting and adventurous, only to be forced to watch his classmates and superiors die before his eyes and in his arms, and from the perspective of those trying to defeat America.

"I didn't have a problem with that at all (playing a German in WWI)," Thomas says. "It's one of the great anti-war novels and stories of our time; that's a more important affiliation than a national affiliation. I wanted very much to play that part. It's a great story, it's a great part. I don't know of any other young actor who didn't want the part."

He took home the Baumer Sweepstakes, and checked out Lew Ayres' work as Paul in the original film to get ready. Then he and the rest of the "troops" headed to boot camp in Prague for another round of getting in character. But just as with most other professions, acting has some aspects that can only be learned on the job.

"You can't really prepare for that, because all you can bring with you are your feelings, your desires, and your knowledge of the area," Thomas says of the role. "In a situation like that you're shooting under extreme conditions. We prepared by going to boot camp for a couple of weeks, and then we were shooting in the mud and the rain and the trenches. You just had to show up and stay alert!"

Ironically, that becomes Paul's fatal downfall; entrenched in the trenches in the film's final sequence, he's killed after taking his eyes off the action to draw a passing bird.

Keeping with the tradition of bringing novels to the screen, Thomas had one of his other more well-known roles in the 1990 adaptation of Stephen King's book *It*, the story of a group of friends in a small Maine town who reunite to battle the nightmarish evil that terrorized them and slaughtered several classmates during their childhood.

"I hadn't read the book before," says Thomas, who played the adult Bill Denbrough, whose little brother Georgie becomes one of the creature's first victims early in the film, "but it was another great story, a very popular novel. I got to work with some of my pals, like Annette O'Toole, John Ritter, and Richard Masur, people who I'd worked with before and liked very much (Ritter had played Rev. Matthew Fordwick on *The Waltons*). I'd never made that type of picture before, so I decided to do it."

Though the monster changes shape throughout the film to fit the kids' worst fears, it's often personified in the form of a wicked clown, always a popular fixture of maleviolence in films and television – played by Tim Curry in all his evil cameo glory.

Viewers – and readers of the novel – first meet the main characters, soon to be called the "Losers Club" in their younger forms, as longtime child star Jonathan Brandis plays the younger Bill. Brandis' character displays the stuttering that would make Bill a lifelong target for bullies, and plague Bill throughout his life, culminating in his subtly scary repetitive "He thrusts his fists against the posts and still insists he sees the ghosts," scene, just after Bill returns home to face the enemy that killed his brother.

"We met each other, but we didn't really work together," Thomas says of Brandis, who would tragically fail to make the same child-to-adult transition that Thomas himself made, dying by his own hand in November 2003. "But I thought he did a terrific job."

Perhaps showing a bit of King himself, Bill's a horror novelist, one of his works being *The Glowing*, a not-too-subtle reference to a certain other writer's *Shining*.

"I had to work on the stutter and figure out how I was going to make that work," Thomas says. "I had to research a little bit about stuttering. I also had to brush up my bike riding, because I hadn't done that since I was a teenager." There's a great scene near the middle of the film when he and childhood friend Mike Hanlon (Tim Reid) take a huge jump back to childhood by cruising their street on a bike together. For Thomas, the film was more about the value of lifelong closeness, rather than beating monsters.

"I think it's a story about friendship and community in the face of adversity, and that interests me," says Thomas. "I didn't have such an interest in the supernatural aspect of it; it was more about the kids and what they go through and the way the childhood experience bound them together made it an interesting thing to watch." Ironically, he'd bring King's work to life again over a decade later, appearing in an episode of the TV adaptation of the 2006 miniseries *Nightmares and Dreamscapes*.

Thomas hasn't stopped appearing on the small screen; throughout the 90s, he appeared on *Touched By An Angel* (1997), *The Practice* (1999), and other shows, including 1993's *Waltons Thanksgiving Family Reunion*. But one of his most memorable standouts was a 2001 episode of *Law and Order: SVU*, "Scourge."

Looking incredibly different from his other roles, Thomas plays Daniel Varney, a family man turned serial killer, given to fits of psychotic rage throughout the episode. Eventually, it's learned that Varney's insanity is caused by syphilis, and the justice system goes easy on him.

"What you do is you study a little bit about the symptoms of end-stage syphilis and put some of that physicality into the work," Thomas explains, "in terms of how you physically move and the speech patterns and how that particular disease affects the brain.

The rest of it is just internal work, internalizing the anguish that the character was in. You try not to see him as a killer and a psychopath, not to think of him as evil or a villain, but to understand his anguish."

It's devotion like that that has helped Thomas become one of the most successful performers to make the jump from young to adult star, as well as a top name on the unofficial "Hollywood's Best Character Actors" list.

"I consider myself a character actor because I never thought of myself as a tall, sexy, leading man type," Thomas says. "I always felt like the character was the most important thing. I like to consider myself a character actor, and I think that most actors do nowadays, because what they want to be seen to be doing, and what they want to do, is to enter as fully as possible into the life of the character. The long and the short of it is that you can say that a typical star is famous for being themselves on screen; a character actor becomes famous for immersing themselves in the part, rather than the star who appears as the star all the time."

But there's one person who's never really been a big fan of seeing Thomas in action, no matter the size of the screen.

"I'm not a particularly good judge of my work," he admits. "I went through a period when I didn't watch myself for years. For several years, I just wasn't interested in it. I watch myself kind of like other people watch horror movies: with my fingers over my eyes.

"I don't really enjoy watching myself very much. If I feel like I've done a particularly good job and not upset myself too badly, then I feel pretty good about it."

Beverly Todd

It wasn't hard for Beverly Todd to prepare to play a drug-addled mother in 2004's Best Picture; to an extent, she'd been preparing for the role for three decades.

Now don't get the wrong idea here – Todd wasn't a user herself, nor were any of her family members: not anything like that. It's just that, for a period in her life, she was around those who'd fallen into the deep trap that drug use can become.

Living in New York "about 30-some-odd years ago," the up-and-coming actress wanted her son to get a diverse education.

"New York was not the best place for public schools at the time," Todd remembers. "Every private school I took him to had no other black children and no black teachers. I wanted him to go to a school where he saw people like himself, to help him know that he was valuable."

So when Todd couldn't find such a school, she decided to make one, opening the private facility Sunshine Circle on the third floor of an office building.

A few doors down on the floor, the facility had a built-in "Scared Straight" program – a methadone clinic resided on the structure's base. Every day, Todd encountered women who'd thrown their lives away to drugs, and now were trying to get them back.

Beverly Todd's druggie mom helped cornerstone *Crash* all the way to 2004's Best Picture Oscar.

Decades later, she'd be asked to take on such a persona, playing a drug-using mother of two sons in *Crash*. Todd played the mother of a police detective (Don Cheadle) and a street hood (Larenz Tate), although viewers didn't find that the two were brothers until the plot twisted in at the end.

Recalling her time in the Sunshine Circle, Todd says, "I watched these women in the elevator, going to exchange one drug for another drug. I studied them. I studied their behavior and their posture, and the look of them."

For her audition, Todd not only took on the personas of these people, she actually headed to a thrift store and picked up some "appropriate" attire. When she got the role, director Paul Haggis – who'd win Oscars for both the film itself and his screenplay – asked her to show up in the same clothes she'd worn to the tryout.

A film as diverse – and a cast as loaded down – as Haggis's study of subtle bigotry in Los Angeles couldn't spend too much time on character development, which may be why it garnered only a single nomination for acting (Matt Dillion got a Supporting Actor nod for his portrayal of a pissed-off cop who remembers how to do what's right, just in time). The anger of Todd's character (not actually named in the credits) at her police officer son for his refusal to communicate with his estranged brother might not have a clear meaning for viewers that don't notice the table full of drug paraphernalia at her house.

"Unless people saw it, they didn't associate it with me being a druggie," Todd says. "At the time, *Crash* was a unique film, with different people going different ways and their lives intertwining, unbeknownst to them. It became a universal film with so many different situations that people could relate to."

For many in her line of work, fame can become a detriment. Once one's face gets too familiar to the public, he or she can be forced to sacrifice privacy for popularity, forced into seclusion by those wanting to meet, greet, photograph, interview, and everything else with the person. But that doesn't often happen to Todd — and she's just fine with it.

"When people see me, they know the roles that I played," she says, "but they may not know it was me doing it, because I don't look like the character. My role is to leave Beverly somewhere else and be the character I'm playing. In order to bring a character to life, I have to know the character and know as much about them as I can, to make it internal, so I'm not just playing the character — I become the character."

In Todd's career, she's taken on enough characteristics to drive a multiple-personality expert crazy. A sad, downtrodden woman who couldn't relate to her gay son in *Six Feet Under* (2002). The wife of a baseball legend in the 1981 TV film *Don't Look Back: The Story of Leroy 'Satchel' Paige*. Acting alongside Oscar winners Sidney Poitier, Whoopi Goldberg, and, a few times, Morgan Freeman.

And lest we forget one of her first big (quite the understatement there) roles, one that made her a part of television history: playing Fanta in an episode of the legendary 1977 miniseries *Roots*. Alex Haley's literary creation told the centuries-long story of slave Kunta Kinte and his family's move to America, and their ascension through time.

Since then, Todd's enjoyed steady work in television, with occasional forays onto the big screen; the frequent school speaker remarks that young people can often recite her lines from her work as Mrs. Levias in 1989's *Lean on Me*. Nearly two decades after appearing together in the inner-city school drama, she and Freeman would depict a much closer relationship.

In a role that some said should have snared her a Best Supporting Actress nomination, Todd played Virginia Chambers, the wife to Freeman's Carter in 2007's drama (with quite enough warm-hearted laughs) *The Bucket List*. Learning that they each have cancer, Carter and Edward Cole (Jack Nicholson) embark on a world trip to accomplish everything they've ever dreamed up, from skydiving to auto racing to biking across the Great Wall of China (a scene of Carter realizing his lifelong dream of winning big on *Jeopardy* was deleted, Todd says).

With her husband gone, Virginia tries to figure out if she did wrong, or what she'll do if he comes back (the couple's son was played by Freeman's real-life son Alonso, who'd played him as a youth in 1994's *Shawshank Redemption*).

However, once Carter returns, Virginia tosses her inhibitions to the wind, and shows the wild side that children like to pretend their parents don't have. Together in the bedroom, Virginia coyly asks her husband to sit and wait; there's a special surprise waiting. Stepping into an adjacent bathroom, she comes out in some sexy night-wear that turns this lady into an impromptu Victoria's Secret model.

"I had specifically asked for it to be nylon lining so you could see through it, but not really," Todd recalls. "It gave the illusion that my character purposely found that gown to be really sexy for that moment that we would be together again as man and wife. It was about the excitement of being with my husband again, so that I could touch him and hold him."

Finally, she shows us the strong, stoic side that spouses are forced to find when their longtime loved ones pass, as Carter dies during cancer surgery.

"I was a drama mama in that film because for most of the film," Todd says. "I was upset because my husband had gone off to have his last laughs with a stranger."

Musetta Vander

Throughout this book, and even this chapter, we've met quite a few performers who have taken diversity to a whole new level. But Musetta Vander goes even farther.

For this performer, it's not just about accents, voice tone, or facial expressions. Of course, all those things are important to Vander, but she doesn't seem satisfied with all that. Her top roles are known just as much, if not much MORE, for the physicality versatility. Dancing, brawling, weaponry at top speed... she's done it all and more.

Shortly after making her way to the Golden State from her native South Africa, Vander turned heads among tunes, showing up in music videos to the sounds of Tina Turner, Elton John, and dozens of others.

"Music videos only required me to show up and do what they asked for in the moment," she recalls. "You get hired because you fit the profile of what they are looking for. All you have to do is be yourself."

Vander helped launch the TV tomes of a certain bloodsucker-slaughtering, dropkicking lass in 1997. As *Buffy the Vampire Slayer* rolled onto the small screens, she showed up to put the movies on the Buffster's pal Xander on her way to taking him down, and then out as Ms. French – the alter ego of the ominous She-Mantis.

"All teachers make an impression on their students in some way or another," she jokes. "I just hoped that Natalie French would have that effect also. The role was extremely well written and it was hard to keep a straight face in some of the scenes, like the seduction scene with Xander."

Later that year, she took the first steps toward the new trademarks of her career – actually, it was more of a few high-kicks. Vander was the deliciously evil Queen Sindel in *Mortal Kombat: Annihilation*, playing the top female general of the evil emperor Shao Khan. In a trek to wreak havoc on the Earth, Khan, Sindel, and the rest of the Outworld's in-crowd take on a group of the planet's top warriors, including Sindel's daughter Kitana (Talisa Soto).

"Sindel was a larger than life character and powerful," explains Vander, less than four years older than Soto in real life. "I loved her wild streak and limitless boundaries. She'd been seduced by the dark side but was inherently good, which provided an opportunity to show both sides of her. I also looked forward to the opportunity to combine my dancing skills with martial arts."

After years of showing off her physical prowess on the action side, Musetta Vander (center) displayed some seriously seductive strength in 2000's *O Brother, Where Art Thou?*

Thrust into the role over a month into filming, Vander landed in London already in overdrive, determined to hit the ground fighting.

"Everyone had been training for three or four months," she says, "so I had to rely on my dance skills to pull me through. I received fight training a few days before we shot the action scene." The film ended with a high-class battle royal with possession of the planet on the line, as Sindel and Kitana went head to head and boot to boot.

"The great thing about *MKII* is that we traveled extensively," she says. "It was amazing! We worked in London, Thailand, and Jordan and got to experience different cultures and parts of the world in a very unique way. I love traveling and made the most of my downtime by exploring and experiencing the surroundings and local culture. We, the cast, got along great and are still friends to this day."

Then she sent Will Smith and Kevin Kline on the run as weapons guru Munitia (what a wonderful name for a lady gunner!) in 1998's *Wild Wild West*.

"Training started right away and I spent at least a month constantly training with all sorts of weapons," Vander recalls. "I remember my fingers being raw from continually spinning guns and learning how to load, cock, and fire practically every imaginable weapon. Some were really heavy. Seeing the special effects added is incredible as the detail and realism they add is just amazing. All we see is a green screen when shooting, and this really brings the movie to life."

Perhaps determined to throw down with just about every big name in Hollywood in every area imaginable, Vander headed back to ancient Greece – in character; in reality it was New Zealand – to take on another groundbreaker headsmashing honey, playing the lovely faced and dark-hearted Ilainus in a one-shot (with an arrow and spear!) deal on *Xena: Warrior Princess* (2000).

"I really looked forward to doing the show and getting to fight Xena," Vander says. "It was exciting to be part of such a popular show and also getting a chance to see New Zealand at the same time. Lucy (Lawless) and the rest of the cast were wonderful to work with and made the whole experience very memorable."

"The football player doesn't play the game differently because it's being shot on a video, film, or still camera," Vander explains of flipping back and forth from one broadcasting medium to another. "To me it's the same with acting. I just try to be as real as possible under imaginary circumstances. We're all human beings sharing similar experiences on the planet regardless of our looks, background or culture. Emotions run through everyone and that's what an actor reflects back to the audience on screen."

Taking a safe step away from the physical world, Vander made Robert Duvall the envy of quite a few young men, playing his trophy wife in 2005's *Kicking and Screaming*. John Turturro got a similar gift in *O Brother, Where Art Thou?* in 2000.

The Cohen Brothers film veteran is Pete Hogwallop, on the run from the law alongside a few brothers in crime, like George Clooney's Ulysses McGill. Trucking through the deep south, Pete suddenly finds his mind distracted by the most appealing of sounds, a tune that draws he and his colleagues not just off the road, but through the woods and into a nearby lake.

And this is just too good to be true; there's three caroling beauties, taking a break from washing their most intimate attire to entice and seduce the fellows with their song. Vander's the leader, casting a spell on Pete that doesn't quit until all three fellows are on the wrong side of consciousness.

"I would've accepted a role as a fly on the wall in any Cohen Brothers movie!" Vander exclaims. "I think they are genius filmmakers. I was called in as a dancer on *O Brother, Where Art Thou?* and auditioned in a hotel room near the beach. This was unusual in itself. We were given the lyrics to the siren song while waiting and asked to get familiar with them. Then we were called in three at a time and asked to lip-sync and dance to the music while pretending to be washing laundry and seducing a man. We rehearsed for a week in a studio in L.A. and then left for Jackson, Mississippi, where we shot on location. It was an incredible experience and I was thrilled to be part of it."

Jacob Vargas

Most middle-school age boys may not like to admit this, but just about the most important thing on their priority list is finding a way to attract the ladies. A boy like that may brag to all their pals about how all the girls are after him, but chances are, we wouldn't know what to say if one of them so much as made eye contact.

Perhaps that's why Jacob Vargas put that extra effort into getting down on the playgrounds in his youth. It would be the first step (or stutter step, if you will) toward becoming the envy of young men across America: getting to marry Jennifer Lopez – or at least pretending to.

"I got discovered breakdancing in the schoolyard by my manager," he recalls. "I had my own crew, doing events for neighborhood kids. (My manager) introduced me to an agent, who told me about an audition for *Diff'rent Strokes*. I was twelve years old; it was amazing. I knew at that point it was what I wanted to do for the rest of my life."

As the lady who evolved into J-Lo got her career rolling in the mid-90s, Vargas played her husband in the 1995 generational drama *My Family* (they played the youngest version of a married couple in a film that stretched over a 30-year epic). It wouldn't be the last time they'd share the screen.

After small parts alongside Denzel Washington in *Crimson Tide* and John Travolta in *Get Shorty* (both in 1995), Vargas grabbed the roll of Abie Quintanilla, brother to the title character in the 1997 biopic *Selena*, which lit the rocket that Lopez's career would become. An integral character in one of music's most tragic stories, Abie helped launch his little sister's career and went on to his own lyrical livelihood.

"I was a fan of Selena's before she passed," Vargas explains. "My brother was in the military, and he brought back CDs and videotapes of her concerts, so we'd sit around and admire her." Abie was one of Selena's top songwriters in the early parts of her career, which roared through Mexico like a brushfire and was knocking on the American border before her shocking murder.

"I really wanted the role of (Selena's husband) Chris originally," Vargas recalls. "Eventually, the director decided I wasn't, quote unquote, *hunky* enough for that role, so they offered me the role of the brother." Former Golden Gloves champ Jon Seda snared the husband role, but Vargas wasn't disappointed.

"I wanted to show Abie's growth as an artist," he recalls. "He really is a musical genius. The way he could come up with a beat and a song at the drop of a hat really showed to me. It was hard for him; he lost his sister and best friend and he had to get out of that and continue with his music." Abie, who'd later go by A.B. on the labels, became a part of the bands Kumbia Kings and Kumbia All-Starz.

Like Lopez, Vargas spent time with the Quintanilla family to prepare for his role.

"I was very fortunate that the family was open and involved with the film," he recalls. "I went to Corpus Christi and stayed with the family. We sat around, talked about the old days, and watched a lot of family movies. I became very close to (Abie) and the family, and I'm close to him to this day."

Still, when the cast, crew, and family got together to film the scene when Selena's stolen from them, there was no way to easily bridge the gap between performing and reality.

"That was probably the hardest scene that we had to do," Vargas recalls. "I don't think anyone was really prepared for it. When you have a script, it's there in words, but when you're there in a hospital, and you see the gurney, and everybody's in character, and it really just brings it home." Many of the singer's true family members were on set during the scene, and no one could stop the memories.

"Her father just broke down," Vargas says. "It was hard to watch. It was a fresh wound for everybody."

It was soon off to the Academy Awards for Vargas and his colleagues – a Screen Actors Guild cast victory for *Traffic* pushed the 2000 flick all the way to the top, as the film snared three Oscars and a nomination for Best Picture. Channeling the spirit of *Pulp Fiction* (1997) of the past and *Crash* (2004) of the future, the film tied together several stories of America's war on drugs and showed us exactly who fights on either side – and why. Alongside Benecio del Toro's Supporting Actor-winning work as drug-dealing Javier, Vargas was his partner Manolo.

Jacob Vargas landed on the wrong side of the law as a juvenile in *Ernest Goes to Camp* (1987) and a grown-up in 2000's *Traffic* (below, left as Manolo).

"I always try to read as much as I can about subject matter," Vargas recalls of getting ready, "and I read as many books as I could about Tijuana, border towns, police, and drug cartels. I immersed myself in that world. I watched a lot of Spanish television. The thing that was difficult was that the Spanish phrases we speak in the movie were the border town slang. That was hard."

He and a friend went down to Tijuana and spent time with police officers in a real-life fight with the narcotic knockers of the time and place.

"I picked up their slang," Vargas says. "It was so different than what's spoken in novels or police stations. It's a whole different language."

And he, like those who put the film together, saw the "bad guys" as more than just heartless villains.

"When I look at (Manolo)," he explains, "I don't approach it as a bad guy. Even if he is the heavy antagonist, it's not in their heart for me that they are bad. These people are living their lives with the hand that they've been dealt. This guy was a family man, trying to provide for a better life for his wife, and the choices he made came from that, to help his family, and unfortunately, it backfired."

It was a different kind of war and reality for 2005's *Jarhead*, the story of a young man (Jake Gyllenhaal's Anthony Swofford) who took his audience, and his co-stars, inside the Persian Gulf War that captivated America in the early 1990s. Playing Swofford's trench associate Juan, Vargas turned towards his family to prepare.

"I had two brothers who were former marines, so I had a certain responsibility to make this as real as possible," he says. "*Jarhead* was an amazing experience. It took us a week to read through the script, page by page, line by line." He and the rest of the cast, including Jamie Foxx, fresh off a pair of Oscar nominations in 2004, spent time with a sergeant major to walk them through the basics of military jargon.

"He explained the different between a squad and a platoon," Vargas says. "He told about the different types of guns, such as the velocity of the rounds. He had us sit around and create a backstory for our characters. This was in 1991, and we had to think about what our character would do in that area. He wanted us to create tapes of music our character would listen to." In a makeshift boot camp, the cast ran through drills, carried packs, learned how to fight in and out of holes and clean out weapons.

Going back and forth between becoming fictional and real people can be tough, he continues. It's a choice between choosing your own creational direction for a fictional person and hoping it's the right one, and breaking through the limits of simple impersonation in realism.

"Playing a fictional character," he explains, "there is the freedom to do whatever you want with this guy. You have to have a blank canvas, which in a way is stimulating. You have to create and find everything.

"But when you're playing a real person, you have a responsibility to play the character as strongly as you can. It's a different kind of research. You try to find as much information; did they have some kind of vice? What about them will help you perform them as a character? In the end, you're not trying to do a caricature of this person, and you're not trying to mimic somebody. You just get the essence of this person and bring some of your essence into this character, and trust what you're doing." Vargas hit the inspirational side of reality in 2015's *The 33*, playing Edison Pena, one of the title character miners, trapped for sixty-nine days under Chilean ground before being rescued in October 2010.

Of course, we can't ignore the role that put Vargas on the acting map, the same one that helped a certain lovable savant janitor switch from TV success to the big screen.

"As a young actor, I was just hungry," he remembers of his role as a juvenile delinquent who comes to care (as did most people around Ernest Powertools Worrell) in 1987's *Ernest Goes to Camp*, "so I would have auditioned for anything. For the role of a tree, I would. I didn't care what it was, whatever, I'd audition for it. First of all, I didn't know what I was doing. I'd just been discovered, so I would have auditioned for anything. They wanted a delinquent with some heart, and I figured, 'Hey, that's me!'"

On a jaunt to the camp that Ernest's just looking for work at, Vargas and his pals, like most who met the unlucky schlub, take pleasure in tormenting him before Ernest's kindness wins the day. And the deviance the kids showed on the screen sometimes jumped off into reality, Vargas jokingly recalls.

"We had a blast, but we were terrible kids!" he laughs. "We just caused mayhem, almost got kicked out of our hotel room. We went to the mall, bought a bunch of ninja stars and nunchucks, and practiced in our hotel room. We messed up the wall, and another actor almost burned the room down, playing with matches and hair spray. We were just thugs!"

Still, he and his friends got to learn from both sides of the good-evil acting equation in the flick. On the screen, Jim Varney's Ernest and former football champ Lyle Alzado's evil construction foreman were the worst of enemies. But each helped Vargas and his acting apprentices get started.

"Jim Varney would invite us into his room," Vargas says, "and he had this hi-fi audio equipment. He played Beethoven, Bach; we picked up different sounds. I picked up an appreciation for classical music from Jim Varney. Then we'd walk over to Lyle Alzado's room, and he had a full-on gym in his room, and he'd ask us if we wanted to lift some weights. It was great. It was a great introduction to Hollywood for a kid. He showed us his Super Bowl ring. Everybody on that set was great."

Even though his acting career got started doing schoolyard hijinks, Vargas still can't help but wish he'd spent a bit more time inside. It's why he's more of a student of acting than back in history and geometry classes.

"I remember going to acting classes in high school drama," he remembers, "but I was a kid and I wanted to have a good time, and I wish I would have learned the techniques and all of that. I wish I would have been more disciplined in that. I read as much as I can on the subject that I'm doing, on the character. I'm always reading a book on acting. You never stop learning."

Darlene Vogel

A few years ago, in the Santa Monica neck of Los Angeles woods, a cop noticed a car going a bit faster than speeding limits of the area allowed. Flashing his lights, he pulled up behind the driver, who hauled off to the side of the road.

Strolling up beside the driver, the cop prepared to explain the rules of the road to the driver. Then the lady behind the wheel showed her true identity, and the officer couldn't believe it.

This was Chris Kelly, who had trained with the police department in the past. The department had shown her how to arrest those who had been harming others. They had been teaching her the ins and outs of everyday police life, and it was always important to take care of everyone, especially those who had been in the game themselves.

The officer couldn't believe what was being seen, and quickly strolled back to the patrol car. After all, cops don't ticket their own, right? Well, maybe.

In the car, Darlene Vogel thanked her lucky acting stars. Four years of being Kelly on the California streets had paid off – and kept her from paying out.

Of course, her first big role would be on the other side of the law. After stepping before a different type of camera for a brief modeling career, Vogel played Spike, the sole female representative of *Back to the Future* villain Griff's (every single relation to Biff, of course!) gang in the film's first sequel in 1989, out to bully every generation of Marty McFly.

"They didn't tell us what the audition was for or anything," Vogel says of her *BTTF2* tryout. "I went in, and they paired me up with two other guys. We did improv, but we still didn't know. But even when we got it, they said it was going to be a two-week job." They ended up staying in character for the next four months.

She may have played a lovely lawbreaker in *Back to the Future 2* (1989), but Darlene Vogel had a much longer turn as a cop on *Pacific Blue* (1996).

Hey, Urban Legend Debunking Alert! You know those hoverboards that Biff's gang and McFly were soaring around on through the year 2015? Though America's youths of 1989 were certainly on a hot hope streak for the time being, those things weren't real then, and never were – contrary to hot gossip, they *weren't* banned because a kid went over water, fell off, and drowned!

"We had two classes, on a ranch, with the hoverboards," she remembers, "being strung up on harnesses and piano wires, up in the air and twirling, which would be a blast. We would stand on the hoverboards for hours, singing songs. We were there from 6 a.m. in the morning until 6 p.m. at night. It just kept lasting and lasting. They said, 'Can we have you back next week and next week and next week?' and we said sure. Basically, it was a lot of spinning around and waiting – with big budget movies, you can do a lot of that."

Of course, there was still a character to develop, and villains in sci-fi comedy can't be too evil or scary; Thomas Wilson made Biff (and Griff, Mad Dog, and every other Tannen he became in all three of the films) evil without actually being too fearsome or hateful, except for his slapping of Marty's mom Lorraine in *BTF2*. Vogel – along with Billy Zane, who played Match, another member of the goon squad – tried to make herself intimidating, but not quite sinister.

"All we had to do was be these tough characters," she says. "They gave me a red contact in my eye: I have one eye half brown, half blue, so they wanted me to have two completely different eyes."

Over the next few years, Vogel's career switched mainly to the small screen, though millions of Universal Studios visitors saw her every year as the hostess on the *Back to the Future* ride. She showed up on *Coach* (1993), *Boy Meets World* (1994), *Northern Exposure* (1994), and several other shows.

Then, in 1996, came a lady named Kelly.

Vogel's friend Paula Trickey called to tell her that Trickey had just snared a role on the USA network's newest show, a series about beautiful cops cycling up and down the Santa Monica beach district.

Trickey said that the producers were looking for a tough blonde to pedal alongside her. Producers had checked out Vogel's failed pilot *Misery Loves Company* and seen what they were looking for. A longtime avid cyclist, Kelly headed for the tryout.

"Went I went in to read," she says, "the producer said, 'You are the prototype for this character.' (Kelly) was very much geared to me, very tough, very independent. I grew up fighting with my brother for my entire life, so I could do all the fight scenes."

But there's a pretty thick line between being a member of the gangs that break the law and the officers that enforce it – and these weren't the type of brawls that Spike might have gotten into off-screen. Vogel and Trickey rode along with the Santa Monica police department in both the cars and the bikes. They were taught how to carry and fire off guns.

"The writers all wrote it around the characters we actually were in life," Vogel recalls. "But the preparation was in the physicality. The one thing I couldn't do was handcuff anybody. It would take me forever. If Chris got the handcuffs, the camera would go off of me, and the camera would focus in on someone else. Someone else's hands were used in the closeups."

Over the next few years, future *Shield* (2002) star Walton Goggins, up-and-coming Terminatrix Kristanna Loken, and B-movie princess Shannon Tweed, among others, showed up to hang out with the girls in blue. Kelly married fellow officer T.C. Callaway (Jim Davidson) in the fourth season opener, and the show made it one past the 100-episode mark before it ended in April 2000.

As just about any longtime actor will attest, acting is the most unpredictable of employment choices in all kinds of ways. Ever watched a film or a TV show, and thought to yourself, "Good grilled cheese, how did they get someone to invest their hard-earned money in *that*?"? On the inside, the opposite rules apply. Tons of scripts come into studios every day, and only a fraction of them will get anywhere near the cameras. An even smaller fraction will be on the air for half a season. All too often, screenwriters will work forever on a script that gets turned down everywhere for years. Actors will be totally sure that the pilot they're making will be the next big hit in TV, only to be told that it's not good enough. Even those that get made and approved are often forced into metamorphosis before they get anywhere, as characters, storylines, directors, producers, and the rest are rearranged in an effort to catch and carry the attention of audiences. Vogel's been there, and done that (and that, and that, and that, and probably a few more things).

Remember *Misery Loves Company*? It wasn't her only pilot that didn't move to a sophomore show. Vogel worked with the writers from the 2001's Best Picture-winning *Beautiful Mind* on *The Cure*, a 2007 shot that attempted to snare the audiences that *E.R.* and other medical dramas soon left behind. It didn't fly. She appeared with Christian Slater in Jerry Bruckheimer's crime drama *The Forgotten* in 2009, but that show also stopped soon.

But also with anyone who ever wanted to make a mark in entertainment, Vogel knows that giving up can never be the answer.

"You can work really hard on these projects, really hard, get excited, and then they never make it to the screen," she says. "The first script that you get will be nothing like the last script that gets put on TV. (But) if it's something you want to do, then you have to take classes, you have to do plays in school, and just really persevere. If you think you're good, you really have to work at it. You have to have some kind of a niche. You have to work for anything in this world."

Special Spotlight: Acting Without Sound

Decades ago, the hearing impaired weren't taken seriously at all in the performing world. *Playing* a deaf character is something that performers would go to the mat to try; loads of young women acted their hearts out to become Helen Keller when *The Miracle Worker* came to the screen in 1961, and Patty Duke snared an Oscar for the role. Alan Arkin's work in *The Heart is a Lonely Hunter* was one of 1968's most acclaimed performances.

Still, actually *casting* a deaf performer? That's still considered an awfully big risk, although Marlee Matlin undoubtedly broke some serious ground with her 1986 Oscar, and others are making waves as well. Here's hoping they continue to do so.

On the outside looking in, we might look at the deaf acting community and see obstacles. Problems. An extra hurdle, an unavoidable one, lifted straight up before those looking to make it in a business that's just about impossible for *anyone*, let alone for people who, right away we assume, find even their possibilities extremely limited.

That's a matter of opinion. Let's look a bit deeper. Let's hear from those who are in the business, or even the battle, if one wants to put it so. We might be a bit surprised.

Linda Bove

To many in the deaf acting community, a lack of hearing isn't considered a handicap. It's not an impairment. It shouldn't even really be considered a problem.

It's more along the lines of a challenge, just one more that needs facing on the already-difficult road to acting stardom.

"Deafness doesn't identify who I am," Linda Bove insists. "It's not a label. I am me. I am a person, just as any actor is, and the one exception is that I have to work a little bit harder to help increase my credibility and the credibility of the project or the program, the production."

For about 40 years, she's been helping a certain production maintain its credibility for generations of America's youths, and even its youths at heart.

"In the late 60s," Bove recalls, "the buzzword was 'multi-cultural,' a new word that people were being introduced to." A new show was helping the public learn the meaning of the term, along with a few fun lessons about lessons and numbers.

Linda Bove and some of her *Sesame Street* neighbors took
their story from TV to theaters in 1985's *Follow That Bird*.

"For the time, it was so innovative," Bove says of *Sesame Street*'s beginnings; it came out in 1969; she arrived two years later. "It was the open-mindedness of the people involved. It was a daring process, and lucky enough, I was involved." She became the first deaf regular character on an American television program.

"Here I was, a deaf person, and I thought of what I could contribute to the show, and how I could enhance the show. They were open to working with me, and there was open dialogue between the writers and myself. They were interested in my way of life, and I thought it was important for children to watch this, to learn to become tolerant of people with differences."

Over the first few years of the show, *Street* visitors met cast members in wheelchairs. They learned what it means to live as a blind person. Many had their first encounters with those afflicted with Down's Syndrome, and eventually autism.

"All sorts of people were included," Bove says, "and that impressed me with the ability to represent an open-minded approach. (Eventually) we all agreed that the concept (of the show) was for kids age two, three, four, or five, and we realized that there needed to be something more concrete for my character than an actor." She took over the street's library, just down the street from Mr. Hooper's grocery store and Big Bird's nest.

"That was quite cool, because there was a deaf person running the library. It taught the value of books and the value of reading to both hearing and deaf children. Kids needed to learn the enjoyment of books. When I became the librarian, the name stayed the same, because people already knew me. I was 'Linda, the girl that signed.'"

Over the next few years, hundreds of children learned about the wonders of reading and got a few special sign language lessons along the way. They learned about how deaf people see and interact with the world and those around them, even without sound. *Sesame Street*'s writers and researchers are known as some of the most thorough in television history, and Bove worked with them to develop fresh ideas about helping others feel at ease around the deaf population, often through friendly education with bits of humor thrown in.

"The Muppets would come to my (home) door and try to work with the doorbell, not realizing that when they pushed the doorbell, lights flashed to let me know someone was there," Bove says. "When I opened the door and the lights flashed, they thought it was a Christmas event. There were many unique instances that evolved in a natural way."

Once when a deaf friend came to visit Linda, the two couldn't communicate without stopping to put down their suitcases until Linda's friend Bob (Bob McGrath) stepped in to carry everything so everyone could sign freely. Bove even got the chance to portray others who, while not deaf, made their own marks in the entertainment world without their voices, becoming silent comedy legends Charlie Chaplin and Harpo Marx in street skits.

McGrath, who underwent a crash course in sign language at New York University to relate to his colleague, called "Christmas Eve on Sesame Street" one of his personal favorites. A devious Oscar sends

Big Bird to the roof to wait for Santa, scaring the grownups into searching for him, and eventually getting Oscar to grow a heart and help out. Grover raps with small children to find out where Santa really comes from. Bob teaches a group of children the song "Keep Christmas With You," and Linda shows them how to do it in sign language. In a heartfelt parody of the legendary short story "Gift of the Magi," Bert and Ernie turn in their prized possessions to buy things for each other, only to have Mr. Hooper return them as gifts. The Dec. 1978 episode, which continued to air long afterward, brought the show one of its 100-plus Emmy awards.

But it wasn't only the children who received a special type of education – the show opened the doors for millions of adult viewers who might never have interacted with the deaf community themselves. In 1985, the lessons hit the big screen, as the show's cast joined up for the full-length cinema production of *Follow That Bird*, the story of the group's plight to find Big Bird as he strolled nonchalantly across the country, much like the overgrown child he personified.

"The movie was loads of fun, and I felt very much a part of the group," Bove says. "We were looking for Big Bird, and all trying to help each other. It felt very normal.

"There are so many memories that can show the diversity and the different sides of myself within that show. I had an opportunity to work at the library at the show and make a living from that, and then I had what my life at home was like. I was able to demonstrate a lot of my different skills and show that deafness had no limitations for me as a member of the neighborhood."

Nor should it for anyone else looking to find their own acting niche, she continues.

"I don't use the word 'hearing-impairment,'" Bove says. "For myself, I use the word 'deaf.' That means that I can't hear, but it doesn't mean that I can't do other things. I can be assertive in my search for work. I don't feel that the deafness should interfere with my work or my career." Along with performing on stage productions of *Children of a Lesser God*, Bove had a small role alongside Matlin's Oscar-winning work in the 1986 film version, and stayed with the *Street* group until 2003.

In 1991, she started spreading such a message to the rest of the deaf community's performers; Bove and her husband Ed Waterstreet, also deaf, founded Deaf West Theatre, the west coast's first sign language-based professional theater. The North Hollywood establishment has become a national touring company, putting on shows across the country and bringing home dozens of awards along the way.

"Deaf West is one of the highlights of my career," says Bove. "We are showing that our theater is competitive with any other theater in terms of quality and production, and acting talent and recruitment of deaf people."

Deanne Bray

As we discussed a few pages ago, playing a deaf character can be a goldmine of acclaim for performers. Sadly, it's still too rare to cast one of the non-hearing persuasion.

However, rare doesn't mean never: a year after playing a doctor on a 2001 episode of *CSI*, Deanne Bray learned that the story of one of the deaf community's most beloved members was being adapted to the small screen.

After dancing with the group Prism West all over Southern California, Bray had felt the chomp of the acting bug on television, along with Bove's DeafWest Theatre. Now she was getting a chance at a small-screen biopic of sorts, another of the most prized treks in the acting world.

After losing her own hearing as a child, Sue Thomas became one of the first hearing-impaired employees of the FBI, and spent nearly four years working in undercover surveillance, mainly through lip-reading. In 2002, the story of her life, *Sue Thomas F.B. Eye* hit the TV screens, and Bray, herself born deaf, took the lead.

Sue Thomas (right) instructs Deanne Bray on portraying her during
Sue Thomas: F.B. Eye (2002-2005).

"I met the real Sue Thomas and asked her many questions," Bray recalls. "I watched how she interacts with hearing people. I studied her facial expressions when she read lips and in how she reacts to people she interacts with."

Like Thomas, Bray's deafness brought her some tough classroom times as a youngster, something that viewers saw early on in the series.

"Some scenes of what happened to Sue Thomas when she was a little girl in the first episode reached out to me," Bray says, "as part of it was my story as well, as (for) much as many of the other deaf and hard of hearing individuals who went to mainstreamed schools and are also from hearing families. There were many scenes in the first episode that were true."

As she got ready to become a makeshift FBI agent, Bray visited the FBI building in Washington, DC, where Thomas had work. She spent time with agents at the FBI building in Los Angeles, and took part in a shooting drill that helps keep agents sharp behind the trigger.

While some of the show might have been manipulated for dramatic purposes – unlike the real Thomas, the lady Bray played had a romantic relationship with a fellow agent, for example – it gave many in the hearing-imparied performance community their own special chances, Bray says.

"Other episodes or the show did well by hiring many deaf and hard-of-hearing characters to be a part of the show. The writers developed many characters for deaf performers, which I felt extremely proud of. There was a range of a four-year-old girl to a 96-year-old deaf woman in the show! There were about 100-plus different deaf/hard-of-hearing actors who worked on the show." Thomas cameoed on a May 2003 episode, chatting with her own portrayer.

After the show's run ended in 2005, Bray appeared on *Law and Order* (2007), *Curb Your Enthusiasm* (2007), and *The L Word* (2007-8) before snaring a recurring role on *Heroes* in 2009.

"Nowadays, there are more professional writers writing roles for deaf and hard-of-hearing actors," she says. "Hollywood is opening up their minds about deaf characters and giving equal access to the deaf and hard-of-hearing's needs in facilitating communication, such as making sure they look at the actors with eye contact and/or providing certified (American Sign Language) interpreters if needed."

Anthony Natale

As he watched the final product of *Mr. Holland's Opus* (1995), Anthony Natale almost found it biographical.

Like his character Cole, the son of Glen and Alexis Holland (Richard Dreyfuss and Glenne Headley), Natale was inexplicably born deaf. Like Cole, Natale had an overly difficult time adjusting to a world without sound – and music wouldn't be the only problem he'd face. But fortunately, like Cole, it was a tuning he'd finally perform – and use the sounds of others to help him along the way.

"I cried during parts of it," Natale said of the film. "I experienced a lot of the similar things that the character did."

"I saw myself in the character," said Natale, who played Cole as an adult in the films (Nicholas Renner and Joseph Anderson – himself afflicted with a hearing problem – performed Cole's childhood and teenage years). "He's similar to my personality." Like Cole, Natale was born into a musical background, and still considers himself quite the Police fan. After getting his start in the theatrical department of his Ohio boarding school for the deaf, Natale spent some time working in dance theater as well.

Then his first shot at the big screen came calling.

"I was excited when I had the opportunity to play for a bigger production," Natale said. "I've always been a big fan of Richard Dreyfuss. He has a big theatrical background, so I felt that there was a kinship there."

Pretty soon, he'd feel the same way about his character.

"I was able to identify emotionally with the character," Natale said. "I identified with the transformation of the character. I used my own personal experience a lot as well, because it really reached home with me. I come from a large Italian family, so I had to learn Italian and English in sign language. It was even more difficult for me to communicate and fit in."

Just as the Hollands do for the first three-fourths of the film (Dreyfuss was Oscar nominated), Natale's family had a tough time learning an unspoken language.

Anthony Natale (right, here finding love with Andrea Farrell in 1996's *Jerry Maguire*) has spoken for the deaf on screens large and small for decades.

"It was harder for my parents to learn English and sign language too," he said. "When we sat around at dinner, I felt left out, but that's normal for deaf kids who have trouble keeping up with a conversation. I found myself frustrated with the language."

That's another reason why Natale could see himself in the scenes where a frustrated young Cole throws a temper tantrum over a kitchen dispute, or fiercely explains to his father why John Lennon's death meant just as much to those who couldn't hear his voice.

"Growing up, with my experience at different age levels," Natale said, "the first few years, I remember being very shy. I didn't have the confidence that I have now, but as I grew, I realized that I would be able to give ideas and be more creative. The experiences that I've had now, I enjoy having more input into the changes in the writing." His 2002 role in the television show *Any Day Now*, he says, wasn't originally supposed to be for a deaf person, but he convinced the producers to change the role. 2011's *Switched at Birth* made quite a bit of history for being the first mainstream show with deaf regular characters, with Katie Leclerc, herself hard of hearing, playing a lady who finds her world flipped when she and her family find she was mixed up with another gal during infancy, causing the groups to raise kids they hadn't birthed before everyone moves in together. Matlin, Natale, Bray, and others from the deaf public have appeared on the show.

When Michael Jackson kicked off his final concert tour, his representatives asked Natale to teach sign language to dancers and choreographers performing the song "Will You Be There." After Jackson's untimely death in June 2009, Natale was invited to his memorial service, where he saw the performers utilizing his teachings to the song.

"I was deeply touched," he says, "and of course I cried. It was emotional. It touched everyone's heart."

One of his other big acting roles was quite a bit shorter – but it would be seen by a larger audience, and require quite a bit of preparation on his own.

As Jerry Maguire and Dorothy Boyd (Tom Cruise and Renee Zellweger, for the three or four people that didn't see *Jerry Maguire* in 1996), still in employee-employer mode, wait in an elevator, a hearing-impaired couple comes in.

Beaming down at his shorter mate, the man makes a set of gestures to his partner. There's no closed-captioning, so the uneducated in sign language (like Jerry) might not know what he's telling her – although his lady's reciprocation of a romantic kiss gives us a pretty good idea.

Fortunately, Dorothy's to the rescue.

"My favorite aunt is hearing-impaired," she explains to Jerry and millions of viewers. "He just said, 'You complete me.'"

For his one-scene performance, Natale didn't even have a name. But little does anyone – in the film or the audience – know that his line will become the one that ties Jerry and Dorothy together in every sense of the word in the finale.

And for Natale, it required its own preparation (Andrea Farrell, his "scene-mate," is also deaf; *7th Heaven* viewers saw her play Heather for a few recurring appearances during the show's 1996-2007 run).

"The language was important," he said. "I had to find the translation in American Sign Language. It was only three words, but I needed to find them in ASL. I didn't want to use the English word order, because the concept wouldn't have been the same to deaf people. It required a lot of transitions to make things match, that the concept was created accurately. There were five signs to convey that very short thought."

In sign language, the word "complete," is often signed as "finish." Therefore, if Natale had done the literal translation of "You complete me," in sign language, deaf people would probably have seen, "You're finished with me," which conveys QUITE a different message.

"In English, you say the word that you mean, but there's a specific connotation around the word," he explained. "It doesn't always express the full meaning of the English word if you just use one sign. You have to find the right meaning for the English concept."

Chapter Five:

OK, So We're Famous – Now What?

Many people believe that success is the result of 'lucky breaks.'
There may be something to that, but if you depend on luck you will almost
certainly be disappointed. The only 'break' anyone can afford is to rely on a self-
made 'break.' These come through the application of persistence. The starting
point is definiteness of purpose."   ~ Hill

You've made it! You've finally reached the top of the acting world! You're a box-office smash, a sensation. Your picture's in the magazines, you've got gorgeous dates on your arm, you're at the highest demand.

So where do you go from here? Well, here's a few pointers to keep you at the top of your game, and the acting world:

a.   Keep branching out — and don't worry!

For an actor or actress, diversity is a magic word.

It would be wrong to say that comedy and horror are the easiest films to perform in, but they're usually where big-time actors get started. But there's a time and a place to change our roles, if only temporarily, and show our talent in other areas. Many feared that Kristin Wiig might have acted herself into a comedy corner even after years of being one of *Saturday Night Live*'s brightest lights – even with the screenplay Oscar nomination she received (and acting nom she *should* have gotten) for 2011's *Bridesmaids*. Then she walked into sci-fi with *The Martian* in 2015 and almost won an Academy Award. That laid her diversity doubters straight down. After years of comedy on the small screen, Mila Kunis shot to dramatic success with *Black Swan* (2010). Jim Carrey may have let his rubber face do the talking and expressing with *Ace Ventura* (1994), but he eventually went elsewhere, and I'll go right back on record as saying that his 1999 Academy Award snub for *Man on the Moon* was one of the biggest Hollywood disgraces of the 1990s.

The point is that it's always better to try and fail than to never try. And remember how early we talked about how rejection isn't something to fear? Same thing applies here.

In acting, as with any other field, you can't please everyone. Sooner or later, everyone gets a bad review, makes a film that doesn't get critical acclaim or box-office success. But one wrong step doesn't doom a career, or even hurt it, too much. Remember, you may get a bad review or your film might have a bad opening – you may even see a harsh headline about yourself in a tabloid, though some consider that a rite of passage – but things like this are the epitome of "here today, gone tomorrow." *Showgirls* (1995) became Hollywood's personal soccer ball, but just about everyone in it is still around. John Travolta and Forest Whitaker recovered from *Battlefield Earth* (2000), Travolta with *Wild Hogs* (2007) and *Bolt* (2008), and Whitaker with an Oscar. It took Kevin Costner making *Waterworld* (1995) and *The Postman* (1997) to learn that the post-apocalyptic genre is a toughie, but he did, and he's still going strong. George Clooney came back after *Batman and Robin* (1997) to win an Oscar; Sandra Bullock recovered from *Speed 2* (1997) to grab her own statuette.

If you make enough movies, enough appearances, you'll eventually hit on one the critics use for target practice and doesn't quite get back to its own financial bottom line. The crowds may not always come and the critics won't always be nice – bad reviews get more feedback than good ones! – but new roles, new tasks, new quests are always there for the acting out and on.

The acting public and the people who write about it have notoriously short memories. Something's always happening. Scandals, affairs, rehab stints, it's all there for the writing about. What's new and innovative to talk about in the morning might be old news by lunchtime, or at least dinner. Unfortunately, that means that a lot of good is forgotten, but the bad is forgotten as well.

Your film was a bust? Big deal. Next week or sometime soon, someone else will make another bad film, and you'll be in the forgotten past and free to move toward the welcoming future. If people tell you that your career is kaput, just keep asking until you find someone with a slightly brighter attitude.

Making my way to and occasionally through the inside of the acting world, I learned of a job that's never particularly easy, at least to most. Acting is an escape from reality. It's a chance to become someone, or something else. It can be one of the most frustrating jobs in the world, and those obsessed with making it rarely get there; those that dream of it are the ones that do.

In order to make it in the acting world, we rarely know which path to take. In pro sports, we have the minor leagues, the major leagues, even the Hall of Fame. Acting doesn't have that.

We've heard a lot, and I read even more, about the big performers who were true deviants, who played by their own rules and didn't follow anyone's lead. But while that makes for a cool story to write just to sell a few more books and garner a few more readers, it's the exception to the rule.

As with any success, sometimes we must walk a fine line between society's rules, and our own. In these pages, we've learned about the non-conformists and the conformists, but the majority of those who made it in the acting world knew when to say enough was enough, and when to say nothing at all. Sometimes it's best to get in line, sometimes it's best to step out, but sometimes it's best to spend our time half in and half out, so the ones behind can glance up and see us and those far ahead can look back and know who's following.

"You'd drive yourself crazy trying to please everyone else," says Tina Majorino, who's stolen scenes as both a child (1995's *Waterworld*) and an adult (2004's *Napoleon Dynamite*). "In this business, people always have something to say about what you're doing. Sometimes it's positive, sometimes it's negative. In the end, you just can't give a shit. You've gotta go with your gut and do what's right for you, you know?"

Do you know now?

b.   Make yourself accessible – to an extent

Throughout this book, you've met a multitude of people who represent the finest in Hollywood. Why? Because they realize that it's the fans that keep actors visible. It's the people who buy the tickets and write the reviews who keep a career going. Talent is important and hard work is a necessity, but it's always important to keep yourself open and visible not just as a performer, but as a person as well.

That's not to say that we should invite the paparazzi into our homes every day or jam our children in front of the cameras. That's an extreme that we don't need to go to. But once in a while, it's good to show your face in front of the cameras. Hang out at a charity benefit. Go volunteer at the Special Olympics. Do an interview with a small-time newspaper or budding author. Just do little things here and there to let people know that you appreciate your good fortune.

The WORST thing to do is go to the negative side of accessibility, meaning to say something like, "I DON'T do interviews, no matter with whom! I DON'T make appearances. I'll NEVER do things like that!"

With that attitude, eventually, you're going to run into trouble. Eventually, you're going to rub the wrong person the wrong way. Soon enough, you're going to get a bad reputation with someone, someone who can hurt your career.

That's not to say that we should fulfill every request, do every interview, answer every piece of fan mail. That's neither possible nor expected. But an interview here, a handshake there, a charity donation somewhere, and an autographed picture somewhere else, that's enough to keep the public happy. It's enough to show a performer's obligation to his or her fans. It's enough to make them like us not only as the people they see on the screen, but the people they meet in public as well.

c.   Stay out of trouble!

For the love of God, PLEASE stay out of the problems in the world. I can't stress this one enough. When you're a public figure, you're wide open to the self-righteous, holier-than-thou folks who just love to point out the flawless in the well-known. Actors, like any other public figures, are held to a higher standard than the not-as-well-known, because their faults can instantly become front page or top headline web site news.

All too quickly, in our ludicrously image-obsessed culture, it doesn't take much to do serious damage to a career. Tons of people in Hollywood have the mindset of "Oh, that person might be looked down on by others, so I *can't* be seen with them." This doesn't necessarily mean that you're doing anything illegal or immoral, just something that others might get and take the chance to take a shot at someone who already is where they'd kill to be.

Is that fair? Of course not. But it's the way life is, and always will be as long as people go for fame and fortune. Many people get their joys out of bringing others down, and that's just something that famous people have to deal with. People forget that famous people are human too, and turning on the television or seeing the front page of a tabloid, being humiliated and badmouthed in front of a nation, has just as much of an effect on them as anyone else.

So how do we deal with this? Well, making ourselves accessible – to an extent, at least – as we discussed in the previous step, can help; media folk are less likely to badmouth those they like on a personal level, and that tend to give them something to work with in their stories.

Also, for the first few years of your acting career, it might be a good idea to lead a sheltered life. Don't go to clubs, don't spend too much time shopping or dining out, and, if you're married, try not to get caught in public even hanging out with friends of the opposite sex. Sorry, but that's just how it works for a while. It might get you fans and win popularity contests, but fans aren't casting films, and polls don't always translate into paychecks.

If you are out in public, be with your spouses, children, pets, or even your parents – the tabloids LOVE the mama's boys and girls (ask Justin Timberlake about that one)! Live as ordinary a life as you can; the media gets bored fast writing about normalcy.

The media tends to go after the new blood in Hollywood, people whose star has just begun to shine. When you've been around for a while, they're more likely to leave you alone, unless you put yourself in the public eye from the start, the mistake that made Britney Spears, Lindsay Lohan, and so many like them unfair and overused targets of the press.

There's no real secret to maintaining a standard life while balancing the pressures of public figure-hood. It's better to look at those that have managed to do so, like Denzel Washington, who has been one of America's most recognized faces for decades, yet has been married for over a quarter century and has managed to keep his name and visage out of the tabloids. But as much as the papers get accused of taking things out of context and blowing them out of proportion like a tornado, they can't exaggerate what doesn't exist, and the less you give them to play with, the better.

Epilogue

asketball Hall of Famer Isiah Thomas once compared the chances of becoming a star in his profession to walking through the jungle and not getting bitten by a mosquito. To an actor looking to be the next A-plus-lister, the odds might be even higher.

The March 2012 merger of the Screen Actors Guild and American Federation of Television and Radio Artists into a single labor union left about 160,000 actors on the books — and out of that, "only about fifty might be considered stars," says coach Clay Banks. "The average income that SAG members earn from acting — less than $5,000 a year — is low because employment is sporadic."

Life's never going to be easy for an aspiring actor, searching for a break that's only going to come once in every 33,333 tries. Sometimes our own worst enemy is the person we see in the mirror. Some actors' skin isn't tough enough to withstand the pounding that critics and even fans seem to enjoy laying on it. A person with several box-office smashes can hit a dud once in a while, and there's always going to be those that wonder at high volume whether one bad film is enough to wreck a career (history says it's not).

"There's three things that you must accept as the downside (of acting)," explains coach Eric Stone. "You must be willing to live in repetitive fear of, and experiencing of, humiliation for the rest of your life. When you walk into an audition, when you make a movie, when it's all on the line, there's a world that loves to humiliate you. That fear can cripple you.

"The second thing is the experience of being rejected. You better be ready for it. You can take as many iron pills as you want. You can pray to Allah, you can do whatever. But you are going to live a life of being rejected, and with the fear of being rejected. That fear of being rejected is a cancer of the creative soul.

"The last thing is the fear of being ignored. It is painful to go to a place, and everyone's swirling around to make a movie, or to celebrate a movie, and you look like the guy who's holding the hors' de ouvers. You go, 'I came from Smalltown, USA, and I was King of the Campus, and I was hot stuff.' But when you come to Hollywood, someone's personal assistant tells you to step outside. It's a lonely world. Those are the three poisons to watch out for."

But every problem has a solution. Every question has an answer. And every dream can be realized, one way or another. Sometimes we have to walk through hell to get to heaven, and there's a great deal that actors (at any stage of their career) can do to be ready for the journey before we take the first step, Banks continues.

"The anecdote is to work, work, work, work! Do student films, do non-union films, come to (an acting school), get in front of the camera! TRAIN! Your experience is indicative of how much you can get in front of the camera. It's just like being a pilot; the more time you spend in the air, the more likely they are to give you the 747 to fly."

That's because, before the prestige shows up, before an actor's name lands on the pages of *Entertainment Weekly*, before the four-, five-, and eight-figure checks start rolling in from anywhere and everywhere, something else needs to grow and flourish inside every budding actor.

The desire. The drive. The reasons for acting, the incentive to give one's best performance, can't come from the hopes of taking home lottery-esque checks. Actors can't think, "Hey, if I do well, maybe I'll get to meet Steven Spielberg or Martin Scorsese, or date someone who's a heartthrob to millions, or *become* that heartthrob." That's not why people should get into acting.

"I've seen kids who have a lot of desire, but not a great work ethic," says longtime performer Jason Alexander. "I've seen kids who have a great imagination, but not a lot of life experience. I've seen kids who have a lot of life experience but no imagination, and all of them have to come together to make an actor."

Ask the question: why do athletes get into their sports? Why did the best baseball players of all time first pick up a bat? Why did an elementary school-aged Michael Jordan shoot his first layup? Wayne Gretzky hoist his first stick? Tom Brady toss his first downfield bomb?

The answer's simple — for the love of the profession. The joy for what they were doing. The enthusiasm. Of course they had talent. Of course they had natural ability. But it was the passion for success, to be the best they could, that carried them as far as they went.

The same concept applies to acting. It's not enough to watch a film and say, "You know, I could do what he does!" It's not enough to read over a script, and expect to snare a roll right away. It's not enough to have one film role, and start planning an illustrious career alongside the ranks of De Niro, Eastwood, Streep, and Nicholson.

It's the gusto to never give up, to never say die. To never let a blown audition, a bad critical review, a negative response from a coach (or anyone else) get in the way of one's dreams. If we're born to act, we'll act, and we'll know that we're doing exactly what we wanted to do.

"There's this great line," says longtime performer Joe Mantegna. "(that) the three greatest professions in the world are professional athlete, rock 'n' roll star, and actor. The actor's the best because you can play the other two."

And if we don't make it to the big time, if our name never goes up on the marquee, well... that's not why we got into the game to begin with. Success can't lie in the fame we receive from others — it's got to come from the confidence, the pride, the accomplishments that we make and meet for ourselves.

Don't ever think of yourself as a failure if you don't become a big star, because the fact that you even made the attempt puts you so much farther up the accomplishment ladder than legions of others.

Becoming an actor is like any other dream – it's going to take time and effort, and sometimes it may not feel worth it. But in the end, no one's going to stop you from doing anything you ever wanted. That person staring back at you from the mirror can be your worst enemy or your greatest asset; that's all up to you. One thing's for sure: the acting world's not going to come knocking on your door. You've got to go find it, and sometimes you're going to have to play the world's hardest game of hide-and-seek.

And as this former budding actor learned, sometimes you find something you never knew how much you'd enjoy.

As I walked off the stage as the curtains fell on my first few high school plays, a sense of energy and pride swept over me, and a huge grin suddenly grabbed hold of my face and didn't let go.

What was going on? Was I glad it was over? Was it because I liked getting cheered by the crowd, and the hugs and high-fives I'd received from my fellow castmates as we congratulated each other on a job exceptionally performed?

That was definitely a part of it. But in my senior year, after the final call of my own theater swan song, a production of *Godspell* (always popular around schools because of its simple setup and outstanding storyline), I started to realize that there was more to it than that – and while I can't speak for any other performer, if this is a common thing, it's more than enough reason to want to stay with acting for the long haul, no matter where it takes us.

It's the ultimate feeling of accomplishment. It's the pleasure of a personal transformation, a feeling of stepping outside one's emotional being and, for only a brief period, taking on a whole new persona.

For the first time, I realized that Jason Norman had just ceased to exist for the time being. He'd become someone else. He'd become Hawkeye Pierce from *MASH*, a soldier from *South Pacific*, and Jesus Christ's buddy during *Godspell*. When an actor's on stage, in front of a camera, or even in front of a mirror at home, he's literally not himself anymore. He gets to become someone else, taking on their way of thinking, their personality, and even their physical being at times. That's one of the greatest feelings in the world.

And it's reason enough to try acting, even for a short while. Like just about everything else, acting's not for everyone. But it can be for someone who wants to know what it's like to live outside their heart, their mind, their body for a while. It's for those who want to feel the ultimate sense of accomplishment, of meeting a strong challenge, and doing so just to see if we can.

Finishing up my research for this book, I found that I wasn't the only one who took this feeling from a performance.

"You'll hear many stories of people feeling really sick backstage, flu, cold, whatever," explains Kevin Pollack, of *The Usual Suspects* (1995) and *A Few Good Men* (1992), "and then ten minutes into their act, they're completely well. It's a euphoria that can't really be described, other than to say it transcends all illness, it transcends all stress, and problems of your day."

"A real actor knows that this is what they have to do; they're not concerned with the odds," acting coach Fran Montano says. "They know that anything else they do with their life is just not going to make them happy, and if they can find something that makes them happy, they should do it. It's not about being a Tom Cruise. There's a difference between the craft of acting and being a star; a big difference. There are actors that are working all over the world, in theater, in television. Most people who want to be really famous don't make it; they drop out, or burn out, because they don't like what they're doing anyway – and they're doing it for the wrong reasons."

Because, coaching colleague Eric Stone gleefully reiterates, the only right reason comes from within.

"It all comes down to this," he says. "You gotta love it! You gotta love what happens to you when you're in front of a camera! The only way to do that is to get in front of a camera and hear 'Action!'"

And what better way to end our journey together than to hear that call from the opposing side, to read the words of someone who will never get tired of hearing them?

"The thing," explains two-time Oscar victor Al Pacino, "is doing it. That's what it's all about. Not in the result of it. After all, what is a risk? It's a risk not to take risks. . . I don't feel like a person who takes risks. Yet there's something within me that must provoke controversy because I find it wherever I go. Anybody who cares about what he does takes risks."

Acting's your dream, eh? Go for it – and don't let anything, anyone, anywhere slow you down!

References

A history of residential schools in Canada. (2010, June 14). *CDC News*. Retrieved on Oct. 20, 2010, from http://www.cbc.ca/canada/story/2008/05/16/f-faqs-residential-schools.html

Abit, Otoja. Phone interview. March 17, 2016.

Adolfi, Kristen. Phone interview. April 10, 2010.

Ashton, Tracy. Phone interview. June 18, 2010.

Avari, Erick. E-mail interview, June 19, 2013.

Badham, Mary. Q+A session, *To Kill a Mockingbird* event, Onancock, VA. Sept. 29, 2013.

Banks, Clay. Phone interview. Aug 20, 2008.

Barron, Dana. Phone interview. January 22, 2015.

Batson, Susan. (2007). *Truth: Personas, Needs, and Flaws in the Art of Building Actors and Creating Characters.* Rugged Land, LLC.: New York.

Bentt, Michael. Phone interview. March 11, 2016.

Blommaert, Susan. E-mail interview. Oct. 20, 2010.

Bodison, Wolfgang. Phone interview. Sept. 4, 2009.

Bogdanovich, Peter. (2004). *Who The Hell's In It*. Alfred A. Knopf: New York.

Bove, Linda. Phone interview. Nov. 12, 2009.

Brando, Marlon. (1994). *Brando: Songs My Mother Taught Me*. Random House, Inc.: New York.

Bray, Deanne. E-mail interview. June 26, 2009.

Brown, Dwier. Phone interview. Aug. 10, 2009.

Burt, Clarissa. Phone interview. Jan. 16, 2015.

Burstyn, Ellen. (2006). *Lessons in Becoming Myself*. Riverhead Books: New York.

Caine, Michael. (1990). *Acting in Film*. Applause Theater Book Publishers. New York.

Cardone, Vivien. E-mail interview. April 27, 2014.

Carpio, T.V. Phone interview. April 7, 2016.

Cartwright, Nancy. (2000). *My Life as a 10-Year-Old Boy*. Hyperion: New York.

Cates, Darlene. Phone interview. June 23-24, 2014.

Chapman, Mark David. Phone interview. January 13, 2010.

Chilcoat, Joanna. E-mail interview. April 4/15, 2016.

Cole, Julie Ann. Phone interview. Oct. 13, 2009.

Crewson, Wendy. Phone interview. July 28, 2015.

Crosby, Mary. Phone interview. Sept. 21, 2015.

D'Abruzzo, Stephanie. E-mail interview. May 25, June 2, 2010.

D'Alessandro, Richard. Phone interview. Dec. 15, 2009.

Davis, Julienne. Phone interviews. Oct. 5-6, 2012.

Davis, Michael. (2008). *Street Gang: The Complete History of Sesame Street*. Penguin Group Inc.: New York.

Deats, Dayni. Phone interview. March 4, 2015.

Dempsey, Patrick. Phone interview. March 15, 2016.

Dolenz, Ami. Phone interview. April 22, 2010.

Dotrice, Karen. Phone interview. Oct. 19, 2009.

Dourif, Brad. Q+A session at Monster Mania horror film convention, Cherry Hill, NJ. Aug. 1, 2015.

Dreyfuss, Richard. Speech at Old Dominion University. March 25, 2009.

Edwards, Luke. Phone interview. Jan. 15, 2016.

Eichenbaum, Rose. (2011). *The Actor Within*. Wesleyan University Press: Middletown, Conn.

Ellis, Roger. (2003). *The Complete Audition Book for Young Actors*. Meriwether Publishing LTD.: Colorado.

Englund, Robert. (2009). *Hollywood Monster: A Walk Down Elm Street with the Man of Your Dreams*. Pocket Books: New York.

Ferra-Gilmore, Christina. (2006). *The 7 Steps to Stardom*. Applause Theater and Cinema Books: New York.

Fitzpatrick, Leo. Phone interview. Dec. 11, 2009.

Flynn, Colleen. Phone interview. Dec. 11, 2015.

Friedman, Andrea. Phone interview. July 24, 2009.

Fuller, Kurt. Phone interview. July 8, 2009.

Gammon, James. Phone interview. June 19, 2009.

Garlington, Lee. Phone interview. Feb. 5, 2010.

George The Animal Steele. (2006). Retrieved on Aug. 1, 2010, from http://www.georgetheanimalsteele.com/

Ghigliotti, Marilyn. E-mail interview. April 9, 2015.

Goodwin, Deidre. E-mail interview. January 14, 2015.

Graves, Karron. Phone interview. Feb. 2, 2010.

Hall, Irma. Phone interview. Dec. 18-19, 2014.

Heard, Shawnette. Phone interview. May 26, 2016.

Heller, Randee. Phone interview. March 10, 2015.

Hill, Napoleon. (2004). *Think and Grow Rich: The 21st Century Edition*. Bill Hartley (Ed.). Highroads Media, Inc.: Los Angeles.

History. (n.d.). *Indian Residential Schools Survivors Society*. Retrieved on Oct. 20, 2010, from http://www.irsss.ca/history.html

Holihan, Ryan. E-mail interview. June 9, 2015.

Hollister, Lindsay. E-mail interview. June 7, 2010.

Holton, Mark. E-mail interview. Aug. 30, 2009.

Horn, Delton T. (1991). *Comedy Improvisation: Exercises & Techniques For Young Actors*. Meriwether Publishing LTD.: Colorado.

Howey, Bill. (2005). *The Actor's Menu*. Compass Publishing. Lakewood, Colorado.

Hudson, Ernie. Q+A session at Tidewater Comic-Con, Virginia Beach, VA. May 21, 2016.

Irvin, Laura. (Nov. 13, 2006). "Mary Badham, on a 'Mockingbird' mission." *SF360*. Retrieved on Jan. 17, 2010, from http://www.sf360.org/features/mary-badham-on-a-mockingbird-mission.

Jazwinski, Peter. (2003). *Act Now!* Three Rivers Press: New York.

Jessie, DeWayne. Phone interview. Sept. 9, 2014.

Johnes, Alexandra. Phone interview. Oct. 21, 2015.

Jones, James Earl. (1993). *Voices and Silences*. Macmillian Publishing Company: New York.

Joosten, Kathryn. Phone interview. Jan. 25, 2010.

Kanes, Benjamin. Phone interview. May 27/Aug, 25, 2015.

Kapelos, John. Phone interview. March 19, 31, 2010.

King, Adrienne. Phone interview. April 22, 2009.

Konno, Kelly. Phone interview. May 18, 2016.

Lassez, Sarah. E-mail interview. June 1, 2016.

Litteer, Heather. E-mail interview. Nov. 10, 2015.

Luttrell, Kent. Phone interview. May 6, 2015.

Marcus, Stephen. E-mail interview. Aug. 7, 2015.

Martin, Andrew. (2012). *All for the Best: How 'Godspell' Transferred From Stage to Screen*. BearManor Media: New York.

Matlin, Marlee. (2009). *I'll Scream Later*. Simon Spotlight Entertainment: New York.

Matuszak, John, & Delsohn, Steve. (1987). *Crusin' with the Tooz*. Charter Book: New York.

McGrath, Bob. Phone interview. May 8, 2009.

McMahon, Keana. Phone interview. April 3, 2016.

Mdelar. (Oct. 30, 2009). "Paranormal Activity" Interview with Micah and Katie. Retrieved on May 20, 2010, from http://www.youtube.com/watch?v=Y_9jOZkOhhQ-&feature=related

Michelle, Shelley. Phone interview. June 22, 2010.

Mitchell, Alice Barrett. Phone interview. Oct. 26, 2009.

Montano, Fran. Phone interview. Aug. 28, 2008.

Moreau, Marguerite. Phone interview. July 27, 2009.

Morgan, Cindy. Phone interview. Sept. 8, 2015.

Mulligan, Robert. (2005). *To Kill a Mockingbird*. DVD. Universal.

Natale, Anthony. Phone interview. June 25, 2009.

Nayyer, Harsh. E-mail interview. Aug. 31, 2016.

Parker, Kelley. E-mail interview. Aug. 12, 2014.

Patterson, Marnette. E-mail interview. June 30/July 6, 2015.

Pena, Elizabeth. Phone interview. Dec. 3, 2009.

Perera, Fia. Phone interview. March 2, 2010.

Powell, Michael. (2010). *The Acting Bible*. Barron's Educational Services: New York.

Pozniak, Beata. Phone interview. Aug. 16, 2009.

Pugatch, Jason. (2012). *Starting Your Career as an Actor*. Allworth Press: New York.

Rosenblat, Barbara. Phone interview. Feb. 19, 2015.

Rivas, Sara. Phone interview. Sept. 16, 2014.

Sampson, Tim. Phone interview. Sept. 17, 2009.

Schatz, Howard. (2006). *In Character: Actors Acting*. Bulfinch Press: New York.

Scheine, Raynor. Phone interview. June 8, 2016.

Schwimmer, Rusty. Phone interview. March 17, 2016.

Shields, Charles. (2006). *Mockingbird: A Portrait of Harper Lee*. Henry Holt and Company: New York.

Sloan, Amy. Phone interview. March 8, 2010.

Spacek, Sissy. (2012). *My Extraordinary Ordinary Life*. Hyperion: New York.

Spignesi, Stephen J. (2003). *In The Crosshairs*. New Page Books: New Jersey.

Squibb, June. Phone interview. Sept. 7, 2010/June 1, 2014.

Sroka, Jerry. Phone interview. July 16, 2010.

St. John, Michelle. E-mail interview. Dec. 10, 2010.

Steele, George. Phone interview. July 27, 2010.

Starr, Mike. Phone interviews. July 22, 2009/June 26, 2014.

Stone, Eric. Phone interview. Sept. 2, 2008.

Stronach, Tami. E-mail interview. Sept. 3, 2009.

Struycken, Carel. E-mail interview. July 18, 2009/May 9, 2015.

Swayze, Patrick, & Niemi, Lisa. (2009). *The Time of My Life*. Atria Books: New York.

Taylor Gordon, Hannah. Phone interview. May 23, 2016.

Thomas, Richard. Phone interview. Oct. 13, 2009.

Tibbetts, John C. & Welsh, James M. (1998). *Encyclopedia of Movies into Film*. New York: Facts on File, Inc.

Trujillo, Raoul. Phone interview. July 27, 2009.

Vander, Musetta. E-mail interview. Jan. 11, 2011.

Vargas, Jacob. Phone interview. Jan. 14, 2011.

Vetter, Pam (2008, June 14). Actress Tracy Ashton: Making Strides for Performers with Disabilities on 'My Name is Earl.' *American Chronicle*. Retrieved on June 21, 2010, from http://www.americanchronicle.com/articles/view/65059

Vogel, Darlene. Phone interview. Oct. 26, 2010.

Wakkechinsky, David, and Amy Wallace. (1993). *The Book of Lists: The '90s Edition*. Little, Brown, and Company: New York.

Waters, Harry. Phone interview. May 4, 2015.

White, Cheryl. E-mail interview. May 10, 2010.

Willig, Matthew. Phone interview. April 2, 2016.

Index

www.ingramcontent.com/pod-product-compliance
Lightning Source LLC
Chambersburg PA
CBHW060324100426
42812CB00003B/874